Accountant's Guide

to Profitable Management

Advisory Services

Accountant's Guide to

Prentice-Hall, Inc.

Profitable Management

Advisory Services

CONON D. WHITESIDE

Englewood Cliffs, N.J.

Accountant's Guide to Profitable Management Advisory Services
Conon D. Whiteside

PRENTICE-HALL INTERNATIONAL, INC., *London*
PRENTICE-HALL OF AUSTRALIA, PTY. LTD., *Sydney*
PRENTICE-HALL OF CANADA, LTD., *Toronto*
PRENTICE-HALL OF INDIA PRIVATE LTD., *New Delhi*
PRENTICE-HALL OF JAPAN, INC., *Tokyo*

LIBRARY OF CONGRESS
CATALOG CARD NUMBER: 69–14584

PRINTED IN THE UNITED STATES OF AMERICA

X

WHAT THIS BOOK CAN DO FOR YOU

This book is intended to accomplish two distinctly different but related objectives:

- To help the small pracatitioner to improve his personal effectiveness, expand his practice and strengthen his position as a professional man with his clients.
- To provide the necessary information and guidance to enable the ambitious practitioner to enter the challenging and fast-growing field of management services with confidence.

Publications expressing the views of the public accounting societies consistently express grave concern in recent years about the deteriorating competitive position of the sole practitioner and small accounting practices as compared to the large public accounting firms. One reason is that the large CPA firms have added special management services departments to assist clients of all types and sizes in many different areas of business operations.

By contrast the small or medium-size practitioner finds it very difficult merely to keep up with the routine demands of his profession. He may have very little time to invest in acquiring new skills, or offering new services. However, changing conditions require positive action to meet the situation. One such action is to expand the scope of services and personnel and engage in management services. This positive step will help assure the continued existence of the small practitioner, a valued member of the business community.

To accomplish the two objectives stated above this book covers a wide range of subjects. You will note that the first group of chapters covers many vital aspects of management services. For example the first chapter presents an outline and description of what management advisors do—with special emphasis on how clients benefit from advisory services. Section One chapters make available the inside techniques of successful, professional advisors:

   . . . How to sell management services to clients
   . . . How to write effective, selling proposals
   . . . How to prepare and write reports
   . . . Different ways of quoting fees; typical fee schedules

The chapters on professional salesmanship are a unique addition. A knowledge of the principles and techniques of communication and persuasion has a definite and concrete value in almost all lines of endeavor. In the field of management services the ability to make effective presentations and sell services to client managements has a proven value. As Roger Schleider, Treasurer of the Crane Company, so aptly stated the situation: "You qualify as an advisor because of technical skills and experience. You become a Partner only when you can *sell*."

The material on salesmanship, to a large extent, is based on my seventeen years of experience in the field of office equipment and computers. Starting out in the public accounting field in 1935, I switched to selling office equipment in 1937. Eight years of on-the-job experience in training professional salesmen produced much of the information presented in these special chapters.

The second group of chapters covers the broad field of Financial Services. One chapter introduces the practitioner to Credit and Collection functions and policies—a virtually unknown field to many accounting-trained professionals.

Section Two is intended to provide instant access to information on office and manufacturing systems. The last section is a guide for modern data processing. The information here is based on many years of day-to-day experience in this fascinating field; you will be able to advise your clients on many phases of this increasingly important aspect of business operations.

Summary

In summary the objectives of this handbook are to enable the small and medium-sized practitioner to compete favorably with large CPA firms that have management services departments. At the same time the one objective is to help the practitioner upgrade his services through increased personal effectiveness, train a staff, and increase gross and net income as he builds his professional image with his clients.

Conon D. Whiteside

FOREWORD

The individual accounting practitioner, who traditionally works closely with proprietors of small business organizations, is becoming increasingly important to the health and effectiveness of a large segment of American business. He works hard to implement his principles and philosophy of business, and influences his clients to follow sound business practices.

The practitioner planning on entering the management services field should not be over-awed by the large monolithic advisory firms with extensive and impressive manpower resources. Advisory services are *personal* services; results are obtained by the application of knowledge and experience to the problem at hand by *the man doing the job*. A well-known firm backed up by many partners in the firm's office has little to do with producing valuable results for the client. Therefore, the individual practitioner should not underestimate the importance of his role in today's increasingly complex business community. It is still the little man with ideas, initiative and a willingness to go all out for his clients who is in the best position to provide effective personal services to those clients.

Capitalism and individualism are almost synonymous in meaning. In this nation each individual is still important. As an individual practitoner you have every right to enter the management services field—to broaden your services and increase your value to your clients, for their benefit. If practitioners as a group lose, through inaction, their unique personal relationship with leaders in the business community, then the American economy will lose some of the dynamic force that has pushed the free enterprise system to world leadership.

Two Categories

Advisory services may be divided into two different categories:

    . . . The application and use of technical skills and experience to effect problem solutions.

    . . . The provision of counsel and guidance to management—assisting with policy formulation and the decision-making process.

Now, public accounting houses are apt to consider management services as an extension of their public accounting services; this is "technical" advising. It is probably true that most successful advisors specialize in one or more technical fields, in order to supply concentrated knowledge and experience not available to the client within his own firm, to solve client problems.

In which category can you qualify as an advisor? A highly specialized technical skill provides a good foundation for entering the advising field. If, in addition, you can qualify as an advisor to top management, because of intensive training and experience in the business world, you will be well equipped to make an outstanding success in this challenging profession.

Qualifications of a Consultant

What are the qualifications of an advisor? To answer this question, let's examine the characteristics and background of a typical, successful management advisor:

- He has had concentrated exposure to one or more fields in the business world.
- He brings a broad body of detailed knowledge to bear on any problem in his chosen field.

- He knows other leaders in his field, and can go to them for aid and assistance when needed.
- He tends to be a leader and is accustomed to influencing the thinking and actions of other people.
- He gains the respect of people in the client firm at all levels by exhibiting knowledge and ability—and never shows a superior attitude.
- He always considers the viewpoint of the other man, and recognizes the self-interest motivation behind all human actions.
- He recognizes the importance of each person as an individual and is emotionally mature so that he gladly gives due credit for ideas and suggestions to the originator.
- He practices and excels at the art of communication to inform, persuade and motivate.
- He avoids the appellation of expert because he knows his own limitations.
- He has the courage to say "NO" to his client whenever this becomes necessary for the best interests of the client.

Ethical Conflict

The practitioner about to enter the field of management services should be aware of a severe ethical conflict which may arise because of his role as a public auditor in certain client firms. An advisory assignment (or the prospects of an assignment) may place the practitioner in a very awkward position.

For example, suppose the audit reveals damaging information as to the activities of company executives which forces the auditor to report irregularities to the Board of Directors. How can he fail to reflect upon the fact that carrying out his role as a professional auditor properly will eliminate any opportunity to obtain a lucrative advisory assignment?

The large public accounting firms have found a solution. They organize and set up separate and independent departments to specialize in management services. Many medium-sized accounting firms have followed this pattern of operation with success.

The CPA firm of Squires & Rinehart in Albuquerque, New Mexico solved the problem along similar lines. One partner, Don Reinhart, specializes in management services; the other partners carry on the tax services and audit engagements.

CONTENTS

Accountant's Guide

to Profitable Management

Advisory Services

1

What Management Advisors Do and How Clients Benefit

Consulting is an ancient profession. In the past, the word "consultant" has been associated predominantly with the activities of engineers, architects, scientists and other members of the professions. For our purposes the terms management "advisor" and "consultant" are synonymous.

Today, with the constantly increasing complexities and demands of the business world, the consulting profession is enjoying a very rapid growth. Total billings constantly increase and the number of individual firms that utilize consulting services are becoming more and more numerous.

In recent years, large public accounting firms have been expanding their client services by entering the consulting field with great success. These firms frequently set up and staff special departments to engage in "management services." By contrast, professional firms that render consulting services only—that is, their services do not represent an extension of a public accounting practice—call themselves "consultants." Therefore, the word "consultant" is used quite often in this book interchangeably with "management services."

This chapter does not stress the benefits or profits to be gained by the practitioner who enters the growing field of consulting. By contrast, it focuses on the benefits of consulting services to clients—when the job is done by a competent consultant who is fully qualified for the assignment by background, experience and education.

The basic reason for concentrating on client benefits in this chapter is that Chapter 2 introduces the techniques of professional salesmanship; and it tells how to effectively present and sell your services. Now, a prime requirement of salesmanship is that the seller must be fully aware of the *benefits* that the prospective buyer can expect from his product and be able to explain them. At all times, he must be aware of the prospect's unspoken question, "What's in it for me?"

This means that the practitioner must fully understand and appreciate the wide range of benefits that the prospective client stands to gain from the services he offers; he must be able to discuss and explain the specific benefits which he believes will stem from the particular assignment under consideration.

Since this chapter concentrates on benefits that accrue to clients who engage professional consultants, it serves as a foundation for the next two chapters on professional salesmanship.

Definition of a Consultant

A management consultant may be defined as, "an individual qualified by education, experience, technical ability and temperament to advise and assist management on a professional basis in identifying, defining and solving specific management problems." (This definition is found in Wilson Seney's definitive book on consulting entitled, *Effective Use of Business Consultants,* published in 1963 by the Financial Executives Research Foundation in New York City.)

Other criteria which apply to a consultant:

- A consultant serves the client as an impartial, objective advisor, and is not an employee of the firm in any sense of the word.
- A true consultant serves fundamentally as *staff to management.*
- A consultant assists in defining problems, outlines alternative solutions, evaluates the impact of various alternative approaches and suggests or recommends the best solution or solutions.
- A consultant guides, advises and counsels; he does not assume line authority, nor control the conduct of the client's business.

Benefits and Basic Values

As mentioned before, the practitioner who expects to become proficient at selling management services must know the major benefits which usually stem from consulting services. In order to find out what the *users* of consulting services deemed the most important benefits, the Financial Executives Research Foundation in New York City conducted an extensive survey. The executives who were polled mentioned the following five points most often:

1. The consultant brings *concentrated experience* and a body of knowledge to bear on a problem or a project.

2. The consultant brings an independent, impartial and objective viewpoint to bear on problem definition and development of effective solutions or recommendations.

3. The services of one or more consultants frequently make it possible to speed up the completion of a project, avoid detours, and eliminate the cost of trial and error that may occur without experienced, professional guidance.

4. The consultant, in many instances, is free to do a better job than a staff man, since he can ignore interdepartmental boundary lines without internal, political repercussions.

5. The consulting firm offers manpower flexibility; it can select and assign men to handle each phase of a project quickly and objectively, so the client doesn't need to incur a long-term budget obligation by hiring additional people for his own staff.

Analyzing Each Benefit

Now, let's examine each of the major benefits, one at a time in detail, and explore each one's potential value to the client.

1. *Concentrated Experience:* Depending upon the specific assignment and the situation, this one benefit may well be worth many times the total fee of the consultant engaged for the project. For example, "feasible fallacies" seem to exist in nearly every line of business and in every aspect of a situation. Any individual or group, when faced with a specific problem for the first time, may tend to embrace the solution which is readily apparent and attractive for various

reasons. This may lead in turn to a firm's investment of considerable time and work for implementing the solution or concept that seemed to be the best answer—*not aware that other firms and groups had tried a similar approach to the same problem*—with unsatisfactory, costly or even disastrous results!

This is one way of saying that quite often, the client can benefit greatly by learning from the consultant WHAT NOT TO DO. One excellent case history which will serve as an illustration of this is found in the application of an electronic computer to trade accounts receivable. Here is the story:

Nearly everyone who ponders over the question of how to apply an electronic computer to customer trade receivables (where the customer is a business firm, not an individual) decides initially that the computer should "apply cash automatically"—that it should, thereby, reduce clerical costs by eliminating the manual identification and marking of paid items. However, implementation of this concept, before it can be tried out in practice, is usually quite costly. For example, one firm with some 40,000 customers found that the complex programs for this concept required the full time of four programmers for one full year. In addition, it was necessary to increase the size of the computer's core memory—which increased the monthly rental costs—to implement this attractive-sounding approach to the problem of applying cash to specific paid items.

Finally, the new system was put into effect. Even though payment data was keypunched directly from the check or voucher apron, the computer was unable to find, match and delete a considerable number of items on customer checks. As a result, the number of entries on customer accounts representing unapplied cash began to mount rapidly. After four months the past-due statements were found to be very misleading, and credit evaluation for order approval began to deteriorate. Ultimately, the general credit manager forced the discontinuance of the system.

Now, here is the key point: A consultant who specializes in this field would have reviewed with the client group—at the *beginning* of the project—the various approaches to utilizing a computer for receivables in general, and for cash application, specifically. He would have pointed out the experiences of other firms, and the costs and results obtained from each method of applying cash. Thus, he may have steered the client completely away from a costly approach which would have little, if any, possibility of working in actual practice.

This type of specific guidance, based on concentrated experience, has a direct and tangible dollar value to the client. This is one prime benefit of your services in a field in which you specialize.

2. *Independent, impartial, objective viewpoint:* A practitioner just entering the field of management services may not, at first, fully appreciate the value of this aspect of his services to the client. Let's now discuss the perimeters of the usual situation and typical problems facing a client.

Top management typically has access to the opinions, suggestions and the viewpoints of many people at various levels of management—ranging from vice-presidents down to department heads. The length of service and experience representd by such a group may be very impressive. In view of this, why are the services of an outsider or a group of outsiders a desirable adjunct to this in-house counsel and advice?

To answer this question and thereby explain the value of an independent, objective viewpoint, we must briefly explore the organizational structure and political nuances of a typical business firm, and even examine certain aspects of human nature.

The top executive in a typical American business firm usually does not establish policy or set up rules and procedures arbitrarily and autocratically. He has an advisory committee, or he may consider himself to be just one member of an executive operating group. Policies are not determined, nor are key decisions made until one or more protracted meetings are held at which each individual has an opportunity to voice his opinions, ideas and suggestions.

In this type of organization and environment the personal ambitions and objectives of each executive or department head must be recognized and reckoned with. In other words, the motivation of an individual within a firm may stem from a strong desire of personal advancement and recognition, rather than from a strong desire to sacrifice personal interest to the best interest of the firm. This is another way of saying that internal politics is a formidable factor in management decisions—and this may create a severe internal problem for top management.

This problem centers around the fact that a member of top management knows from past experience that he cannot fully accept at face value the suggestions or recommendations of his contemporaries or subordinates without considering the possibility that the suggestion or recommendation stems from personal bias, politics or a self-interest motivation.

By direct contrast, he feels that he can fully rely on the independent, objective viewpoint of a competent, outside professional consultant who is immune from influences of the internal organization and power structure of the client firm. For this reason the consultant sometimes becomes a trusted sounding board, another pair of trained ears to listen to the problems, ideas and opinions of the top man who lives in a rather lonesome environment.

We can logically conclude that *many consulting assignments have been, and will continue to be, authorized by executives; primarily, because of the basic need to communicate with a trusted outside adviser and gain the benefit of his objective viewpoint and suggestions.*

3. *Consulting services make it possible to speed up a project, avoid detours and eliminate the cost of trial and error.*

The presence of an outside consultant tends to speed the completion of a project for a combination of reasons. For example:

- When a consultant is selected for an assignment or a project, the client usually assigns one or more staff men to work closely with the consultant. This frequently has the effect of freeing these men from other duties, with the result that they can concentrate on the job at hand, and not be bothered with diversionary problems or frequent changes of plans.
- A competent consultant with broad experience and an accumulation of knowledge in his field can easily earn his fee by helping the client eliminate most of the trial and error which he would otherwise experience. When you read this paragraph you can surely think back to many instances in which you have been able to persuade a client not to take a course of action or adopt a solution which seemed to have merit, because you knew, from prior experience, that he was about to make a mistake.

In recent years, I have conducted six major seminars for the American Management Association on the application of computers to receivables, credit and collection functions. The most common comment we have had from registrants who had already gone through the systems work, conversion and programming required to computerize receivables has been: "If only we had known all this *before* we started on our project!"

4. *The consultant can ignore interdepartmental boundary lines:* This political mobility may add great value to a project, since many new plans and policies, to be truly effective in a firm, are dependent upon an overall, integrated approach, rather than a limited departmental approach.

Experience has shown clearly that employees of the firm, regardless of title or position, may have great difficulty obtaining assistance and full cooperation of department or division heads. By contrast, the consultant is usually recognized to be a representative of top management and easily obtains the full cooperation of key people—if he is properly introduced by top management at the time the project begins.

In addition to organizational mobility, a competent consultant should be able to help the client do a better job in many ways. A consultant with the necessary broad experience can explore with the client ways of reducing costs, improving gross profit or increasing the productivity of personnel. For example:

In one recent assignment involving a basic review of all office operations, policies and procedures, I was fortunately able to increase the net profit of the client firm by $15,000 per year— simply by pointing out to the vice-president certain policies in use by other firms in the same line of business. The client was not aware of certain trade practices which were being followed in the industry. Furthermore, this was only one product of the basic review, which resulted in 14 written reports dealing with many recommendations, some of which had larger profit potential than the change in policy mentioned above.

5. *Manpower Flexibility:* The ability of the consultant to add manpower to a project quickly, and on a selective basis, adds greatly to the value of his services. Consider the usual situation in which a client has decided to develop and install new systems and procedures in his office or plant. When surveying his own supply of skilled and experienced manpower, he increasingly finds that the requirements of the project (which may offer very substantial improvements and benefits) exceed his resources.

This situation represents an ideal condition for the use of consultants. That is, the client can buy, on a short-term basis, the necessary experience and manpower required to implement the project and complete it in a reasonable time frame.

The controller of a medium-sized electronics manufacturing firm recently remarked that he was finding it increasingly difficult to find, hire and train the necessary manpower for his staff that he actually needed to meet the increasingly difficult projects and assignments generated within his expanding firm. He said that his only "practical recourse was to an expanding use of outside consultants to complement his staff from time to time."

WHEN CONSULTANTS SHOULD BE CALLED IN

Several independent surveys have been conducted by various organizations recently in regard to when and how consultants should be used profitably. These surveys were directed at the executives in hundreds of companies which had, at one time or another, engaged consulting services of one or more firms.

One questionnaire was directed to more than 600 companies. The replies represented the condensed experience and conclusions of several hundred *users* of consulting services. As a result the information gathered from these replies has great potential value to all practitioners and management consultants alike.

For example, the clients said that it was their policy to use management consultants in the following situations:

1. When the internal staff does not have technical experience to solve a specific problem or handle a contemplated project.

2. When the staff not only needs assistance on an urgent, technical project, but is faced with a backlog of unfinished jobs, or a shortage of people.

3. As an aid to management when faced with critical decisions.

4. To develop specific programs.

5. To obtain an objective viewpoint and recommendations; to reconcile opposing or conflicting views voiced by internal groups or individuals.

Types of Services

As you know, consultants offer a tremendous range of services which cover nearly every aspect of business operations. An elderly consultant in New Jersey concentrates on working with newly-appointed company presidents—to help the new president learn what a president is supposed to do!

One specialist travels all over the world to assist laundries with various difficult problems that may occur in the laundry business.

Several large consulting firms specialize in corporate organization, or reorganization projects. Some are experts in executive compensation plans—others concentrate on executive search and placement.

In recent years, a number of firms have developed, along with the broad acceptance of computers by the business world, to aid with systems design and development, programming, conversion of existing records and other aspects of a computer installation. One survey showed that nearly 30% of the firms, both large and small, utilized the services of outside consultants in connection with one or more aspects of their computer installation.

HOW CONSULTANTS HANDLE ASSIGNMENTS

Since this chapter serves as an introduction to the field of consulting, the remaining pages cover fundamentals, such as how to prepare for an assignment, the importance of a specific action program and working guidelines for the practitioner.

Sequence of Events

The sequence of events in performing an engagement are:
- Preparing for and beginning the assignment.
- Performing the work as outlined in the written proposal.
- Bringing the project to a close.
- Writing all necessary reports.
- Reviewing the reports with the client and discussing and planning implementation of all recommendations made in the reports.

Starting the Project

Three actions are necessary to begin an assignment:
- The consultant prepares and submits an engagement plan—unless this plan was an integral part of the detailed proposal previously submitted to the client.
- The client makes all arrangements for the assignment of company personnel and designates physical sites and facilities for the project team to use during the engagement.
- The client introduces the consultant to members of the organization who will be directly or indirectly affected by the project.

Engagement or Action Plan

The engagement or action plan is a comprehensive, written outline of the work to be done. Frequently, it includes a complete list of work phases or action steps that develop from preliminary conferences with the client and his staff. These conferences usually precede the preparation of a written proposal that covers the job to be done as understood by the consultant.

This written action plan is even more vital, if the consulting firm's head who made the presentations to the client must assign to one or more of his staff men the responsibility for doing the work as defined and agreed to by contract.

If the assignment is to cover a long period of time, elements of time should be allotted to each work phase. This converts the action program into an overall Master Schedule for the assignment, and it provides a continuing check on progress.

Exhibit 1-A illustrates a Master Schedule developed for a client in connection with a plan to convert a large accounts receivable installation to a computer.

Exhibit 1-A

MASTER SCHEDULE

This schedule covers the planning, systems development work, setting up new departments and other activities required to convert accounts receivable from accounting machines to a computer.

Work Phase No.	Description	Estimated Time Period	Month Numbers
I.	Interviews, Systems Planning and Systems Development and Documentation	6 months	1-6
II.	Programming, Testing and Debugging	16 months	5-21
III.	Set up Customer Coding System, convert ledger names and addresses to computer Customer Master File	3 months	12-14
IV.	Prepare physical site for computer	3 months	12-14
V.	Establish New Operating Departments:		
	A. Account Coding	1 month	16
	B. Input Department	1 month	16
	C. Proof and Control Group	1 month	16
VI.	Begin partial operation for parallel testing of programs	2 months	17-18
VII.	Convert first section of receivables	—	19
VIII.	Final conversion of all receivables	—	21

COMMENTS:
- The estimated time period for this program was 21 months
- The work phases are broad in scope; it is frequently desirable to develop a more detailed action program for each major work phase.
- Many work phases will overlap others, or the work is done on more than one phase concurrently.

Client Arrangements

It is the client's responsibility to make all arrangements for assignment of company personnel and use of company facilities by the consultant and his project team. However, this is not as important as the appointment of a liaison officer to whom the consultant reports.

The designated executive should fully recognize that overall supervision of the activities of the project staff and guidance of the project are an important part of his management responsibility. This member of management becomes the intermediary between top management and the consultant. There will be times when the consultant will appropriately seek conferences with top management in connection with the assignment, but his day to day contacts are with the liaison officer. This officer should realize that the consultant is an additional resource available to the company; and he should strive to make full use of the consultant's time and abilities. This arrangement is also of value to the consultant who occasionally needs to make specific requests or arrangements to further the progress of the assignment. The consultant needs this support, since only the client has authority. A consultant analyzes problems, conducts interviews and holds discussions; he offers guidance and counsel, but he has no authority to order or direct the client's employees.

WORKING GUIDELINES FOR THE PRACTITIONER

Extensive reviews of completed consulting assignments, analysis of results from the viewpoint of clients, and consideration of the problems involved from a consultant's viewpoint have led to ground rules which the practitioner should weigh very carefully. Here is the list:

- *Be convinced that you can deliver substantial benefits to a client before starting an assignment.*

If you have serious reservations about the potential for developing savings or benefits for the client as a result of an engagement, perhaps it would be better to candidly discuss this with the client, and look for an assignment elsewhere. This is effective public relations and seldom fails to pay dividends in the long run.

- *Make sure that the client is ready and willing to support a project adequately.*

Management should appoint a top-level liaison officer, assign competent personnel, and provide satisfactory working conditions for the consultant about to begin an assignment. These actions commit top management firmly to the project and serve to indicate its interest and support.

- *Be sure to keep top management informed of progress.*

It is not only courteous but good business to keep top management informed from time to time of the progress being made on the assignment. Invariably a member of top management must approve your interim billings, and he should be informed of progress and results, whenever possible.

One way to do this is to prepare interim reports, and then request a meeting to review the findings to date—while the report is *still in rough-draft format*. If it is not feasible to present interim reports with specific information and conclusions in a reasonable length of time after starting the job, then prepare periodic "progress reports," outlining what you are doing and why.

- *Check your proposal and action program occasionally to determine if the anticipated benefits are developing, fading or have gotten out of focus.*
- *Do not lose sight of the original purpose, scope and objectives of the engagement as agreed upon initially and outlined in the proposal.*

Carefully review the stated purpose, scope and objectives of the engagement as the work is being done. It would seem that this suggestion is unnecessary—that any practitioner would do this without being reminded. However, on-the-job experience shows that it is surprisingly easy to digress from the purpose and scope of the original assignment and become involved in one or more side aspects of the basic project.

If a mid-engagement review indicates that the project is, in fact, changing in scope and purpose—because of unexpected, significant findings during the basic-review work phase—you should immediately request a special conference with the client.

Before presenting the altered situation to the client, you should carefully evaluate the project in view of the new situation and develop written notes and suggestions on what should be done next. The client will appreciate the fact that you are reporting the new developments, and that you are asking his guidance, suggestions and approval of the next steps to take.

The conscientious practitioner will report the pertinent facts, even if he has reason to believe that the client will cancel the assignment at once.

- *Never ignore subordinate executives and department heads.*

It is difficult to comprehend the thinking of a consultant who tends to ignore subordinate executives and department heads involved in the area of operations logically covered by the assignment. For one thing, you are apt to find most of your answers at this level.

Never fail to acknowledge the *source* of good suggestions or answers. Build up the position of people at all levels, wherever possible. You become a bigger individual by so doing. As Gene Benge, of Benge Associates points out: "Giving due credit to others requires emotional maturity on the part of the consultant."

A final point: The implementation of a new policy, a new system or set of procedures requires the full assistance and cooperation of people at many levels. If the consultant and the project staff have ignored lower-level department heads during the engagement, it probably will be very difficult to secure their full cooperation when the time comes to put the new policy, system or procedures into effect.

- *Maintain good human relations at all levels.*

It may not be possible or even necessary for a consultant to win a popularity contest while doing a job for a client, but it certainly makes good sense for the consultant to create goodwill throughout the assignment. The opinions and viewpoints of subordinates often play a large part in shaping the client's ultimate judgment as to the competence and performance of the consultant.

Practitioners with extensive audit experience should recognize that the environment and approach to a management services engagement is completely different from that inherent in an audit assignment. A large New York CPA firm which secured a lucrative consulting assignment failed to coach two young auditors assigned to the job, with disastrous results. These young auditors were selected to make a diagnostic review of a client's credit and collection department which was a very sensitive area of the firm headed up by a vice-president.

From the beginning, these young men adopted the attitude that they were the outside experts and that all client personnel had to do whatever they said with no questions asked. Their attitude and approach generated intense resistance and resentment at all levels within the client firm; the client terminated the assignment after a couple of weeks.

Desirable Attributes

Gene Benge lists the following as desirable attributes of a successful consultant:
- Always consider the viewpoint of the other person.
- Be tolerant and open-minded at all times.
- Maintain a sense of modesty.
- Don't talk down to anyone. Remember: The mail boy may be the company president's son who is working his way up in the firm's management hierarchy.
- Move slowly on an assignment to build a climate of *confidence*.
- Pay more attention to the social relationships involving client people.

Summary

This first chapter covered, in broad terms, what consultants do and what benefits they bring to clients. Then we explored in detail *why* utilization of a consultant should produce results of a very tangible nature and with a direct, dollar benefit to the client.

Next were outlined the situations or conditions usually prevailing in a firm when outside consultants are brought in, according to the views of hundreds of executives who continually use consultants in the operation of their businesses.

Finally, we discussed the sequence of events in actually handling an assignment, followed by working guidelines for the practitioner.

2

The Art of Salesmanship

Public accountants are technically trained professionals who are engaged in performing a wide variety of services for businessmen in the business community. They handle extensive and complex audit engagements, prepare certified financial statements, prepare income tax returns, offer advice and counsel on mergers and consolidations, assist with securing financing and offer many other services to their clients. The value of their services now is universally recognized and fully accepted in the business world.

Because of this recognition and general acceptance, it would seem that any capable practitioner would have little difficulty in expanding his client list and increasing the size of his practice over the years. However, the single practitioner still outnumbers accounting firms consisting of two or more principals.

It is noteworthy to find an accounting practice that steadily increases its client list and requires comparable increases in the size of its staff and the number of partners to handle a growing, successful practice. An interested observer of this common phenomenon may well wonder why one firm finds it easy to grow and expand; while another equally competent firm, offering virtually the same services in the same area, remains somewhat stagnant.

The missing ingredient is frequently the lack of *salesmanship*. It is a fact that most professionals in nearly any of the better-known professions are deficient in knowledge of the principles and practices of the art of selling. For example, in the early days of electronic computers, the manufacturers made a basic mistake by assigning the selling job to young electronic engineers. These men knew how the computer was designed and of what materials each part was made. They were professionally competent but were not very successful at selling computers. You will learn why as we expand on the fascinating subject of selling.

A working knowledge of the principles and practice of salesmanship has a tangible value to people in all walks of life, since it is a fact that everyone must sell himself and his services to others at all times. And, in the business world the ability to sell is the mark of the true executive.

The practitioner in business for himself soon realizes that technical competence alone does not guarantee a successful, profitable practice. If the practitioner seldom gets the opportunity to demonstrate his skill and competence on an assignment, his income will be limited and his business will stagnate.

11

Some of the most competent men in the consulting and accounting professions find it necessary to work for others—because of their lack of sales ability. If they had the ability to sell enough engagements to keep a staff busy at a profit, they would not find it necessary to take down their shingle and look for employment with those firms that have the demonstrated ability to continually secure enough work to keep a staff busy on a productive basis. Roger Schlieder, Treasurer of the Crane Company, sums up the situation this way: "You become a consultant because of technical skills; you become a partner by being able to *sell.*"

Wilmer Wright, President of Wright Associates, sums up his 34 years' experience in the consulting profession by stating: "A successful practitioner must be a good salesman—because a report not acted upon by a client *has no value.* Therefore, the consultant who accomplishes worthwhile things for his client is the man who convinces the client to put his suggestions and recommendations into action."

The subject matter included in this and the following chapter is intended to assist those practitioners who are ambitious and determined to be an outstanding success in their chosen field of accounting and management services. These men will carefully study the principles of professional salesmanship explained in this handbook—and will diligently practice them until the techniques become second nature. They will be rewarded by being able to obtain a large percentage of the management services assignments that they strive to obtain for their firms.

The Salesman

Many professional men dislike thinking of themselves as "salesmen." This bad image of the salesman probably stems from the type of person often seen on stage or screen, playing the part of the "travelling drummer" of many decades ago. He was nearly always cast as a jolly, but empty-headed, fellow who had a large collection of off-color jokes for entertaining his customers and prospects. This image of the salesman has not been valid for a long time; things in the sales field have changed rather dramatically in the past fifteen or twenty years.

Today's professional salesman is, quite often, a specially trained, well-paid company representative with a competent, technical background of engineering, accounting, chemistry, metallurgy, medicine, etc. As business has become more competitive and complicated, firms that want to expand their business have found it necessary to render specific services and offer technical guidance to their customers. Hence, the emergence of the professional, technically-trained sales representative to aid the businessman with a wide variety of problems.

In subsequent discussions of selling techniques and the principles of salesmanship, the nouns "seller" or "salesman" are used to designate any person offering any product or service for sale. Likewise, we will refer to "prospect" or "client" in broad terms of any person who needs the product or service, that is, the one who must be sold by the "seller."

For you to benefit most from this chapter and the one following, put yourself in the place of the salesman, and visualize a typical prospective client as being the man who is listening to the sales presentation. This chapter covers the principles of salesmanship in general as they apply to presenting and selling *any* product. The following chapter deals with selling management services as a special "product," and it outlines the special situations peculiar to selling personal services.

The Selling Process

Regardless of the product being sold, or of the varying conditions under which a sale begins, a successful sale represents a definite sequence of events or steps:

- The Approach
- The Presentation
- The Close
- The Action Phase

Before discussing each phase of the selling process, it is essential to recognize and understand the reasons why people buy *any* product or service. These fundamental reasons underlie each of the steps leading to a successful sales effort; the successful practitioner of professional salesmanship must know what these reasons are and how to work in harmony with the buyer's basic "buying motives."

The Buying Motives

A person's decision to buy a product results from a mental process based on emotions which generate a personal desire to buy. Can these emotions be clearly identified? Can the seller learn how to consciously work in harmony with buying motives and appeal to them deliberately?

The LaSalle Sales Training Program, published by the LaSalle Extension University of Chicago, answers these questions in the affirmative. This course on salesmanship says that there are only four basic buying motives:

- To gain something of personal value; to *profit* from the product or service being offered. (The Profit Motive)
- To protect property or persons. (The Protection Motive)
- To win the approval of others. (The Personal Approval or Prestige Motive)
- To gain comfort or convenience. (The Comfort/Convenience Motive)

There you have them. All products bought by anyone at any time are based on the motives listed above. Reflect on these four basic BUYING MOTIVES for a few moments and then attempt to determine *which* buying motive (or combination of motives) influenced your most recent major purchase—ranging possibly from life insurance, a new automobile, new furniture, a set of sterling silver tableware, a new typewriter for your secretary, etc.

After you have identified your own buying motives in each instance, practice recognizing these motives by scanning the advertisements in any magazine or newspaper. You will quickly find that most of them are aimed solely at the "profit motive." Writers of advertising copy seldom appeal to any of the other three buying motives. Even though appeals to the profit motive are greatly overworked, they obviously are still very successful on a continuing basis.

However, it is interesting to realize that the giant insurance business and the flourishing cash register business are both based on the proven existence of the "protection motive." This is, indeed, a powerful, basic human motive—the desire to protect one's self, family, physical possession, business position, health, etc. Subsequently, in this chapter you will learn how the seller of management services can successfully appeal to this motive of protection to win approval of a consulting assignment.

One intriguing fact about the protection motive is that experts in the field of motivation research claim that people are far more apt to take prompt action to protect something than to gain an equivalent or greater amount of profit, or some other benefit. For example, a businessman will invest a considerable sum of money in a safe or a cash register to protect a small amount of cash, such as $100, much more readily than he will take action to merely add another $100 to profits.

The most overlooked buying motive of all is the desire to gain the approval of others. It exerts a very powerful influence on human activities. A wide range of products depends upon this motive to remain in existence. For example, firms in the sterling silver, fine china, cut glassware and related industries are a testimonial to the tremendous power of this buying motive. Consider the hidden reason for the purchase of an expensive set of sterling silver tableware for the home . . .

Will the purchaser save money, or profit from this purchase?

No.

Will it add to his comfort or convenience?

No.

The real, underlying motive is to set an impressive dinner table; and thereby, gain the silent or spoken approval of friends, relatives, business associates, club members and others.

Analysis of the advertising message found in nearly every advertisement for Cadillac automobiles reveals that the advertising agency understands very well the real reason why people buy Cadillacs; it is *prestige*. "Prestige" is a single word expressing the desire to gain the approval of other people. It is, indeed, a powerful buying motive.

The desire for comfort and convenience is self-explanatory. Many purchases are made solely to satisfy this desire. For example, the purchase of a larger refrigerator, a better washing machine or dryer, an air conditioner for the home or office, an electric adding machine bought to replace a manually-operated model for the office force—all of these illustrate purchases made primarily for comfort or convenience.

Sometimes a purchase is based on a combination of two or more buying motives. Consider the instance of the small business owner who buys a better typewriter for a valued employee, even though the old machine is working reasonably well. The motives here may be twofold: the owner's desire to gain the approval of this employee, coupled with his desire to enable the employee to turn out more and better work—and, thereby, profit from the investment in the typewriter.

Significance of Recognizing Buying Motives

Analyzing buying motives is indubitably foreign to the normal thinking of most public accountants. Let's pause here and review the reasons why we are stressing this subject to such an extent:

- The buying motives are at the root of every sale that is made anywhere.
- Management services are personal services. They must be sold to the client—*before, during and after* the assignment.
- A few practitioners accidentally and instinctively follow the principles of good selling without a conscious realization of the techniques involved. It is obvious that they would be much more effective salesmen if they understood the principles of salesmanship and deliberately planned their client presentations accordingly. (The successful management services practices are invariably headed up by men who have learned how to present and sell proposed services.)
- For those practitioners who are technically-oriented, the information found here should be very helpful. The thousands of graduates of sales training courses have conclusively proven that virtually anyone can study and practice the principles outlined in this chapter —and use them to produce sales.

If it is possible for you to study and consciously learn specific techniques that will bring in a higher percentage of engagements to proposals made, then mastering the art of salesmanship obviously has a tangible value.

Applying Your Knowledge

A thorough knowledge of the buying motives is also very helpful during initial conferences relative to the assignment under discussion, and in the preparation of the "benefits" section of the proposal—found in subsequent pages of this chapter.

When the practitioner consciously recognizes (through the constant application of selling techniques) the existence and the power of the buying motives, he will strive to weave in appeals to such motives when he discusses the proposed assignment. He will concentrate on pinpointing and explaining possible benefits, rather than dwell on details.

Make no mistake about it; many assignments that would have resulted in substantial benefits to the client have been lost irretrievably because of poor selling techniques on the part of the consultant, such as failure to present properly and prove the benefits to be gained by the client. In other words, the consultant failed to sell the client; both were losers as a result.

The Buying Process

The action steps in making a sale are:
- The Approach
- The Presentation (of the selling proposition)
- The Close
- The Action Phase

Now, let's cover each step in making a sale one by one, with special emphasis on examining the buying process—to gain some insight into the prospect's thinking at each step.

The Approach

The approach is the beginning of the selling process and is the most crucial step, since no sale can be made unless you get the prospect's attention; an opportunity to present your case. If you strike out on the approach, any possibility of a sale is gone, regardless of the many worthwhile benefits which you stand ready to offer the prospect.

The principle involved in an effective, successful approach is a very simple one; however, more salesmen violate this principle than observe it:

Arouse the buyer's self-interest motivation by stating, suggesting or implying that he will GAIN something of value, PROTECT something he already has, WIN THE APPROVAL of others, or GAIN COMFORT OR CONVENIENCE. In other words, the seller simply appeals —consciously and directly—to the prospect's buying motives. That is all there is to it.

(The seller must be fully aware of the typical, self-centered attitude of the prospect. He is not really interested in anyone but himself; he is always probing (silently) for an answer to this question: "What do *I* get out of this? " Also remember that he is examining everything you say with a very skeptical "So?"—because he knows you are trying to sell him something.)

The appeal to buying motives is accomplished by mentioning or claiming potential *benefits* to the prospect—available to the prospect if he buys your product or services. This implies that you have prepared a list of major benefits, and that you are ready to discuss and explain these benefits very convincingly at any time with very little additional preparation. (Since you know that benefits are the foundation of all sales appeals, you will understand why Chapter 1 devoted several pages to a general discussion of the primary benefits which consulting services bring to clients.)

While we are on the subject of benefits, note that Exhibits 2-A and 2-B at the end of this chapter includes lists of benefits taken from actual proposals to clients.

A CASE HISTORY

Before proceeding to the second step in the selling process, let's examine an actual case history where a public practitioner saw an opportunity for selling a new engagement, after completing the one which brought him into the client's business.

This young practitioner was about to complete a systems assignment for a wholesale distributor which involved a thorough review of the order and billing procedures, with a view toward mechanization of invoice-preparation and posting accounts receivable records.

While studying the order-filling procedures in the shipping department, he had observed several significant things:

- The shipping clerks used unnumbered bill of lading forms for truck shipments.
- The shipping clerks had separate forms for railroad shipments and Railway Express shipments.
- The clerks wrote the product description in pencil on the face of the bill of lading forms hastily and without reference to the prescribed legal description found in the Interstate Commerce Commission's *Manual on Tariffs*.

The practitioner recognized the possibility that freight charges applied by the carriers to outgoing freight were higher than necessary, and that internal control over shipments was lacking. There was the possibility that shipments were being made and never invoiced—and a concomitant potential for diversion of valuable products through unauthorized shipments from the warehouse.

The practitioner now began to think and plan like a salesman, and to "prepare his case" for presentation to the client. He secured examples from his firm's library of what other firms had done to cut freight costs in comparable situations and to gain positive, internal control over all shipments at the same time. He prepared a written list of potential benefits which would accrue to the client if he were given the assignment to review and correct the situation. He then practiced what he was going to say and how he would say it.

He made an effective approach to the client—by naming the potential benefits to be gained from a study of the major products sold and shipped, by showing how the products were packaged and described, and by designing new forms to provide better internal control. He explained how the use of authorized tariff descriptions of products shipped on bill of lading forms would reduce freight costs. Then he pointed out how the present system failed to control warehouse shipments—and how the new system would provide positive control at all times.

Next, he made his presentation by showing examples of forms used by other firms that once had been faced with similar problems. He reviewed the potential benefits once more, estimated the length of time and the fee for the proposed assignment—and he made the sale.

Summary

To summarize, the basic principle behind an effective approach is to suggest, state or indicate to the prospect that you have something of potential value and benefit to offer him. You then request an opportunity to explain and prove the potential benefit or benefits. This initial step leads into the presentation phase of the selling process.

Before covering the presentation phase, it is essential that we mention what not to do on an approach. Do not use all of your "ammunition" in the approach. A successful approach is usually based on only one or two major benefits which you mention to the prospect. For example, if you have prepared a list of six benefits which you honestly believe would accrue to the prospect as a result of buying your services, do not mention more than two of these in your approach. Save the others for the presentation and for the "closing step."

The Presentation

The presentation logically follows a successful approach. The prospect may decide to listen to your story at once; or together, you may plan a time and place for a subsequent meeting. The prospect may decide that he wants other key people to attend the discussion and presentation.

In broad terms, the presentation requires that you present, explain and *prove* each benefit to be expected from your product or services. You *present* each benefit; you *explain* each benefit— and you *prove* each benefit.

For this step in the selling process, specially-prepared presentation aids are helpful. These can take many different forms.

Presentation Binders and Visual Aids

After you have defined the nature and type of management services which you will frequently offer to prospective clients, you should build special presentation binders or portfolios for use in interviews and selling presentations. The material in these binders or portfolios is assembled to help you explain your service, describe the benefits, and prove, wherever possible, the benefits which will result from your services.

As you gain experience in the practice of professional salesmanship, you will begin to realize fully that *conversation alone* is a very poor selling tool. A prospect's mind has a tendency to wander when he is exposed to a lengthy conversation. Further, his ability to remember key points covered during your selling presentation may be limited.

By contrast, visual aids and exhibits, professionally done, which are clean and neat are of tremendous potential value in presenting and selling your services. This is so, because impressions and information received through sight make an almost indelible impression on the prospect's mind. And, if you present specific examples of what your services are and the potential benefits to him, he is not apt to forget them easily.

Discussion Memos

Preliminary or exploratory sales calls and interviews can be made much more effective through the use of typed discussion memos. This technique requires that you organize the material for a call on a prospective client by preparing in advance a "discussion outline." Make several copies. When the interview begins, hand a copy to the prospect and a copy to other executives or members of his staff who attend the meeting. Your prospective client will be favorably impressed; here is why:

- You will be able to discuss the client's problem and your proposed assignment in a well-organized sequence. No key points will be overlooked, since all parties concerned follow the discussion memo.
- The typed memo remains in the client's possession after the meeting is completed. This means that he will be reminded of the key points discussed, and the major benefits covered by your discussion.

- The typed sheets provide an excellent basis for review and discussion between the prospective client and his staff members, associates or superiors after you have departed.

You will find a condensed discussion memo illustrated at the end of this chapter; see Exhibit 2-C.

A CASE HISTORY

In one instance, a consultant who is an effective salesman had three interviews with the president of a prospective client firm, discussing his proposed services. Competition for this assignment was keen, since other major consulting firms were under consideration by the client.

For each of the three meetings, this consultant prepared a set of memos, "Topics for Discussion." He always left the original with the company president after concluding each meeting. His final written material which was submitted to the client included a letter that outlined the parameters of the project, plus a complete list of the benefits to be derived by the client from the project. He won the contract from the prospect.

Sell Benefits—Not Services

The title of a popular book on salesmanship, written by Elmer Wheeler and published by Prentice-Hall, Inc. in 1940 is *Sizzlemanship*. The gist of the subject matter throughout the book was "SELL THE SIZZLE, NOT THE STEAK." Interpolating this admonition as it applies to consulting, it says, "Sell the BENEFITS, not the service."

You will find it surprisingly difficult at first to force yourself to think in terms of benefits, rather than concentrating on *what* you do, and how you do it. But you must learn to do this if you expect to sell a high percentage of the prospects to whom you offer your services.

One way to learn to do this is to force yourself to sit down and prepare a list of all possible benefits which you think may accrue to the client as a result of your doing a job for him. Always do this before you meet with the prospect to discuss the proposed assignment. This practice will build your self-confidence, increase your enthusiasm, and make you a more effective salesman when you make your presentation.

The Importance of Evidence

As you have seen, the sale hinges on the presentation of enough benefits to make the client want to buy your services. However, you should always be aware of the fact that businessmen, from long experience, disbelieve or question at least 50% of all unsupported claims or general statements made to them by salesmen, or by anyone who has something to sell. (In making this sweeping statement, we exclude the special situation where a practitioner has built up, over a period of years, a strong reputation with a client for integrity and dependability.)

You should expect the prospect to be skeptical, and adopt a "Show Me" attitude. He is both judge and jury; you should be prepared to go "on trial" in front of the prospect and prove your case. You should prepare your presentation in the same way a competent attorney prepares for a jury trial. Assemble your evidence carefully; be prepared to prove each of the major benefits that you claim.

A training film on salesmanship, used by firms to train salesmen, stressed the need for proof and evidence by dramatizing a sales presentation in the following manner:

When the salesman comes in to call on the prospect, the latter is shown sitting at "the bench," clad in judicial black robes. The salesman makes his selling points one by one. Each time he stretches the truth just a little, a blast from a referee's whistle halts his verbal claims. The film continues to show that the salesman should be well prepared to present his case in a systematic, logical manner, with conclusive evidence to back up each and every sales claim that he makes.

Gain Commitment

As you explain a benefit and offer evidence, attempt to gain a commitment from the prospect that he understands and accepts the stated benefit. Remember that a benefit has no value if the prospect does not understand it—or does not believe that it would apply to his situation.

In summary, your sales presentation will be successful if you:
- Demonstrate a thorough knowledge of the subject matter pertaining to your services.
- Show evidence of having carefully thought out and prepared your presentation.
- Explain and prove major benefits.
- Offer evidence of having made valuable contributions in the past to the profitability and success of other firms with similar problems.

Types of Evidence

Evidence comes in many forms. Take with you on a sales call such important aids as work binders and reports that have been prepared for prior clients. These may include feasibility reports, organization studies, surveys and resulting recommendations, or any other material which can be used without violating the confidential relationship with clients.

Show the prospect a list of satisfied clients; offer to provide names and telephone numbers, if he wants to check your past work and credentials. Try to obtain testimonial letters from clients that are as specific as possible in regard to savings, cost reductions, general improvements and other benefits which these clients have received from your work.

If you have written articles or books that have been published, show a copy to the prospect. If you have participated in seminars on technical subjects, show the printed program as evidence of your activity in your professional field.

Prototype List of Benefits

Obviously, a list of potential benefits must be carefully tailored to each specific, proposed assignment. You should invest considerable time in developing the list, since your sale hinges on the number and the potential value of the benefits which will accrue to the client, if he buys your consulting services.

Because a list of potential benefits are those which will result from the implementation of personal services, you are forced to appraise your own work with high esteem—in advance of performance. This is unavoidable. One helpful technique when detailing your proposed services is to use the pronoun "we" rather than "I."

This correctly implies that even a lone practitioner should adopt the position that he is a "consulting firm." Since consulting is such a demanding profession that covers a wide range of special services which require competency in many fields, the lone practitioner should make a determined effort to associate himself with other reputable men in the field, even on an informal basis. This capability of calling in experienced associates in various fields, when needed, lends credence to the use of the pronoun "we" when you write a proposal. And, it will improve the practitioner's image in the eyes of the client.

The benefits listed in the following exhibits were taken from two different proposals dealing with proposed services in the data-processing field. Quoting the exact words is not as important as illustrating the format of a list of benefits for your guidance and use in the future.

Looking Ahead

In the next chapter we will continue to discuss the principles of salesmanship by covering the known techniques for "closing sales." We then will explore the two common mistakes made by salesmen in general; the remainder of the chapter deals with special situations found in selling management services.

Exhibit 2-A

Introductory note: The list of benefits presented below was included in a proposal to a client as a separate exhibit. The exhibit was captioned as shown below. (Note how each benefit was summarized and enclosed by parentheses.)

BENEFITS TO BE DERIVED FROM OUR SERVICES

1. *Guidance* in avoiding the many internal problems and hazards which have so often been associated with a punched-card receivables system.
   (Safer, fewer operating problems.)
2. Special techniques and procedures to derive definite *dollar benefits* from better control over unauthorized deductions, unearned discounts, remittance shortages, etc.
   (Better control, better system.)
3. *Experienced assistance* in planning for a smooth and comfortable conversion from present ledger records to punched cards.
   (Avoid the trouble and cost of operating a duplicate system for a period of time.)
4. *Counsel* on system design and special reports required to meet the genuine information needs of the various departments served by the new system, such as the credit and collection departments.
   (Improve the operation and effectiveness of these departments.)
5. *Solve the reference problems in advance*
   We have learned how to solve the vexing backtracking and reference problems commonly associated with punched-card systems. We will outline all runs and reports required to "fill in the gap" in this very important area which is usually overlooked until the problem is encountered in full force.
   (More satisfactory system for all concerned; fewer customer queries and complaints.)

Exhibit 2-B

Introductory note: The proposal from which this exhibit was taken included one page which covered present methods in use, the limitations of the existing system—and the known plans of the prospective client. The problems of transition from the present system to a different type of computer system were then outlined. The following benefits appeared on page three of the memorandum:

MEMORANDUM TO: *John F. Doe & Company*
The Benefits of Consulting Service in Connection with the Design
and Installation of an Electronic Computer System

The overall benefits are that the system development will be done FASTER, the transition will be SAFER, and the new system will be MORE PROFITABLE.

1. *FASTER.* Because of concentrated, specialized experience in this application, the new system can begin to operate several months sooner.

2. *SAFER.* It is not necessary to repeat some of the mistakes of others. Our research files contain details of the case histories of costly oversights, wrong approaches and detours with the new types of data storage devices applied to the same applications as those required for the John F. Doe system.

3. *MORE PROFITABLE.* Since our firm has specialized in researching every phase of profitably applying the new types of computers to your line of business for many years, programming time will be reduced and the cost of re-programming changes will be minimized.

Also, by having continuing, full access to the experience of many firms that have already installed similar computer equipment on receivables, we can select the best and most profitable procedures and techniques which fit into a custom-tailored system to produce the best possible results for your management.

(The remainder of the memorandum provided further explanation of the benefits claimed. In addition, the memorandum included a special exhibit which featured specific examples of major contributions made to systems planning work that was done for other clients on prior assignments. This exhibit covered six pages of information presented in double-spaced format. The examples were attuned to the client's business and to his own requirements, since they covered work that was done for clients with almost identical problems.)

Exhibit 2-C

Introductory note: This exhibit presents an actual *discussion memo* that was prepared for an interview with a committee of three executives, dealing with a possible assignment to assist in developing a complete electronic computer installation. Such a memo is usually typed on a letterhead.

Topics for Discussion

The ABC CORPORATION

PROJECT: ELECTRONIC COMPUTER INSTALLATION

A project leading to the ultimate installation of a full-scale electronic computer covers many different activities, over a long period of time. These various activities are described below as "Project Phases."

ACTIONS TO BE TAKEN

Phase I. Establish and Document Management Objectives
- Conduct interviews with management.
- Determine special management reports wanted.
- Determine data contents of reports—by working with users.
- Prepare Master List of all management and operating reports.
- Document all policy decisions and interviews.

Phase II. Systems Development Phase

This phase covers many important activities and is extremely important, since all subsequent programming rests on this systems foundation. In fact, the ultimate success of the entire installation rests on the thoroughness of the job done in this phase.

1. Prepare a Master List of all computer runs.
2. Prepare a Master List of every conceivable transaction.
3. Draw prototype forms and reports—with sample entries.
4. Prepare punched-card formats.

5. Lay out all tape files and records.
6. Write program specifications in detail.
7. Draw work flow diagrams for each computer run.
8. Write procedures for all related clerical operations.
9. Prepare. . . .
10. Document . . . etc.

Phase III. Programming, Testing and Debugging

After a group of related computer runs has been completed to the satisfaction of the systems team, the documentation is turned over to the programmers. Phase III covers the approximately 20 steps known as "flow charting, coding, testing and debugging."

Phase IV. Customer Coding

Several months before the first test runs are ready, the existing customer accounts should be screened and numbered.

This involves. . . .

Phase V. Planning the Customer Coding Department

The daily coding work requires. . . .

Phase VI. Planning the Input Department

Various methods of input. . . .

Relative costs of each method. . . .

Proof and correction procedures. . . .

Phase VII. Preliminary Conversion Problems

This is a very critical phase. . . .

Phase VIII. Selecting the Appropriate Computer

Phase IX. Site Planning and Environmental Requirements

Phase X. Other Considerations

Summary

This chapter is the first of two chapters that cover the subject of professional salesmanship. You have learned the basic buying motives, the steps in the selling process—and have examined the reasons why the seller must know how to work in harmony with the personal motivations of the prospect at all times.

Selling is both stimulating and interesting. It is also financially rewarding. Even though professional ethics prohibit the solicitation of engagements, the practitioner who learns how to sell effectively has a very bright future.

3

How to Sell Management Services

Before delving into the unique aspects of selling management services, we will conclude the subject of professional salesmanship by examining that phase of the selling process known as "closing." This is an intriguing aspect of selling and has baffled thousands of experienced salesmen and observers over the years.

It is safe to assume that the art of closing a sale is not known to most public accountants or to professional men in kindred fields. These professionals should not feel alone in this respect, since the closing technique remains a mystery to many salesmen with years of selling experience.

This should not be the case, however, since the principles involved in closing were first analyzed, defined and tested many decades ago by sales leaders of the business world, such as Patterson of the National Cash Register Company, Watson of IBM, Charles Roth, Elmer Wheeler and many others.

Charles Roth's book, *The Secrets of Closing Sales* offers an excellent study on this fascinating subject (available to anyone who is willing to invest a modest amount of money and time by buying and reading the book). As Roth points out, the technique of closing is not some mystic process that suddenly impels the prospect to buy the product that is being offered; it is not actually a separate step in the selling process at all. It is, rather, a continuation of the process of explaining benefits to the prospective buyer—and of *gaining commitment* from him, in one way or another, that he understands the benefits and accepts them as being applicable to his situation.

Roth does an excellent job of explaining this by asking the reader to visualize a pair of delicately-balanced postage scales which represent the prospect's mental process of weighing each benefit that is presented to him by the salesman. On one side of the scales, the prospect places the dollar cost of the product or services, and adds known disadvantages which are sometimes a part of a selling proposition. On the other side, he weighs the value of the benefits as presented to him by the salesman—and as *accepted* by him mentally. Now, when the value and desirability of the benefits to be gained outweigh the cost and any related disadvantages, the scales figuratively tilt—and the decision to buy is formulated in the prospect's mind.

23

Win Agreement and Close Sales

The technique of winning agreement is far too important to pass over lightly. It is one thing to present and lucidly explain a benefit—it is quite different to *obtain agreement,* by the use of deliberate, planned questions or otherwise. To repeat, you are *closing* only when you present a specific benefit, prove the value of the benefit—and *win agreement* from the prospect that it is a desirable benefit.

The theory is that by selling each part of a selling proposition, you end up selling the whole. And it works.

A CASE HISTORY

As an illustration of this theory, let's examine a selling proposition which I once used successfully in an office equipment proposal. One product which was especially suitable for my retail territory in the Southwest was a small, relatively inexpensive desk model posting machine. This machine had unusual merit; it was easy to operate and was designed for posting charge sales invoices to a *ledger and a statement* with one operation. This process required only that the operator feed the forms into the machine, index the last old balance, and copy the invoice number and amount to the keyboard of the machine. It proved the amount posted and the account balance as the posting work was done.

In preparing to sell this product to retailers and small wholesale firms, I analyzed the benefits usually derived from an installation of this desk model posting machine. The analysis revealed that the selling proposition included six major benefits to the user:

1. Accuracy.
2. Time Saving.
3. Work Saving—by eliminating the separate step of preparing customer statements at month-end.
4. Reduced accounting costs.
5. Improved cash flow through better collections.
6. Machine-prepared statements gained prestige for the firm.

As further preparation, I used a special portfolio of documentary material—such as letters from users, pictures of installations, sample forms with actual entries on them, and testimonials from users as to speed, accuracy, time saving, etc.

Armed with this type of selling ammunition or "evidence," I would demonstrate in the prospect's office how the machine worked—taking care to *interpret* what the machine did in terms of a *benefit* to the user.

The closing technique practiced was simply to present and explain one benefit at a time—and *win agreement* from the prospect that it was a benefit, and one that he would like to enjoy. Only then would the next benefit be covered.

The secret of the closing process was this: The prospect, by *buying each part* of the six-pronged selling proposition, found it easy to decide to *buy the entire proposition,* which meant he signed an order for the desk model posting machine.

This statement does not mean that the prospect will always sign up immediately and automatically. Many extraneous considerations may cause the prospect to delay an actual purchase for weeks or months. However, this does not alter the fact that an effective selling and presentation technique, which can be learned and consciously practiced by anyone, induces the prospect to reach a favorable decision on the product or services being offered to him at the time.

You now realize the importance of including a list of benefits in each of your proposals for management services. The listed benefits are your "selling ammunition"—the very foundation for winning approval of the assignment from the prospective client.

Side Benefit

The technique of inviting agreement on each major point has a significant side benefit; it uncovers situations in which the prospect does not understand clearly what you are claiming. Or, he may understand it but disagree in regard to its applicability to him or his situation. Pressing for agreement brings out into the open the prospect's thinking and his reasons for rejecting the point under discussion. Once you have identified the problem, you can take steps to review the benefit again, examine it from his viewpoint—and perhaps, win agreement on it after further exploration. If you are able to do this, you have moved one step closer to final approval of your selling proposition.

The Leading Question

A prime method of winning agreement is to ask leading questions. Let's see how this technique is put to use in the field of management services:

Suppose that you are proposing an office systems study to a client who has several problem areas in his office. His office force is not able to keep up with the current volume of work; preparation of invoices is delayed; customer statements are mailed late in the month; collections are decreasing and delinquent accounts are increasing.

You have made a brief preliminary study of the situation, and you have discussed certain solutions with the client. You now propose that he authorize you to develop and install a mechanized system for the office to enable the personnel to process the work volume on a current basis.

"Mr. Client, proper mechanization of the invoicing and posting of accounts receivable records will make it possible for your office staff to handle the current work load, plus enabling it to handle an increased volume in the future. This step will reduce clerical costs, provide better control over billing, and improve collections." (Statement of benefits.)

"You will then enjoy more peace of mind, and you will be able to discount your bills and meet your payrolls better. You would really appreciate being in that financial position once more, *wouldn't you*, Mr. Client?"

The leading question, which invites or even requires a direct affirmative answer, tacked onto the end of the last sentence, *asks for agreement* by the prospective client. Since this is the hidden key to selling anything—products or services—*be sure to WAIT for some word or gesture that indicates agreement*. DO NOT PROCEED to a discussion of another benefit until you have *positively obtained agreement on this point*.

List of Questions

The sales-minded practitioner who recognizes the importance of gaining agreement will prepare his own list of leading questions to be used in typical selling situations, wherever appropriate.

Here are some typical questions which require affirmation:

"Don't you agree, Mr. Client?"

"You can see what this (benefit) would mean to you, can't you?"

"Isn't this the type of valuable result you had in mind when you first considered having this job done?"

"You recognize the value of this approach to the problem—don't you, Mr. Jones?"

"Do you agree that the results (benefits) as outlined here are possible to attain? Are they overstated?"

The latter type of question invites the prospect to discuss his ideas, opinions and other aspects of the benefits under review. This can be invaluable, since it so often happens that the prospect knows of reasons why the potential benefits are of far greater importance than the consultant realized.

Trial Closes

A trial close is a technique for finding out where you stand; to determine how you are doing during or after a selling presentation. Suppose that you have gained enthusiastic agreement on several key benefits; you have received an indication that the sale has been made. Yet, the prospect has not actually authorized your proposed assignment, nor has he given you any definitive clue as to what decision he has reached. Rather than ask him directly for his decision, it is tactful and effective to resort to the use of one or two "trial closes."

A trial close is a question based on the assumption that the prospect has mentally reached a favorable decision, although he has not voiced this decision. Therefore, the technique is to ask a leading question—which is intended to elicit a response from him that will undeniably reveal his unspoken decision.

For example, suppose you study your pocket calendar, mentally select a date two or three weeks in the future, then slowly ask the prospective client: "Mr. Client, what do you think of our starting the assignment on or about Monday, June 21?"

If he indicates agreement on the date, or suggests an alternate date—then he obviously has approved your proposed assignment!

The trial close can be effected by any one of many types of logical questions. Here is another one which fits the usual situation encountered when selling consulting services: "Mr. Client, what individual on your staff would you appoint as the Project Manager to work with us on this assignment?" Again, if he names one or two men as possible candidates and discusses their qualifications for the job, he has probably bought the assignment.

Only rarely will a prospect resist the trial close technique, or indicate that he feels he is being pressured into a decision. If this should happen, you simply express appropriate apologies for assuming that he had made a decision, and pursue the subject no further at the time.

Value of Trial Closes

Note that a trial close induces the prospect to make definitive decisions and take action on your proposition. Therefore, trial closes have a definite place in your arsenal of selling techniques; consistent use of them should increase your selling effectiveness.

Two Common Mistakes

Many people involved in selling make two common mistakes which are very costly in terms of lost sales:

1. Covering details rather than talking about benefits.

2. Presenting *all the benefits* before trying to win approval of the selling presentation.

Let's consider the first mistake: You will find that you will have a strong tendency to tell the prospective client *what* you plan to do for him, *how* you are going to do it and *why*. There is nothing wrong with this in itself—but it is not selling. You will probably lose your client's attention and interest, if you dwell on details too long before explaining the benefits he can expect to gain from your services.

In the office-equipment business we labeled typical machine-feature presentations as "Nuts and Bolts" demonstrations. The new, untrained salesman would first learn a "canned" demonstration of the machine. He would find a prospect and make arrangements to demonstrate the machine to the prospect. When the prospect came in to see the machine in which he was interested, the salesman would proceed to show him *how the machine worked,* feature by feature—but he would fail to explain how or why the machine would produce savings and benefits of far greater value than the required investment in the machine. Result: NO SALE.

You should never forget that, although it is good practice to explain the "how" and the "why" of a selling proposition, you must not fail to interpret and explain the *potential value or benefit* of each point to the prospect. You see, the prospect wants to know why he should part with his money to buy the particular product or service being offered to him. And, he wants the seller to outline and present good, solid reasons—backed up by as much proof and evidence as the seller can muster.

Now, the young electronic engineers who tried to sell computers in the early days of the computer industry, were not successful at selling computers. They talked about how the computer was built and told how it worked—but they seldom explained what it could do for the user. It is true that the prospects were interested briefly when the engineer pointed out with pride that the computer hardware was "cadmium plated" or that the control circuitry included "germanium diodes." But, this type of detail information alone will not motivate the prospect to buy the product.

See if you can now recognize the difference between details and benefits. Let's study an ad which appeared in an office-equipment magazine. Determine for yourself if the following ad is made up of "nuts-and-bolts" details—in contrast to naming benefits which would appeal to the buying motives of a businessman who needed a cash register. Here are the featured points listed in the ad underneath a picture of the register that was offered for sale to the readers of the magazine:

1. Automatic total and subtotal
2. Automatic receipt and business record
3. Durable inked ribbon
4. Movable cash tray lid
5. Made of all steel

I think you will agree that this ad positively fails to appeal to ANY of the basic buying motives; the points listed are strictly hardware details. It may get results if the reader of the ad has already decided to buy a cash register, but it does no creative selling.

The Second Mistake

The second mistake stems from the belief that it is necessary to present ALL of the benefits before "asking for the order." This is not so. It has been stressed by leaders in the selling field that the prospect may well be ready to buy after recognizing and accepting only ONE major benefit; it all depends on the situation. To prove this possibility, I will refer once more to my personal experience in selling the small posting machine to retail and other small firms:

Although the selling proposition for this machine included six major benefits, I quickly discovered that the prospect in this type of firm bought the machine, primarily, because of only *one benefit* he wanted most!

The most powerful buying motive invariably was the desire to eliminate the preparation of customer statements as a separate job at month-end.

Here is why this was the most desired benefit: In many typical small businesses that permit purchases to be charged, the job of preparing several hundred customer statements must be done at the end of the month. This usually requires that the owner and his wife or chief clerk spend two or three nights after hours to post the charge tickets for the last few days of the month, to balance the ledgers, and to type or handwrite statements to be mailed upon completion of the job. This is an onerous, dreaded month-end task. When the prospect realized that the low-priced posting machine would eliminate this work, he was strongly motivated to buy it.

SPECIAL SITUATIONS IN SELLING MANAGEMENT SERVICES

It is an interesting fact that selling principles and the basic buying motives remain unchanged, regardless of the type of products or services being sold. However, selling management services involves certain special situations and considerations. This chapter discusses the climate in which management services are sold and performed—and several of the unique selling problems encountered.

One prime difference between selling a product and selling management services is that the latter represents *personal services* offered to the prospective client. In effect, the prospective client is "buying" the firm and/or the individual making the presentation. If the assignment is later turned over to one or more staff members, the client must "buy" these individuals also by approving them for the assignment.

The Personal Touch as an Aid to Selling

After pondering over the foregoing paragraph, you will realize why it is essential for the "salesman" of management services to strive to make a good personal impression—to develop personal habits that improve his demeanor and appearance, and that enhance his stature as a mature, responsible businessman who has something of value to offer the prospective client.

The salesman will avoid a cocky, arrogant attitude during the interview. He will observe the usual amenities expected of a visitor in the client's office, and he will attempt to avoid any friction with the prospect or with members of his staff. He is "on trial" during the presentation; he should meet the test with confidence and enthusiasm, and exhibit a firm conviction that he can bring worthwhile benefits to the client and his company.

Show Enthusiasm

A multitude of things, both large and small enter into the making of a sale. Books have been written about the power of a selling personality, what to do and what not to do, etc. However, from my own years of experience in professional selling, and after training scores of men in this fascinating game, one thing stands out as a prime requirement of a successful salesman—he must show *enthusiasm*.

Enthusiasm acts as a catalyst to induce the prospect to act. It is contagious; if the seller is not enthusiastic, he cannot expect the prospect to get excited over the potential benefits to be gained by buying the seller's product.

It is easy to tell another person to be enthusiastic. But just how do you do it? Can you develop this valuable trait, or is it something possessed only by a fortunate few?

Fortunately, the ability to show enthusiasm is not restricted to a few people; anyone can quickly learn how to show enthusiasm—*if* you have a deep-seated, sincere belief in yourself and in your product. As an authoritative book on salesmanship expresses it: "To *be* enthusiastic you must *act* that way. Acting enthusiastic somehow generates genuine enthusiasm."

You may ask "How do you act enthusiastic?" Here is how:

- Sit up straight in your chair during an interview or presentation. (You can't register enthusiasm if you're slumped down, sitting on the end of your spine with your head resting on the top of the chair back.)
- Your face must show interest—sincerity—and animation.

To register animation may require practice in front of a mirror. A dead-pan expression seldom sells anything and produces a negative reaction from the observer. A truly enthusiastic person usually smiles, makes appropriate gestures, leans forward toward the listener in his eagerness to tell the good news, and concentrates his entire attention on telling his story, while he watches the prospect's reaction at the same time.

To repeat: You must have a strong, sincere belief in the benefits behind your product or services to serve as the foundation for your enthusiasm. If you do not, the prospect will quickly detect this fact and will not react favorably to your proposition.

Climate and Environment

Since consultants work at the top-management level, and do, in fact, represent top management directly when performing most assignments, it is essential that you fully understand and recognize the organizational and political structure of a typical American business corporation or firm. You can profit greatly from an understanding of the rules of the game.

You should realize that each department head and each company official, in one way or another, plays the internal political game—which means that he tries to fit into the group as smoothly as possible and is not prone to rock the boat too much by sponsoring radical ideas. He wants to protect his valued position in the organization.

Now, personal security is a major objective of any individual at any level; therefore, it is one of the motivations of the company official with whom you will be dealing as a consultant. Do not forget that this man will naturally be motivated by self-interest to some extent at all times; he subconsciously wants to advance himself and increase the security of his position within the firm at every opportunity.

At this point you may be asking yourself, "What does all this mean to me?" Here is the crux: You must consciously realize that any proposal you make for management services to the firm will probably be evaluated and analyzed by each official of the firm from a self-interest viewpoint. That is, the executive may ponder over how the proposed consulting assignment will affect him and his position personally. He may read certain implications into the assignment that he feels will adversely affect his personal fortunes; or, he may conclude that the assignment might benefit both him and his firm.

This aspect of the selling situation should prompt you to analyze each circumstance in an attempt to determine the benefits that will accrue to the key individuals—besides the benefits which will accrue to the firm, as a result of implementing the proposed assignment.

Happily, there is no conflict of interest involved in most consulting assignments. What is good for the company is also good for the individuals, and vice versa. However, this is not always the case.

Occasionally, a consultant will be called in by top management to straighten out a situation brought about by someone at a lower level of management. This situation puts the consultant in an awkward position with the person directly responsible for the problem. The practitioner should be tactful, but he must remember his basic obligation to the client—to develop the facts and present appropriate solutions and recommendations, regardless of the side effects on certain individuals.

This type of situation is not as delicate as that which develops when a trained auditor uncovers evidence pointing to defalcations by a person in a top-management position within a firm. Under these circumstances, the auditor's position is strengthened by the fact that he represents the stockholders of the company.

Selling Yourself and Your Firm

A consultant should be prepared to answer the unspoken question which always occurs to the prospective client: "Who is this man? What are the qualifications of this consultant or his firm?"

In the chain of decisions that lead to a sale, one of the last questions to be decided is the *source*. In the sale of a product, this means that after the prospect has decided to buy the product, he focuses on *where* to buy it. This accounts for the shopping around in various stores or in automobile agencies where the same or comparable products are sold.

In the sale of personal services, this aspect of the sale causes the prospect to decide WHO or WHICH FIRM will be selected to perform the desired services.

To answer this question, you should have pre-printed "Personal Data Sheets," covering the background and experience of yourself and each member of your staff, to present for the prospect's inspection. (See Exhibit 3-A and 3-B.)

Incidentally, there are two types of personal data sheets. One is in outline form, as shown in Exhibit 3-A. The other type is in narrative form; see Exhibit 3-B.

Other Credentials

If you have had articles published in recognized trade journals or magazines; or, if you've conducted seminars or workshops for associations or groups, you should tactfully exhibit the published articles, brochures or leaflets which indicate your competence and recognition in your field.

A typed list of references, complete with names, titles and telephone numbers of clients for whom you have done work, is sometimes required, because the prospective client may request such a list.

Competition

Members of CPA firms frequently find themselves on the inside track with clients whom they have served for years on audits and tax work. When a potential consulting assignment arises, they have an ideal opportunity to indicate capability in the particular field pertaining to the assignment—and they probably will get the job. However, it is a common failure for the practitioner to rely too heavily on his built-in advantage, and fail to talk about the benefits which he can produce for the client.

The representative of an outside consulting firm is aware that he must really do a selling job in order to overcome the built-in advantage of the other firm; therefore, he will concentrate on selling results—thereby *proving* why his firm is the best source for experienced, competent personal service that's required to get the most benefits from the assignment.

Exhibit 3-A

PERSONAL DATA SHEET

CONON D. WHITESIDE

Consultant to Management

President	Whiteside Associates, Inc. 300 Madison Avenue New York, N.Y. 867-7487

Summary of Experience	Entire career dedicated to designing and installing *practical and profitable* management control and accounting systems in diversified industries.
	27 years experience includes:
	  3 years—electronic computer specialist
	  2 years—manager, industrial systems department
	  2 years—dept. store & retail systems specialist
	  13 years—accounting machine systems specialist
	  2 years—forms & records specialist
	  2 years—public accounting
	  3 years—military & government service

Author of Detailed Systems Manuals	Wrote the following published procedure manuals:
	  (1) "Production and Inventory Control"
	  (2) "Industrial Accounts Payable Plan"
	  (3) "Insurance Agency Accounting"
	  (4) "General Accounting Plan and Procedures"

Input Techniques	Wrote and taught a 60-hour evening course on "Computer Input Techniques."
System for Automobile Dealers	In 1953, developed a complete, mechanized accounting system for automobile dealers. Wrote detailed procedure manual. More than 3,000 dealers, representing all major makes, installed the plan.
Published by Prentice-Hall:	Author of *Accounting Systems for the Small and Medium-Sized Business* published by Prentice-Hall. Now in seventh printing. 30,000 copies sold.
Seminars	Under the sponsorship of the New York Credit and Financial Management Association, presented three all-day seminars: (1) "Application of Electronic Accounting to Factoring" 4/22/63 (2) "What the Credit Executive Should Know About Electronic Computers" 5/8/64 Attendance: 350 (3) "Computers and the Credit Man" 4/21/65 Seminar leader for American Management Association on ten different seminars on Mechanized Receivables, Credit and Collections.
Member	New York Credit & Financial Association—New York Institute of Credit
Wartime Service	Special Agent, Federal Bureau of Investigation Staff Sergeant, United States Army
Education	Wayne University, Detroit, Michigan F.B.I. Academy, Quantico, Virginia New York University—evening courses Correspondence courses: LaSalle Extension and I.C.S.
D.P. Certificate	Certificate in Data Processing D.P.M.A.—1965

Incidentally, there are two types of personal data sheets. One is in outline form, as shown in Exhibit 3-A. The other type is in narrative form; see Exhibit 3-B.

Exhibit 3-B

WRIGHT ASSOCIATES

WILMER WRIGHT
Biographical Data

(PERSONAL PHOTO HERE)

In his twenty-nine years of business and professional experience, Mr. Wright has conducted or supervised improvement programs in almost every phase of industrial and business activity. He has been particularly active in developing modern techniques for providing management with the "tools" for profit planning, decision making and control. He formed Wright Associates in order to provide management with a more specialized service in this area.

His training and experience include twenty-five years of service with Stevenson, Jordan & Harrison, where he was one of the "Senior Partners." Prior to joining their staff in 1933, he spent three years with Western Electric Company and a year as an independent consultant in Baltimore, Md. During World War II he took leave to serve in the Ordnance Department (Captain to Lieutenant Colonel) and to fulfill a special mission for the Reconstruction Finance Corporation as Budget Director of the Budd Company.

Mr. Wright has worked with executives on over one hundred specific consulting assignments. He was consultant-in-charge of a number of notable studies, including the following:

Reorganization and Cost Reduction Program
New York Stock Exchange
Basic Cost Installation
Pittsburgh Plate Glass Company
Direct Standard Cost Installation
Universal-Cyclops Steel Corporation

He participates actively in the development of modern management. Eight of his technical papers have been published and he has delivered more than two hundred speeches before business and professional organizations. He holds memberships in the Society for the Advancement of Management, the National Association of Accountants, and the American Management Association.

Mr. Wright is a graduate of the University of Michigan, class of 1929. His course of study included mechanical and industrial engineering, accounting, and business administration. The University, as part of its Centennial Celebration in 1953, awarded him a citation in recognition of his contribution to advanced concepts of profit planning and control.

Conclusion

At first, you may be self-conscious and bashful about putting the principles of salesmanship, as described in these two chapters, into actual practice in your daily work. If you find this to be the case, you must convince yourself thoroughly that you are working for the best interests of the client. Once you have done this, you will register sincere enthusiasm—and you will be eager to make your presentation and explain the potential benefits to the client.

4

How to Write Proposals for Management Services

"Management Services" is defined as consulting work performed for a client by a public accounting firm or an individual practitioner. Since it is essentially consulting work, it connotes personal services rendered to the owner or management of the client firm.

These services may range over a broad and diverse area of business problems; the requirements of each assignment can vary tremendously. Therefore, the *definition* and nature of a specific job assignment may be very vague, until the practitioner takes certain steps to pinpoint the objectives of the assignment and strives to outline what will be done to achieve those objectives. Then, he presents to the client his understanding of the job to be done, the overall objectives and an "action program" in a *written proposal.*

Basic Purpose of a Proposal

Authority to perform management services usually follows the submission by the practitioner of a written proposal to the prospective client. As defined by the subcommittee on methods of preparing proposals, under the auspices of the Association of Consulting Management Engineers, Inc., a proposal is a "means of creating a clear understanding of the job assignment between a consultant and a prospective client, and can lead to the retaining of the consultant's services. Usually the preparation of the proposal does not involve any cost to the organization for which it is made."

Preliminary Steps That Lead to a Proposal

A proposal is usually the culmination of several preliminary meetings between principals representing the client and the consulting firm. Let's discuss what usually precedes the preparation of a formal proposal.

In public accounting firms, many management services engagements stem from the regular work done for the client, such as balance sheet audits. Perhaps a major problem area has been casually mentioned by the client as one that needs special study and review. This opening leads to one or more meetings between the partner who represents the management services section or department and the client and his staff or assistants.

33

During all such meetings, it is essential for the consultant to take extensive notes, and concentrate on *defining* the problem—and *defining the work to be done*. He should encourage the client and his staff to discuss the probable scope of the assignment under consideration from all angles. Discuss related areas to determine whether they logically should be a part of the assignment or excluded.

Define the Scope of an Assignment Carefully

The vice-president of a firm doing three and one-half million dollars' worth of business annually, when discussing the prospective assignment with a firm of consultants in a preliminary meeting, stated that his accounting system needed updating in order to meet the demands of increased volume and greatly increased monthly reporting requirements. He identified the problem as consisting of two main areas:

1. Inadequate facilities for distribution of income and expense to several hundred accounts found on the Chart of Accounts.

2. Inadequate reporting; departmental reports were being prepared on a quarterly basis only.

The consultants then reviewed the apparent objectives of the proposed assignment, and secured his agreement on the scope of the job as follows:

1. Develop a new system to handle the income and expense distribution work.

2. Develop reporting methods to enable present personnel to prepare monthly operating reports for all departments.

Since the vice-president had referred casually to a cash-control problem in one of the departments which did a cash business in excess of one-quarter million dollars each year, one of the consultants queried him about this; the consultant asked if the vice-president considered this to be part of the assignment. If so, it would require a review of all cash sales procedures, inventories and development of new inventory and cash-control methods.

The prospective client replied emphatically that a review of the sales operation should be part of the assignment. This was then added to the list of things to be covered by the assignment.

Define Areas Not Included in Scope of Work to Be Done

It is equally important for the consultant to pinpoint areas NOT to be included in the assignment to avoid future misunderstandings. One proposal that was submitted relative to doing extensive systems-planning work for a factoring firm included the specific paragraph: "This assignment does not include any proposed systems work for the Commercial Finance Department."

Here is an excerpt from another proposal, rendered in connection with proposed systems-development work leading to the eventual installation of a magnetic tape computer system:

"One of the first things we will do is develop a Master Work Project and Installation Schedule.

This Schedule serves several purposes:

1. It provides a foundation to guide all subsequent work included in the project.

2. Provides a time table for evaluating actual progress against scheduled progress.

3. Provides a precise definition of exactly what work is to be done by us, and *clarifies our total assignment responsibility.*"

Make a Preliminary Study

Quite often, it is necessary to make a short, preliminary study of the situation, before the information necessary for an intelligent proposal is available.

Be prepared to invest one-half day, or a full day in determining:

a. Paperwork volumes.

b. Number of people involved in present operation.

c. Present policies and procedures from a broad viewpoint.

d. Physical facilities.

e. Office or other equipment in use, paper flow and other related considerations.

A preliminary study benefits the practitioner in several ways:

1. This provides the consultant with still another opportunity to discuss the apparent problem, to find out the objective of the client, and, in general, attempt to *determine the proper scope* of the assignment.

2. Just as important, such a preliminary study frequently uncovers the presence of special problems that should be discussed before writing the proposal or starting the assignment.

3. The practitioner is better able to establish the probable scope of the assignment and will be better prepared to estimate time and work requirements.

General Rule: The consultant should always invest enough time in studying the indicated problem to be able to:

1. Prepare a very specific and intelligent proposal.

2. Estimate the total time required to fulfill the proposed assignment and plan staffing requirements.

3. Determine the full scope and other implications of the project.

4. Determine major benefits and results expected, as a result of performing the work.

Paid Study May Be Indicated

If the problem area is complex and involves a large number of departments or interrelated functions, the consultant should propose that a preliminary study be made and he should quote a fee to the client.

The result of such a study is a special report on what the preliminary study disclosed and data on the scope, time and estimated costs (as well as projected benefits) to be used later in the formal proposal, when it's prepared for the major assignment. Or, the net result of this preliminary, broad-gauged study may be a recommendation to the client to proceed no further.

A consulting firm specializing in data-processing systems-development work made such a recommendation based on a short, free, preliminary survey and discussion with the prospective client. The client wanted to computerize the accounts receivable, credit and collection functions. During the short review, the consultants quickly found that the firm had only 2,000 customers who bought heavy equipment very infrequently; two posting-machine operators kept up with the receivables postings very easily. Collection work was relatively efficient and under the control of only two people.

After the consultants pointed out the large number of computer programs that would be necessary for a complete automated system—plus the estimated time and cost of the required programming work and the staff it would take to continue such a project—it was mutually decided to retain the old method of handling receivables. The benefits from mechanization could not possibly offset the cost factors involved in such a step.

Use of a paid preliminary study as an approach to a major, complex assignment is excellent psychology in that it enables the client to obtain a sample of the consultant's approach to a problem, plus presenting the client with the opportunity to evaluate the competence and experience of the consultant and/or his staff. It enables both parties to concentrate on a short, but important, preliminary step before embarking on a potentially long, complex job that requires a considerable outlay of fees on the part of the client.

Equally significant—one result of the preliminary study may well be that the entire nature and scope of the major assignment originally under consideration is radically altered, because of concentrated attention focused on the problem area during the initial study, for the ultimate benefit of all concerned.

A CASE HISTORY

A consulting firm was asked by a prospective client in the publishing business to undertake a computer feasibility study and to evaluate a computer proposal which had been submitted by a computer manufacturer.

A senior in the consulting firm made an initial study, noted the physical arrangement and operation of the warehouse and the billing section, and observed many other basic problems that needed correction. After a series of meetings with the client and his staff, the assignment objective was changed to a review of all present operations and procedures, with recommendations for changes which would correct many deficiencies. The computer feasibility study was postponed indefinitely, since it was mutually agreed that much basic work was necessary to provide a sound foundation for a computer system.

Contents of a Proposal

The usual headings found in a properly organized proposal are outlined here for your guidance. On subsequent pages the contents of each section are discussed in detail.

SAMPLE OUTLINE OF PROPOSAL CONTENTS

1. Identity of document submitted to the prospect.
2. Outline of the existing situation.
3. Nature and scope of services to be performed—backed up by a comprehensive Action Program attached as an exhibit.
4. Benefits and results to be obtained for the client.
5. Statement as to the *time period* to be covered by the assignment.
6. Fee structure and billing arrangements.
7. Other major considerations—such as staffing, physical facilities required, special services and supplies needed, client personnel to be assigned, etc.
8. References and personnel data sheets if requested by the client.

PROPOSAL CONTENTS

Following are examples taken from actual proposals, plus additional comments or explanation of the proposal section being reviewed.

1. First paragraph *identifies* the document as a letter or as a proposal, such as:

   "This is a proposal to render professional consulting guidance in connection with the planning and preparation for a punched-card computer system for the accounts receivable of your firm."

   Another example: "We propose to provide management consulting guidance and assistance in connection with a comprehensive diagnostic review and analysis of operations, policies and procedures in your company."

2. The next paragraph defines or reviews the *existing situation,* such as:

   "The accounts receivable are now kept on bookkeeping machines. The receivables volume has been increasing for several years, and overall clerical costs have kept pace with volume increases. Your management has made the basic decision to automate receivables by application of the IBM 1401 computer, now used primarily for sales analysis and payrolls, to the receivables operation in order to gain substantial benefits in several areas. . . ."

   Another example: "You have been investigating the mechanization of your office procedures for some time. Proposals have been obtained from manufacturers of equipment, such as Friden, National Cash Register, Burroughs—and from data processing service bureaus.

   Each proposal was based on a different systems approach and recommended the use of different equipment. Equipment costs and personnel requirements varied from one proposal to the other. And some proposals failed to provide adequately for Inventory Management records—an essential aspect of your overall systems requirements.

   Further, we believe it is correct to state that when you checked with other firms in the same line of business, you probably found each of them using a different system. All of this has probably induced considerable confusion into your situation and makes your decision difficult."

This paragraph is very important. A review of the prevailing situation provides a reason or foundation for the proposed services. The practitioner may outline here all the background information and facts deemed sufficient to explain to any interested reader of the proposal why and how the proposed project originated.

3. The next section outlines the *Nature and Scope* of Services to be Performed.

Here is an example of this section taken from a proposal to render services in connection with a computer receivables system:

SCOPE OF WORK TO BE PERFORMED BY JAMES/RIVERS AND SMITH.

Phase I. Conduct Basic Review

Conduct a comprehensive basic review of present operations, forms and procedures to obtain the necessary factual foundation for subsequent systems work.

Phase II. Prepare a Series of Special Management Reports

After completion of the basic review, we will prepare a series of special management reports, dealing with special problems found in the review, and planning memoranda to be used in the subsequent accounts receivable systems development work.

Phase III. Provide a Foundation for the Planning and Systems Development Work

While the actual systems development work will be a team project, we propose to provide certain basic written reports, forms and other material to serve as the initial foundation, including a list of steps and instructions for the conversion operation.

COMMENTS ON "NATURE AND SCOPE" SECTION

Quite often, the details of the nature and scope of the proposed services appear at the back of the proposal as a separate exhibit. However, this paragraph remains a part of the first page of the proposal; it then includes only a general statement as to the scope of the work proposed, with a reference to "Exhibit A (B, C or D) found in the back of the proposal."

4. Benefits and Results to be Realized

As pointed out in the special chapter dealing with selling consulting services, this is a very important section of any proposal. In many instances, a separate exhibit does a better job, since the list of benefits may cover several pages. Please refer to Exhibit 4-A or B at the end of this chapter as an example. (In this case, the numeral "4" refers to the chapter number of this book.)

The practioner should devote his best efforts to writing this section of the proposal. Since the average public accountant normally does not think in terms of "selling" benefits, this section may be difficult to write at first.

However, the proposed services either have—or they do not have—potential benefits for the client. If the practitioner is sincerely convinced that he can help the client with a problem, he should exert considerable effort to put down on paper exactly *what those benefits are.* If the practitioner *cannot determine what the benefits are,* the odds are that the *client cannot determine them either*—and there is no basis for the client to authorize the work to be done.

A good, solid list of benefits provides a solid sales foundation (Refer to Chapter 2 on Selling Your Services.) for presenting and selling the assignment to the client. The direct and tangible potential job benefits to the client should outweight the total estimated fee by more than 2-to-1. Otherwise, why should the client bother having the work done?

5. State the Time Period Required for the Work

EXAMPLE: "Assuming no unforeseen major delays, we estimate that the total calendar time required for the work to be done as outlined in prior paragraphs is four months. This estimate is based on the assumption that you will assign to the job one full-time Project Manager; our staff man will work closely with him two or three days each week."

6. Outline the Fee Structure and Billing Arrangements

"We offer to provide consulting guidance, assistance and service throughout the entire Systems Development Phase for a total fee of $_____. We contemplate that the fee shall be billable proportionately over the period of time the service is rendered, which we estimate at four mounths. Accordingly, as a matter of administrative convenience, we propose to submit semi-monthly invoices of $_____ each."

ADDITIONAL PROPOSALS

It is normal for an experienced consultant to uncover problem areas not connected with the job at hand, when performing a specific assignment. And the potential benefits to the client of an assignment to work on these new problems may be substantial. The question arises whether a proposal should be made to cover the situation; and, if so, when.

As a general rule, it is preferable to complete the present assignment before proposing additional work. If the consultant comes in with a proposal for further work before the current assignment is well under way, the client may react unfavorably.

Also, by deferring such action until the initial job is completed, the consultant has the opportunity to get better acquainted with the client, to develop an atmosphere of competence and professional integrity, and, if possible, to develop and deliver major benefits to the client as a result of the first assignment. Under these conditions, acceptance by the client of a suggested corollary assignment becomes very easy and natural for him.

REQUESTS FOR PROPOSALS INVOLVING HIGHLY SPECIALIZED WORK

Occasionally, a consultant will have the opportunity to make a proposal on a job which is actually beyond the experience of the consultant and his staff. What should the practitioner do in this instance?

This situation spotlights the desirability of an alert, aggressive practitioner maintaining constant contacts with a wide range of professional people in many different types of business. Here is where membership in professional organizations can pay off—in that the practitioner who is faced with this problem knows where to look for competent assistance on various specialized problems.

The consultant should suggest to the client a joint assignment to be handled by two (or more) consulting firms. There is no reason for the consultant to be hesitant about suggesting a joint effort, whenever part of the problem involves highly technical areas. In fact, the client will gain increased confidence in the consultant when the consultant explains why he alone should *not* handle the entire assignment.

A CASE HISTORY

Here is an actual case history in which a small consulting firm was invited to undertake a joint assignment:

The basic assignment consisted of an extensive study of a very large charitable organization (with a complete, functional restructuring of all administrative activities as the probable result to be accomplished). The consulting firm which specializes in such work realized that a significant part of the study would involve reviewing a large data-processing installation. Not possessing any qualified people for this phase of the project, the principal of the first consulting firm approached the principal of a small consulting firm which specializes in data-processing applications to request its participation in the engagement. Details were worked out, discussions were held with the client and approval of the joint assignment was obtained. The work was performed to the full satisfaction of the client.

The practitioner should not conceal such participation by other firms or individuals. All of the facts should be made available to the client before the job begins.

Summary

Since a written proposal is the primary working tool of a practitioner who is striving to perform management advisory services, it is difficult to over-emphasize the importance of writing a well-organized, impressive document that will win the client's approval of the proposed assignment.

(Other major considerations and aspects of proposals are covered in the next chapter.)

Exhibit 4-A

EXAMPLES OF BENEFITS FOUND IN GOOD PROPOSALS

Chapter 2 includes sample benefits taken from actual proposals, since the subject matter deals with selling techniques. Because this chapter deals with the preparation and contents of written proposals, we are including this exhibit dealing once more with benefits.

Proposal No. 1 was submitted to a manufacturer of textiles and the benefits were outlined as follows:

"Benefits Sought

The ultimate purpose of this study is to contribute to improving or maintaining profitability, directly or indirectly. We will seek to develop recommendations which will—
- Increase the ability to render good service to customers, thereby cementing good customer relations and strengthening competitive position.
- Reduce the clerical cost of handling present work volume or enable the processing of additional volume without proportionately increasing clerical cost.
- Provide prompt and accurate reports which are *useful* to management.
- Outline factual data on projected costs, savings and benefits if electronic data processing methods are applied to the present work being done manually."

Proposal No. 2 devoted several pages to a general discussion of benefits to be derived by a large chemical manufacturer, if the services of the consultants were engaged. These pages were summarized thus:

"Summary of Benefits

Because we offer concentrated experience and research in this complex application, we can help you to achieve a faster, better and safer system.

Faster: We provide guidance in a straight-line approach, avoiding the wrong decisions and consequent back-tracking which is inevitable the first time a group tackles such a project.

This has a very definite cash value—in several ways:
1. Reduce the time required on the part of your systems people.
2. When re-programming becomes necessary, this obviously involves considerable lost time and actual expense.
3. Substantial benefits have been pinpointed by the initial survey. A delayed installation naturally postpones benefits, and upsets other interrelated job schedules.

Better: We examine each aspect of the new system, and help you make a decision on the basic approach, based on thorough knowledge of the experiences of other firms who have already faced the same decisions and experimented with various methods and approaches. We can assist you in selecting the right method *the first time*.

This has a very definite, tangible value. For example, think about the costs involved in the attempts to automatically apply cash, which required the work of a team of four people for one year (in more than one instance)—and then proved to be unsuccessful!

Safer: . We provide insurance against unsuccessful approaches, unforeseen technical problems and constant changes which affect customers and many internal operating departments."

Proposal No. 3 was designed to assist a firm with the planned conversion of receivables from bookkeeping machines to a computer.

"OUR SERVICES OFFER THE FOLLOWING BENEFITS:

1. Guidance in avoiding the many internal credit and reference problems so often found with automated customer records.
2. Techniques, forms and work flow to derive definite *dollar benefits* from positive control over unadjusted deductions, mis-coded cash credits, absorption of cash differences and errors, etc.
3. Experienced assistance in planning for a smooth and painless conversion from the present system to the new computer system.
4. Concentrated experience brought to bear on designing specific, valuable reports required to meet the genuine information needs of credit men, bookkeepers, collectors and adjusters, as well as top financial management.
5. Provide special forms and reports for answering customer questions and complaints, for back-tracking to detect duplicate deductions taken, duplicate payment of the same invoice, etc. Failure to provide this special collection of forms has actually resulted in needing more personnel to operate the overall system, as proven by the experience of other firms."

Exhibit 4-B

Sometimes it is good practice to remind a prospective client of the benefits to be derived from obtaining professional consulting guidance on a project. This exhibit represents another method of outlining, in summary form, the benefits and basic values accruing to clients from consulting services (as were also presented in detail in Chapter 1).

Benefits generally offered by a competent professional consultant

1. *Time* (Time for concentrated attention to client's problems).
2. Freedom from operating responsibility (and consequent distractions).
3. Understanding of *principles* (From extensive experience).
4. Perspective (A very valuable attribute to bring to bear on a problem).
5. Attitude of being highly interested, but completely *impartial*.
6. Experience with similar situations elsewhere.
7. Technique for applying his skills on a planned basis.
8. Organizational mobility. Free to *move* across departmental lines, at all levels.
9. Freedom from prejudice or favoritism concerning the existing situation.
10. Motivation (Professional, not personal betterment within the firm).

5

Other Major Aspects of Proposals

PART I

SELLING STRATEGY

The purposes of this chapter are to examine several major aspects of proposals and to offer information and suggestions for improved professional proposal writing. Since this chapter also covers fees, fee arrangements and billing, it will be of considerable interest and assistance to the practitioner planning on entering the management services field.

Multiple-Segment Assignments

Many perplexing questions arise in connection with preparation of a proposal. One of the most difficult, fundamental decisions which must be made involves the *scope* of the engagement to be proposed to a client. Here is the basic question to be resolved: Should the practitioner strive for an extensive, total engagement—or should he divide the work into two or three logical phases or sections and then try to sell the first small assignment as a separate project?

Seldom will you find a definitive, clear-cut answer to this basic dilemma. You will resolve the question only after considering the client's overall situation—by reviewing the personalities of all who will be involved in the final decision on the proposed work and your past relations with them, as well as other factors which point to the feasibility and possibility of gaining the client's approval of an extensive assignment in one package.

A related consideration is the number and duration of engagements you now have on hand or lined up. This aspect of the situation may clearly indicate that the wisest course of action at this time is to go after a small assignment only, because of your own lack of staff or other internal problems.

An Effective Strategy

Dividing a potentially large job into several smaller jobs is sound selling strategy in most cases, regardless of other considerations which may point toward going after the total job. This approach appeals to a client for several reasons:

1. It takes time and clear thinking to analyze a large assignment and break it into logical sections—each one of which can be implemented independently with good results. When a consultant accomplishes this feat and presents a well-planned, logical, overall outline of each section, the odds are that the client will be impressed.

2. The client instinctively likes the idea of avoiding an all-embracing commitment to a comprehensive, long-term project that involves a substantial fee. He feels more comfortable, if he can approve the job one phase at a time. This also makes it easier for him to obtain budget approval, if his firm operates under budget controls.

3. The client also knows that this approach will permit him and his staff to become familiar with the consultant's method of working on an assignment, and enable him to evaluate the experience and competence of the man or men assigned to the first phase of the project—before approving further work on subsequent phases of the master plan.

How to Price Job Phases

Be sure to place a price on each phase or section of the job that is higher than the pro rata amount would be for the entire job—if undertaken and approved as one integrated project. It is only logical that the price of the job, when handled as a separate, independent phase, will be higher than if it were undertaken as one continuing project. This technique provides the prospect with a monetary incentive to go ahead and authorize the practitioner to do the entire job.

Prepare Proposal in Rough-Draft Format First

Here is a very successful technique of potential value to any consultant:
PREPARE THE PROPOSAL IN ROUGH-DRAFT FORMAT—and review it with the client while it is in rough form.
This technique offers many benefits:

1. It provides the prospective client with an opportunity to *participate* in drafting the final version of the proposal. He may detect inaccurate statements and figures in the proposal material; he may want to add sentences or paragraphs pertaining to certain internal circumstances or situations of a delicate nature. He will have the opportunity to eliminate phrases or reference to subjects which he knows will arouse unnecessary issues not pertinent to the proposed work.

2. If you are dealing directly with the key executive of the firm, you gain his personal participation and ideas through this technique. If he, in turn, must sell the project to one or more executives higher on the corporate or management ladder, he *will help you* explore all possible benefits and will make them more explicit and more forceful.

3. The review of the proposal offers still another opportunity for both parties to define the scope of the assignment further, to understand the objectives better and outline them even more clearly. One outcome of the review may be discovery of additional major benefits which will help sell top management!

PART II

FEE ARRANGEMENTS AND OTHER CONSIDERATIONS

Businessmen usually think of per diem rates in connection with fees for consulting work. And, they know that the total fee for a typical assignment is usually based on an estimate of the total number of work-days required to complete the assignment.

Even so, consultants are frequently requested to quote either a fixed fee for a specific, well-defined assignment—or to quote minimum-maximum figures, referred to as a "bracket quotation."

From the business executive's viewpoint, this approach to quoting fees makes sense. Quite often, a consideration of budget exists. That is, the cost of the proposed services must be covered by a budget request, with subsequent approval by a budget officer or committee. Or, the businessman may consider his request for a bracket quotation to be a prudent step to guard against an unexpectedly large fee commitment.

A bracket quotation protects the consultant by stipulating a minimum fee for the job, and it also protects the client by stating the maximum fee. If unforeseen situations or problems force the assignment into new areas, then the consultant and the client will sit down and redefine the nature and scope of the assignment, set up new objectives—and simultaneously, renegotiate the fee arrangements.

Why does the consultant need "protection" by stipulating a minimum fee for a job? This necessity arises from intense and long-term specialization in a certain field. For example, if a consultant has invested four years of time and effort—literally studying one type of application or problem for six or seven days a week—he becomes too proficient in that a fee which was quoted strictly on a per diem arrangement would probably be *too small* to adequately compensate him for his skill and ability to deliver very beneficial results for the client. It would be most unfair for a professional man's earnings to decrease in direct proportion with his ability to do an outstanding job in a highly technical field—merely because he was able to do the work in a short time span!

Per Diem Rates

Per diem rates vary considerably from one consulting firm to another, and they vary according to the age, experience and classification of the person doing the job. A recent study conducted among members of the consulting fraternity revealed the following detailed data about fees:

Classification of personnel	Fee Range	Normal Average
Partner	$175 to $400	$250
Principal or Senior	150 to 300	200
Management Consultant	120 to 250	150
Junior Staff Consultant	80 to 160	125

The "normal average" reflects those rates most commonly applied.

In connection with this sensitive area of per diem rates, fees and billings, there is a number of significant points to observe:

1. It is accepted practice to quote a per diem rate for a staff man or men, then add a specified amount to cover supervision by a partner or manager of the consulting firm. *Note—* When you hear that a partner or a principal in a firm charges $350 to $500 per day for his services, this rate applies only when he is performing in a short-term supervisory capacity. Such rates normally do not apply if the same individual is performing normal consulting services on the level of a staff consultant.

2. There should be a relationship between the work progress and the number of billings rendered. Any engagement which seems to produce more billings than visible results is subject to a critical review by the client.

3. The nature of an assignment may be such that a very heavy investment in the number of man-days is positively necessary in the early stages of the assignment, with a distinct

tapering-off to occur in the latter weeks or months of the project. In this case, it is desirable to eliminate the "front-end load" by deferring some of the billings from the early stages and picking up the unbilled time and costs with invoices rendered as the project is nearing completion. This type of arrangement can be presented to the client in such a way that you will gain his full approval and cooperation in most instances.

4. Do not present your final invoice until the job is completed. It is much better business practice to withhold the final invoice (even though the quoted time period has elapsed) if the project remains incomplete. Your client may pay the invoice when it's submitted to him, but the possibility of hidden resentment or hostility always may result from your request for payment in advance of completion of the job. Your client is well aware of the criticism that will be his lot from his superiors if you fail to deliver the final results as outlined in the formal proposal.

5. Do not propose or accept an assignment for which your fee is based on a percentage of results or savings achieved. This practice is unprofessional and it will create friction between you and the client. The client will have a definite tendency to play down all benefits and savings, since your compensation is based on the agreed-upon savings. You will receive no credit for intangible benefits, which may far outweigh those with direct, admissable dollars-and-cents savings.

It is much more appropriate to quote a per diem rate, or a fixed fee for a job; then, the client has no reason to understate actual benefits or savings which he derived from the assignment.

Out-of-Pocket Expenses

A proposal should include some mention of out-of-pocket expenses, even if none is anticipated. It is customary for all travel expenses to be paid for by the client. Air travel, hotel rooms and meals are all in this category. Billings for such expense should be clearly identified to avoid future misunderstandings. Since the client is usually faced with budget considerations, he is entitled to a reasonably accurate estimate of total fees and costs involved in the proposed project.

A major point in connection with these expenses is that such items are usually billed at cost; no profit markup is added.

Rates for Management Services

Many practitioners who are just entering the field of management services tend to under-price their services. They have a tendency to apply the fee schedule normally used for accounting services. This fee schedule is based on an hourly rate. For pricing accounting services, this may be adequate, since the CPA has the advantage of continuity year after year with his clients. He can depend upon continuing assignments from the client. Therefore, the per hour or per diem rate can legitimately be lower than the appropriate rate that should be charged for management services. Here is why:

In the management services field each job is a unique assignment. There is no continuity—no "repeat" business, so to speak. The practitioner soon learns that he must charge enough to cover the unbillable time of the staff which he maintains to handle assignments.

The ratio of unbillable time to billable time is sometimes rather high. It is normal to find that 35% to 40% of the staff's total time cannot be billed. When a firm is able to bill 75% of the time of its staff, it is doing an outstanding selling and performing job.

Guidelines for Establishing Rates

Because of the high cost of unbillable time as outlined above, experienced consultants have developed a couple of basic guidelines to use whenever they quote per diem rates for staff members:

1. *Multiply the man's daily salary by a factor of 2½ to 3.*

   Suppose that the salary of a staff man is $12,000 per year. Dividing by 50 weeks, we find that he is paid $240 a week, or $48 per day. Applying the factor of 2½, the firm must bill this man's time at $120 per day. If we apply the factor of 3, the per diem rate is $144, which probably would be increased to $150.

2. *Decimal-Point Method.* Write down the man's yearly salary, then move the decimal point two places to the left; the result is the per diem rate. Here are two examples of this:

   - The per diem rate for a staff man with a yearly salary of $10,000 is $100. (Move decimal point two places to the left.)
   - The rate for a man with a yearly salary of $12,000 is $120.

These examples indicate that the decimal-point method is actually based on a factor of 2½ to 1.

HOW TO PREVENT UNDER-ESTIMATING JOBS

Estimating the number of man-days required for an assignment is admittedly a difficult problem—since each assignment is unique, even though it may resemble prior jobs. Many factors enter into this problem. We will discuss some of these on subsequent pages.

One significant factor is that the client should assign a qualified project manager to work with the consultant. This is especially important when the consultant contracts to provide guidance and counsel to the client's staff, as opposed to doing the work himself. If the client fails to assign a man who is both competent and willing to assume responsibility for the project, the work load and responsibility shifts to the consultant—even though the proposal clearly specified the nature and scope of the work that he was supposed to do. This one factor can easily increase the estimated number of work days by as much as 25% to 50% over the original estimate.

Here is one way to guard against under-estimating: When you discuss the proposed assignment with the client, ask him which one of two types of service he wants you to quote on: A guidance and counseling type of job, or a complete "turn-key" job, where you receive minimum assistance from his staff and project manager.

Be sure to point out that if the second approach is the one the client wants—possibly because of a staff shortage or too many other projects—then the total fee will obviously be increased over that which is applicable to the first type of service. If the client wants his staff to do the work, with your services consisting primarily of guidance and counseling, you should protect yourself in the following ways:

1. Interview and qualify the project manager and staff men. Determine their background, experience and attitude toward the project. Try to ascertain their ability to perform as expected, with the active assistance of your guidance and counsel when and where it's required.

2. Discuss with the client the fact that better long-term results will be obtained if his staff assumes the responsibility for the project—with your participation being that of providing experienced direction at each step and of guiding the project to its stated objectives. The

reason for this is that your part of the project eventually comes to an end; someone must take charge of the project and manage it after your participation has ended.

Cost of Reports; Time Required

A number of written reports usually result from a consulting assignment. One of the skills which a practitioner must develop when he does management services work is the writing of clear-cut, forceful management reports that are a basic end-result of his studies and recommendations.

A completed assignment may result in one major report—or several interim reports on various subjects, followed by one final report which summarizes the entire assignment. The main point to stress in estimating fees is that the preparation of these reports take time. Reviewing each report while it is still in rough-draft form, plus the rewriting, requires special appointments with the client, followed by considerable time and work in the office. The experienced consultant always increases the estimate of man-days required to do the basic work by a factor which provides for time to write reports.

Check List for Estimating an Assignment

Here is a check list of action steps which are usually included in an assignment—all of which tend to increase the total number of man-days required to do the total job.
- Conduct interviews with department heads and top management; take notes and document each interview.
- Plan and hold information meetings at various stages of the project to invite ideas and suggestions from department heads and middle management. Prepare memos of each meeting and document all decisions and policies that have been established or agreed upon.
- Organize and conduct review-and-work planning sessions.
- Perform project development work, outline methods and procedures.
- Prepare charts, forms or other material and present them to users; make changes when necessary.
- Review survey notes and restructure detailed notes according to function, area or department.
- Draft final reports and review them at various levels of management.
- Provide time for implementing solutions on an interim basis to problems uncovered during the basic review work.

Don't Do a Rush Job

Beware of doing a rush job on a project. Even if your concentrated background and experience qualifies you to move very, very rapidly on an assignment, slow down. Business men are prone to distrust fast decisions and hastily-done work. Treat their problems with care and with due respect; be cautious about making major recommendations based on impulsive solutions. Cross-check your thinking with your associates in the firm and do some field research, as mentioned in other sections of this handbook, before going on record with suggested major changes.

Time and Personnel Correlation

In the field of work reviews and systems analysis, there is some justification for charging a large firm a larger fee than you would charge a smaller firm for an almost identical job. The reason is that job time studies indicate that survey time actually does increase proportionately with the number of people who perform a given function or work in a department.

How to Increase Accuracy in Quoting Fees

The only sure way to increase the accuracy in estimating time and fees for each job on which a proposal is made is to keep accurate and complete records of time and costs involved in each assignment handled. These records can subsequently be reviewed and evaluated in comparison with the apparent requirements of the job under consideration; fairly accurate estimates can then be made.

Many practitioners have found that keeping a running diary, as the work progresses, provides the best type of record for future analysis when estimating a similar job. Such a diary provides invaluable reminders of and clues to unforeseen work which, as it developed, required considerable time and special attention.

SUGGESTIONS FOR PROPOSAL PREPARATION

The suggestions for proposal preparation listed in subsequent paragraphs represent a blend of points found in a study made by the Association Planning Committee, Association of Consulting Management Engineers, Inc., plus other points distilled from the combined experience of several practicing consultants.

Proposal Check List

Most proposals should contain the following elements or sections:
- What the consultant proposes to do.
- What benefits the client will receive—why the consultant proposes to render the service.
- How the consultant proposes to do the work; where it will be done; how many members of the consultant's staff will be needed; and what client facilities will be required.
- Period of time covered by the project, from starting date to completion.
- How much it will cost. Include fee schedule and billing arrangements.
- What specific accomplishments can be expected (expressed in terms of savings, cost reductions, benefits, increased profits, etc.).
- Why the consultant is qualified to do the work.
- Planned or suggested starting date.
- References that include consultant's qualifications and experience—if client has requested this data.

Proposal Format

In many instances the consultant is faced with a decision in regard to the proposal format—should it be in report format, or a business letter?

Suggestions:

- Use letters for small assignments unless client requests that your proposal be in report format.
- For a formal and extensive proposal, use a report format in a bound cover—and include exhibits,* if necessary.
- Use center headings for major subjects, plus side headings for minor subjects.

Cover Letter

When the proposal is prepared in report format, it is customary to attach a cover letter to it. Quite often, the fees are quoted only in the cover letter and are omitted from the proposal. There are several good reasons for this.

- The client may want several people in his firm to review the proposal and evaluate it. At the same time he may not want these people to be concerned with the fee structure, billing arrangements, or the total expenditure required.
- The consultant himself may favor this format, since he can provide a copy of the proposal accepted by the client, and the action program to a staff man for guidance on the job—without revealing the special fee arrangements made with the client.

Other Key Points

The proposal should include very little, if any, outright selling phrases or sentences. However, a list of the benefits and results to be obtained (which have been reviewed and verified by the prospective client while the proposal was in rough-draft form) is an essential part of the proposal.

Do not use the passive tense for describing scope of the work to be done. Use action verbs fully; note excerpts taken from an "Action Program" found in a successful proposal:

Action Program for Systems-Development Work to Be Done

Prepare a Master Planning and Installation Schedule.
Construct a Master Transactions List.
Survey existing operations and procedures.
Interview key individuals representing all levels of management.
Determine information requirements for all reports.

(Notice the crisp tone and authority of a proposed action program when action verbs are consistently utilized to begin each sentence. If you substitute the passive tense to describe the work to be done, you will notice a distinct difference in the effect on the reader.)

Do not use the pronoun "I" in a proposal. The proposal is supposed to represent a commitment by the entire firm—not that of any one individual.

Avoid the use of nicknames when referring to individuals, either those employed by the clients, or members of the consulting firm that's submitting the proposal.

When naming officers or executives in the client firm, refer to them formally.

---

* Exhibits may be used for the "Action Program" (an outline of the scope of the assignment) for the list of benefits and for special purposes.

(The basic reason for these admonitions is that proposals are circulated among the top echelon of management. They are read by officials who may never meet the consultant or members of his staff face to face. The unseen executives will inevitably form certain opinions and conclusions about the consulting firm—based strictly on reactions generated by the proposal itself. A formal, businesslike format is more apt to create the good impression desired by the consultant.)

Determine WHO in client's firm will read the proposal—and HOW it will be used. This is a key point which is easy to overlook. Accurate, advance determination of the WHO and HOW may alter the contents and format of a proposal, depending upon the particular circumstances surrounding the proposed services. Furthermore, a second proposal, prepared for a firm after completion of a prior assignment, may necessarily be quite different from the original proposal which was accepted by the client.

Special Arrangements

A proposal should be as specific as possible. If certain equipment or facilities of the client are needed during the engagement, this should be stated. Arrangements for staffing should be spelled out, along with other pertinent aspects of the proposed engagement.

Here is an example taken from a proposal:

a. We understand that you will assign one man to the Project on a full-time basis; we are to review and evaluate the background and experience of the man proposed by you.
b. We request the use of a fully-equipped work room to be used as an office; equipment to include a typewriter and a dictating machine.
c. It is agreed that typists in your firm will type survey notes and prepare necessary copies of interim reports and planning memoranda for the project team as the work progresses.
d. We warrant the experience and capabilities of the man to be assigned from our staff. We will provide you with a complete Personal Data Sheet for your information and advance approval.

If paper, printing, supplies or overtime clerical work will be required, it is well to specify who bears the cost. (Normally, the client does.) In fact, anything that will avoid future friction and misunderstandings should be carefully outlined.

References

If the prospective client specifically requests references, then it is appropriate to enclose pages which list the names, titles and telephone numbers of key executives in firms for whom the consulting firm has done work in the past.

When such a list is made part of a proposal, it is good practice to telephone the executives whose names appear on the reference sheets, and inform them that you have listed them as references in connection with a proposal which you've prepared for a specific firm (state the firm's full name). This is not only a courteous act, but it gives your references an opportunity to formulate in advance a reply when the anticipated visit or telephone call takes place from your prospective client.

Personal Data Sheets

It is good practice for any consultant to have on file a set of printed Personal Data Sheets for each principal or partner in the consulting department, plus sheets for each staff man. Copies of these sheets may be routinely supplied in the back of each proposal. (See Chapter 3 for examples.)

Method of Proposal Transmittal

In most instances a proposal should not be mailed. It should be delivered to the prospect in person and presented by a principal of the consulting firm.

It is an excellent idea for the staff men who will do the work (or supervise a group) to accompany the principal on this call, and participate in the review of the proposal with the prospective client.

Maintenance of Project

Caretaking and maintenance of a project, after the consultant has completed his assignment, is obviously of great importance and value to the client. The proposal may appropriately refer to arrangements for the consultant to return at certain intervals to review the project's status and its results, and to assist with further refinements or problems.

6

How to Write Reports

In management consulting it is difficult to over-emphasize the importance of superior report writing. The essence of consulting is rendering personal services. The visible evidence of the work that's done for the client is the written report, or reports produced as a result of performing the work.

Sound suggestions and recommendations, resulting from an assignment, will lose their value if they are presented in such a way that the client fails to understand them fully, or if he fails to recognize their merit. On the other hand, suggestions and programs that represent only modest improvements can be "dressed up" and presented in such a way that they will receive enthusiastic acceptance.

It is easy to conclude, then, that a successful practitioner must develop the ability to write superior reports for all assignments that he performs for clients. The purpose of this chapter is to provide information and guidelines for effective report writing.

Now, it is unfortunately true that most people, including many professionals, dislike writing anything. Even the writing of an informal letter to a relative or a friend is something that many people dread. And, when faced with the necessity for writing a voluminous report to a client, many consultants feel that this is the worst phase of the consulting profession.

What Is a Management Report?

A report is an important document for those who are to use it. It is fundamentally the written communication of information or counsel which is desired by the recipient, and which will be used by that person, or persons, to accomplish one or more specific results or objectives. The way a specific report is to be used and the requirements of the user should determine the structure and contents of the report.

Further, the success of the report depends on how intelligently it has been planned to meet all the conditions it must serve. For example, the report must make it possible for the reader to easily obtain the essential ideas and information presented in the report in a logical, orderly sequence.

General Principles of Report Writing

1. Express each idea in a separate sentence. Avoid the use of long, rambling sentences.

2. The length of a paragraph is related both to the subject matter and to the natural limits of a reader's attention. In other words, a short paragraph which contains simple, short sentences will convey your ideas better than massive paragraphs that consist of long, involved sentences.

Each paragraph should include a "topic sentence," close to the beginning of the paragraph. Once the reader has identified the subject of a paragraph, the writer must hold his attention by elaborating on that particular subject until he has fully covered it.

If the subject matter covered in the paragraph is of unusual importance, one technique used to close a paragraph is to repeat or summarize the subject toward the end of the paragraph.

Report Requirements

A report should satisfy the following requirements:
- It should present all material that is pertinent to the subject.
- It should present the subject matter according to a preconceived plan, based on a logical analysis and classification of the pertinent material.
- It should make this plan so evident that it can be easily understood and eliminate confusion.
- It should be written in a simple, concise style that permits no possibility of misinterpretation.
- It should be intelligible to all who are likely to read it, even though the reader may not be especially well versed in its technical detail.

How to Make Reports Interesting

The ideas which are presented here have been taken from the Rudolf Flesch book, *A New Way to Better English*. The author spent several years analyzing various books and magazines to determine why some magazines are very difficult to read. He then studied articles and magazines which were easy to read; and, by a comparison of the characteristics of each, he was able to pinpoint the elements that make written material difficult or easy to read.

This is definitely an important consideration to you as a consultant. If your clients find that your reports are difficult to read and understand, they are not apt to act on the recommendations found in the reports. If this happens, you will not enjoy a good reputation as a consultant who gets things done for his clients. So, let's review briefly what to do to make written material easy to read.

- Be very specific in the use of facts, names, dates and places. Use illustrations whenever possible.
- Keep your sentences short. Each sentence should average about 16 words in length.
- Emphasize certain words by underlining them. One underlined word may raise the effectiveness of a sentence or paragraph enormously. This writing technique corresponds to a speaker who raises his voice to emphasize a key point.
- Use numbers whenever it's logical to do so. Identify an event by its date.
- Use at least eight periods within a hundred words; use commas only where necessary.

- Use as many question marks as you can. If you deal with a question, formulate it as a direct question with a question mark.
- Use parentheses freely to play things down.
- Use dialogue wherever it's applicable. This adds interest to written material.
- Keep your paragraphs short. Don't put more than two, three or four of your 16-word sentences into one paragraph.

The Four Steps in Report Writing

There are four distinct steps in the evolution of a report.

1. Preliminary study
2. Careful planning
3. Actual report writing
4. Refining and polishing

The first step involves reviewing, assembling and sorting all of the material that's to go into the report. The consultant must evaluate all his facts and material of all types to decide what conclusions and recommendations are indicated.

The second step is the period of careful planning. In this stage it is essential that you keep the prospective *reader's point of view* constantly in mind, and structure the report accordingly. One discipline which tremendously helps you do this is to force yourself to write a concise sentence or paragraph, stating the *purpose of the report*. This is sometimes surprisingly difficult to do. The end result may make it appear easy to write such a summary. For example, consider the following one-sentence summary in a report to a client:

"The purpose of this report is to provide factual data, guidelines, evaluations and conclusions relating to the desirability and feasability of installing an electronic computer to replace the tab equipment."

This one-sentence summary was distilled from 34 typewritten pages of material. It took the consultant several days to condense the material down to a single sentence. He had to review his notes several times to determine what the client wanted as a result of the assignment, and how the client would use the report.

The third step, or actual writing of the report should be viewed as a process that requires several steps or stages. First, you should simply get down on paper, as quickly and easily as possible, all the ideas and material which seem to belong in the report. Don't worry about grammar, sentence structure or continuity. You will correct all of these things during the rewriting and polishing stages.

Most authorities on written communications agree that writing a report should be done in a single, uninterrupted period of concentrated effort—rather than by a part or a section at a time. Thus, the writer achieves a unity of style and a proper proportion of parts that are impossible to come by otherwise. This indicates the desirability of using a tape recorder, so that the ideas can flow without delay or interruption.

The fourth step is usually easier than the actual writing stage, since it involves a critical review of your rough draft, so you can make additions, changes and deletions. One helpful suggestion is to read aloud the key paragraphs. This sometimes reveals incomplete thoughts or awkward sentences.

The Outline

An effective report is one that is logically and systematically organized. That is, the presentation of information flows from one topic to another, with no awkward digressions and interruptions. The easiest way to achieve the desired result is to outline the subject matter—then test and review the outline for any overlapping ideas or duplicate subjects as well as for continuity.

Use 4″ × 6″ index cards to record the topics that must be covered in the report, writing one topic on one card.

Test the cards with reference to the limits of your assignment, to determine those subjects which are extraneous to the assignment. Add anything that you have omitted or have temporarily overlooked.

Now classify your material represented on the cards. Put all the subjects together that logically belong together.

Finally, decide on the most effective sequence of presenting the subjects included on the unit cards. One way to assist yourself with this critical problem is to arrange the cards in various sequences, and then write the subjects in outline form on a pad of paper. This technique frequently indicates which subjects have been duplicated in the various areas, or it may spotlight whatever is out of sequence.

Suggested Report Format

Here is the recommended format for a formal, lengthy report which is to be accompanied by a letter of transmittal to the client:

- Title display.
- The letter of transmittal which also serves as the introduction—and *a summary of conclusions and recommendation.*
- Table of Contents.
- An introductory report section presenting the method of approach or any other introductory or explanatory material that should not be included in the letter of transmittal.
- The body of the report, carefully organized, so that it gives the impression of organization, order and system—and which will stand the most critical analysis and examination.
- A terminal section, summary, conclusion or final comments.
- An appendix that segregates voluminous detailed information—such as dates, graphs, charts, and exhibits which serve to back up facts, conclusions and recommendations included in the body of the report.

Exhibit 6-A shows the Table of Contents that was taken from a report on a computer feasibility study. Notice the *flow* of subjects—from the introductory material to a review of the present situation, to a review of the various computer types and makes, followed by specific recommendations.

A well-organized report never combines a discussion of what you did or what you found out with what you recommend. Be very careful to segregate these two subject areas—to avoid confusion and to obtain the reader's full concentration on your suggestions and recommendations. (This is so important that I repeat the point: *Do not scatter your recommendations throughout the report for various areas or segments of the client's business; bring all recommendations together into one group whenever this is possible.*)

Exhibit 6-A

TABLE OF CONTENTS FROM A REPORT

I   INTRODUCTORY
        Scope and Objectives
        Interviews
        Computer Requirements
        Evaluation of Data Storage Methods
II   REVIEW OF PRESENT SITUATION
        Present Work Load
        Other Aspects of the Work Load
        Circulation Department
        New Applications Considered
        Review of the Master File
        Possible Use of a Service Bureau
        Conclusions and Recommendations
III REVIEW OF COMPUTER TYPES AND MAKES
        Magnetic Tape Computer
        Environment
        Environmental Costs
        Typical Monthly Rentals
        Random Access Computer
        Punched Card Computer
        Our Recommendation
IV THE CASE FOR A PUNCHED CARD COMPUTER
        Ease and Speed of Programming
        Facilitates Rapid Change-Over
        Processing Speed
        Requires No Special Environment
        Requires No Tape Library
        Cost Differential
        Other Benefits
V   SPECIFIC RECOMMENDATION AS TO COMPUTER MAKE AND MODEL
        The Model No. XXXX Card Processing Computer
        Suggested Action Program

APPENDIX

EXHIBITS

How to Gain Client Participation in Report Writing

Here is a good general rule: DO NOT SUBMIT ANY REPORT IN FORMAL AND FINAL FORMAT WITHOUT FIRST GOING THROUGH THE PRELIMINARY STEPS LISTED BELOW.

- After you have gained all the facts and figures necessary for report preparation, type the report in ROUGH-DRAFT FORM and double spaced. First, review it with someone on your staff or in your office; glaring errors of omission or commission may be detected this way.

- Take the rough draft to the client and review it with him. First, stress to your client the fact that the report *is* a preliminary draft, and that you want your client's reaction, opinions and possible corrections, before proceeding any further.
- If the report deals with technical, operating functions or procedures, it may be advisable for you to review it first with a department head or line supervisor *before* presenting it to the client.

Now, this obviously takes time and work. It may seem unnecessary. Therefore, let's review the two basic reasons for these preliminary steps:

1. The first reason is to protect you from making a ridiculous mistake. If a report is based on facts and figures which prove to be incorrect or incomplete, the accompanying recommendations may be completely invalid.

2. The second reason is equally important. The successful consultant must always be aware of the importance of the *human equation* in his professional work. The finest, most accurate report that deals with an extremely vital subject, may be rejected or ignored if the people involved in the project do not participate in any phase of the report; and, if they're given no opportunity to express their views, or to display their knowledge and importance.

Obtain the full participation of some key person who will be on hand to supervise the new procedures or suggested methods after your assignment is completed. Be sure that your suggestions and recommendations are not yours alone: Enlist the support of line supervisors and other experienced people, who will, in return, adopt a proprietary attitude toward the new system or new approach to old problems; and who will strive to make the suggestions and recommendations a practical reality.

General Rule: A FINAL REPORT SHOULD CONTAIN NO SURPRISES TO THE CLIENT.

Report Copies and the Status Problem

After the client and his staff have helped you develop a report to the point of final typing, the problem arises in regard to how many carbon copies are needed and for whom. This problem involves seniority and status considerations.

For example, suppose that the liaison officer who is supervising your assignment is a corporate vice-president. All final reports are submitted to him. However, he has requested three sets of each report—one for the president, one for himself and one for the treasurer.

If you prepare an original and two carbon copies, do you give the original to the president, or does he get carbon copy No. 1? What will be the reaction of the treasurer if he receives carbon copy No. 2?

One acceptable solution is to provide three xerox copies, which, in appearance, compare favorably with the original typed report.

Do Not Use Pronoun "I"

Any formal report is presumed to represent the best thinking of several members of the accounting or consulting firm which you represent. For this reason, the plural pronoun "We" is usually preferred over use of the pronoun "I" when you're writing reports.

Reports Should Be Formal

It is recommended that reports be worded in a formal manner, and that use of first names or nicknames be avoided.

The reason for this assertion is that consulting reports are usually perused by owners or officials of the client firm other than those members who arranged for the work to be done, or those who are participating in the project. Since these anonymous officials will inevitably reach certain conclusions and form certain opinions about the consulting firm—based entirely on the written reports that they read—it is very important for the practitioner to make each report as factual, concise and valuable to the client as possible.

Use Action Verbs

Many reports that deal with business operations will include in them the details of any suggested new procedures to be followed. Or, these proposed changes will be submitted as a separate exhibit.

One of the most common mistakes that is made by untrained writers is the constant use of the passive voice. For example, suppose that the practitioner is describing procedures that deal with receiving and applying cash. His version will probably read something like this:

1. The envelope *is* opened; the check *is* removed.

2. The checks *are* sorted by remitter's name, then matched to corresponding customer ledgers for application of cash.

By contrast, the use of ACTION VERBS makes the written procedures come to life. Write the proposed procedures thus:

1. *Open* the envelopes, *remove* the checks.

2. *Sort* checks alphabetically, then *match* each check to the corresponding customer ledger.

The same principle should be applied to those sections of a report which describe what you did during the survey, review, analysis or other work phases connected with the assignment. In other words, when you describe the steps you've taken or any work that's done, always use ACTION VERBS. For your benefit, and to save yourself time, a comprehensive list of action verbs that are frequently used in various final reports appears below.

Determined
Reviewed
Studied
Evaluated
Examined
Analyzed
Discussed
Covered
Traced
Verified
Noted
Interviewed
Balanced
Observed
Checked
Established
Recommended
Held (group meeting, etc.)
Participated (in)
Provided (list for guidance, etc.)
Conducted (an overall review)

Note the wide choice of applicable action verbs. By selective use of verbs from this list, the final report will clearly state all the work that's done, without the use of repetitious verbs or phrases.

Another Sample Report

The final exhibit in this chapter is the Table of Contents from a lengthy report that was prepared for a client by a large, well-known firm of management engineers.

Note the arrangement of the subject matter, as well as the interesting handling of suggestions and recommendations. After the findings are presented for each major department, the consultants present their recommendations. Then, in Chapter 7 of the report, they bring all suggestions and recommendations together into one consolidated listing. (These totaled 19 in the report.)

The Transmittal Letter

The letter of transmittal does more than merely accompany the report. It gives the reader his first contact with the subject and prepares him to receive the subject matter. It does the following:

- It states the subject of the report.
- It indicates the purpose for which the report has been prepared.
- It summarizes, in a few words, all of the conclusions and recommendations made.
- It explains the plan of treatment.

Busy executives demand that the gist of the report be presented to them in the first few pages. To satisfy this requirement, the letter of transmittal provides the introduction and the summary of conclusions and recommendations. In other words, the client should be able to grasp the purpose of the report, and the conclusions and recommendations * without reading the report itself. He wants to know what the proposition is, how the writer proceeded to investigate or study it, what he found out, what he concluded and what he recommends.

When trying to meet the requirements of the transmittal letter, as outlined above, you will quickly find that there is a tendency to provide too much detail. The letter should contain nothing except the briefest, most compact sentences and statements. The backup data and details are provided in the body of the report; they do not belong in the letter of transmittal. Further, the Table of Contents makes it easy for the reader to turn to those sections of the report which contain full details of the subjects in which the reader is most interested. (See Exhibit 6-B.)

---

* As a professional management consultant, don't act as a gatherer and a reporter of facts, leaving the decisions to the client. MAKE CONCRETE RECOMMENDATIONS, and be prepared to back them up.

Exhibit 6-B

REPORT TITLE AND TABLE OF CONTENTS
(Taken from a Report Made By a Large Firm of Management Engineers)

THE COMMONWEALTH EDUCATIONAL CORPORATION

A GENERAL APPRAISAL
OF
ORGANIZATION AND BUSINESS METHODS

TABLE OF CONTENTS

Adams, Brown and Charles
Management Engineers

7

How Clients Evaluate
Management Advisors

The first chapter outlined what management consultants do and the business situations which most frequently lead to the engagement of outside consultants. Other chapters have covered the mechanics of proposal writing, fee arrangements and billing, how to write effective management reports and other subjects connected with the practice of consulting.

One purpose of this chapter is to present guidelines for a critique of your own work (or work that's done by your staff) *from the client's viewpoint*. And, the last section of this chapter provides an insight into how clients who frequently employ outside consultants *rate themselves* on the effectiveness of their use of the services of outside professionals.

Learning how clients—with a considerable accumulation of experience in working closely with consultants—evaluate and rate consultants should be of great interest to everyone in this challenging field. Also, the rating criteria included in this chapter may serve as a convenient check list for reviewing each assignment as it nears completion. In effect, this check list will enable you to rate your own performance—before the client does! It provides the basis for your diagnostic review or critique of each assignment before you prepare the final report to the client.

One valuable use of this check list is to enable you to determine quickly which work phases have not yet been begun or completed; it will assure quality control over incomplete assignments.

Philip Shay, executive director of the Association of Consulting Management Engineers, in an article in the *Business Management* magazine, lists the following fifteen questions which the client should ask about a completed assignment, in order to determine whether the consultant really helped the client's company.

The Fifteen Points for Client Evaluation

1. Did the consultant prepare a written statement of the nature and scope of his work—and the objectives?

63

2. Did the consultant carefully plan the work?
3. Did he submit progress reports, or interim reports to appropriate executives?
4. Did the consultant and his staff operate in a professional manner?
5. Did the consultant work constructively with our people?
6. Did our staff work well with the consultant?
7. Did the consultant teach our employees so they could implement and control the improved methods?
8. Are we more competent managers as a result of the assignment?
9. Did the study achieve our objectives?
10. Did the recommendations incorporate the best collective judgment of the consultant and our own executives?
11. Are we satisfied with the way the consultant presented his findings and recommendations?
12. Did the consultant maintain close contact with our staff when it was considering and implementing the recommendations?
13. Was the consultant's work done in a reasonable time for a reasonable fee?
14. How do our executives rate the consultant and his work?
15. Would we retain the consultant again if we needed this type of service?

Item number five in the list above involves human relations. If a consultant is not adept at getting along with people at all levels, and if he antagonizes various members of the client's staff, his services may have limited value, even though he is competent and knows his business.

The Time Element

It is admittedly difficult for a client to evaluate objectively a consultant's work shortly after the job is completed. This is true because of the very nature of consulting work. For example, the consultant may have made eight important recommendations during the course of the assignment, or in the final report. The client may have accepted two or three almost at once; action on the remaining recommendations may be pending. As time passes, the client probably will implement two or three more of the written recommendations. The point is that the client really should not evaluate the consultant's performance in total until most of the recommendations have been put into practice—and the results have been determined.

Major Purpose of a Consulting Assignment

Your chief goal, after completion of an assignment, is to get the client to implement your major recommendations. Remember that the "ACTION PROGRAM" resulting from the recommendations is the major output of all the work you have done on the project. Unless action follows recommendations, the assignment may well be rated a failure by the client.

Why Reports Lie in a Desk—Unused

Why does a client fail to act on a report which outlines logical action steps of potential value to him and his firm? The answer involves elements of human psychology, poor salesmanship and other aspects of management services.

Five major reasons have been given to explain why reports are not implemented:
1. Poor definition of the problem and the objectives.
2. Consultant failed to gain the confidence of the client.

3. Operating personnel and other key people on the client's staff failed to participate in the project.
4. Liaison with the client broke down during the work phases.
5. An unsatisfactory relationship developed between the client and the consultant.

The Sixth Major Reason

The sixth reason is surprising, since it would seem to be an integral component of the client's planning for a consulting engagement. If the client fails to plan for and set up procedures for the "action" stage of the report—that is, he does not plan for the implementation stage—the project may never bear fruit.

The *Acme Reporter,* published by the Association of Consulting Management Engineers, says flatly: "Implementation does not just happen. It has to be anticipated and planned for during the time the report (or reports) itself is taking shape."

Because of the importance of this point, the intelligent practitioner will add this to his list of things to discuss with the client during the early stages of the assignment. This will assure everyone concerned that the client will be prepared for the implementation stage, that he will get the best results possible from the study, and that the consultant will earn a good reputation from the assignment.

Evaluating Benefits

Businessmen should regularly evaluate the worth of each consulting assignment. And, the client should estimate the total costs, including the cost of company time and talent invested, and measure those costs against the known accomplishments and benefits resulting from the job.

Intangible Benefits

In some instances the intangible benefits accruing from the consultant's work may be the most valuable—but they are difficult to measure. Some of these intangibles are:
- Has our staff learned how to solve problems of this type that may arise in the future?
- Have internal relations improved since the study?
- Did our people get new ideas or new insight into operations?
- Did the study reveal costly internal situations or organizational problems which had not been recognized before?
- Did the study lead the firm toward new and profitable endeavors?

Greatest Contribution

The greatest contribution of a consultant may result from his role as a teacher. If he went beyond the particular problem on which he was working, and if he demonstrated new ways of attacking problems—focusing on concepts and principles rather than details; if he has added management skill and power to the client's staff, then he has made a great contribution to the firm.

A NEW LOOK AT THE BUSINESS-CONSULTING RELATIONSHIP

Here is a roundup of advice from businessmen—based on their own experience as to how they and their colleagues can make the best use of the experience and advice of consultants.

One vital function of the Association of Consulting Management Engineers is to educate both the businessman and the consultant with respect to the appropriate and most valuable relationship; that is, to point out how the services of the consultant can be utilized to maximum benefit. The following pages are taken directly from the *Acme Reporter* (an official publication of the Association). The information presented in these pages is priceless both from the viewpoint of the businessman and the consultant who desires to acquire a better understanding of the field of personal, professional services.

FROM THE *ACME* REPORTER

In recent months, the federal government has begun to study the role of outside consultants for its many departments and agencies. Given the tremendous growth in such assistance in the years since the war, a systematic look at the operation would seem to be called for. This survey does not, of course, imply that the basic concept of outside help is in question; actually, it is an accepted fact of modern government management. Rather, the *use* of the system is to be re-examined in an effort to make sure that it is being handled effectively.

Business has long since come to realize that the use of management consultants is an essential tool in the running of an enterprise. But it behooves many companies to follow Washington's example and take a look at the practice in terms of their own operations, to make sure that they are reaping the *maximum benefit*. Like any other part of the administrative process, this one should be examined from time to time and such adjustments as are necessary should be made in light of changing circumstances and increased knowledge and experience. As a matter of fact, some observers have said recently that such a new look is way overdue.

Though some people trace the practice of consulting back to Joseph and the Pharaoh, the great expansion of this kind of assistance came with the formation of the first consulting firms a half century ago. Since the war, the volume of activity has increased tremendously; according to one reliable source, there are some 2,000 firms—most of them small—doing consulting on a full-time basis in addition to perhaps 6,000 individual practitioners. The fees earned by established firms now run over $500 million annually, and their activities cover every conceivable area of management concern.

With growth has come an increasing body of experience and information about how to use this kind of help most effectively. Business managers no longer have to experiment for themselves; they can profit from a backlog of ideas and information that has been developed over the years. This article will review that material in an effort to stimulate managers to re-examine their own use of consultants and thereby improve their practices in this field.

SEVEN QUESTIONS

Generally speaking, an analysis of a firm's use of consultants should be broken down into seven questions:

How thoroughly do we establish our need for outside help and define our problem?

How careful are we about selecting the consultant?

How effectively do we brief the consultant we have chosen?

How well do we brief our own people, and how skillfully do we introduce the consultant into our business?

How good are we at working with him once he is on the job?

How good are we at evaluating his recommendations, making conclusions about them, and implementing those which seem most helpful?

How meticulous are we about evaluating our total experience with the consultant and using the information the next time we call on outside assistance?

THE NEED

The variety of managerial, operating, and technical problems on which a consultant can be helpful is, of course, vast. The practice of these specialists touches every phase of a business operation from systems and procedures to long-range planning. One company may need help in over-all marketing strategy; another might want advice on plant layout. One can be worrying about how it can maintain controls now that it has decided to decentralize; another might want a program for more effective recruiting of senior managers. "Cinderella" companies which have experienced sudden growth that has outpaced their management structure and the competence of their top people may be asking for organizational help; others—and this is an expanding area of concern—may be looking for ways to upgrade their executives in view of the new knowledge available and new challenges confronting today's administrator.

But whatever the specific issue at hand, it needs to be identified in advance. Even now, some companies still call in consultants "just because everyone else is doing it"; and too many others have failed to think through their situation and sharpen up the issue on which they want help.

One of the most successful management consultants focuses his first interview with a client on the single issue: "What is your problem?" Almost invariably he is forced to push his potential client to face up to this apparently obvious question; instead, the businessman usually wants to talk about possible solutions, peripheral matters or his hopes about what might come out of the consulting assignment.

The identification of the problem is, in many ways, the most difficult of a manager's responsibilities. Yet it is an essential first step, and one that only he can take. Few consulting assignments that started off with marching orders like "Come and look us over," or "I have a feeling something is wrong; see if you can find it," were ultimately successful.

It is true, as indicated below, that the full dimensions of the problem may not be clear until the consulting process has gone down the road a certain distance. Sometimes what appears to be the issue is, in fact, not the heart of the problem at all. But some kind of clear definition of the objectives and scope of the assignment is needed right at the start if the consultant is to make profitable use of his time and his client's money. Sometimes the client will not know exactly what his problem is and will need the consultant's help in defining both the problem and the objectives he hopes to accomplish by its analysis and solution.

Some businessmen have found it helpful to start the process of defining their problem by considering whether they are looking for *information* or for *assistance*. The common assumption is that the former is what they need; but many times it is not a lack of specialized knowledge that is tying them up but rather a breakdown in the process of putting it to use. One firm, for example, called in a team of consultants to advise it on the establishment of better data-collection techniques. The excellent set of recommendations which emerged from this study ended up in the organization's library; the real problem lay in the controller's office, which was headed by a man who was unable to think about his job in the way the new approaches demanded. If this firm had asked the question: "How can we improve our system of developing and presenting the numbers on our financial situation?" instead of "What are the most up-to-date ideas on data collection?" the end result might well have been more successful.

Experience shows that the majority of problems which call for outside help are like this one; that is, they fall in the category of need for assistance rather than need for mere information.

Thus, as a part of the process of delineating the problem, the manager should ask himself what he hopes to get from the consultant. Does he want new ideas, improved performance, lower costs, better-equipped management people, concentrated attention on some issue which he is too busy to handle himself, or the advantages of a fresh look at some barnacled dilemma that has been irritating him for a long time? What kind of help, in short, will best enable him to solve his problem successfully?

Inevitably, in framing the problem, management is going to find itself hip-deep in the tall grass of company objectives and basic policy. The consultant cannot determine whether the firm prefers to diversify or not; whether it wishes to become an international company or continue to be domestic; whether it wants to concentrate on immediate profitability or long-range growth. He can, of course, indicate the implications and results of these alternatives, but he cannot select one over the other. Management must therefore have thought through its objectives and identified the problem on which it wants help in terms of them before it can expect much concrete assistance from its consultant.

It is true, of course, that consultants can be of real assistance in isolating problems. But it is also true that when they perform this function they are generally doing so by urging and guiding management into doing the kind of thinking about its operation that it could do for and by itself. This preliminary investigation is often simply a prelude to more specific help and, while it has real benefits in training managers to do the job for themselves in the future, it is not necessarily the most profitable use of the advisor's time and skills.

One further point should be made here: wise managers have discovered that bringing in a number of their key people for discussions on the issue to be presented to the consultant not only gives the outsider a better picture but saves a great deal of misunderstanding and possible friction later on. The assignment then becomes a cooperative one instead of a suspected scheme of the front office. Working relationships with the consultant up and down the line are more likely to be constructive and produce really meaningful results.

SELECTION OF A CONSULTANT

In looking at its practices in the use of consultants, a company should satisfy itself that it is going about the process of selection in a businesslike way. Many managers apparently fail to appreciate the significance of this decision. The choice should be based on criteria more orderly than price or a chance evaluation tossed off by a fellow businessman at a club luncheon.

By and large, managers can have confidence in the honesty and reliability of consultants today. The time is passing when quacks and charlatans are able to secure substantial blocks of business. But it is still wise to be alert to the possibility; to check with *ACME* because one can be sure its members are competent and ethical; to run standard clearances with agencies like the Better Business Bureau, Dun & Bradstreet, and the credit associations. But the dangers of mistakes in selection are not generally caused by falling into the hands of dishonest operators; they are more often the result of casual assessment of the merits of a firm or an individual practitioner in terms of the *particular issue* with which the company is faced.

The prime consideration, of course, is the resources of the proposed consultant in terms of the particular problem with which the company is faced. While many firms handle a broad range of issues, others are more specialized. Unfortunately, some companies fail to realize that successful performance in a technological area does not *necessarily* mean that the same firm is equipped to do an equally solid piece of work on a human relations question, or that it isn't.

Accordingly, some direct conversations with managements who were given help on similar problems in recent years are advisable. Written commendations or long lists of former clients with no dates indicated are not sufficient; a few telephone calls are much more reliable.

At the same time, it is well to bear in mind that the heart of the consulting process is the analysis and solution of problems by independent and objective professional staff men. Management consultants enter the field largely because they like to solve problems, particularly new ones. They find a new problem more challenging than one they have solved many times before. They will work harder and with a deeper interest on a new problem than an old one. There is also a tendency for each company and each industry to believe that its problems are unique. They fail to see how industrial experiences all deal with the same material, financial and human factors—all representing variations on the same underlying system. So emphasis should not necessarily be placed too strongly on previous experience with the *same* problems, although a record of success in solving *equally difficult* problems of course means a lot.

Some businessmen seem to have built-in prejudices which limit their freedom of choice. They steer away from younger men who have obviously not had senior operating experience, failing to realize that skill in sizing up a situation and helping others to handle it does not necessarily coincide with the ability to do the job oneself. Consulting is a professional field, just like managing, with its own practices and techniques; many top-flight teachers of business administration do not make good administrators, any more than all-effective managers make good teachers. The question to ask here is "How good are these people at *consulting?*" not "How good are they at managing?"

Others refuse to deal with newer firms, although they may be made up of experienced and imaginative people. Conceivably, on some problems you might get excellent service out of a newcomer simply because he would be anxious to establish a reputation for himself. The fact remains that reputation is a useful guide—but it must continue to be earned.

Still others look primarily at fees. This can be misleading for many reasons. One company received six different proposals from consulting firms with a spread of 600% between the estimated costs of the project. Upon investigation they discovered a substantial variation in the approaches suggested by the competing firms, and they made their selection on the basis of a combination of the two factors—price *and* approach. In consultant services, like anything else, the important factor is the result. A good job is well worth the cost; a poor one is a loss, no matter how attractive the price tag may have been. Consultants do not come cheap, and they should not.

The practice of asking several management consultants to bid on proposed assignments may have real disadvantages for the client. It has a tendency to encourage overly optimistic estimates of costs and savings and other conduct of doubtful professional caliber and almost always puts the more conscientious firms at a disadvantage.

Getting proposals from several firms to determine the approaches they expect to use in the solution of a complex problem, however, is a useful course to follow, especially if the client compensates the firms for the work they do in preparing their approaches. But if the problem is relatively uncomplicated, and the approach which should be taken to solve it is well known, it is usually more satisfactory for the client to follow the same procedure he uses in engaging other professional services. He should satisfy himself by appropriate inquiry of the reputation and qualifications of any firms he wishes to consider. If he finds that a firm has a good reputation, he will be safe in working with that firm alone, for it will regard its continuing good reputation as far more important than anything that could possibly be gained by failure to serve the best interests of the client.

There are many checklists, including one prepared by *ACME*, which will help a firm select a consultant. Some companies will prefer one, some another; and many will draw up their own. But it is vitally important that this choice be made on the basis of some kind of formal evaluative procedure, rather than quickly or "intuitively."

A CLEAR MAP

Once a company has selected a consultant, it should turn its attention to making sure that he has a clear picture of the total situation into which he is moving. It is true, of course, that he has some preliminary ideas about the problem from the discussions held during the selection process. But these rough sketches are not enough; the time has now come for a detailed map of the territory.

Too many managers do not think through this stage adequately. They do not spend enough time planning and presenting the story to the consultant; apparently they assume he is all-seeing and all-knowing and somehow can absorb the full dimensions of the problem from a walk through the plant. Here, again, valuable time and talent may be wasted in a gearing-up stage that could have been reduced by some more thoughtful preparation.

Many times this part of the consulting relationship is weakened by a deliberate policy on the part of management. Executives may be afraid that the consultant will "leak" facts to a competitor, although most businessmen are now too sophisticated in the use of consultants to take this spectre very seriously. Obviously, good consultants respect the confidences of their clients and will not violate them.

Far more common, however, is the tendency of businessmen to cover up unpleasant facts because of normal human feelings of guilt. Businessmen would naturally rather present a picture of competence and efficiency to an outsider; they dislike to paint in the corners of the picture that which they fear might reflect poorly on their ability. But the consultant is not on board to judge or to criticize; he is there to help. His job is to analyze the total situation as it is and give the manager a hand in improving it.

Furthermore, he will probably uncover the dust that has been whisked into the corner eventually, anyway. The wise manager will save time by honestly looking himself and his organization in the face and admitting that everything is not perfect.

As the businessman studies his use of consultants, he will do well to check and see that his briefing sessions cover the *human elements* in the landscape as well as the economic, organizational, and technical ones. What kind of people are involved, how do they act on and affect each other, what are their strengths and weaknesses? Incidentally, some attempt at evaluating one's own role in this regard can do no harm, either. We like to act and talk as though the problems in our company are all external to ourselves, the results of other forces, even when we honestly know that we, too, are major factors in the equation.

The briefing process should include discussions with a variety of key people. They should be encouraged to describe the problem as they see it. The quicker the consultant can get a total view of the company, the more effective he will be. Like a detective searching for clues, the more data—albeit some of it may appear to be irrelevant at first glance—the closer he will come to a realistic answer.

INTRODUCING THE NEWCOMER

Sometimes there is a tendency for managers down the line in an organization to look on the consultant as an outsider, as a cop or a spy for top management. They may suspect that the boss does not like the way they are doing their jobs and is checking up on them. They worry about being shown up by "this hot-shot guy from New York (or Chicago, or San Francisco)".

One consulting firm tackled an engineering assignment in good faith only to find itself blocked at every turn by the in-house personnel. The consultants were unable to get the data they needed, found their comments along the way resented, and were disappointed to learn that their work was finally wasted because none of their suggestions was actually put into effect. Only later did they discover that the chief engineer was not in on the project when it started, and had never been adequately acquainted with the problem under study, nor the purpose of the review. His entire effort during the period of the examination had been aimed at proving that he was just as good as anybody that "the old man could bring in to check up on me," and he was vigorously resistant to the consultants both personally and professionally.

The literature on the use of consultants frequently tells the reader to "instruct your people to talk freely and to cooperate." But as any experienced manager knows, cooperation and effective participation cannot be secured simply by grinding out a mimeographed statement from the Executive Suite. The operating people have to be involved from the very beginning and have to be a part of the whole process from the definition of the problem to the final study of the report which includes a suggested specific plan of action for implementing the recommendations. They need to feel confident that this is a joint venture designed not to needle or to dredge up evidence to go in an efficiency report but rather to strengthen and improve the company and to help them do their jobs better.

All this is much easier to describe than it is to accomplish. But businessmen who have had the most successful results from consultants have found that concentrating on the introduction problem, and taking some concrete action that goes beyond simply bringing the consultant and his group around from desk to desk on the first day, can pay off handsomely when the score is tallied.

ARM IN ARM

Managers vary considerably in their view of the consultant once he is on board. One small company president was so uncomfortable at having an "outsider" working with him that he literally hurried him out of the office when anyone else appeared at the door. The whole performance took on a conspiratorial air to the point where both the consultant and the principal were highly ill at ease during the entire relationship. Another man treated his new "partner" as though he had all the answers and knew everything there was to know; rightly or wrongly, he soon found himself locked into such a relationship of dependence that he was incapable of making a move without checking first. When an emergency developed, and his consultant couldn't be reached by telephone, he was lost.

A third way of thinking about the relationship has been described by one observer as the "purchase and sale" type of attitude. The manager looks on the consultant as someone who can supply a package of techniques or procedures in response to a set of specifications, much as his purchasing agent orders a certain quality and quantity of copper tubing from a supplier. When the "shipment" ultimately arrives, he is likely to be disappointed.

For consultants do not take the place of managers. They supplement and complement them. They are associates who need to maintain a continuing relationship with the key people all along the line if they are to come up with meaningful interpretations of what is going on and what can be done to improve it. "After all," says one analyst of the client-consultant relationship, "the problem is management's, and the consultant can do no more than assist in its solution—which he is likely to do not only to the best of his ability but also in proportion to the cooperation he receives."

Many companies assign liasion teams to work closely with the consultants throughout the project, comparing notes and ideas and helping to bridge the gap between the outside participant and observer and those who have had both the opportunity and responsibility of dealing with the situation on a day-to-day operating basis. Whether this particular device is suitable in a given situation is not the point, however; the significant idea is that the two parties must work in close association for the duration of the undertaking.

As mentioned earlier, it is likely that the study will turn up questions and implications which had not been seen at the beginning. As a matter of fact, this change of scenery and props is one of the results which managers should hope for and expect from an outside, objective analysis of their company's performance. Without a continuing close contact with the consultant, management will not be able to adjust its perspective accordingly, supply the new data, introduce new personnel, and prepare the way for resulting changes.

THE MORNING AFTER

More than one consulting firm, looking at its own operations, is unhappy with the final outcome of some of its assignments. Although the project was well handled, the recommendations sound and the presentation well planned and thorough, the actual results in the company were imperceptible. At least one major organization in this field, while recognizing that the major responsibility of implementation usually rests with the client's management, has given serious thought to the possibility of making a parallel study on each of its projects on how it should go about increasing the probability that its suggestions will bear fruit in new decisions and new policies.

This article has touched on many of the reasons why reports lie unused: poor definition of the problem, poor selection of a consultant, lack of participation of operating personnel, a breakdown of liaison with the client during the study, a misunderstanding of the true nature of the relationship between client and consultant, and so on. But the failure of management to set up machinery for serious consideration of the product of the survey can also be blamed.

One institution hired a group to do a major over-all examination of its program, facilities, personnel, and long-range plans. It worked fairly closely with the consultant during the process, and the top people gave careful thought to the final document. All of a sudden, they realized that they had a detailed set of recommendations before them without the foggiest notion of how they were going to go about submitting them to lower-echelon personnel, do their own audit of the suggestions, evaluate them, and execute the necessary changes. As a result, except for some perfunctory passes at a consideration of the report, they soon became caught up in the press of other business. And the carefully developed report became just another item for the company historians to note.

It seems almost ridiculous to have to say that the implementation and installation of the recommendations contained in the report are essential parts of most consulting assignments. The whole purpose of most assignments is action; unless that follows the report, the effort is barren. Implementation does not just happen. It has to be anticipated and planned for during the time the report itself is taking shape.

Thus, a major portion of the self-study on a company's use of consultants ought to be an analysis of the operating impact of the studies that have been made. How many recommendations have been accepted? How many rejected? How many modified? Is there anything to be learned from the fate of the major proposals as opposed to the minor ones? Why were some turned down and others adopted? What should be done to build a higher batting average for the future?

THE LOOK BACKWARD

A hard-headed evaluation of the worth of the consulting assignment to the company should be a regular management practice. Businessmen should not be satisfied with a "general impression" on the usefulness of the relationship and the results it achieved. They should systematically review the whole experience from the dollars-and-cents standpoint, including the company time invested, and measure it against the accomplishments they had set out to register when they first established the operation. Granted it is difficult to attribute savings, increased orders, reduced overhead, or higher productivity to any one factor; yet even a crude judgment is better than none at all. And the discipline of reviewing the program with an eye to similar arrangements in the future is beneficial to all concerned.

But the evaluation should include intangible results—or failures—as well. What has happened to internal relations within the company? Have we learned anything about solving this particular kind of problem which will stand us in good stead the next time? Did our people get some new ideas or approaches, which they have adopted? Did we uncover some kinds of problems which we never suspected existed before? Are we off on some new paths of company activity which have not yet become profitable but which show real promise? Have we identified some personnel situation of which we were not aware? In short, are we a better, wiser company?

It is true, of course, that this kind of evaluation does not have much meaning until a reasonable amount of time has passed. The first reaction may be a false one; it may not be until after recommendations have been evaluated and put into effect that an accurate reading can be taken. Depending on the nature of the project, a year may not be any too short a period to wait before attempting a real evaluation of the usefulness of the relationship. A continuing process of looking at the history of consulting projects may well serve a real purpose so that as the history of the company unfolds the role of the consultant in its progress may be charted.

But the greatest contribution of the consultant will prove to be the hardest to measure. His true worth is expressed in the working efficiency of the men with whom he has dealt. If he has gone beyond the particular problem with which he was asked to work and demonstrated new ways of attacking questions, new questions to be asked, new sources of management skill and power, he will have left a priceless heritage. For in the largest sense the consultant is a teacher, and a company that takes a new look at its system of using consultants should view him in that light.

A brochure describing "How the Management Consulting Profession Serves Business Enterprise" and a list of members or a Directory of Membership and Services may be obtained by writing the Association of Consulting Management Engineers, Inc., 347 Madison Avenue, New York 17, N. Y.

8

Unique Management Services of Special Value

The practitioner most apt to succeed in the field of management consulting is the one who is constantly searching for new ways to serve his clients. This chapter explains two unique ways in which to serve a client. Both of these services offer considerable potential benefits to any client—and they represent a logical extension of the background, knowledge and experience of the public practitioner.

A third service is covered in the following chapter, "Money Management—and Sources of Financing."

PART I

DIAGNOSTIC REVIEW AND ANALYTICAL CHECKUP

When making a diagnostic review of a client's balance sheet, the practitioner plays the role of a business diagnostician who carefully checks the pulse of the "patient." He examines each item on the balance sheet to detect symptoms of a business malfunction, indications of inappropriate business policies, or a lack of internal control. Also, the practitioner deliberately questions policy and procedures in vital areas—and analyzes operations in general, with an eye for spotting all areas that need improvement or overhauling to increase profits.

The purposes of this diagnostic review of major balance-sheet items—plus a critical analysis of operating policies and procedures, as stated above—are to spot areas of weakness and opportunities for profit improvement in general. Another purpose of such a review is to conserve cash and locate sources of short-term capital by the use of special techniques which are discussed in the next chapter.

If you have an audit background, you may find it difficult at first to perform as a business diagnostician. You must place yourself in the position of management when you examine balance-sheet items. Do not evaluate the figures from the familiar viewpoint of an auditor. Your function, when rendering this service, is to act as a trained investigator and guide the management of your client firm to analyze and evaluate each asset and resource, one by one. Ask penetrating, challenging questions; take copious notes; make suggestions. Personally investigate all operating areas which indicate the need for improvements, or changes. Look for

75

clues which indicate problems in the various inventories, production control, credit policies, invoice terms offered to customers, collection policies and functions, excessive investment in fixed assets, etc.

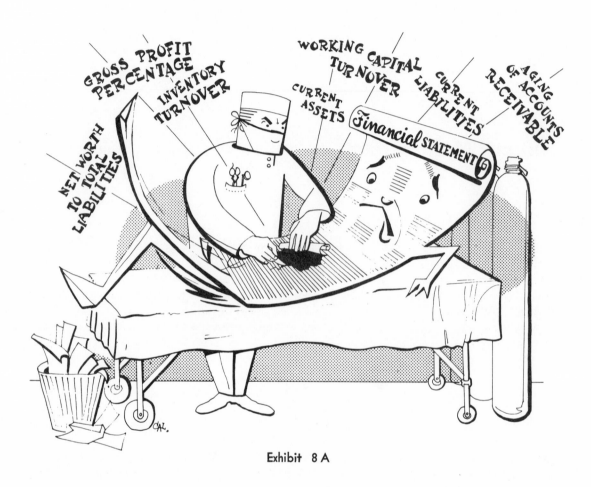

Exhibit 8 A

Exhibit 8-A portrays the public practitioner as an examining physician, looking for symptoms of disease in the business patient. (Taken from a credit department brochure, published by M. Lowenstein & Sons, Inc., New York City.)

On the following pages, penetrating questions are asked about each item on a typical balance sheet to stimulate your thinking. Special pointers are listed and suggested action steps are provided. (Each verb is underscored to *indicate suggested action,* as compared to pointers or supplementary information included in each paragraph.)

Merchandise Inventories

How about the cost of sales as shown by the records? Does the cost seem to be high in relation to sales?

Does the client have any form of inventory control, such as stock records that show the quantity of each item which should be on hand—and which can be compared on a periodic basis with an actual count of items in the warehouse?

(The so-called "cost of goods sold" in a firm which has no book records on inventories is the dumping ground for all types of errors, stolen merchandise, failure to invoice shipments, etc.)

- *Determine* the ratio of average investment in merchandise inventories as compared to the annual sales volume. Is the investment in merchandise unnecessarily large?
- *Ascertain* the frequency of back orders. This data will provide a valuable clue in regard to overstocking merchandise. Inventory should represent a compromise between the demands made on it by customer orders—and management's willingness or ability to maintain a large inventory of practically all items at all times, in which case back orders would be a rarity.

It is feasible to reduce deliberately the inventory on hand by reducing minimums across the board—and by ordering smaller quantities when orders are placed. This policy leads to an occasional stock-out condition and backlog of orders. Even so, the prevalence of back orders is not necessarily a bad condition; it may indicate a well-conceived inventory policy.

To look at the inventory problem in the aggregate, management policy should be to operate somewhere in the middle, between the two extremes of deliberate overstocking in order to render first class customer service, with almost no back orders—and a constant out-of-stock situation with attendant, numerous back orders.

There is a big difference between considering inventory in the aggregate, and in detail with regard to specific products. And, here is where record-keeping can really pay off handsomely. Almost without exception, a small percentage of the total number of products which are carried in stock accounts for a very high percentage of total sales.

You should *make recommendations* to the client, or take steps to *determine* just which products represent the cornerstone of sales. One result which can be obtained by the use of an outside data-processing service bureau for sales analysis and special reports, is a report of annual sales that's prepared in the form of a pyramid. Thus, the product with the largest dollar sales for the year appears as item number one at the top of the report; the product with the second largest dollar sales is the second line on the report, etc.

Such a report should include a column which shows the cumulative $ sales and the % to the total sales as each product is listed. Perusal of such a list nearly always presents the same type of picture; a small number of items provides a very large percentage of the total sales dollars. Here is an example contained in an IBM manual on inventory management; these percentages represent more the norm, rather than the unusual:

- 1% of all products will account for nearly 18% of dollar sales.
- 5% of all products will account for about 40% of sales.
- The upper 20% of all products account for *more than 70% of all sales.*
- Looking at the thousands of items on the last pages of such a report—*about 40% of all items carried in stock produce only about 5% of the annual sales.*

After you have absorbed the impact of these thought-provoking percentages, you will recognize the need to *examine* the client's inventory situation—not in the aggregate, but from the viewpoint of improving the stock position of the upper 20% of the items which are the real income-producers. You will also want to *examine the lower 40%* of all items carefully, because these are apt to be obsolete, and in an overstocked condition.

A corollary analysis may pay very large dividends. When similar analysis figures are obtained on sales and profits BY CUSTOMERS, this data may point the way to significant changes in marketing and distribution. For example, one large soap manufacturer had serviced 40,000 customers on a nation-wide basis for many decades through a field force of salesmen who worked in fixed geographic areas all over the nation—making personal calls on small drug stores to sell the company's varied line of products. When the president of the firm requested an analysis of sales volume by customers, the amazing fact came out that 90% of all dollar sales came from 200 large chain store customers, or the equivalent.

Some 200 customers out of 40,000 produced most of the income dollars! This fact led to some very drastic changes in the firm's marketing and distribution policies which measurably improved operations and profits.

Referring again to the 40% of all items which accounts for only 5% (typically) of the sales, what are the possibilities for a write-down of certain items to reduce inventory value, in line with the conservative accounting practice of valuing inventories at "cost or market, whichever is lower"?

Manufacturing Inventories

Does the client maintain a sizeable working inventory of piece parts and small subassemblies. most commonly used in manufacturing finished products?

Does the client maintain bills of material lists—and post production requirements to piece part records as soon as requirements are established by the planners? This makes it possible to function with a minimum investment in inventory—if the system is properly set up to provide signals that warn of "impending shortages." The mathematical formula usually applied to obtain the automatic warning signal is:

> Quantity on hand plus quantity on order . . .
> Less: Quantity Reserved . . .
> Equals the *Quantity Available* (for further production commitments).

When the quantity available is less than the minimum amount to be kept in stock, the planning department goes into action to procure additional quantities of the part to meet future production requirements. (For additional details see page 161 of my Prentice-Hall book, *Accounting Systems for the Small and Medium-Sized Business.*)

Does the purchasing department make use of annual purchase agreements, frequently referred to as "blanket purchase orders"?

Negotiating annual purchase agreements with major vendors who are supplying repetitive items may reduce the cost of purchased inventory items by as much as 15% each year. This enables the purchaser to secure favorable, low unit prices without being required to order and accept large quantities at any one time.

Such agreements offer benefits to the suppliers, as well as to the buyers. These major benefits are:

- The supplier can forecast and schedule his sales, production and inventory requirements.
- Quantity sales to the customer are assured with no further bidding or expensive paper work.
- Handling and shipping costs may be reduced by consolidating orders.

Annual price agreements have the following characteristics:

- Once-a-year purchase.
- Negotiation on annual requirements, at quantity discount prices.
- No commitment to purchase specific quantities at specific times.
- Price-protection clause.
- Termination clause.

Accounts Receivable

In recent years, the investment in this prime asset has been increasing in many firms. This increase is usually attributed to an expansion of credit sales; but, in some cases, it is caused by granting invoice terms of increasing length or by a slowdown in customer payment of invoices.

There are many aspects of receivables which *should be analyzed;* for example:

1. *Invoice terms:* On what terms are most goods sold? What is the average number of days offered to customers before payment is due?

Compare terms-days with actual days. To do this, calculate the average number of days that invoices are outstanding before payment is received. One simple method is to *divide the average amount invested in receivables at the first of each month by the average amount of daily charge sales. The quotient is the average number of days that capital is being tied up by customers before they make payment.*

Example: Average amount invested in accounts receivable is $100,000.00.

Average daily charge sales are $2,500.00; therefore, receivables represent an average of 40 days' sales.

If sales terms are net 10 days, then receivables are in bad shape. If, however, terms are net 30, then the collection of receivables is in reasonably good shape.

2. *What price invoice terms?* ANALYZE all terms being offered to customers from several viewpoints:

- What is the cost (in terms of discounts allowed) of quickly converting receivables to cash by offering cash discount terms, such as *2/10* net 30?
- Are customers observing the terms—or abusing them? (If terms are 2/10 net 30, and you find that receivables are outstanding an average of 45 days before payment is received—and you also determine that most customers are improperly deducting the 2% cash discount anyway—then you may recommend to the client that all invoice terms should be carefully reviewed, and possibly changed.)

3. *Determine* the percentage of remittances that include unauthorized deductions—sometimes referred to as "claims."

Analyze the reasons for such deductions—and prepare a list of all major reasons. The ones commonly found are:

Freight claims (damaged goods)
Freight allowances (customer paid the freight, but deducted it from invoice payment)
Merchandise returned
Advertising allowance
Merchandise shortage
Price difference
Parcel post
Sales taxes
Unknown

Study the follow-up and paperwork procedures for deductions. (Deductions result in reduced cash flow and represent a dubious asset, since the amount of the deduction remains charged to the customer's account only until a settlement of the claim is reached.)

Consider the possibility of reducing income tax liability by setting up a special reserve for deductions, since experience indicates that more than one half of all deductions are eventually allowed.

Collection Policies and Procedures

Receivables are only one step removed from cash. The collection department is the department that's charged with the responsibility of converting receivables to cash on hand. *Study* the policies and procedures of this department carefully. (Refer to Chapter 11 for a complete discussion of collection department policies and suggested procedures.)

Examine the contents of past due statements, and determine the *time* between follow-up cycles. Perhaps a change or two will markedly improve collections. For example, collection techniques suitable for retail accounts may not be effective for wholesale customers. Here is an actual case history to illustrate this point:

A CASE HISTORY

A firm that offered about twenty different sets of invoice terms to its customers (which meant that invoices were coming due from certain customers every day during the month) had long used a so-called past-due statement that included current invoices (not yet due) as well. A simple change in procedures—showing ONLY past due-items—improved collections immediately.

Analyze Credit Memos

One source of information, commonly overlooked, about the operations of a firm is an analytical review and tabulation of credit memos for a representative period of time. The idea is to discover the trouble spots within a company by studying the *reasons* for the credit invoice documents. For example, I once studied 1,675 credit memos covering more than a dozen textile manufacturers. Here are the trouble symptoms and conclusions drawn from them, without going near the companies represented by the documents:

Price errors—problems in the order department, or in billing.

Damaged goods—freight line is careless, or packaging of goods is inferior.

Goods returned—"stains, spots, soiled, flaws, oil spots, etc." Careless manufacturing operations, dirty facilities, poor warehousing, shipping.

Wrong color, style or sizes—careless shipping department.

Shipped short—careless shipping department.

Freight allowance—salesmen may be promising to ship goods prepaid or allow freight charges, if paid by customer upon arrival of goods.

Find out if invoice terms are applied to credits. This is most important. Failure to apply applicable invoice terms to credit invoices represents a potential source of loss, since discount terms that have been applied to a credit have the effect of reducing the credit amount. Examine how one firm lost in excess of $30.00 through a chain of transactions:

- Customer orders merchandise at a purchase price of $1,000.00 subject to terms of 3% net 30.
- Customer paid the invoice promptly, by remitting $970.00.
- Customer examined the merchandise and returned all of it.
- Supplier prepared a credit invoice for $1,000.00 with net terms.
- Customer requested a check and received one for $1,000.00.
- Supplier lost the prepaid freight, the cost of employee time in selecting, packaging and shipping the merchandise, plus the time of putting it back into stock when it was

returned. He lost $30.00 in cash besides, because of the policy of not applying invoice terms to credit invoices.

Note: The policy of applying net terms to credits may stem from the fact that more than 50% of all credits are unidentified; in many instances it is difficult to relate the credit to one or more specific invoices. However, any credit for returned goods should bear the terms most commonly granted to the customer, in the event that no invoice is referenced by the credit.

Freight on Outgoing Shipments

If the client firm pays the freight costs on merchandise shipments to customers, the total freight expense for the year may represent a substantial charge against profits. Since you may be able to *show a client how to reduce his freight costs* as much as 45% or more, this item of freight charges is worth considerable investigation.

Freight charges are based on weight, distance and classification of the goods shipped. Several factors determine the technical classification, which is controlled by the Interstate Commerce · Commission (ICC). Basically, the classification is based on the composition of the commodity, its bulk and how it is packaged for shipment.

By application of appropriate, official descriptions to each commodity shipped, it is frequently possible to reduce freight costs from 15% to 45%, or more. The details of what you can do to accomplish these results for a client are found in Chapter 7 of my book, *Accounting Systems for the Small and Medium-Sized Business.*

Review Sales Compensation Plans

"Salesmen's compensation plans are coming up for review now more and more by management people. The compensation plan can be a very important factor in a highly competitive field."

This statement, which first appeared in the author's book in 1959, is even more pertinent today than it was then because of the increasing pressure to increase sales volume without regard to the profitability of sales. As the chapter points out, most salesmen are paid a salary, or a salary and a commission—*based on a percentage of sales.* This is the fallacy in most compensation plans.

When a salesman is paid a percentage of sales, there is no incentive for him to concentrate on and sell high-profit merchandise. He may not even know which products produce a substantial margin of gross profit—and which ones do not. If the compensation plan offers no reward or penalty, the salesman probably will not be too concerned, even if he does know the facts.

On the other hand, a compensation plan which pays a commission that is based on a percentage of *Gross Profit* gives the salesman a direct incentive to promote and sell high-profit products. "When a salesman's commission is based on the gross profit involved in each sale, he becomes, in effect, a direct partner in each sales transaction. If he holds the price line and sells high-profit merchandise, his commission will be substantially greater than his commission on a sale involving price-cutting or special allowances due to a sharp decrease in gross profit."

Such a compensation plan is predicated on the basis that the unit cost of each item in stock is known and recorded. This does not necessarily mean that the firm employing the salesman maintains an elaborate system of inventory control. It is possible to maintain price catalogues which reflect the latest invoice cost for each product in the product line.

In today's business world it is very easy and economical to secure extensive sales-analysis reports of many types—because of the advent of data-processing service bureaus which are dedicated to bringing the benefits of computers to businessmen by offering special services such as sorting, tabulating and printing sales-analysis reports.

If the unit cost is recorded on each product that appears on each invoice, the service bureau can easily provide comprehensive reports as to sales, costs and GROSS PROFIT on every invoice. This, in turn, makes it easy to maintain records of *customer profitability* also.

Finally, the reports will group all sales, costs and profits according to each salesman—and these reports are the basis for commission payments based on gross profit.

Sales Forecasting

Sales forecasting is becoming an increasingly important management tool. It is useful for budgetary planning, and it also ties in with forecasting purchase requirements for the year—which is necessary for the savings to be effected by the use of annual purchase agreements, as already outlined.

The use of a competent data-processing service bureau makes it easily feasible to maintain the necessary monthly quantity-sales figures, product by product, customer by customer, or in other ways over a long period of time. Such data should cover a minimum period of two years of prior sales (1) so that past sales, month-by-month, will reflect *seasonal variations* and (2) so that recent sales can be compared with a moving average of prior sales *covering a comparable period* for the prior year to reflect adequately a possible *trend*.

PART II

THE ADVISORY COMMITTEE—A MEANS OF OPENING THE DOORS TO NEW MANAGEMENT HORIZONS

Any client enjoys working with a practitioner who brings in fresh ideas, especially when those ideas will produce direct and immediate benefits for the client. The concept of assisting the owner or chief executive of a small-to-medium-sized business with setting up an advisory committee is an intriguing idea because of the many complex problems faced today by businesses of all sizes.

This idea has been implemented with great success by a well-known firm of certified public accountants. The story is told here by Theodore Cohn, CPA, and a partner in the firm of J. H. Cohn & Company of Newark, New Jersey.

The following is a reprint of an article which appeared in the *Journal of Accountancy* under the title of "Management Controls and Information."

THE ADVISORY COMMITTEE: OUTSIDE VIEW, INSIDE MANAGEMENT

THEODORE COHN, *CPA, is a partner in the Newark, N.J., office of J. H. Cohn & Company. Mr. Cohn is chairman of the Management Advisory Service Committee of the New Jersey Society of CPAs. He has written articles for professional and association journals, including* THE JOURNAL.

WHERE does the president of a small- or medium-sized company turn to get answers to these questions:

- *What* are the areas of our business that require strengthening?
- *Where* can I find the technical skills that are missing in my company?
- *How* do I go about making plans for the next three or five years, or even for the next month?
- *What* do we do best competitively on which, if we spend our major efforts and resources, we would realize the greatest profits?
- *Where* can I get some fresh ideas to perk up my own and my executives' thinking?

These are common middle-of-the-night concerns of intelligent managers. Merely raising the questions in many cases provides the hint of the answers. In other cases management of small- and medium-sized business is so concerned with day-to-day operations that these basic and long-term problems and opportunities are quickly shunted aside in favor of the ease and pressure of solving today's and yesterday's problems.

Yet without intelligent consideration and practical answers to basic questions business cannot maximize its potential or even—sometimes—survive.

Through the diversity of personnel and the use of an active board of directors, large companies have the inner resources to consider long-term management problems. Smaller businesses struggle to find or retain people with sufficient experience and skill to solve all their problems. However, the need for counsel on special marketing, financing, organization, foreign trade, pricing, etc., is great in all businesses.

How then to attract on a continuing, noncrisis, basis people with the skill and experience in special areas and general management outlook which small business needs? Competent people rarely want to serve on the board of directors of small companies in which they have no financial interest. The reason for this is the wish to avoid the legal and moral responsibilities that go with membership on a corporate board of directors. In the case of the CPA his independence *prohibits* membership on the board of a client.

One answer to this problem that we have found to be most successful is the establishment of an *advisory committee*. Individuals with skills not present in the internal management of the business, or with general management knowledge, are asked to join the committee on an experimental basis. They are told that the first meeting will be exploratory; they will be paid a fee of $50 to $100 for their two- to three-hour participation; and management will reserve judgment on how it wants to use the advisory committee in the future. Payment of the fee puts the relationship on a professional basis and permits management to drop a member who is incompatible.

Meetings are generally held quarterly for luncheon and with a time limit to prevent irrelevant discussion. Financial statements with comments are sent monthly to committee members. Members are also available for phone calls on specific problems between meetings.

The president of the company, usually with the help of the person who has recommended the forming of the advisory committee, prepares an agenda and background information which are submitted to the members of the committee a week or so in advance of the meeting. It is wise to have the first agenda longer than the time permits so that, in addition to new subjects that may come up, the second meeting has some major questions to consider.

What are the sources of good people for an advisory committee and why should they serve? Most of the committees we have been involved with chose their members from the following: a partner of the accounting firm; a business-minded attorney; possibly an outside management consultant; a senior officer in the company's bank who has contact with the business; a retired executive in the same or related industries; executives of companies in different industries; and senior loan officers in nonbanking financial institutions, such as insurance companies, investment banking houses and stock brokerage firms.

Because the invitation to join an advisory committee is a flattering one, the ratio of acceptance is high. In effect, you are telling the potential committee member that he is smart enough so that other people are eager to listen to him. Subsequently, his judgment may turn out to be otherwise, both in the sense that his ideas and other contributions to the committee may not be relevant or acceptable and that internal management, although willing to submit to an advisory committee, may not want to listen to it.

The word "submit" is used with forethought; the process of using outside people to question the basic philosophy and aims of a small business can be a disturbing, as well as an exhilarating, experience. Management must be both tough-minded and open-minded enough so that criticisms of the most basic type, even when presented objectively, do not destroy management's self-esteem. For this reason care is required in the selection of committee members.

We had an experience with a small company whose president was excited about the idea of the committee, but was unable, rather than unwilling, to submit to a second meeting. He found the questions of the three outside committee members so fraught with danger to his self-image as an executive that, although he admitted the questions were relevant and subsequently immensely valuable, he could not tolerate the experience again.

More commonly, internal management finds the opportunity to discuss and the pressure to decide basic questions an experience of great educational, as well as immediately practical, value. In one case the first meeting was concerned entirely with the basic question: Why did this company make a profit? After an hour of discussion and a tentative answer (its executives were extraordinary in their ability to price the product), the committee suggested—and management decided—that the following steps should be taken:

1. Assistant salesmen should be hired to learn the selling techniques of the principals and to free the latter for finding new customers.

2. A competent secretary should be hired to relieve one of the principals of routine administrative work.

3. One principal should be relieved of 50 per cent of his selling duties and be charged with the responsibility of developing new products and markets.

Finally, because the company had recently suffered a loss of salesmen who had gone into business for themselves, the accounting firm was asked to develop a method of compensation which would attract and keep good men.

All of these decisions were tied in with specific individual responsibilities and dates for their accomplishment and measurement.

NEW MANAGEMENT DECISIONS

In another case the advisory committee was used in the same way as a routine physical examination—to pass on the assumed good health of the client. Although management had made long-range plans, the two principals were so closely involved with day-to-day operations that they wanted help in clarification of administrative procedures, definition of executive functions and improving communication between executives. As a by-product of the committee's questioning, two ideas came out of the overall discussion of the business which management volunteered were worth $100,000 each.

Facing basic problems in a creative and structured situation, in which solutions can be explored, responsibilities assigned and follow-up procedures instituted, is a management approach which an advisory committee helps to implement. For internal management the advisory committee opens the doors to new management horizons without usurping the decision authority of the board of directors and the corporate officers. To the outside members of the advisory committee the experience is usually immensely satisfying.

Benefits of an Advisory Committee

Many benefits, both tangible and intangible, accrue to management of a firm that adopts this "board of directors" plan. Here are a few which experience points to as being significant:

- Management's circle of influence is widened.
- Valuable new contacts are opened up for the business through the combined influence of leading businessmen represented on the committee.
- Management establishes a better relationship with the firm's banker; the banker gets in on the ground floor of future financial requirements, and actively participates in the planning of business growth and solidarity.
- Committee members provide guidance and education to management in many broad areas, and bring an objective viewpoint to bear on pressing problems.
- Management gains the benefit of the combined experience of the members of the committee, plus valuable new ideas which may be the key to expanded sales or more profitable operations.

This concept is more valid today than it was a decade ago. Here is why. In recent years, more and more firms have instituted liberal retirement plans that are based on insurance contracts which provide the retirement funds as employees are retired. These contracts usually *force* the employee's retirement at age 65. This policy has removed many very able, competent and highly experienced executives and business specialists from active business participation. This has created a large pool of unusual talent—just waiting for an invitation to serve as a valued member of the advisory committee!

9

Money Management—and Sources of Financing

The prime purposes of the diagnostic review and analytical checkup as described in the prior chapter were to find clues as to malfunctions in business operations and to develop opportunities for profit improvement in general. The diagnostic review should include one other major objective—to uncover sources of short-term cash as a by-product of analyzing balance-sheet accounts. A corollary subject included in this chapter is "money management"— which explains how to speed up the flow of incoming cash and slow down outgoing cash, plus ways of putting idle funds to work.

A bulletin issued by the American Institute of Certified Public Accountants states: "One of the most valuable services a CPA can give his clients is guidance to sources of funds. Although there are many sources, the smaller business often looks only to its commercial bank for capital. If a proposal is rejected by the banker, plans for growth, product additions, or new plant and equipment may be discarded."

The following paragraph also appears in this same bulletin entitled, "Financing the Small Business":

"To function as a public treasurer to small business managements, a CPA must know at least as much about methods and sources of financing as the treasurer of the private company, as his knowledge must extend to the many sources available *only to small business.*"

There is no doubt that finding money with which to grow and expand is a major problem for most small business entrepreneurs. It is traditional for the new business to be long on optimism and ideas, but short on cash. And, as the business becomes increasingly successful, the supply of operating cash is apt to dwindle, because of commitments all along the line which are necessary to produce and handle an increasing sales volume.

This chapter, plus the following chapter entitled, "Accounts Receivable Financing," provides a review of the financial world and information as to where the small-to-medium-sized business client may find capital—both from sources within his company and from outside sources.

INTERNAL SOURCES OF FUNDS

When you are performing the diagnostic review of balance-sheet accounts, you will be searching for various ways to secure additional funds, or to free up funds, as indicated by the

87

following test questions that may be applied to each asset under examination:

1. Can this asset be used as collateral to raise cash? (To secure operating cash.)
2. Can we reduce the funds invested in fixed assets? (To free up frozen cash.)
3. Can we develop legitimate adjustment entries for certain accounts which will reduce book profits and reduce the income-tax liability? (A means of reducing cash outgo.)
4. Is it possible that certain changes in policy or procedures (or both), or installing a new system will reduce funds that are tied up in inventories or other asset accounts? (Reduce funds now unavailable for operations.)

Balance-Sheet Accounts

Accounts receivable are only one step removed from cash and can be sold or pledged to raise cash. If the list of customers meets with the approval of a factoring firm, there is a possibility of selling the receivables outright to a factor who also assumes the credit risk, plus handling all accounting and collection functions connected with the purchased receivables.

Commercial finance is another method of raising funds by pledging receivables as collateral for a loan. This arrangement differs considerably from factoring; the lender does not buy the receivables—he advances funds against them up to 80% of the total value.

These two sources of cash from receivables are of prime importance to you and your clients. So, the following chapter is devoted exclusively to detailed coverage of these two financing methods.

One other possibility should be explored in connection with receivables fund raising. Do the products that are sold to customers lend themselves to installment sales? If so, sales finance companies are a potential source of funds.

Investigate fully the use of negotiable paper, such as trade acceptances and bankers' acceptances. A trade acceptance is a draft upon the buyer which accompanies the invoice. The buyer must accept the draft and sign it. He returns it to the seller, who can use it to improve his working capital position since it is negotiable.

A bankers' acceptance is a time draft. These can be discounted by the seller at his bank to raise funds at once.

While the use of these two types of negotiable paper may not be feasible for all customers, the client should consider their use when shipping goods of substantial value to marginal accounts.

Inventories as a Source of Funds

Quite often, it is possible to pledge inventories as collateral for loans. A commercial finance company will consider loans against inventories as part of a package plan which includes financing receivables.

Investigate the possible use of public warehouses and *warehouse receipts* as a device for pledging inventory as security for loans. Under this plan the inventory is actually delivered to the lender, or put into the hands of a public warehouse for safekeeping. Inventory is moved in and out of stock, covered by legal documents that are known as trust receipts. For flexibility, the "public warehouse" is sometimes set up in a corner of the borrower's own warehouse.

Look into the feasibility of obtaining prime materials or goods on a *consignment basis*. For example, during a recent visit to a small electronics plant which uses more than $100,000 of aluminum materials each year, I noticed that one area of the warehouse was segregated. The aluminum bars and rods stored in this area belonged to a supplier. The president of the electronics firm had made arrangements years before with the aluminum supplier to put in large stocks of the material on consignment. The user firm merely reports and pays for all materials removed from the enclosure.

Fixed Assets

Mortgages on machinery and equipment, land and buildings represent a conventional source of borrowed funds. However, in recent years a device known as "sale and lease-back" has been increasing in popularity.

Suppose a firm has built up a considerable equity in fixed assets, such as land, machinery and buildings. One cash-raising device is to arrange a sale of such facilities for cash, with a lease-back arrangement stipulated in a long-term contract, whereby the seller pays a yearly sum for leasing the facilities. This arrangement has many benefits and is quite popular with large firms that operate on a large scale, geographically—as a means of avoiding the tying up of large amounts of capital in fixed assets.

A fast-growing type of business is the company which specializes in leasing equipment. More and more firms are leasing office equipment, computers, delivery equipment, aircraft and other assets which would tie up substantial amounts of capital if they were purchased.

Depreciation Reserves

An obvious source of conserving funds is to check into the basis used for depreciating fixed assets and the corollary reserves. See if the depreciation can be speeded up. Study the possibility of taking the 7% investment-tax credit on large, recent purchases of machinery or equipment.

Special Tools Charged Off

The controller of a large electronics firm in 1965 was looking for ways to improve reported profits. He checked into special tools which had been purchased for a particular production order that involved defense equipment of custom design and manufacture. These tools represented an original investment of more than $100,000 and they were stored in the basement of the manufacturing plant. The controller looked them over and called firms which were engaged in similar types of manufacturing activity. He successfully sold the forgotten tools to a firm for $45,000.00.

Officers' Life Insurance

Insurance specialists say that it is possible to raise cash from an insurance policy without reducing the amount of protection provided by insurance. This is done by re-programming the policy or policies—in order to set up adequate coverage with new policies and to permit the insured to obtain cash from the old policies.

Bad Debt Reserves

Review the size of the bad debt reserve in relation to the size of the receivables asset. And, as mentioned in the prior chapter, perhaps the reserve should be increased to take care of a large number of unadjusted deductions which are a dubious asset, but are a part of the receivables.

Prepaid Insurance

If you find substantial sums tied up in prepaid insurance, investigate the possibility of paying insurance premiums on an installment basis.

Reduce Financial Costs

Sales terms frequently produce a very large charge against profits on the Profit and Loss Statement in the form of discounts allowed. Cash discount terms such as 3/30 net 31; 2/10 net 30; 1/30 net 31 offer an inducement of a stated discount percentage for early payment of the invoice.

A thorough review and examination of sales terms quite often reveals that such terms do not produce the desired cash flow—that they are *not* essential to meet competition, and result in large financial costs.

In today's tight money market more and more executives are taking one of two steps to reduce these costs:

- Change the terms to fit the facts.
- Increase the selling price of the product just enough to cover the loss of the discount.

What is meant by "change the terms to fit the facts"? Here is a representative situation which an analysis of terms, and a study of how the terms are administered in the collection department, may reveal: `

Suppose that sales terms are 2/10 net 30 which theoretically will bring in the invoice amount less 2% in 10 days from invoice date. However, the facts gathered in regard to the condition of receivables show that only a small percentage of invoices are paid on a discounted basis—open receivables are outstanding for an average of 42 days, and the customers deduct the 2% regardless of lateness of payment. Further, if the collection department attempts to collect the unearned 2% discount deducted improperly by the customers, it meets with little success and, therefore, has almost quit trying to enforce the terms being offered on the invoice.

Changing the terms to fit the facts, as outlined above, offers many benefits. Suppose that terms are changed from 2/10 net 30 to net 30. This eliminates the large sums charged to discounts allowed, and makes it easier for the collection department to administer terms, since no unearned discount is in the picture. It also eliminates a bone of contention between the customers, the sales department and the collection department.

Examine Accounts Payable Policies and Procedures

One way to conserve cash outgo is to divide payables into three categories of invoices:

1. Invoices subject to substantial cash discounts (and owed to firms which enforce their discount terms) are placed in the first group for quick payment on or before the discount due date.

Where the vendor permits, such invoices may be paid even earlier than the discount terms require, and anticipation (interest earned) may be taken in addition to taking the discount.

2. Invoices subject to net terms of less than 30 days are placed in a folder marked for payment in approximately 30 days from the invoice date.

3. Invoices subject to trade discounts and end-of-month (EOM) terms are grouped together for payment about the middle of the month, following the month shown on the invoice as the

date of purchase. This group may include the invoices subject to cash discount terms, but are from firms which obviously do not enforce their terms.

FINANCIAL MANAGEMENT

Raising funds should be an activity which takes place after determining financial requirements, unless the client is chronically short of funds and is perpetually in need of capital from any and all possible sources.

As the American Institute bulletin says, "The forecasting of financial requirements lies at the heart of the financial management of any Company." And, as the bulletin points out, successful financial management of any firm involves these factors:

1. Determination of the financial requirements, in advance of need, including both short-term and long-term requirements.

2. Establishing various sources for funds of the right type, available at the right time.

3. Proper use of the funds after they are made available to the businessman.

Determining Financial Requirements

Some form of forecasting is the foundation for determining financial requirements. The importance of cash forecasting and planning is difficult to exaggerate—since more firms enter bankruptcy while *earning a profit* than those showing a loss! The reason for this phenomenon is that a shortage of operating cash creates the existence of overdue bills to vendors, contractors or government agencies in many instances. One disgruntled, impatient creditor may blow the whistle on an over-expanded firm with a short cash position, regardless of the fact that it may be showing truly excellent book profits.

Forecasting Methods

Although there are several methods of projecting short-term cash requirements, one familiar method is the direct estimate of cash receipts and disbursements.

A formal operating budget provides the basis for the most accurate forecasts. If such budgetary detail is not available, estimates can be established from a review of events expected to take place in the future, based upon historical events for a comparable period of time in the past.

The CPA bulletin summarizes the process of cash forecasting with this statement: "Financial planning of short-term requirements should include estimates of events throughout an entire cycle of operations. A forecast of financial condition at widely spaced intervals can be entirely inadequate because of seasonal and other fluctuations. Like budgeting as a whole, cash forecasting is a spiral thing. It must be reviewed continuously and should continually project the entire cycle of the business. If this is not done, most of its advantages will be lost."

Benefits of Cash Forecasting

1. Forecasting reveals the need for obtaining funds from outside sources well in advance—and it will enable management to determine the probable *duration* of loans.

2. It provides for the preplanning of the owner's salary or drawing account, or for dividends and bonuses; plus the payment of taxes, insurance and other major obligations.

3. Adequate cash forecasting may enable the small business to take cash discount on bills

or to purchase large quantities of raw materials, parts or supplies at reduced prices. Both steps increase profits.

4. The technique of cash forecasting indicates good business management; lenders will be favorably impressed.

Integrated Money Management

Most firms are not organized for effective money management. It is not uncommon to find several different executives or partners in a firm involved in bank relations, bank loan arrangements, commercial financing of receivables and possibly factoring arrangements. Then the application of cash to receivables records (and the subsequent deposit of checks) is left to the office manager to administer. The supervisor of the accounts payable department is left to his own devices in processing vendor invoices, and in getting them ready for payment. Also, cash flow from receivables is under the control of the credit and collection manager, who may, or may not be doing a good job of converting receivables to cash when payment is due. It is not unusual to find such a firm losing thousands of dollars each year because of loose, informal money management.

By direct contrast, the firms that have done the best job of money management in this time of high-cost capital are those in which management has centralized the responsibility for coordinating all the functions that involve cash flow, both incoming and outgoing.

There are many opportunities for profit improvement through effective money management. Let's discuss a few of them.

Lock Boxes

In recent years we have seen an ever-increasing use of bank operated "lock boxes." The remitter is instructed to send his check to a designated box number. The mail in the box is regularly picked up by a bank and the remittances are deposited at once to the credit of the payee firm. For firms that operate in large geographic areas the use of centrally-located lock boxes may well speed up the deposit of remittances from one to three days.

Put Idle Cash to Work

For many years I worked in banks of all sizes as an outside bank specialist, analyzing checking accounts as to activity, average balance and profitability to the bank. I have long been impressed with the number of firms that leave substantial funds in banks which are not allowed to pay interest on open checking accounts.

An enterprising money manager will attempt to put all available funds to work by transferring idle funds from outlying branches by draft in order to invest them in interest-bearing municipal or government securities, or in preferred stocks.

(One limitation on putting idle funds to work is that loan agreements with a bank may require the maintenance of a substantial balance in the bank accounts. However, any excess over the stipulated amount should be put to work as suggested.)

Another technique of transferring funds is to use drafts when paying large sums to vendors. The difference between paying by draft and paying by check is based on legal requirements.

When the drawer of a check writes and mails a check, the funds are legally supposed to be in the bank *at that time*. Yet, the firm receiving the check or checks may not be able to deposit them for several days. By contrast, a draft may be drawn and mailed with no legal requirement that funds are available at the moment. When the draft is presented to the drawee bank, the bank will notify the firm that issued the draft; funds are then advanced to cover the draft or drafts.

Convertible Debentures

Many businessmen are seemingly unaware of the many benefits offered by investing in convertible debentures. These unique securities offer a fixed rate of coupon interest—AND an opportunity for capital gains!

More than 250 well-known firms have issued this type of interest-bearing securities in the past two decades or less. Here are some typical characteristics of convertibles:

- The face amount of the bond is in multiples of $100.
- They pay a fixed rate of interest through attached coupons.
- They include a "convertibility" feature which specifies that the debenture can be surrendered to the treasurer of the issuing company and the bond owner will receive a stated number of common stock shares in return. This feature assures that the market price of the convertible will move upwards in relation to the total cash value of the stock shares represented by the bond—when the market value of the common stock increases enough to establish a cash value for the bond which is greater than its face value.
- They represent excellent collateral for loans.

(Many banks will lend up to 80% of the market value of convertibles issued by blue-chip corporations. This means that the firm owning them can unfreeze most of the funds invested in them for operating purposes; yet retain the possibility of earning substantial capital gains, which will accrue if the price of the corresponding common stocks rises on the stock market.)

Summary

A check list of internal sources of funds to refer to during a diagnostic review follows:

- *Accounts Receivable*
     Sell the receivables
     Pledge the receivables
     Discount installment sales paper
     Secure negotiable documents from customers in lieu of cash
- *Inventories*
     Pledge inventories
     Use warehouse receipts
- *Fixed Assets*
     Utilize sale and lease-back arrangements
     Increase depreciation reserves
     Investigate special, charged-off tools
- *Officers' Life Insurance*
     Raise funds by reprogramming
- *Bad Debt Reserves*
     Increase reserves, if possible

- *Prepaid Insurance*
  Pay premiums on an installment plan
- *Reduce Financial Costs*
  Change selling discount terms—or increase selling prices
- *Accounts Payable*
  Analyze vendor invoices—group into 3 categories

10

Accounts Receivable Financing

Most articles dealing with the subject of business financing usually allocate only two or three pages to accounts-receivable financing. By contrast, this entire chapter is devoted to the two major types of receivables financing; commercial finance and factoring.

The reasons for the extensive coverage of the subject are several. First, the ability to convert receivables to cash quickly is increasingly important to many businesses operating in today's high-cost environment. Secondly, it is important for any practitioner to understand the fundamentals of financing and factoring to qualify as a financial consultant to clients—to qualify as an adviser in regard to sources of funds when operating capital is required.

FACTORING: WHAT IT IS AND HOW IT WORKS

Factoring is frequently either unknown or misunderstood in the business community. Yet, the dynamic businessman with a growing business should understand and use the unique services rendered by these financial firms, because of the valuable contribution that a good factor can make to the growth and prosperity of a manufacturing firm which is short of working capital.

Factors do more than offer a source of financing; they supply several unique and useful services to clients in addition to providing financing. Since they are an adjunct to any business offering extensive trade credit to customers, one purpose of this chapter is to remove the mystery surrounding this time-honored industry, and to explain the benefits accruing from factoring services.

Definition

An "old-line" factor is a commercial enterprise which *buys* acceptable receivables outright. The factor buys the invoices from the mill or manufacturer without recourse, unless the credit standing of the client's customer is questionable, in which case the factor will accept the invoice with recourse—at "client risk."

In addition to supplying ready capital, the factor performs a credit checking function, and handles all bookkeeping and collection activities. A factor with 150 to 200 clients may process up to 400 million dollars or more of receivables in a calendar year.

Origin of Factoring

More than 100 years ago the typical factor was a sales agent in the New York and New England textile industry. These selling agents represented the leading textile mills in England. Their customers were the dyers and converters in the United States who continually purchased English fabrics for conversion to piece goods in this country.

The English manufacturers were naturally dubious about making open, unsecured shipments of large amounts of textile goods to customers of unknown integrity and financial resources in the United States. As one solution to this problem, the sales agents began the practice of guaranteeing payment for all sales made to their customers. This was the origin of the practice of old-line factoring as it still exists today.

Growth of Factoring

For many generations, according to Mr. Jerome Harber, Senior Vice-President of Mill Factors, the firms using factors were confined almost exclusively to textile mills, selling agents and converters. But, within a relatively short time, this method of financing was accepted by other branches of the textile industry—and it spread to unrelated businesses such as bedding, cosmetics, furniture, shoes, toys, paint, rubber, etc.

The sales volume of a typical firm that uses factoring ranges from $100,000 to more than $40 million annually. A factored firm is one that is apt to be an energetic, fast-growing concern which needs additional working capital because the management is concentrating on product development, increased production and earning more profit from increased sales.

In 1941, factored receivables amounted to scarcely more than $500 million; by 1964, the total exceeded $6 billion. In 1965, factors handled more than $8 billion in receivables, according to an article in the February 4th, 1966, issue of the *New York Times* which quoted Mr. Walter Yankauer, President of Mill Factors in New York City.

Factoring Arrangements and Procedures

The mechanics of factoring are outlined in detail for the information of the practitioner. Some of the highlights are:

1. The manufacturer (the client of the factor) bundles up all of his invoices daily or periodically and prepares an Assignment Sheet—a legal cover sheet which assigns the receivables invoices to the factor. Then he mails or sends the assignment sheet and the invoices to the factor.

2. The factor groups the invoices by invoice terms, calculates the applicable discount amounts, and credits the client with the net total of the invoices after discount. To the factor, accounting for sales invoices received represents an accounts payable situation; the client record is known as an "Account Current."

3. The client's customers are instructed to send their remittances directly to the factor. Each invoice is clearly stamped with remittance instructions.

This arrangement is known as "notification factoring." (There is another method whereby the customer is not aware that his supplier has sold the invoices to a factor; this is "non-notification" factoring.)

4. The client may draw cash advances during the month against his sales which have been assigned to the factor. Cash payments to the client, before the end of the month, are considered to be an advance because of the prevailing practice of settling with clients at the end of each calendar month.

5. At month-end, the factor prepares a sales statement for each client; this statement shows gross sales, credits and cash discounts deducted from sales. Please refer to Exhibit 10-A, which shows that the statement is divided into three sections—gross sales, credits and net sales—followed by sections for discount analysis and commission rates, and commission amounts.

ANY MANUFACTURER, INC.

MILL FACTORS CORPORATION
380 PARK AVENUE SOUTH
NEW YORK 10, N. Y.

Recapitulation of Account Sales for the month of_____ MARCH 195_

	SALES	CREDITS	NET SALES	
	42,952.48	2,580.65	40,371.83	
DISCOUNT RATE	NET SALES	DISCOUNT	NET SALES LESS DISCOUNTS	
NET	40,371.83		40,371.83	
COMMISSION RATE	NET SALES LESS DISCOUNTS	COMMISSIONS		
1 3/8 %	40,371.83	555.11	39,816.72	

VALUE	JUNE 14 1967		39,816.72
VALUE OF TERMS	MAR 31/67 TO JUNE 14/67		721.68
VALUE	MARCH 31 1967		39,095.04

MF 102-3M-8-65 W P

E. & O. E.
MILL FACTORS CORPORATION

Exhibit 10-A
TYPICAL SALES STATEMENT

In the "analysis for discount" section, sales are shown by discount percentage groups, since the factor deducts the discount before he computes the net amount payable to the client.

Average Due Date

The lower section of the statement shows the "Average Due Date" of all sales, and the time period used to figure interest, followed by the interest amount. Factors utilize an ingenious averaging method for determining the average due date—based on the *discount option* of multiple option terms—for all invoices received during an accounting period, which is usually one calendar month. (As is explained in Chapter 12, when invoice terms are applied to invoice dates, two due dates result: the discount due date and final due date.)

The average due date is the basis for interest "pro and con" (interest credited or charged to the client). The number of days from the end of the current month to the average due date is the time period for interest calculations.

The Dollar-Day Concept

The method used to calculate the average due date is known as "dollar day" accounting. *Multiplying the number of days from a base date to the discount due date (the earliest due date in multiple-option terms) by the invoice amount produces a result called "dollar-days."* You will soon see how this technique produces the average due date for all invoices received for an entire month—even though the manufacturer (the client) may be sending in groups of invoices every day during the month, representing a constantly-advancing invoice date and many different sets of terms.

Focal Date Concept

One of the essential tools for averaging is a base starting point for calculating the number of days; factors use the concept of a "focal date" as the base. Although it is feasible to select any arbitrary fixed date as a focal date, most factors select one of two calendar dates, such as the end of the prior month—or the last day of the current month. For the illustrations which follow, the last day of the prior month is the focal date.

Dollar-Day Calculations

Now let's see how the dollar-day technique works. Suppose the factor receives a batch of invoices dated June 10th, which represents an assignment by a client of invoices that total $5,000; all bear the same terms, 2/10 net 30. Here are the procedures for dollar-day calculations:

1. Apply the terms to the invoices and figure the short-term or discount due date. (Add 10 days to the invoice date of 6/10; short-term due date is 6/20.)

2. Working backwards from the due date of 6/20 to the focal date of 5/31, we find that the time period is 20 days.

3. Now multiply the invoice batch total of $5,000 by 20 days. *The result is 100,000 dollar-days.*

During the remainder of the month of June, the factor receives a second batch of invoices, totalling $10,000; these are dated June 15th and terms are net 30. Let's calculate the dollar-days:

1. Add 30 days to invoice date of 6/15. The due date is 7/15.

2. Counting the days from the focal date of 5/31 to 7/15, we find that there are 45 days between the two dates.

3. Multiply 45 days by the total amount of the invoices; the result is 450,000 dollar-days.

How to Calculate Average Due Date

Now let's recap the sales and dollar-days represented by these two batches of sales invoices, then calculate the average due date.

Batch # 1	$ 5,000	Sales	100,000 Dollar-Days
Batch # 2	10,000		450,000
Totals	$15,000		550,000

Divide the total number of dollar-days by the amount of sales; the result (to nearest whole day) is 37. Adding 37 days to the focal date of 5/31 produces an *average due date* of July 7th. However, since the current month ends on June 30th, the average due date is compared to this cut-off date to determine the actual number of interest days, as explained next.

Interest Charge or Credit

The average due date is the base for figuring an interest charge or credit to post to the client's "Account Current" ledger. When the month-end settlement date is compared to the calculated average due date, one of two conditions applies:

1. If the average due date is later than the end of the current sales month, there will be an interest charge to the client. As determined earlier, the average due date is July 7th. The factor applies an agreed-upon interest rate to the amount of net sales, and calculates the interest for 7 days. The factor then posts the interest amount to the client's account.

2. However, if the average due date falls on a date PRIOR TO the end of the current sales month, the factor calculates the interest on the number of MINUS DAYS—and CREDITS INTEREST to the client's account.

In the first instance, the factor charges interest, since he is crediting the funds from sales to the client's account SEVEN DAYS before the customers are supposed to remit. In the second instance, the factor credits interest, since the client's customers will be remitting funds to the factor several days before the end of the month.

Collection Days

The average due date shown on the sales statement is increased by an arbitrary number of days stated in the factoring contract, and identified as "collections days."

The number of collection days may range from 4 to 10. Theoretically, they represent the time period from the mailing date of the average customer's remittance to the date that the factor's bank credits the factor's account with the funds. If no collection days are added to the actual average due date represented by the aggregate invoice terms, the factor loses the use of his capital during the time period represented by collection days.

If the number of collection days stated in the contract seems to exceed a reasonable period for receiving and processing remittances, the additional compensation to the factor may be justified as an offsetting factor to the cost of late payments made by the client's customers. For example, in the retail trades many customers ignore invoice terms, pay their bills late—and refuse to pay late interest. By negotiation, the factor may secure a partial offset to such costs by increasing the number of collections days.

Credit Invoices

Credits are processed in separate batches from invoices. Invoice terms are applied to credits, but the base date is the date of the applicable invoice. The client is supposed to make reference to the applicable invoice—when preparing a credit document. However, many credits do not apply against a specific invoice or it is not possible to determine the applicable invoice. So, the factor may arbitrarily back-date the credit for purposes of interest calculations.

Since credit invoices are the reverse of a sales invoice, interest calculations may result in an interest credit—unless the credit document applies against an invoice which was issued in a prior month, and the discount due date of the invoice falls *before* the focal date currently in use.

Maturity Clients

Some clients do not want cash advances from the factor before their invoices mature. They factor their receivables to gain the benefits of the credit and collections services of the factoring firm. Such clients are known as "maturity" clients. At month-end the factor calculates the net amount that is due the client on the average maturity due date, but holds the check until the maturity date arrives. No interest is charged or credited under such an arrangement.

Credit and Collection Fees

A factor makes a special charge based on sales for servicing the client's receivables. The charge is improperly called "commission"; it is actually a credit guarantee and collection service fee. The rate ranges from ¾ of 1% to 2% of net sales.

This fee includes the credit risk which the factor assumes when buying the invoices without recourse. The factor sets up a receivables record for each customer, and handles all remittances, correspondence, deductions and all other matters pertaining to the account plus collection followup.

A significant item of expense to the factor is the handling of deductions from remittances. The client's customers frequently deduct amounts as claims for various reasons, such as: *damaged goods, returned goods, incorrect pricing, short shipment, freight allowance, advertising allowance, etc.*

The factor must obtain approval of each deduction from the client—since the client remains responsible for handling and settling all claims, and will be charged for all deductions allowed to customers.

Benefits from Factoring

The benefits of factoring vary from one type of manufacturer to another. Let's take a look at some of the outstanding, major benefits of a factoring arrangement:

1. *Convert Orders or Invoices to Cash:* A factor will advance cash at once against sales invoices when received. It is even possible to secure advances against customer orders, since the factor usually approves credit on orders before they become invoices. This can be of great significance to a firm which finds it necessary to invest a considerable amount of capital

in materials, supplies or labor before the order can be converted to a completed, shipped sale.

2. *Eliminate the Cost of Credit and Collection Functions:* Even a small firm may find that two or three people are required almost full time to post receivables, prepare customer statements, pass credit on orders, maintain credit and collection records, and perform collection follow-up work on the telephone and by mail.

All of these functions represent a direct continuing overhead cost to a growing business. If the factor accepts all, or nearly all invoices without recourse, the expense of this department can be eliminated. One person may be retained to telephone customers' orders to the factor for credit approval, and to handle deductions and other related problems when necessary.

Quite often, the factoring firm is able to save the salaries of several people by assigning the receivables to the factor who performs all the subsequent accounting, credit and collection work.

3. *Increase Sales Volume Safely:* Landing a large order may pose a potentially serious problem to a small, under-financed firm. The mere possibility of a large credit loss may deter the firm from accepting such orders. By contrast, a factored firm will cheerfully go after orders of all sizes, since there is no credit risk if the order is acceptable to the factor.

The factor, in many instances, will accept marginal risks because of extensive credit files built up over the years—plus the vast resources of the factor, which enables him to spread the risk over a huge volume of sales.

4. *Provides Cash for New Facilities and Increased Sales:* Many well-known firms were once factored during their period of growth from small to large companies. In many instances they were unable to secure adequate funds at the local bank, and they turned to factors for badly needed funds for expansion of facilities, new products, market research, etc.

5. *Availability of Funds Increases Profits:* The firm with adequate operating funds earns profits by taking cash discounts on paid bills. But even more important than that, an improved Dun & Bradstreet credit rating, plus money in the bank, enables the purchasing department to obtain more favorable prices on raw materials, parts and supplies that are required in the manufacturing processes.

One small firm in 1964 paid approximately $30,000 additional for necessary raw materials— because of a very unfavorable D & B credit rating. Stock options were given to some suppliers to obtain desperately needed materials to fill orders. On top of these measures, approximately $6,000 in available cash discounts were lost when paying vendor invoices.

6. *Eliminate Credit Losses:* Unexpected credit losses hit a small business where it hurts. Factoring the receivables passes the credit exposure as well as most clerical costs to the factor.

7. *Consulting Services:* Some "client affairs" executives of major factoring firms are excellent, competent financial consultants in their own right. Case histories attest to the ability of these men to help their clients work out serious financial and production problems with great profit to the firm receiving such assistance.

Misunderstood Aspects

It is a common misconception that factoring costs range as high as 15% on the funds advanced by the factor. This conclusion can be reached only by an incorrect interpretation of the facts.

There are only two types of charges—interest and commission. Let's first review the situation regarding interest charges:

- Interest is charged on cash advances made during the month in response to a client's request. Interest is figured from check date to the end of the month. The rate is usually only slightly higher than the prevailing bank rate.

- Interest is deducted from the client's net proceeds at month-end only if the average due date of the sales falls on a date later than the end of the current month. When interest is charged in this situation, it discounts funds which the factor cannot collect from the client's customers until the due date matures.
- The "commission" charge on sales is not interest. It is actually the fee charged for assuming the credit risk and doing all the bookkeeping and collection follow-up on all invoices purchased from the client.

The commission charge on sales varies with each client (to some extent), since it is a negotiated percentage of sales. However, certain ground rules help establish the appropriate commission rate. For example, a client who sells his product to wholesale customers, or to other manufacturers will receive a favorable rate in the range of $\frac{7}{8}$% to $1\frac{1}{4}$%. By contrast, a client who sells to retailers may have to pay from $1\frac{1}{4}$% up to 2%. Broad experience in factoring reveals the reasons why retail accounts are less desirable:

a. Many retail customers habitually pay invoices on a delinquent basis, and also refuse to pay late interest assessed.

b. The average invoice amount is relatively small in the retail field. This means that more paper work for each dollar of sales and commission is necessary to handle the sales of clients who sell to retail accounts.

c. The number of credits issued by a "retail" client is always greater than those credits processed for a wholesale client.

d. Retail customers usually make more deductions for claims from remittances than wholesale customers. Such deductions tie up capital, and require extensive paper work and clerical follow-up to remove them from the receivable records.

Working Arrangements with Factors

Factors try to expand their sales and services in various ways. One favored method is to encourage the accounting practitioner in any area to understand and accept the potential benefits of factoring for his client who is short on operating capital—and to recommend that a factoring arrangement be investigated.

Several key factoring firms have branch offices located in the larger cities in the nation for this purpose. They will be glad to send an account executive, at your request, to evaluate your client's business operations, analyze the customer list, terms of sales and other aspects of the situation to determine the feasibility of arranging a factoring contract for your client's firm.

The factors named below have their main offices in New York City. Some have a network of branch offices; others will send an account executive from the main office to visit your client.

Crompton-Richmond Co., Inc.—Factors
111 W. 40 St., New York, N.Y.

Mill Factors, Inc.
380 Park Avenue South, New York, N.Y.

Rusch Factors, Inc.
1430 Broadway, New York, N.Y.

James Talcott, Inc.
Sperry Rand Building
6th Avenue & 51st St., New York, N.Y.

COMMERCIAL FINANCE

While factoring has experienced a substantial growth in the past decade, its offspring—commercial finance—has far outpaced its parent in dollar volume. For example, the two types of receivables financing accounted for $23 billion in volume in 1965; $14.8 billion of the total were commercial finance loans secured by receivables.

Growth Rate

During the past twenty years, factoring and financing were finally recognized by the business community as legitimate businesses which offer valuable services in the financial field. The stigma formerly attached to these sources of financing began to disappear.

The growth rate of the commercial finance industry in the past two decades has been phenomenal. While the Gross National Product was increasing 200%, the combined value of commercial financing and factoring grew 670%.

How It Started

According to an article in *Credit and Financial Management* magazine, dated November 1965, titled "Finance and Factoring—A Backward Glance," the original concept of commercial finance came into being in Chicago in 1904. The author, Mr. Jerome Harber, is Senior Vice-President of Mill Factors Corp. of New York City, and is a well-known executive in the commercial finance field.

"It seems that in Chicago, back in 1904, two men named Arthur R. Jones and John L. Little were selling the *Encylclopedia Americana* on the instalment plan, and soon found their capital exhausted. Although they were using all their own funds and available sources of credit, they felt they could do more business if they had more cash—a common problem. They finally resolved their problem by organizing a specialized financial institution, which would follow factoring practice."

The Differences

"However, differences soon began to creep in, which changed the shape of their operation into something quite different from that of factoring. For one thing, upon purchasing the accounts receivable represented by open-book accounts for various firms, Jones and Little found that the procedure of notifying their customers of the financing arrangement made them uneasy. Business firms outside the textile field seemed to think that such an action might be construed as a sign of financial weakness. The two met this situation by formulating a plan whereby they financed the receivables of the borrowing companies, but these concerns continued to carry the accounts as though they had not been sold or assigned, keeping their own credit and collection departments.

Nor did Jones and Little assume the bad-debt risk, but instead, bought accounts with recourse (the borrower was responsible for delinquent accounts and credit losses). Firms also took care of their own collections, giving the original collection payments, as received, to Jones and Little. This became known as "non-notification" financing to differentiate it from old-line factoring, where companies were notified that the accounts receivable of their customers were being bought."

How It Works

Under a commercial finance arrangement funds are advanced by the finance firm to clients on a revolving basis against their accounts receivables. Clients collect from customers in the usual way without the customers being aware that their obligation to the vendor or manufacturer is involved in a financial arrangement.

The primary difference between financing and factoring is that the lender does not purchase the receivables; they are merely pledged as *security* for the revolving loan.

The borrower signs an agreement stating the maximum amount of receivables pledged, the percentage of cash to be advanced against sales, the interest rate to be charged on the loan balance, etc. Other details of the financing arrangement are outlined below.

1. *Invoices*: The borrower lists sales invoices on an assignment sheet, attaches the actual invoices and sends them to the commercial finance company. (The borrower has already posted these invoices to his own detailed receivables records in the usual way.)

When the finance company receives the invoices, the credit department checks the status and credit of each customer, and it accepts or rejects the invoice or invoices as collateral. If accounts with customers of the borrower are kept on a "detail" ledger basis, a bookkeeper then posts each invoice to an accounts receivable ledger sheet.

If the borrower has a standing request for a full cash advance against all sales assigned, the finance company will draw a check at once for an amount equal to the stated percentage of gross sales; 75% to 80% represent typical arrangements with clients.

2. *Checks:* The client is obligated to send all customer checks promptly to the finance company. (The client has already applied cash from these checks to his own receivables records, and has audited each remittance.) The client lists all remittances on a transmittal cash sheet, and sends the sheet and the actual checks to the finance company.

A bookkeeper in the finance company examines each check, applies it to open invoices appearing on customer ledgers, and posts it to the ledger records.

A special endorsement stamp is applied to the back of each check so that the remitter is not aware that his check was deposited by a firm other than his supplier. For this reason, this type of financing is known as "non-notification."

How Finance Firms Account for Receivables

When a finance company maintains receivables in "detail," it sets up unit ledger records for each customer of the client. It posts sales, applies cash and maintains receivable controls the same way that the client handles his own receivables records.

However, the finance company follows procedures which are quite different with respect to customer deductions and past due invoices.

Deductions

When a customer makes a direct deduction from a remittance, and refers to a credit memo—or to his own debit memo—and there is no open credit on the receivables ledger, the transaction is frequently referred to as a "claim," or as an "Unadjusted Deduction."

The client bookkeeper will usually accept the check, key off the indicated paid invoices—and set up the deduction amount as a temporary charge-back to the customer's account, pending investigation of the claim, or pending receipt of the referenced credit document.

The bookkeeper in the finance company is not concerned with later disposition of such items; the policy may be to ignore the deduction entirely, since it has no value as collateral.

Aging Open Invoices

When aging unpaid invoices on an Aged Trial Balance, the client's bookkeeper will add invoice terms to the invoice date (or to the "as of" date) and develop the actual final due date to determine the appropriate aging category. By contrast, the finance company simply applies a period of time (such as 60 days) on all invoices dated during the current month. Any invoice that's still unpaid 60 days after the current month is considered to be past due and is deducted from the collateral available for cash advances.

Verification Procedures

Lending firms are well aware of the possibilities of being defrauded in various ways by clients. One of their defensive procedures is periodic verification of open items through audit statements mailed to a selected small percentage of the client's customers.

The statement form usually indicates that an independent audit firm is verifying the receivables of the customer's supplier (the client of the finance company). This is how the customer remains unaware that his supplier has pledged his receivables.

Bulk Basis

Many commercial finance firms do not maintain detailed customer receivables records. They operate on a "bulk" basis, keeping summary records of total sales assigned and total cash received from each client; no detailed customer records are kept. When client records are kept on a bulk basis, the lender relies heavily on his field auditors, who go into the borrower's office at frequent intervals to make spot checks of the General Ledger and review outstanding items on the borrower's detailed customer records.

The lender usually requires that the borrower provide a detailed, monthly-aged trial balance as soon as possible at month-end for analysis and review.

Summary

When receivables are pledged as collateral for a commercial finance loan, the borrower still maintains the usual credit and collection personnel, and continues to maintain complete accounts receivable records. Invoices must be posted and cash applied as always. The bookkeepers continue to audit remittances, and account for errors and differences as usual.

In summary, the borrower is not able to effect any operating savings in receivables, nor shift any responsibilities connected with receivables to the finance company.

HOW COMMERCIAL FINANCE DIFFERS FROM FACTORING

There are several major differences between factoring and a commercial finance arrangement. Reviewing a list of the key features of each financing method will cause the major differences to stand out clearly.

Key Features of Commercial Finance

1. Borrower still operates his own credit, collection and bookkeeping departments.
2. Borrower pledges his receivables as collateral for a loan up to 80% of the total collateral acceptable to the finance company.
3. The finance company takes no responsibility for credit or collections; the receivables remain the property of the borrower.
4. Past due invoices are charged back to the collateral account by the lender which reduces the amount of funds available for loan.
5. Customers of the borrower remain completely unaware of any pledging arrangement involving their liability to the supplier, the client of the finance company.

Key Features of Factoring

1. The client sells all, or most of his receivables outright to the factor, without recourse.
2. The factor passes credit on each sales order, does all bookkeeping and collection work.
3. On sales accepted without recourse, the client remains responsible only for customer deductions.
4. The factoring arrangement is known to the customer, since the invoices are stamped with instructions for the customer to remit directly to the factor.
5. The client is able to convert his receivables asset to a cash asset.

11

Management Services for Credit and Collection Departments

Introduction

As a member of the New York Credit and Financial Association, in recent years, I have had the good fortune of becoming acquainted with many members of the credit fraternity. And, while developing computerized receivables systems for clients, I have had the opportunity to work closely with the general credit manager of several, different large firms over a period of time. Through the sponsorship of John Lynch, General Credit Manager of Prentice-Hall, Inc. (Publishers), I have been a guest lecturer in the New York Institute of Credit from time to time over the years. But I have never been a credit man.

For assistance I turned to Morton Reitman, Vice-President and General Credit Manager of M. Lowenstein and Sons, Inc., a large textile manufacturing firm in New York City, who assisted greatly in the preparation of this chapter. Therefore, as a direct result of his participation, this chapter includes a wealth of information, guidelines and valuable suggestions based on his many years of experience both as credit man and as Credit Manager.

Today's well-educated and trained public accounting practitioner is very capable of assisting clients in many diverse areas of business problems and operations. He is accustomed to working on tax problems, budgets, internal control systems, and cost accounting; he prepares and interprets financial statements, counsels on financing and plans for expansion, and acts as an adviser in many special situations. However, the functions of the credit and collection departments remain a mystery to many people in the accounting profession.

Evidence indicates that many businessmen, corporation managers and executives really do not understand this area of business either. Thus, the practitioner should be—but seldom is— equipped to step in and make a basic review of credit department operations and policies for a client, followed by specific recommendations for changes and improvements.

Objectives

The major objective of this chapter is to cover the functions and duties of a typical credit and collection department—and to present information about the modern techniques of creative credit management. This will broaden your capabilities to be of service in this relatively overlooked, but increasingly vital, area of business operations. You will learn little-known techniques of effective and profitable credit and collection management. You will find in this chapter guidelines and measuring devices for evaluating the efficiency of an existing credit department. Further, you will find out how to set up a new credit department, and how to help select the policies that are most appropriate for the particular financial situation in which your client firm finds itself.

You will quickly feel that you are in familiar surroundings, since credit management deals with financial statement analysis, statistics, customer pay habits, special reports and other tools which you will readily recognize as familiar concepts in the financial functioning of a business.

Importance of the Credit Department

The amount of capital invested in receivables has been on a steady climb since 1949. In early 1967, the total outstanding manufacturers' receivables exceeded $50 billion. In recent years, the amount of capital invested in receivables has exceeded the amount invested in inventories for the first time in business history. Management attention has been increasingly directed toward the efficient management of receivables, since the era of high interest rates and tight money began to pinch nearly every operating business after the midpoint of the 1960–1970 decade.

An efficient, progressive credit department can contribute toward developing new sales outlets—as well as toward expanding sales to established customers. The credit department acts as the custodian of capital invested in this key asset of receivables and it increases the profitability of the firm by effecting a quicker turnover of capital.

Small or medium-sized firms need effective credit management just as much as the larger firms—and possibly more. Credit losses that could be easily absorbed by a large, well-capitalized firm might be disastrous to a small firm, which must use its limited available capital to its best advantage.

It is interesting to note that many of the concepts and functions of credit management today are fairly new. They have developed hand in hand with the tremendous upsurge in economic growth and the parallel increase in the volume of trade-credit sales in recent decades. In today's business environment, credit administration is, indeed, a very important and specialized function which can contribute greatly to the success and profitability of any firm that's engaged in credit sales. And, today's professional credit administrators receive specialized training through courses in financial management offered at many leading universities under the auspices of the Credit Research Foundation.

FUNCTIONS OF A CREDIT DEPARTMENT

The primary functions of a credit department are to evaluate the credit worthiness of customers, to control the extension of credit by approving (or disapproving) sales orders, and to convert receivables to cash as speedily as possible, through efficient collection activities. When checking credit on orders, a credit man acts, in a sense, as a trained arbitrator between the three parties to each sales transaction—each of whom has a conflicting self-interest:

- The salesman wants to sell as much merchandise as possible to any and all customers so he may earn maximum commissions.
- The customer wants to buy goods on the best possible terms and operate on the seller's funds as long as possible to increase his earnings on investment.

● The seller wants to increase sales volume; yet, he wants to avoid credit losses and to convert credit sales to cash as quickly as possible.

Exhibits 11-A and 11-B were taken from an illustrated brochure on credit published by M. Lowenstein and Company, Inc.

Exhibit 11A

THE QUESTION IS OFTEN ASKED, "WHAT IS A CREDITMAN?"

We have had numerous experiences where the weakness of one business was offset by the strength of another business through a merger or an acquisition arranged in the credit man's office. An apparent weakness of a business, when recognized by the astute credit man, can frequently be resolved by an imaginative approach. To accomplish this, the credit man must gain the confidence of the customer through an understanding of complexities that can run the gamut from human psychology to management consulting. The policy of rehabilitation of weak concerns through the medium of a well-balanced business marriage has resulted in tremendous good will and sales for our organization.

Duties of the Credit Manager

A monthly newsletter published by the New York Credit and Financial Management Association recently had this to say about the credit manager:

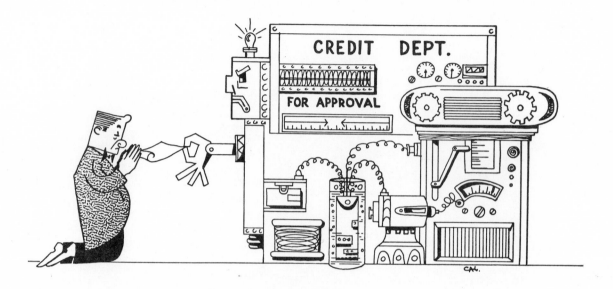

Exhibit 11B

THE CREDIT DEPARTMENT IS OFTEN VIEWED AS A COMPLEX MECHANISM

Once the order reaches the Credit Department it is assigned to a specific credit man. The account is then subjected to a comprehensive credit evaluation. Naturally there are some concerns which enjoy such a strong credit position that very little time is spent arriving at a positive credit decision. Unfortunately, not all businesses have reached this stage of success; therefore, more time must be spent to evaluate the elements of risk and arrive at a credit decision.

"The credit manager is an important member of the management team. As such, he is interested in helping his company achieve its objectives, including the earning of a satisfactory profit. He can do so by being alert to the development of maximum, sound sales volume and profits."

Upon the credit manager falls the chief responsibility for guiding the credit and financial policies of the company's overall planned program for greater sales volume, customer satisfaction and increased profits through credit sales. The credit manager is increasingly recognized as a financial executive in his own right. He usually reports to the owner, treasurer or financial vice-president of a company.

Quoting once more from the newsletter: "The purpose of credit management in a company is to enable the credit staff to recognize and understand underlying credit and business problems, search for and find the necessary facts; and then, by thorough exploration of possibilities, consider alternate courses of action. All the while, there is an awareness of the risks and probable consequences of each alternate proposal, particularly its impact upon company profits. Finally, with balanced judgment, vision and skill, there is exercise in the art of selection, choosing the best alternative available under given circumstances, within the framework of company policy objectives."

Aids in Re-examining Policies

Now, one of the continuing functions of an aggressive, alert credit manager is to review and reappraise, on a continuing basis, the existing credit policies in the light of current conditions. Credit policies which are too tight or restricted can be even more detrimental to profits than those which are too loose.

The credit manager should be as sales minded and profit-oriented as any member of the sales management team. He should work closely with the sales department since both deal directly with customers. However, there is one important difference in emphasis between the sales and credit managers. The former is interested in the increased turnover of inventory; the latter, in the increased turnover of accounts receivable.

HOW A CREDIT DEPARTMENT EVALUATES AND CONTROLS CREDIT EXTENSION: IMPORTANCE OF WORKING CAPITAL

Any firm which does a large volume of short-term trade credit (sales on credit to other business firms) views the customer's working capital as an indicator of the customer's ability to pay. As the author of the famous H. A. Finney books on accounting (published by Prentice-Hall, Inc.) states it, "The working capital ratio is indicative of short-term solvency."

As you know, net working capital is the excess of current assets of cash, receivables and inventories over current liabilities. Both the amount of working capital and the ratio are important to the credit man who is considering granting short-term credit to a business.

- The *amount* has a bearing on the highest credit which may be extended.
- The *ratio* is indicative of the degree of safety—since it reflects the relation of current assets to current debts, and thus, reveals how much shrinkage in current assets can occur before the interests of the current creditors would be jeopardized.

Example	*Company A*	*Company B*
Total current assets	$200,000	$1,000,000
Total current liabilities	100,000	800,000
Working capital	$100,000	$200,000

Company B has twice the amount of working capital as compared to the other firm. However, Company A's position is more favorable than Company B's, since Company A has $2 of current assets for each dollar of current liabilities—whereas, Company B has only $1.25 for each $1 of current liabilities. The ratios are 2/1 for Company A and 1.25/1 for Company B.

Increase or Decrease in Working Capital

Since the security of a short-term creditor is based on working capital, it is essential for a credit man to trace any increase or decrease in this key indicator of business health.

ELEMENTS THAT CONTRIBUTE TO AN INCREASE IN WORKING CAPITAL ARE:

- New contributions of capital funds by the owners.
- New funds received from long-term obligations such as long-term notes or bonds.
- Earnings retained and reinvested in the business and reflected in current assets, such as receivables.

- Writing up merchandise inventories and marketable securities.
- Reserves against receivables.

ELEMENTS WHICH CONTRIBUTE TO A DECREASE IN WORKING CAPITAL ARE:

- Losses incurred.
- Distribution of earnings or withdrawal of capital.
- Use of current funds to acquire fixed and non-current assets.
- Use of current funds to fund reserves.
- Marking down of inventory values and marketable securities.

Basis for Extension of Credit

The amount of working capital is only one factor considered when classifying and evaluating accounts for extension of credit. Other criteria are:

- Selective ratios calculated from information provided by the financial statement, such as working capital turnover (the relationship between the average amount of working capital and total sales), total debt to net worth, etc.
- Past collection experience of the seller, as well as information gathered from other creditors.
- Length of time in business.
- High credit extended by other creditors.
- Dun & Bradstreet rating.
- Character, capacity and capital. Capacity refers to the qualitative aspect of the customer's situation, the ability to pay.

In broad terms, one essential function of a well-operated credit department is to gather financial and other information about each customer, evaluate it, then use it intelligently as the basis for extending, refusing or limiting credit as sales orders are processed through the credit department.

Working Tools

There are many different tools available to a credit man to assist him in arriving at a credit decision:

- Financial statements submitted by the customer on his own form—or blank statements submitted to the customer by the credit department and filled in by the customer's accountant.
- Monthly General Ledger Trial Balance.
- Bank investigations and reports.
- Accountant's Cash Flow Forecast.
- Dun & Bradstreet reports and ratings; and reports from the National Credit Office or other specialized credit agencies.
- Appraisal memorandums based on personal visits to customer's premises.
- Personal Guarantee Documents.
- Aged Trial Balance or ledger sheet which shows latest status of the account.
- Credit Interchange Reports.
- Written memos regarding reported pay habits and high credit—obtained at meetings of industry credit groups.

All of this information is maintained in the "credit file."

Bank investigations and reports tell the credit man the length of time the bank has had the account, the approximate average amount in the checking account or accounts, and how the customer has handled his bank loans.

One important source of credit information is the "credit interchange." This systematized exchange of information between creditors takes many forms. Credit men and credit managers join trade associations; they belong to trade groups and meet weekly at lunch to exchange the latest information about key accounts. Credit interchange reports are written answers to queries received from other firms that extend credit to the same customer, or customers. These reports cover key points, such as terms offered to the account, average length of time invoices are outstanding before payment, high credit, how long the creditor has been selling to the account, etc.

Use of Cash Flow Forecast

A cash flow forecast is a tabulation of the plans of a firm in terms of their impact on the receipts and expenditures of cash in future periods. It may be thought of as a timed prediction of additions to and deductions from the firm's bank accounts.

A cash flow forecast makes it possible to determine, in advance, what the probable needs of the customer firm will be—so that suitable arrangements can be made to obtain the necessary financing, if a cash deficiency is expected in any given period. The seller can offer longer terms, create more sales and gain customer goodwill by working out suitable arrangements with the customer.

Approving Credit by Exception

Several methods of approving credit on individual orders, intended to speed order approval and reduce the cost of credit checking, are in common use.

Establishing a line of credit for each customer is a well-known device for controlling credit. The line of credit is the approximate amount which the seller is willing to risk as outstanding credit to the customer. As a rule, the unpaid ledger balance, plus approved orders in process, should not exceed this figure. Of course, the credit line for many large, blue-ribbon companies is recorded as "requirements." That is, the seller will honor any and all orders from these firms; there is no limit.

The credit line assigned to an account is based on the factors listed earlier in this chapter that are used to classify and evaluate each customer.

Use of a credit line makes it easy to approve orders that do not exceed the established credit line.

Another method for simplifying order approval is to establish minimum shipping amounts. For example, one large firm approves all orders from customers for orders up to $50. No checking is done on these small orders.

Credit Checking with a Computer

An increasing number of firms now utilize a computer for order/invoicing preparation. Since this requires keypunching each order to feed into the mechanized system, it is easy for the computer to check credit, if well-defined tests and parameters have been set up by the credit department. One primary guideline is the credit line assigned to each customer.

The computer will make the prescribed tests for each order, and then report orders which require a decision on an exception basis. According to the guidelines in use at one large, progressive merchandising firm, an order will be rejected if:

- The total exposure (present accounts receivable balance plus orders in process) exceeds the assigned credit line.
- The customer's account includes one or more past due invoices.
- Customer is classified as a marginal account, and has not sent in a recent financial statement.
- The increase in inventory is more than twice that of the preceding year, but working capital has not increased more than 50%.
- Working capital has not increased more than 50%, but current liabilities have increased in excess of 50% of net worth.

The last two tests are based on financial statement information, which has been keypunched and fed into the machine as a basic component of the "customer profile." This is a truly modern development; all indications are that the trend toward using the computer for statement analysis will grow.

Classification of Accounts

The classification of accounts goes hand in hand with the procedures for checking credit on orders. Accounts may be divided into four classes:

1. Excellent
2. Good
3. Marginal
4. Poor

Customer accounts that are rated as "excellent" are those firms which have been in business a long time, are soundly financed and have established reputations for integrity and dealings with creditors. Outstanding examples of firms in this category are J. C. Penney, Woolworth, General Motors, Sears, IBM, Borden's and many others not as well known. This type of firm is usually rated "AAA1" by Dun & Bradstreet.

"Good" credit risks are those firms which are stable and pay promptly. Every indicator used by the credit man points to their credit worthiness—but their financial structure will not permit shipments to them in unlimited amounts. *A credit line is assigned to these accounts.*

"Marginal accounts" are those with marginal working capital, or which have a history of variable pay habits. Special studies indicate that 25% or more of the total number of accounts in a typical list of trade customers are classed as "marginal"—and require a high percentage of the total time and effort devoted to credit checking and related collection work in a credit department.

Each order from such a firm must be approved for credit after the credit man has reviewed the firm's current status. As Morton Reitman says, "The test of a strong credit department is its ability to transact business with companies in this category, with profits earned far exceeding losses incurred. One benefit of selling to this type of customer is that the seller's margin of profit can be maintained; the account is subject to minimum risk of a competitor forcing prices down."

"Poor" accounts are those with limited working capital (or none)—and with a small net worth. Shipments to such accounts are frequently handled as COD shipments.

HOW THE CREDIT MAN CAN CONTRIBUTE TO INCREASED SALES

There are several ways by which the credit man can help increase sales:

1. Provide lists of accounts which justify intensified cultivation and sales efforts.

The credit man can analyze the current position of all accounts in relation to the amount of potential business as well as the progress of the management. Lines of credit may be based not only on the working capital and net worth of the firm, but also on the firm's ability to consume and resell. Such information may be very helpful to the sales department.

2. The credit man can examine the operating and financial backgrounds of firms classed as marginal. Such accounts can produce a large sales volume with minimum losses, if properly handled and controlled.

3. The credit man can review each salesman's list of customers and:
   - Point out potentially good customers who should be cultivated and developed into volume buyers.
   - Identify nuisance accounts where the potential for growth is limited.
   - Identify those firms which should be avoided because of financial or special management situations.

STATEMENT ANALYSIS AND CREDIT EVALUATION

A National Credit Office bulletin states: "Intelligent statement analysis demands not only resourcefulness, but a definite intimacy with the conditions in every line sold, as well as a broad understanding of business fundamentals in general."

To do an intelligent job of credit evaluation based on facts and figures found in financial statements, the credit man should know how to compute the following:
   - Breakeven Inventories
   - Breakeven Sales
   - Changes in Inventory Investment

Breakeven Inventories

A short-term creditor has a primary interest in the customer's working capital. Therefore, when interim trial balance information is obtained, it is important to calculate the amount of inventory required to *maintain* the working capital shown on the last issued financial statement. Here is how to determine the probable amount of inventory on hand—working only from a current trial balance and relating it to the last complete financial statement:

1. Add the amount of working capital from last statement to the current liabilities, established from figures on the current trial balance.

2. Subtract the current "quick assets" (cash and receivables) from this figure; the result is the amount of inventory required to maintain the working capital. For example, here is how the procedures work:

Customer X's Trial Balance as of March 31, 1969

Cash	$10,000	Accounts Payable	$45,000
Accounts Receivable	30,000	Due Bank	30,000
		Other Current Liabilities	10,000
	$40,000		
		Total Current Liabilities	$85,000

Now, let's assume that the amount of working capital calculated from the figures on the Financial Statement as of December 31, 1968 was $50,000. To figure the breakeven inventory amount as of March 31, 1969:

1. Add $50,000 to $85,000: Result is $135,000.
2. Subtract current quick assets of   40,000 (−)

        Breakeven inventory is $ 95,000

This amount of inventory added to the quick assets of $40,000, less the total current liabilities produces working capital of $50,000 which is equal to that of December 31, 1968.

Breakeven Sales

To calculate the volume of sales required for a firm to break even, the credit man must ascertain the gross profit percentage by reviewing prior years' Profit and Loss Statements. The monthly overhead expense total is then taken from the trial balance expense accounts to determine the *minimum* amount of sales required to cover the total overhead expense.

Suppose the expense accounts show that the average monthly overhead is $20,000. If the gross profit percentage on sales is only 25%, then it is obvious that the minimum amount of monthly sales must be $80,000—merely to cover the overhead expense of $20,000.

Changes in Inventory Investment

Many firms lose their liquidity through accumulation of excessive inventories. Normally, the investment in inventory should vary directly with the sales volume. An increase in inventory levels that goes substantially beyond that required to support an increase in sales raises the possibility that further investigation is required. Is such an increase the result of unsalable merchandise piling up; is it from deliberate overstocking of raw materials to avoid expected price increases—or is it from substantially increased costs reflected in inventory values?

One way to detect changes in inventory investment is by development of a simple ratio. Compare the year-end inventory on hand with the cost of goods sold; the resulting ratio provides an indicator for each year. Comparison of these indicator ratios for several years provides trend indications. Note the following example:

Year	Year-End Inventory	Sales	Cost of Sales	Ratio Indicator
1965	$200,000	$ 700,000	560,000	35.7%
1966	290,000	1,000,000	730,000	40.0
1967	340,000	1,000,000	740,000	46.0

Another method of finding the relationship between inventories on hand and inventories sold during the year is based on inventory turnover. For example, in the year 1967, goods valued at $740,000 were sold. The year-end inventory value of $340,000 was turned 2.38 times during the year. By contrast, the 1966 inventory on hand compared to the cost of sales represents a ratio of 730,000/290,000: Result is a turnover figure of 2.5 times.

It is important to note that the credit man who analyzes a customer's inventory position is not working with exact book amounts. He is more apt to use a rough average figure, obtained simply by adding the opening and closing inventories for the year, and dividing by 2.

Inventories Should Be Classified

A breakdown of inventories on hand between raw materials, work-in-process and finished goods provides even more meaningful comparisons. An inventory buildup in finished goods is much more significant than a comparable buildup in raw materials. The customer's financial statement should provide the breakdown required.

WARNING SIGNALS AND SPECIAL CONTROL TECHNIQUES

It has been often said that "experience is the best teacher." The points which follow have been drawn from long experience in the credit profession and may be of value to other credit men in their daily work:

Warning Signals

1. Any customer who does not issue a financial statement within a 3-month period after the date that a financial statement is normally compiled should be reappraised for credit at once.

(It is far better to curtail credit when a satisfactory response for a current financial report is NOT received, than to hope that the figures—when issued—will be OK.)

2. When there is a change of accountants—the new accountant must issue figures within 3 months from the date of the change. ANY DELAY IN GETTING THE FINANCIAL INFORMATION WITHIN THAT TIME SPAN WILL CAUSE WITHDRAWAL OF CREDIT.

3. Post-mortem situations have often revealed the significance of *unanswered questions* on a financial statement form submitted to the customer for completion and return. In one case the accountant who filled out the form was quite selective in answering certain questions; whereas, he failed to answer other questions. THIS WAS A CLUE to the bad state of affairs—which was not recognized in time to prevent a credit loss.

One firm which received a requested financial statement by messenger failed to realize that this method of delivery could be a way to avoid the penalties attached to *mailing* a falsified financial statement. When the firm later went into bankruptcy, and the principals were charged with preparing false financial statements to creditors, the reason behind the personal delivery of the documents became quite clear.

Any person who opens envelopes containing financial statements should write the date of receipt and sign his name on the documents. This is essential procedure in order to comply with Federal law against using the mails to defraud; the creditor firm subsequently may file charges in court because it has extended credit on the basis of falsified financial statements.

Characteristics of a Potential Loss Account

1. Hypothecation of accounts receivable with slow trade payments.
2. Change of accountants in mid-year with the new accountant not issuing figures until about six months later.
3. Relationship of current liabilities to working capital was almost 5:1.
4. Working capital turnover was almost 17 times, on a gross profit of less than 10%.
5. High credit was almost $10,000 in excess of working capital.
6. Personal guarantees not supported by Personal Financial Statements.
7. Credit man made no personal visits to see what was going on.

Special Control Techniques

When an account is in the questionable-risk category—and it is desired to release goods, but the requested financial statement has not been received—the credit man may resort to the expediency of *reducing terms from long-term to short-term*. As Morton Reitman explains it: "The right to accelerate collections when promises are not kept enables us to pull out of a financial embarrassment before a meeting of all creditors is called."

Another advantage of this technique is that the account status is repeatedly called to the attention of the credit man through the medium of past due statements.

If a guarantee is essential for approving credit of a corporation, *Personal* Financial Statements should be obtained. And, these statements should be signed by the wife in all cases—even if she does not appear as an officer for reasons which are quite apparent.

When a customer requests extra time, with interest, for payment of an open invoice, an excellent opportunity is provided to obtain a personal guarantee in return for the granting of extra time.

Refunds to customers for open credits on the books should not be made without approval of the credit manager, especially if the amount is large.

When promissory notes or trade acceptances are received from customers in lieu of cash payments, the credit manager should be notified.

The credit manager should be informed of checks returned from the bank because of insufficient funds.

Orders held for payment of past due items should be disposed of within 30 days. If arrangements for payment cannot be made within that time period, the order should be canceled.

Uncollectible Accounts

- The credit manager should maintain a control over accounts turned over to the legal department or to an outside collection agency.
- Notices of meetings of creditors should be sent to the legal department.

Accounts Which Represent Special Problems

Special problem accounts should be reviewed carefully by the credit manager at least every six months whenever:
- The credit extended at any time is equal to or greater than the *working capital*.
- Any account is, in the opinion of the credit man, marginal.
- All credit exposures exceed a stated amount—regardless of credit standing. (This is to control accounts with large balances.)

NO CREDIT WILL BE GRANTED WHERE THERE IS AN ABSENCE OF WORKING CAPITAL.

Rules for Credit Exposure

- When the amount of credit exposure is high in relation to working capital, the credit files should include at least one *annual certified* balance sheet.
- When a financial statement is received, the accountant should be asked to prepare a verification form to indicate the depth and scope of the audit in connection with the

statement. An inventory verification form may also be used when the inventory investment is sizeable in relation to working capital.

SPECIAL RULES AND IMPORTANT CONSIDERATIONS

Listed below are some special rules and important points based on broad experience in credit management and administration. These rules have been proven sound and instrumental in controlling credit losses.

1. *Control over Credit Exposure:* The credit man should be required to report any credit exposure which exceeds a guideline based on a pre-determined amount or a percentage. For example, when the total credit extended to *any one customer* exceeds 10% of the *seller's* net worth, house policy may require that this be reported to the general credit manager, who, in turn, may refer it to an Advisory Executive Committee.

Other examples of internal control over credit exposure are:

- A junior credit man can extend credit up to 25% of the customer's working capital without referral.
- A senior credit man can extend from 75% to 100% of the customer's working capital with no referral.

2. *Credit Decisions:* Credit decisions should not be predicated upon conversations with management of the customer firm; they should be backed up by specific financial information.

3. *Use of Monthly Trial Balances:* If the customer is classified either as a marginal account or as an active account, the customer's accountant should forward monthly trial balances to the credit department.

- Credit evaluation should include an appraisal of the customer, preferably at his place of business. The credit man will obtain valuable information and impressions—and create goodwill for his firm at the same time.
- Any account which has been rejected for credit reasons should be reviewed every three months. Information may be found that justifies reopening a line of credit for the account.

4. *Accounts with large open balances:* The credit files should contain sufficient, specific information to justify the total credit risk involved in the account.

5. *Control Over Extra Dating:* Sales that are made with 30 and 60 extra days offered as terms, with or without interest, should be approved by the general credit manager.

HOW TO APPRAISE RESULTS OF A CREDIT DEPARTMENT

There are three measurements for evaluating the performance of a credit department in obtaining maximum sales, minimum bad debt losses, and in keeping the receivables investment at a minimum.

1. *Extension of Credit:* Summarize the dollar value of credit decisions made within a stated period of time. Gauge the volume of sales approved—and the volume of sales orders *rejected*.

2. *Determine dollar volume of sales by credit risk categories:* If you find that the majority of sales approved for credit were to blue chip, triple-A accounts, there was practically no credit risk, but the orders turned down may represent a substantial loss in gross profits.

If you find that a large volume of approved orders were from marginal accounts, but that bad debts were relatively small, then you may conclude that the credit department is functioning well.

3. *Determine final outcome of credit extension:* List charge-offs because they were adjudged

Exhibit IIC

THE EFFECT OF A SMOOTH-FUNCTIONING CREDIT DEPARTMENT IS SELF EVIDENT

If our company decided tomorrow to transact all of its sales on a cash basis it would be safe to conclude that our sales volume would be cut down by at least two-thirds. When viewing this reduction in terms of loss of salesmen's commissions alone, it can readily be seen how credit is instrumental in putting more income into the pockets of our salesmen. The intelligent administration of credit, which is a tremendous force in view of the sizeable capital employed by our company, results in more merchandise sold, greater profits earned and benefits of a successful business accruing to all of our employees. Equally as important is the advantage gained by our customers in their being able to use our liberal credit to achieve higher profits.

to be bad debts. Analyze large amounts that were charged off to see if they could have been prevented by better credit analysis, or by more prompt collection efforts.

Collection Performance

Collection performance may be rated by two primary yardsticks:

1. Analyze the total volume of unpaid and past due invoices. The basic report for this purpose is the familiar Aged Trial Balance. For this purpose this report should show each open item, with the amount spread across the page in columns according to the age. These columns typically exhibit the age of each item as to current and future due, followed by the past due categories of 1-30 days; 31-60; 61-90; 91-120 and over 120 days.

Items in the "current" column are those not yet due for payment, according to the invoice terms. Items in the "future due" column are those with extended terms which cause them to come due in a future period of time.

2. Determine the number of days' sales represented by the total outstanding receivables. The relationship of receivables to sales volume is widely used to appraise the efficiency of collection functions. For example, if the usual sales terms are net 30 days, and the receivables total represents 50 days' sales,* then this indicates that the collection operation can be improved.

To figure the number of days' sales, *divide the total outstanding in receivables by the average dollar volume of credit sales.*

Example: Total receivables in a firm are $100,000 and the daily volume of credit sales is $2,000. Obviously, the total uncollected open items represent 50 days' credit sales. As indicated above, you then compare the number of days outstanding with the number of days offered by average invoice terms. (If the firm offers a wide variety of invoice terms, this comparison becomes difficult.)

3. Collection ratio: The ratio of the total amount collected during the month to the total amount outstanding at the first of the month is also used for appraising collection performance. However, the existence of collections on short-term sales tends to dilute the effectiveness of this yardstick.

THE COLLECTION FUNCTION

A sale is not completed until the cash is received in full payment. For this reason the credit manager is usually responsible for the operation of the collection department.

Three things are necessary to obtain and maintain a satisfactory rate of accounts receivable turnover:

1. Systematic and consistent collection follow-up—beginning within five days to two weeks after the invoice is due, according to invoice terms.

2. An efficient method for aging the accounts to detect those which need special attention.

3. A flexible collection system to handle customers with special collection problems.

A truly successful collection operation accomplishes the following objectives:
- Enforces terms of sale.
- Prevents overbuying by customers.
- Provides for specialized or legal collection action on accounts which become seriously delinquent.
- Suspends very slow accounts promptly to limit loss.
- Turns receivables into cash without losing customer goodwill.

Collection Working Tools

The most commonly used collection tools are statements and collection letters. There are several different types of statements; each has, or should have, a specific objective:
- *Full-Account Statements:* These statements show every open item on the customer's ledger or account record. Firms doing business with small retail stores provide such statements, because both the store owners and their accountants request them for their own internal accounting purposes.

---

* If customers are habitually given special "future dating"—the date when the terms become applicable—the results here will be misleading.

- *Past Due Statements:* These statements show primarily those invoices which are, according to invoice terms, *past due*. Received-on-account cash also may appear on such a statement. Invoices not yet due, and open credits are frequently omitted from this type of statement.

The past due statement is considered to be the first notice of a delinquent situation to a customer. If this gets no action within a period of time (two weeks is a popular time period), then a collection letter may be written and mailed to the customer. The first collection letter may, in turn, be followed by letters No. 2 and No. 3—which are usually worded in such a way that the tone of the letter becomes more firm about requesting immediate payment of the past due item or items.

If the customer ignores the past due statement, and all subsequent collection letters, then the collector may resort to the use of telegrams or night letters. (Some collectors use the telephone to supplement or follow up on one or more collection letters.)

What Should Be Shown on a Past Due Statement?

Systems analysts are quite often faced with these decisions:
- What transactions, other than past due invoices, should be shown on a past due statement?
- How about received-on-account cash? Overpayment credits?
- Should open merchandise credits be shown?
- Should invoices *not yet due* be shown?

Answers to these questions enter the realm of personal opinion to some extent—and the type of business has a bearing on the situation. However, a sampling of prevailing practice as found when designing past due statements for computerized receivables indicates the following consensus of opinion:
- Received-on-account cash should be shown as an offset to past due invoices.
- Merchandise credits should not be shown. The reason is that most of these credits cannot be identified as to the source invoice. And, the customer has the privilege of applying and using these credits any time he wants to do so; he can apply them against an invoice of any age.
- Current invoices should *not* be shown on a past due statement. This dilutes the message of the statement, and defeats the purpose of reminding the debtor of past due items.

The Exception Technique Applied to Collections

Statistical studies have consistently revealed that a small number of invoices for large amounts represent the majority of receivables dollars outstanding at any given moment of time—in almost any firm. For example, a recent survey of a large factoring firm which buys receivables from 200 manufacturers showed that invoices in amounts exceeding $1,000 represented only 16% of the total number of invoices received. Yet, these invoices represented *68% of the total dollars* posted to the various customer accounts.

Once these facts are accepted, it then follows that special collection procedures which have been set up to follow and control these large invoices, offer control over a very high percentage of the total receivables—with a minimum of paper work and clerical cost.

Suggested Procedures

After all invoices have been routinely posted to customer ledger records, file all invoices above a stated amount, such as $1,000, alphabetically in a special collection file—BY DUE

DATE. From time to time, a collection clerk pulls the invoice copies which have matured for payment and compares each copy with the ledger record to see whether the large item has been paid when due. If this comparison reveals non-payment, the invoice copy is used as the basis for initiating the usual collection follow-up work, such as writing collection letters or making telephone calls.

Automatic Writing of Collection Letters

Collection letters are usually form letters which follow a consistent pattern. The first letter requests payment, but it is worded carefully so that it doesn't offend the customer in the event he has already paid the past due invoice or invoices.

The second letter—which usually is not prepared until a time period of two weeks or more has elapsed since mailing the first letter—is a stronger demand for payment. The third letter, if used, may contain a rather blunt demand for payment at once, etc.

Writing collection letters has been, traditionally, a routine task which is done after collection personnel has laboriously reviewed every open item on the customer's account record to determine those which are past due. The credit man or his assistant dictates the details to secretaries, who type the various form letters.

This type of routine, memo clerical work meets the test of work which can easily be computerized, because:

- The computer can easily identify each past due item by applying terms to the invoice date, or to the "as of" date.
- The review of accounts is usually on a cyclic basis; it can mark each item according to the number of times it has been reported as past due and identify which form letter should be written.
- The computer can print the form letters at very high speed.

An increasing number of companies that have placed accounts receivable on a computer has also mechanized the writing of collection letters by means of the techniques described above.

Aging of Receivables

An aged list of accounts is a basic working tool of collection and credit management. As stated before in this chapter, accounts become much more difficult to collect as they grow older. As an example, some experts contend that unpaid items which are one year past due have a realizable book value of only 45% of the original amount! Therefore, aging all items on accounts periodically is one of the basic methods used to analyze the status of receivables, and to evaluate the performance of the collection department.

The periodic aging is usually done monthly, when the Aged Trial Balance report is prepared, either in summary format or in detail. The Aged Trial Balance report is simple to prepare; but, it takes considerable time to do so under manual methods—if each open item is shown, which is typically the way it is prepared under data processing methods.

As mentioned, the Aged Trial Balance report may be prepared in detail, or in a summary form. The application of a computer to receivables makes it very easy to print each and every open item on the customer's account, and to show the aging status of each item. This printed report is prepared at high speed, and may serve several different useful functions, such as credit evaluation, data for credit interchange—and as an indication of the status of collection activities.

HOW TO SET UP A CREDIT DEPARTMENT

Concurrently with making physical arrangements for setting up and staffing a credit department, management of the firm, assisted by the accounting practitioner, should establish credit policies which will best accomplish the firm's objectives—and which will be consistent with the amount of capital available for financing trade credit receivables.

Basic Objectives

The *Credit Management Handbook,* published by the New York City Credit and Financial Management Association, states what the objectives should be for any firm:

"To formulate sound and constructive credit policies and practices and to administer all credit operations of the company in a manner that will:

1. Increase distribution and sales volume.
2. Contribute to the profits of the company.
3. Add to customer stability.
4. Provide for prompt turnover and adequate protection of the company's investment in accounts receivable."

These are sound, basic objectives; they deserve the investment of the necessary time and effort on the part of the practitioner and his client to implement them effectively.

Selection of Credit Policy

According to the authoritative *Credit Management Handbook* the choices available to management when selecting credit and collection policies are as follows:

- A liberal credit policy, coupled with a liberal collection policy.
- A liberal credit policy with collection strictly enforced.
- A strict credit policy—with a flexible collection policy.
- A strict credit policy, coupled with a strict collection policy.

Before selecting one of these combinations, the management team should carefully consider the following criteria:

- Nature and size of the business—now and in the foreseeable future.
- Total financial resources available to the company for operations.
- Gross profit on products sold; is there a substantial gross profit against which bad debt losses can be absorbed?
- Credit risk categories represented by customers representing the majority of dollar sales.
- Existing trade practices as to terms, credit and collection policies. (Is it necessary to match competitors point for point?)
- What are the possibilities for pledging or selling receivables to a commercial credit company or to a factor?
- Possible effect of changing business conditions after credit and collection policy has been selected and implemented.

Implications of Credit Policy Adopted

A liberal credit policy implies that the firm is willing to extend credit on a volume basis to marginal risk accounts. This policy obviously stimulates sales, but it also results in slow turnover of receivables, causes increased collection effort and expense, plus an inevitable amount of bad debt losses. However, if the gross profit on products sold on credit is substantial, such credit sales may well prove to be very profitable and desirable.

Management, when selecting a liberal credit policy, should recognize that bad debt losses are an inevitable element of this policy, and it should not criticize the credit manager for such losses. It is an interesting fact that some firms today set up a "loss budget" for each credit man who approves customer orders daily. This budget is not intended to be a restriction—it is an amount which the credit man is *encouraged to achieve!*

At first blush, this may seem to be very strange. However, it means that management has evaluated the potential amount of gross profit available from credit sales to marginal accounts. To obtain the desired gross volume, management sets up a loss budget for each credit man, and for the credit department in total. This gives the credit man the authority to approve large volumes of orders from accounts which might be disapproved, if management had selected a more restrictive policy.

Here is an example of why management adopted the modern credit concept of selling to marginal accounts, even though bad debt losses will be increased:

> A company that needs $1 million in sales each year to break even, works on a 30% gross profit and has a $300,000 overhead. The normal credit loss for the industry is ½ of 1% on average, and this cost is included in the selling price of the merchandise. If the firm finds that sales are $900,000, the resultant gross profit is only $270,000—which does not cover the $300,000 overhead. Net loss for the year would be $30,000. Additional business could only be had from marginal accounts where the bad debt loss would average roughly 5% of sales. Many managements refuse to accept marginal risks that would produce excessive and unwarranted bad debt losses.
>
> However, an enlightened management will remember that profits, not bad debt loss records, are the prime objectives of business. Let's consider what would happen by taking on $200,000 in sales from selected marginal accounts. The gross profit of 30% on this additional sales volume would be $60,000. After deducting bad debts of 5% which is $10,000, the result is an additional contribution toward overhead of $50,000. Add this amount to the $30,000 loss for the year incurred on the $90,000 volume from normal accounts—and the result is an over-all net profit of $20,000 for the year.*

Strict Credit Policy

A strict credit policy implies that sales to marginal accounts are not encouraged—or that they are rejected entirely. This policy speeds receivables turnover, lowers the *amount* of bad debt losses and reduces collection problems and expense.

However, as the previous example illustrates, this policy is not necessarily a more profitable policy than the liberal credit policy. Further, even though the amount of bad debt losses will be reduced, the *percentage* of bad debt losses to sales will be *increased*. When evaluating the two different credit policies, so much depends on the percentage of gross profits on sales—and on keeping bad debt losses on sales marginal accounts under effective control.

Why Policies Must Be Flexible

In today's fast-changing business environment management cannot hold one or two meetings, and establish policies for the credit department to adhere to without change for coming years. Management must be very responsive to changing conditions. For example, the following

---

* Example is taken from a talk by Mr. Herbert I. Mere, who is on the faculty of the New York Institute of Credit.

list reveals certain conditions that call for the consideration of liberal credit to help build profits:

- Inventory is unusually heavy.
- The company's cash position is low and heavy liabilities are to be met in two or three months, with sales income needed promptly.
- Profit margins are large.
- High plant overhead is present and there is the need to maintain a high volume of sales to break even.
- Because of contemplated style or design changes, there is a probability of heavy losses on inventory that may be carried over at the end of the selling season.

The following conditions represent situations in which *restrictive credit* should be considered for a period of time:

- An over-extended financial condition necessitates selling only to very large and financially-strong customers.
- Demand for the product is substantial, but the company can only fill orders over a long period of time because of limited plant facilities. Expansion may be impossible at the time or not advisable in the long run.
- The profit margin is very small and earnings depend upon rapid turnover.
- When a product is made to a single customer's specifications and cannot be sold to any other users.

Implications of Corollary Collection Policy Adopted

A *liberal* collection policy—regardless of whether the credit policy is strict or liberal—has serious implications for any firm. If invoice terms are not enforced by the collection department, if collections are not followed promptly, the firm may be heading into difficulties. Increasing amounts of funds will be tied up in receivables, concomitant with mounting bad debt losses. It is a well established fact that the face value of a past due amount as an asset decreases in relation to its age. That is, the longer an invoice is past due, the less apt it is to be collected at full value.

When terms are not consistently enforced, customers will deduct cash discounts, regardless of lateness of payment. If this is permitted, then no incentive remains for prompt payment according to invoice terms; collections become progressively slower, with a buildup in capital tied up in receivables.

Invoice terms are the basis for administering a credit and collection department. Business firms today offer a bewildering variety of invoice terms and conditions, including "future dating." All too often these terms are offered to customers without adequate realization of the financial implications behind them, and without considering the overall consequences—such as possible difficulties in enforcing terms or the probable amount of capital required for a stated sales volume.

Since a thorough understanding of terms of sale is essential in today's business environment, this book includes a full chapter on the subject. (See Chapter 12, "Analysis and Evaluation of Invoice Terms.")

Strict Collection Policy

A *strict* collection policy implies that it is the opposite of a liberal policy. This means that the collection department attempts to enforce invoice terms as they appear on the invoices, and that it stays right on top of delinquent accounts until they are paid.

MEASURING CREDIT EXPENSES FOR BUDGET ANALYSIS

Guidelines for measuring expenses in a credit department have not been generally available for comparison purposes. To obtain such data on a broad scale, the Credit Research Foundation mailed 300 questionnaires regarding 1961 operations to manufacturing firms. Some 150 replied; the final report represented 108 firms in 29 different industry classifications. The report did not include personal consumer credit; the study was restricted to firms engaging in commercial trade credit.

Significant data revealed by the tabulated survey includes:

	Lowest	Median	Highest
Yearly Sales Volume (Millions)	$2.5	$109.4	$2,215.3
Number of Customer Accounts	267	7,500	160,000
Active Accounts per Credit Employee	57	604	10,000
Number of Invoices per Year	1,200	160,500	5,000,000
Total Credit Department Personnel	2	12	150
Total Volume per Credit Employee	.01%	.10%	.85%
Annual Credit Department EXPENSE per Active Account	$0.89	$13.75	$113.38

Since averages can be misleading when the statistical samples cover such a wide range in sales volume and the number of accounts and invoices, the following table of personnel may be helpful. This table correlates the total personnel in the credit department with the number of active customer accounts.

No. of Customer Accounts	From: To:	1 1,000	1,000 2,499	2,500 9,999	10,000 24,999
No. of Credit Men and Credit Managers		1	2	6–9	16–30

Guides for Operating Budget

The expense data developed from the survey is shown below; these percentage figures may be used for budget preparation, after the total budget for the credit department has been established.

Type of Expense	Percent of Total Expense
Salaries and payroll taxes	69.9%
Credit reporting services	8.3
Other subscriptions	.2
Memberships	.3
Supplies, forms, printing	1.0
Office services (rent, heat, light, power, maintenance, etc.)	4.7
Communications	2.8
Travel, living, entertainment	2.7
Conferences and meetings	.4
Employee relocation and transfers	.6
Educational assistance	.1
Collection agency or attorney fees	2.9
Miscellaneous	.3
Other	5.8
Total	100.0%

Equipment and Facilities for a Credit Department

A credit and collection department does not require much special equipment. For firms that post receivables on accounting machines, ledger trays and properly-designed receivable ledger sheets are fundamental tools of the credit man, and these are also used by the collectors.

The typewriter and the telephone, of course, are essential devices in carrying out the functions of the credit and collection departments. A photographic copying machine is convenient for providing copies of invoices when customers request this type of verification of unpaid and past due invoices.

A desk model adding or posting machine may be the answer for quick preparation of past due statements, showing open items that are past due. A number of filing cabinets for housing credit folders rounds out the equipment generally needed for this department.

WHY SALESMEN SHOULD BE TRAINED IN CREDIT AND COLLECTION PHILOSOPHIES

The credit manager, by definition, is a member of his firm's planning team. One of his essential duties is to guide the credit and financial policies and practices toward greater sales volume in the face of competition and declining profit margins.

As stated very clearly in the manual published by the New York City Credit and Financial Management Association titled, *What Your Salesmen Should Know about Credit and Collections*—"the most potent weapon any company can have in the field is a profit-minded sales force. The quality of the field forces—the salesmen—which any company sends into the arena of competition will determine, in the final analysis, the success or failure of that company's drive for increased sales and greater profits."

Probably one of the most overlooked areas for re-enforcing the efforts of the sales force is training the salesmen—especially the younger, less-experienced men—in the fundamentals of their firm's credit and collection policies and procedures. In such training sessions, the credit manager exhibits and explains the special credit-sales letters which help build business volume; he offers to make field trips to assist customers with problems—and begins an educational program to explain the meaning of invoice terms to the sales force.

Every effort should be made to convince the salesmen that close cooperation between sales and credit means more profitable sales. The salesmen should understand that, through cooperation, they are literally insuring their sales and commissions.

It is not anticipated that such training sessions will convert salesmen into expert credit analysts. That is not the purpose of these sessions. The objective is to teach the salesmen enough to assist them in properly opening new sales sources—which will enable the credit department to provide faster service on new customer orders and to increase the volume of truly profitable sales.

Key Points to Cover

A number of key points should be covered in training sessions to enable the salesmen to develop a better understanding between sales and credit personnel:

- Salesmen must realize that it is not enough to merely bring in an order for merchandise. A profit is *not earned* until the goods are shipped—and the invoice amount is converted into cash.

- The salaries and other costs of the credit department are not paid from profits on orders refused, but from good business solicited, sold, shipped and paid for. Therefore, it is never in the best interest of the credit department to arbitrarily turn down orders.
- Salesmen should understand that a *credit* loss represents a greater loss than the loss of the profit on the sale. Such losses entail the actual direct cost of the goods, plus handling and shipping and accounting costs.
- A sizeable credit loss may wipe out the profit earned on the sale of a carload-lot of goods.
- Extending credit to customers is equivalent to lending money to them. Since most firms do not have an unlimited supply of capital, good customers must be serviced first; extending credit (lending money) to risky, marginal accounts must be checked and controlled very carefully.

12

Analysis and Evaluation of Invoice Terms

Invoice terms are supposedly the result of a firm's trade credit policies, adopted only after long and careful consideration of many factors, such as the financial cost of discount terms, the terms offered by competitors and the financial resources available for financing trade credit sales.

In actual practice invoice terms frequently represent very little logic or common sense. They just seem "to grow." One wonders where certain invoice terms originated, who originated them and why. The purpose of this chapter is to examine the various types of terms, analyze the financial implications of each type and develop a perspective in regard to the true functions of invoice terms.

Terms as a Sales Tool

Credit terms are generally considered to be a sales tool. When a salesman feels that it is necessary to offer a special concession to a customer to obtain an order, he may offer long terms for payment, such as "net 90" or even "net 130" days. Or, if the usual terms are net 30, he may write up the order as "subject to invoice terms of n30 *plus 60 extra.*"

A later section of this chapter challenges the validity of terms—under certain conditions— as a major competitive weapon. But first, let's analyze the various invoice terms and see what they actually mean.

Credit Terms Offer Time

Basically, invoice terms extend to the customer a certain amount of time, expressed in calendar days, before payment of the invoice is due. By contrast, a cash-on-delivery (COD) sale or a cash sale implies that the merchandise sold is exchanged for cash almost at once. This is, of course, what takes place in a retail store when a customer walks in, selects certain merchandise and pays for it before he leaves the store with the merchandise.

In addition, certain types of terms offer the customer a financial inducement to pay the invoice amount before the final due date.

Invoice Terms Create Due Dates

One fundamental aspect of terms becomes very clear when receivables are put on a computer. That is, each type of terms creates *one or more due dates* for each invoice to which terms are applied.

List of Examples

	Invoice Date	Invoice Terms	Discount Due Date	Final Due Date
A.	6/01	net 10	—	6/11
B.	6/10	net 30	—	7/10
C.	6/10	1/10 net 30	6/20	7/10
D.	6/05	5/10 4/70 net 71	6/15	8/15

Reviewing these examples, we see that single-option terms, such as net 10, create only a final due date. Contrast this to example "C" or "D" where the terms create a discount due date, as well as a final due date.

Optional Terms

Optional terms are those which provide two or more time periods. Terms of 1/10 net 30 offer the customer two options: If he elects to pay the invoice within 10 days from invoice date, he can deduct 1% discount for early payment. He can, however, ignore the first option and pay on the basis of "net 30 days."

The word "net" is quite often confusing. This option actually means that the customer is supposed to pay the gross amount of the invoice if he elects to pay on the basis of the second option.

Example "D" above illustrates a 3-option set of terms:

Option No. 1. 5% discount if paid in 10 days from invoice date
Option No. 2. 4% discount if paid in 70 days
Option No. 3. Net if paid in 71 days or longer

Two Basic Types of Terms

Business practice in extending trade credit over many scores of years has developed two basic types of invoice terms:

- Cash discount terms
- Trade discount terms

A very significant and fundamental difference between these two types of terms is explained on subsequent pages.

Certain sets of terms are interpreted differently in different industries. Even within the same industry, there exists a conflict of opinions in regard to the true meaning of certain terms. One of the difficulties in preparing a "terms table" for the benefit of a client is that experienced personnel in various departments of the same firm will sometimes disagree vehemently about the meaning and enforcement of one or more sets of terms.

The interpretations which appear in this chapter are primarily those found in the factoring industry. The reason for using these guidelines is that a typical factor buys receivables from hundreds of different manufacturers, who represent many different segments of American business. Since the factor buys all of the invoices that are subject to the terms as extended by the manufacturer to his customers, the factor is exposed to terms of all types on a broad scale.

Moreover, a factor operates on a tiny profit margin. He must carefully administer and control the terms offered by the clients to customers, since these customers remit directly to the factor. Therefore, the interpretations applied by factors are based on long experience and on a very fundamental basis of financial costs.

For example, when a manufacturer ships goods to a customer on terms of *1/10,* net 60, the factor, as part of his accounting with his client, does the following:

1. Deducts the 1% discount offered to the customer by the terms, since this is a possible discount deduction.

2. Charges the client for 10 days' interest on the invoice amount, since the customer's discount due date is 10 days from invoice date, and therefore, the factor cannot expect to receive payment for 10 days or longer.

Notice that the factor uses the short-term option as the basis for buying the invoice from the client. If the customer, however, elects to pay on the basis of the last option of "net 60 days," this is acceptable to the factor since the customer gives up 1% discount in return for an additional 50 days' time.

Cash Discount Terms

A cash discount set of terms is characterized by the inclusion of the word "Net" or the symbol "N" appearing as the last option where the first option or middle option offers a discount for early payment. For example, terms of 2/10 N30 offer the customer a 2% cash discount on the invoice amount if he pays within 10 days from the invoice date. The "N30" option indicates the following:

- The customer loses the 2% cash discount if he waits longer than 10 days plus a grace period—which is usually 5 days or more—to pay the invoice.
- The customer is supposed to remit the gross amount within 30 days plus the grace period—or the payment will be considered late, which affects his credit rating with the firm. Also, more and more firms are now assessing late interest charges against customers who pay invoices late.

In summary, the cash discount option means that the seller is willing to stand this financial cost in return for prompt payment within a short period of time.

Trade Discount Terms

Trade discount terms never include the word "net" or the symbol "N." They appear as follows:

1/10
1/10 EOM
1/60
2/70, 1/130

The usual interpretation of trade discount terms is that the discount deduction is *not* lost because of the passing of time. In other words, the discount is considered to be a reduction of the selling price, and is not based on the promptness of payment.

The use of trade discount terms came into being as a convenient method to adjust selling prices in order to meet changing price conditions and competitive pressures, without necessitating the expense of reprinting price lists and catalogues.

Notice the last set of terms in the list of trade discounts. The customer is offered a 2% trade discount if he pays the invoice within 70 days from invoice date, but only 1% if he pays after that time. Now, what happens if the customer waits a long time after the final due date before he pays the invoice?—According to the usual interpretation the customer *can deduct the 1% regardless* of the length of time which passes before payment, after expiration of the first option period.

In summary, because of the basic concept that a trade discount is a reduction of the selling price, the customer is basically entitled to deduct a stated discount amount, regardless of the time element—but may be asked to pay late interest if he pays after the final due date.

Trading Days for Dollars

Properly constructed optional terms trade days for dollars. Examine the terms "1/10 N 70" and note that the second option offers 60 days' more time in return for not taking the 1% discount. The foundation of most terms currently in use is the equation: *60 days equals 1%. (This is based on a "banker's year" of 360 days at an annual interest rate of 6%.)*

Manufacturers in the textile trades recognize this trade-off in another way by permitting a customer to "anticipate" an invoice. Suppose the terms are 1/30 N 31. The customer has the privilege of paying before the discount due date and of deducting interest at 6%. See the following example.

Invoice Date	Terms	Discount Due Date	Final Due Date	Invoice Amount
4/05	1/30 N31	5/05	5/06	$1,000.00

Suppose the customer elects to pay the invoice above on 4/15, or 20 days before it is due, according to the discount due date. Where anticipation is allowed, the customer can not only deduct 1% of $1,000 for discount, but he can also deduct $3.33 anticipation, which is the interest value of $1,000 at 6% for 20 days.

Invalid or Questionable Terms

When reviewing a client's list of terms, you should be alert to the spotting of invalid terms. Any set of terms which allows more than 60 days for each 1% of discount given up should be examined, and possibly changed. For example, consider these terms: *1/10 N 90*. This allows 1% cash discount if paid in 10 days—but the second option entitles the customer to wait an additional 80 days if he forfeits the 1% discount.

Effect of Terms Changes

These terms should be changed to *1/10 N 70*—which allow the standard 60-day differential between the two options.

Does such a change involve important financial considerations? Let's find out by examining the situation in a small firm which sells $3 million per year on the basis of 1/10 N 90. Let's assume that 60% of all customers pay on the basis of the second, long-term option, simply because these customers are chronically short of ready cash for discounting their bills.

Now, if all of these customers pay on or about the net 90 due date, the receivables capital will be outstanding for an average of about 95 days, including the usual grace period. If we divide 95 into 360 days, we establish a turnover rate of 3.9 annually. Since 60% of all credit sales amounts to $1,800,000—this is the average amount tied up in receivables because of the 95 day turnover, which is the maximum number of days allowed on the assumption that no invoices go delinquent.

By changing the terms to 1/10 N 70, we have shortened the turnover period by 20 days. The value of using $1,800,000 for an extra 20 days at 6% is $6,000. This provides some indication of the value of a review of invoice terms in any firm doing a substantial volume of credit business.

Financial Costs of Invoice Terms

All businessmen concerned with invoice terms should fully realize that a credit sale is the equivalent of lending money to the customer—and that there is a direct interest cost connected with each "loan." Further, the standard interest rate historically used in developing the various terms options is 6%. Under tight money conditions this figure is too low to be realistic, yet very few firms change their terms to reflect the higher interest costs.

All credit terms represent a definite financial cost even if no discounts are offered to customers. Consider these facts about "net" terms:

Invoice Terms	Financial Costs in Days	Cost Expressed as a % of Invoice Amount *
N10	10	1/6 of 1%
N30	30	1/2 of 1%
N60	60	1%
N60 plus 60 extra	120	2%
N90 plus 30 extra	120	2%

* Based on annual interest cost of 6%.

Future Dating

Many firms offer "future dating" to their customers for two reasons: First, it is used as a means of getting orders before the customer actually requires the merchandise. Secondly, it enables a manufacturer to make and ship goods in a slack period and at his convenience.

The customer will accept delivery on seasonal merchandise long before his customers start buying the goods, because the seller bills him with an "as of" date inserted into the terms section of the invoice. That is, an invoice for school supplies may be dated June 2, but "as of" September 1. If terms of 2/10 N30 apply, these terms are based on the *as of* date, so that the two due dates for this invoice are September 11 and October 1.

"As of" dating increases the financial costs of credit sales since the capital represented by the invoices will be tied up for the additional time, represented by the difference between the invoice date and the "as of" date. Further, the "as of" dating makes it difficult to estimate the average length of time, expressed in days, being offered through sales terms. Only with a properly-structured computer system is it easy to calculate the average due date for each sales period of all invoices, including the effect of the "as of" dating.

SPECIAL TYPES OF TERMS

"EOM" and "Proximo" terms are generally considered to be the same from the viewpoint of administering terms. 2/10 EOM or 2/10 Prox means that the customer is supposed to pay within 10 days from the end of the month in which the purchase is made, and can deduct 2% discount. However, these terms include certain unusual features.

Trade practice dictates that the customer is given an additional month to pay when the invoice date is the 25th of the current month, or later. Also, the discount due date and the final due dates are the same for these single-option terms. Note the effect of the invoice date on the due dates as calculated and displayed in the following table.

	Invoice Date	Terms	Effective Date	Discount Due Date	Final Due Date
A.	6/16	2/10 EOM	6/30	7/10	7/10
B.	6/26	2/10 EOM	7/31	8/10	8/10
C.	7/09	1/10 Prox	7/31	8/10	8/10
D.	7/27	1/10 Prox	8/31	9/10	9/10

Observe that the "effective date" for invoices dated the 25th or later is the end of the month *following* the current month, as in examples B and D. The 10-day terms are added to this effective date to produce the discount due date and the final due date as shown.

Two-Option EOM Terms

"1/10 EOM *N 30*" is a perfect illustration of a set of terms invented by someone who did not take the trouble to analyze the possible results stemming from application of these cash discount terms. For example, consider the unique results when the invoice date is earlier than the 10th of the month:

	Invoice Date	Terms	Effective Date	Discount Due Date	Final Due Date
A.	4/05	2/10 EOM N 30	4/30	5/10	5/05
B.	4/08	2/10 EOM N 30	4/30	5/10	5/08
C.	4/27	2/10 EOM N 30	5/31	6/10	5/27

In examples A and B, we see that the final due date is EARLIER than the discount due date; this is also the situation in example C. Whoever originated this two-option term obviously did not realize that any EOM or Prox term includes an implied *effective date,* which is the end of the current month for all invoices dated from the 1st thru the 24th. For dates of the 25th thru the 31st, the effective date is the end of the *following month.* Applying the 10 days and the 30 days found in the term to the effective date produces due dates as follows:

Invoice Date	Terms	Effective Date	Discount Due Date	Final Due Date
4/05	2/10 N 30	4/30	5/10	5/30
4/08	2/10 N 30	4/30	5/10	5/30
4/27	2/10 N 30	5/31	6/10	6/30

Apparently the N 30 option was intended to be based on the invoice date rather than on the effective date—with the incongruous results as found in the first table, where the final due date comes before the discount due date!

Terms with Extra Days

Quite often, manufacturers' representatives offer the usual terms, but with additional or extra days added to the base terms. One example: "1/10 N 30 60 Extra." Or the terms may read: "2/30 N 31 60X @ 1%." (In this set of terms, the customer is supposed to pay interest at 6% for the additional 60 days.)

Both of these terms offer extra days; however, the application of the days to the invoice date to calculate the due dates is radically different.

General Rule: The number of extra days is added to *both sides* of a two-option term to calculate the discount due date and the final due date. However, when the *extra days are at customer expense*—"60X @ 1%"—the extra days DO NOT AFFECT THE DISCOUNT DUE DATE. See following table.

	Invoice Date	*Terms*	*Discount Due Date*	*Final Due Date*
A.	9/12	1/10 N 30 60X	11/21	12/11
B.	6/05	2/30 N 31 60X @ 1%	7/05	9/04
C.	9/12	1/10 N 30 60X @ 1%	9/22	12/11

In example A, we see that the 60 extra days are added to *both* the discount days and the long-term days, which means that 70 days and 90 days are added to the invoice date to generate the discount due date and the final due date respectively.

Examples B and C show that extra days at customer expense do *not* affect the discount due date, but serve to extend the final due date.

When the cost of money is close to or greater than 6%, alert management will control the granting of extra days with or without the customer paying for the additional time. A rate of 6% is no longer sufficient to pay for the financial costs of carrying the account for the extra days or months.

ENFORCING INVOICE TERMS

One of the prime functions of a collection department is to enforce invoice terms when payments are received and processed. A fair, but firm policy for dealing with customers who habitually pay late and deduct cash discount amounts anyway is essential for several reasons.

In the first place, management should realize that enforcement or nonenforcement may involve rather large sums, and the Profit and Loss Statement reflects the financial cost of discounts allowed for any reason.

A CASE HISTORY

To be specific about financial costs, let's examine an actual case history of a small electronic manufacturing company in the Midwest. This firm enjoys an annual sales volume of $3 million from its wholesale distributors. Invoice terms are 2/10 N 30. A recent review of payment

Exhibit 12-A
ANALYSIS OF TYPICAL INVOICE TERMS

Invoice Terms	Discount %	Discount Days	Total Days	Extra Days Included in Tot. Days	Remittance Audit Rules Disc. Allowed if Paid in X Days	Discount Always Allowed?	Special Notations and Comments
Net Cash			10		None		
N10			10		None		
N 10/10			20		None		
N10-EOM			10*		None		* From end of month
N30			30		None		
N30 plus 30 extra			60	30	None		
N60			60		None		
N60 plus 60 extra @ 1%			120	60*	None		* At customer expense
N90			90		None		
1% Cash	1	10	10		10	YES	
1/10	1	10	10		10	YES	
1/10 EOM	1	10	10*		10*	YES	* From end of month
1/10 Prox	1	10	10*		10*	YES	* From end of month
1/10 EOM plus 30 extra	1	40	40*	30	40*	YES	* From end of month
1/10 N11	1	10	11		10	NO	Cash discount terms
1/10 N30	1	10	30		10	NO	Cash discount terms
1/60	1	60	60		60	YES	Trade terms
1/130 N131	1	130	131		130	NO	Cash discount terms
2/10	2	10	10		10	YES	Trade terms
2/10 EOM	2	10	10*		10*	YES	* From end of month
2/10 EOM plus 30	2	40	40*		40*	YES	* From end of month
2/10 EOM plus 30 at ½ of 1%	2	10	40*				
2/10 N30 plus 30 @ ½ of 1%	2	10	60	30*	10	NO	* Extra days at customer expense do NOT add to the discount due date
3/10 2/70 1/130 N131	3	10	131		3% 10 days—then drops 1% for each 60 days	NO	4-option set of terms
5/30 4/60 N61	5	30	61		30	No—See Footnote	

Footnote: Where terms provide a discount rate in excess of 3%, it is very difficult to enforce cash discount provisions. Such terms are more indicative of a reduction in the selling price of the goods.

practices has shown that the majority of payments are not received until 45 days from invoice date. And, the customers deduct the 2% cash discount anyway. Since terms are not being enforced, this practice is currently allowed. Assuming that 50% of the remitters are not entitled to the discount taken, then the amount charged against profits because of *non-enforcement is $30,000 per year.*

Another serious result stemming from non-enforcement is that the customer has no incentive to pay promptly. When customers realize that they can wait 45 days to pay, and still be permitted to deduct the 2% cash discount, they will soon begin to wait 60 days before making payment. From a collection viewpoint, therefore, the results of non-enforcement can be very damaging, since the intent of the first option in the terms is to produce a cash flow resulting from early payment of the invoices. When customers ignore the first option, and pay late, more and more capital will be tied up in receivables.

Another Reason for Enforcement

The Robinson-Patman Act is a federal law enforced by the Federal Trade Commission in Washington, D. C. The purpose of this law is to safeguard the smaller business entities against discriminatory practices favoring giant corporations. For example, a manufacturer cannot offer more favorable terms or selling prices to a billion-dollar firm than to a small firm, unless specific volume economies can be shown.

At various times the courts have ruled that varying invoice terms is one method of practicing discrimination. The practical effect of this ruling is that any firm which does not uniformly enforce its own invoice terms is favoring one customer over another, and this is a direct violation of the Robinson-Patman Act.

WHY ENFORCEMENT SHOULD NOT AFFECT CREDIT SALES

Enforcement of terms is sometimes handled gingerly by a collection department because management feels that customer relations will be damaged, and that sales will be lost by a firm collection policy. This situation illustrates one of the many "feasible fallacies" found in business at many levels. Let's examine the reasons why enforcement of invoice terms in the "ABC Company" should have no effect on credit sales.

First of all, orders are placed with the ABC Company by some key individual in the customer firm, such as the owner, the purchasing agent, the engineers or plant manager—depending upon the type of product sold by the ABC Company, and how the product is going to be used by the buyer. Regardless of the title or position of the person who makes the decision to buy the product, his order indicates that he is satisfied with most, or all of the elements involved in a satisfactory customer/vendor relationship, such as quality, product performance, service, reliability of the vendor, price, and other considerations.

The order is accepted by the ABC Company after a credit check, goods are shipped and the buyer receives an invoice. Invoices are processed for payment by the buying firm in the Accounts Payable Department. This department is staffed with people who take no part in buying decisions at any time. Their place in the business hierarchy is to process invoices and related paperwork, and eventually to pay invoices approved for payment.

One important point to realize is that people in an accounts payable section are accustomed to receiving past due statements, letters, telegrams or telephone calls about unpaid bills—especially if their firm is frequently short of cash—and they defer payment as long as possible, following instructions from the owner, the controller or some other official of the firm. Furthermore, remember that accounts payable clerks may have standing instructions to deduct discounts from all invoices which bear optional terms, regardless of the lateness of payment.

In firms where most invoices are deliberately held for late payment, systems analysts and consultants frequently find that the firm maintains a special list of the few vendors who vigorously enforce their invoice terms. Such invoices are paid first, and within the discount period. Once a collection manager gets the message to the buyer that he will tolerate no deviation from terms as stated on the invoices, the buyer will soon add the name of the firm to his priority list—without damaging any sales relationships.

How to Get on the List

To get the message to the right people in the buyer's company may require several well-placed telephone calls. Routine collection letters will seldom accomplish the desired result under the conditions just described. The collection manager should call the accounts payable manager personally and explain that his firm expects full compliance with terms of payment from all customers.

If this approach does not get results, the collection manager—or, in some instances, one of the principals in the selling firm—should get in direct touch with the controller, treasurer or a key member of management in the customer firm. This usually results in the customer firm placing the seller's name on the preferred payment list, with no harm done insofar as losing the account to a competitor.

A CASE HISTORY

My firm recently made a survey of the accounts payable department of a major railroad. The railroad had approximately 18,000 suppliers; extensive payables procedures were in use in connection with a computer to process the large monthly volume of vendor invoices. During the study, we found that special clerical and machine procedures had been developed and installed to process and pay the invoices of one major supplier. The reason for special handling was that this one firm would not tolerate the standard practice of the railroad of paying its bills from four to six weeks late.

TERMS AS A COMPETITIVE SALES WEAPON

The primary reason stated most often for not altering or eliminating certain invoice terms which represent an inordinate financial cost is, "We must meet competition."

Now, there are undoubtedly many situations in which it is necessary to meet competition's terms or lose business. However, this reason is probably invalid for many thousands of manufacturing firms that manufacture and market a unique and patented group of products, or for those firms that render special, technical services to customers.

It has been well established for many decades in the business world that the firm offering the lowest price does not necessarily get all of the orders. Likewise, the firm offering the best invoice terms does not necessarily obtain the majority of orders. There are numerous elements in a business transaction that influence the buyer's decision in regard to the product and the source. Some of these include:

- Product features
- Quality and dependability of the product

- Service and backup provided by the vendor
- Reliability and reputation of the vendor firm
- Price
- Terms

From the buyer's viewpoint, terms are often a minor consideration when he is required to make a decision as to the product he should buy, coupled with a decision as to the source (vendor).

Management should review invoice terms at least once each year; the review team should include the sales manager, financial vice-president or owner, and the credit manager. This periodic review offers a potential for substantial profit improvement by reducing unnecessary financial costs and improving cash flow.

13

Accounts Receivable Methods and Procedures

The growth of trade receivables volume since 1949 has been phenomenal. Expansion of manufacturers' sales volume has been accomplished by easy credit terms to a large extent. In April 1967, manufacturers' sales were moving at the annual rate of more than $450 billion. Outstanding receivables stood at more than $50 billion.

In past years, when an accountant or a businessman analyzed a financial statement, he was accustomed to finding that the inventory account represented the largest single investment of capital. Increasingly today, accounts receivable is the largest single asset on the balance sheet.

This prime asset is belatedly receiving increasing attention today from management at many levels and from public practitioners. Recent high interest rates, a shortage of available capital, plus the large investment in receivables—these are the elements which have caused financial managers to concentrate their attention on this asset.

An article in the April 1965 issue of the *Credit and Financial Newsletter,* published by the National Association of Credit Management of New York City, stated: "Recent years have brought an increasing awareness of the importance of receivables in the total profit picture. As a result, more and more top-level management attention has focused on credit policy." The trend continues to be more of the same.

Opportunity for the Practitioner

The need for adequate control over this asset, which involves a review of the client's credit and collection procedures along with receivables policies and procedures, presents an opportunity for the practitioner to render a valuable service to many of his clients in this key area of business administration. The primary objective of the material in this and the following chapter is to open the door to management services assignments involving receivables, credit and collection functions.

Requirements of an Efficient Accounts Receivable System

An accounts receivable system must serve several different groups of people and many related functions. Some of these functions are:

- Provide an accounting with each customer.
- Provide reference as to account status, open unpaid items and a history of prior payments and deductions taken.
- Serve the order approval function in the Credit Department.
- Provide credit interchange data.
- Furnish the information for collection activities, to convert over-due receivables to cash.
- Make it easy to follow up on Unadjusted Deductions or claims.

The Basic Types of Receivables Records

Over the years, three different types of receivables records have been widely used for customer accounting. Thus, the accounting for each customer has centered around:

1. Ledger sheets, either hand-posted or posted by accounting machine.
2. Unit invoice files; a copy of each invoice is filed in a pocket or folder as the accounting media for each open, unpaid invoice.
3. Unit punched cards filed in tubs by customer. These cards are interpreted (printed) across the top edge so that the bookkeeper can read the coded information punched in the card. These cards are also machine-readable for processing on tabulating equipment, the forerunner of data-processing computers.

Exhibit 13-A
TYPICAL PUNCHED INVOICE CARD

The Real Purpose of Receivables Records

Many systems analysts tend to concentrate on the accounting side of receivables operations and they forget that the real reason for maintaining any receivables system is to *collect the money.* In other words, the collection function and requirements should dictate the type of system and related procedures; the details of maintaining the records and applying cash should assist rather than handicap the collection function.

To continue on this theme—if each and every customer paid exactly on time, and took no deductions other than earned discount—and never made an error in the check amount—there would be no need for detailed receivable records. The bookkeeper would merely file copies of invoices by customer, and would find and remove each customer's copy from the file when paid. The requirements for some type of detailed receivable records exist because of customers who pay late, make partial payments, generate unadjusted deductions and claims, and use open credits—which partially offset open invoices, plus other problems of receivables administration and reference.

RECEIVABLE RECORDS AND POSTING PLANS

Before the widespread adoption of tabulating equipment and computers for processing business data, two basic types of receivables records were very popular in businesses of all types and volume categories:

- Customer ledger sheets
- Invoice copies used with the unit invoice plan

Receivables installations featuring individual customer ledger sheets still outnumber all other types of records combined. Development of accounting and posting machines in the late 1920's, continuing with renewed vigor in the late 1940's through today, no doubt contributed to the popularity of machine-posting charges, credits and cash payments to customer ledger sheets.

Use of an accounting or posting machine increases the speed and accuracy of posting; frequently, a customer statement is posted at the same time the ledger record is posted with no extra work. This saves time at month-end when the firm wants to send out statements of account to its customers—which are, of course, collection reminders.

Daily Posting to Customer Ledger Records

The most commonly-used plan features daily posting of invoices and payments to each active ledger sheet. All debit and credit amounts are first recapped to set up control totals— then the individual amounts are posted to each indicated customer's account. Most posting machines have accumulators which accumulate a grand total of debit or credit amounts posted—or separate totals—for proof purposes. When the posting machine operator has completed posting all invoices for the day, for example, she can compare the total actually posted with the pre-list control total. If the two totals agree, then the operator knows that each invoice has been posted in the right amount.

This explanation is an over-simplification of the problem of proving the posting of items to receivables records, since most posting machines calculate and print a "new balance" as part of the posting operation. The operator must list and add into the machine the *beginning "old balance"* before she posts the amount of the current invoice or credit. Since errors may enter the picture at this point, posting machine specialists have devised proof methods which are intended to prove the accuracy of the old-balance pickup, as well as to prove that the right detail amount was posted.

Essentially, this is accomplished by requiring that the operator read and list the beginning "old balance" a second time—after the posting machine has automatically printed the "new balance"—which is the sum of the first old balance and a debit amount, or which is the difference between the first old balance and a credit amount that is subtracted from it. Please refer to the following example of "Direct Proof."

1st Old Balance	Amount Posted Debit Credit	New Balance	2nd Old Balance	Direct Proof Amount
66.20	20.00	86.20 S	66.20—	20.00*
100.00	35.70	135.70 S	100.00—	35.70*
25.40	10.00	35.40 S	25.40—	10.00*
			Total Proof Amounts	65.70*

The posting machine subtotals the new balance, which retains the figure in the machine. When the operator reads the beginning balance and lists it on the keyboard for the second time, the machine subtracts the beginning balance from the new balance—and prints the remainder in the "Proof" column. If no error has entered the picture, the direct proof amount *will always be the amount of the detail debit or credit amount posted to the account.*

Several posting and proofing plans have been developed over the years; the overriding objective of each one is basically the same as that provided by the direct proof plan illustrated above.

Cycle Posting of Customer Ledger Records

Analysis of the steps involved in posting one charge item to a customer record reveals that it takes much longer to find, insert and align the customer records in the accounting machine carriage than it does to post the charge sale amount. In fact, the ratio of time required for the handling of forms to posting is about 4 to 1. This aspect of the receivables posting work in department stores—many of which have huge customer files and a large volume of daily sales transactions—led to the development of cycle posting of charge sales and cash credits, known as "cycle billing."

The phrase "cycle billing" refers to the division of the posting and statement-preparation task into segments, or "cycles." For example, a department store in Dallas, Texas had 60,000 active accounts at the time the store switched over to a cycle billing plan. Each account averaged five transactions per month. When cycle billing was installed, the accounts were divided alphabetically into 15 equal groups of accounts. Each cycle—consisting of roughly 4,000 accounts and 20,000 transactions—was billed progressively, one after the other, on scheduled days during the calendar month. All of the charge sales and credits for a customer were posted with *one handling of the forms.*

(For a complete explanation of cycle billing, refer to my book, *Accounting Systems for the Small and Medium-Sized Business.*)

Unit Invoice Plan

Under the unit invoice plan a copy of the invoice becomes the customer receivables record. When this invoice copy is placed in a folder in a specially-designed account pocket, the bookkeeper has, in effect, "posted" a debit to the customer's account in the receivables file. When this same bookkeeper processes cash, she *finds and removes* the invoice copy paid by the check. Simply by removing the paid item, the bookkeeper has "credited" accounts receivable for the gross invoice amount.

If the customer arbitrarily deducts an amount from the check for freight damage, freight allowance, or for any one of many reasons, the bookkeeper must manually prepare an Unadjusted Deduction Debit form, and drop it in the pocket where it remains until an offsetting credit memo is received to cover the deduction debit.

Accounting Control

The unit invoice receivables file must be controlled the same as any other receivables plan. The total of all invoices added to the file is added to the grand total of outstanding receivables. Remittances must be recapped to establish the grand total of invoices removed from the file, discounts allowed, deductions set up, and the total debit to cash.

A monthly trial balance requires adding the amounts of all open invoices in the file, plus unadjusted deductions or other debit items. From this, the bookkeeper subtracts credit memos, received-on-account slips and other credit items in the file pockets. The net total of all open items should equal the control account total.

Summary of Plan

The unit invoice plan is a reasonably simple plan which requires no accounting machines. If customers make few partial payments, and the number of deductions is relatively small, and invoice terms are for short time periods, this plan has merit.

On the other hand, there is no customer history for order approval procedures, nor for credit interchange requests. Procedures for the application of cash and audit of remittances must be set up very carefully and controlled by competent people—or trial balance troubles will be encountered frequently.

Punched Card Receivables

In recent years, the increasing use of tabulating equipment in offices for many types of applications has increased the number of receivables installations featuring a unit punched card for each open item. All basic information from an invoice is keypunched into a punched card. When this card is interpreted (the punched data is printed across the top of the punched card by a special machine) and placed in special card trays in a bookkeeper desk, we have another version of the unit invoice plan already described.

A very big difference between the two plans, though, is that these cards are *machine-readable*. To run past due statements or an aged trial balance, the trays of punched cards are carried to a tabulating machine and inserted into a card hopper. After the appropriate form is inserted into the print section of the tabulating machine, it begins to read the punched data in the cards and prints the aged trial balance, or print statements for each customer who has a past due item or items.

The most important benefits of punched-card receivables are the automatic aging and the collection follow-up capabilities.

Cash Application

To apply cash, the bookkeeper studies the check, finds the customer's interpreted punched cards—which are filed together with a name and address card—and removes the indicated paid items. The bookkeeper may be required to prove each remittance by adding the gross amounts of paid invoices—then figuring the allowable discount and proving to the check amount.

New cards must be keypunched for deductions and for major differences charged back to the account. After payment codes have been punched into the invoice cards, and remittance cards have been punched, the tabulating machine prints a Cash Received Journal which details each paid item, and records the cash amount and charge-backs.

Exhibit 13-B
INTERPRETED PUNCHED CARDS REPRESENTING INVOICES

TWO OPPOSING METHODS FOR HANDLING REMITTANCES

Procedures for recording and handling remittances are necessarily dictated by the type of receivables which make up the customer file. For example, charge sales to business firms usually represent an entirely different type of receivables problem than charge sales to individual consumers, which is typical of "retail" receivables.

Retail Receivables

Most everyone is familiar with the retail type of receivables. A customer enters a store, makes a purchase and receives a copy of a charge ticket. The store routinely posts the sale amount to the account; cash is posted as a credit when received. There are no terms or special conditions. It is not necessary to associate the cash received with specific charge sale amounts. In other words, cash is simply posted as "on account." Customers can and do make arbitrary partial payments on account without causing any special accounting problems.

Retail receivables feature the "Balance Forward" method of receivables accounting. Since there is no need to identify specific invoice amounts when cash is received, it is practical to carry forward only the balance owing from one month to the next. Let's examine other characteristics of retail receivables before studying wholesale and manufacturers' receivables problems:

- Store charge sales are posted to the customers' accounts daily, or on a monthly cycle basis.
- Charge sales are never subject to invoice terms or conditions; no discounts are involved.
- Customers seldom take deductions or claims; the amount involved in a return of merchandise is simply credited to the account.
- Cash is posted to the account as a credit—it is never necessary to determine which specific charge amounts are being paid by a check.
- At month-end the store sends a complete account statement to each customer, showing the balance forward from last month, current month's purchases, credits and cash received.

Since cash is not applied to specific purchases, aging presents no special problem. The concept is that cash received this month covers all *net purchases of the prior month*—so, all aging is done on the basis of a full month's purchases.

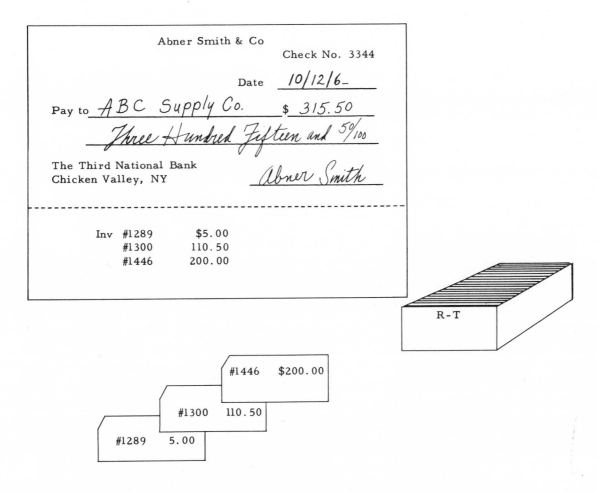

Exhibit 13-C

ILLUSTRATION OF THE APPLICATION OF CASH TO A PUNCHED CARD RECEIVABLES FILE

Trade Receivables

By sharp contrast, wholesalers and manufacturers who sell to business firms rather than to individuals create "trade receivables"—which are usually characterized by *special invoice terms* offered to customers. The existence of invoice terms changes the required cash procedures completely, because—*ALL CASH RECEIVED MUST BE APPLIED TO SPECIFIC, IDENTIFIED INVOICES.*

The reason for this is that the *application of terms* to an invoice creates, in effect, an individual receivables situation for each and every invoice—since terms are the basis for one or two "due dates." Terms are always added to the invoice date, or to an "as of" date when future dating is an element of the terms.

Let's consider several examples of invoice terms and see how the terms create one or two due dates, depending upon the type of terms.

	Invoice Date	Invoice Terms	Discount Due Date	Final Due Date	Invoice Amount
1.	6/05	N 10	—	6/15	315.00
2.	6/05	2/10 N 30	6/15	7/05	500.00
3.	6/10	N 30 plus 30 extra	—	8/09	417.80
4.	6/12	5/10 4/70 N 71	6/22	8/22	1,016.50

Item 2 above has *two due dates* because of the two-option terms offered to the customer. He has the choice of paying on or about the discount due date and deducting 2%, or he can wait until July 5 and pay the gross amount of the invoice—known as paying "net."

Item 4 shows an invoice subject to a 3-option set of terms, but the middle option is ignored for purposes of establishing the two due dates.

Summary

Since invoice terms include different discount rates, variable periods of time and possibly future dating ("as of" date), it is absolutely necessary to determine and *identify* specific invoices being paid by each remittance. In a ledger sheet system the cash application clerks write a code number next to each paid invoice; this code indicates which cash credit amount—posted to the ledger after the cash application procedures—paid the items indicated. This is the "key-off" technique.

This technique is illustrated by Figure 13-1 which shows the use of the Remittance Envelope as the cash application and posting document.

Application of Cash

After the initial step of recording the remittance amount on each envelope has been completed, all envelopes are sorted into alphabetical order and routed to the bookkeeper for further processing. The bookkeeper takes one envelope at a time and first matches the remitter's name with a corresponding ledger record. The bookkeeper then studies the entries on the ledger card and, in the instance of the remittance for $230.08, finds a posted invoice amount of $234.77. This amount multiplied by 2% provides a cash-discount amount of $4.69. The net amount of $230.08 plus $4.69 equals $234.77. It is now evident that the remittance is intended to pay the invoice for the latter amount. The discount amount of $4.69 is then written on the envelope. (Refer to Figure 13-1.)

Keying Off Payments

The total-credit amount later posted to the ledger card is "keyed off" as part of the posting operation; that is, the credit amount posted is assigned a code number, and the same number is written next to the invoice amount "cleared" by the payment. In the illustration above, code number 1 is written next to the invoice amount of 234.77; this same code number is also written next to the credit-posting of the same amount.

Exhibits 13-D and 13-E which follow illustrate the two different control concepts:
- Balance control is the essence of retail receivables.
- Open item control is the characteristic of trade receivables—generated primarily by manufacturers.

FOUR PLANS FOR RECORDING AND PROCESSING CASH RECEIVED

The following four cash-handling plans offer a wide choice of procedures to be selected after a careful study of the client's particular situation and system requirements:

Plan 1: Customer's check (or a photo of the check if client is using the popular "lock-box" plan now being promoted by banks) is used as the basic document for all bookkeeping purposes.

Plan 2: Remittance envelope used for recording and posting cash.

Plan 3: A combined bank-deposit and cash-journal form prepared from the remittance envelopes.

Plan 4: Cash receipt tickets prepared and used for recording and posting cash.

PLAN 1. CUSTOMER'S CHECK USED FOR BOOKKEEPING

Typical Procedures

When the customer's check is the basic document for bookkeeping, some individual in the bookkeeping department does the following:

1. Opens the mail and removes checks from envelopes.
2. Sorts checks into alphabetic order.
3. Matches each check to the corresponding receivables ledger card, then:
   - Identifies each item paid by the check
   - Determines if discount is allowable according to invoice terms
   - Calculates the amount of discount
4. Writes earned discount amount in the left-hand corner of the check.
5. Adds check amount and discount amount to obtain a total of the two amounts. Writes this total credit to the account on the check under the discount amount.

Journalizing Remittances

Checks are now used for writing the Cash Received Journal. The name written in the journal is always the name of the customer receiving credit for the payment. For various reasons familiar to the practitioner, this may not be the name on the signature line of the

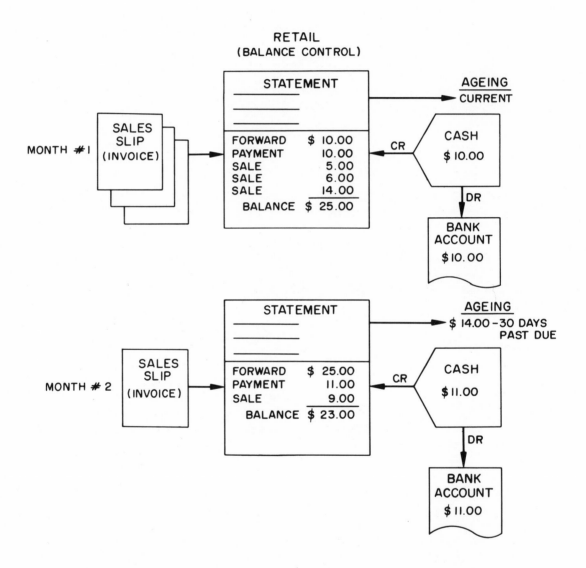

Exhibit 13-D
SYSTEM CONCEPTS: RETAIL vs. MANUFACTURING RECEIVABLES

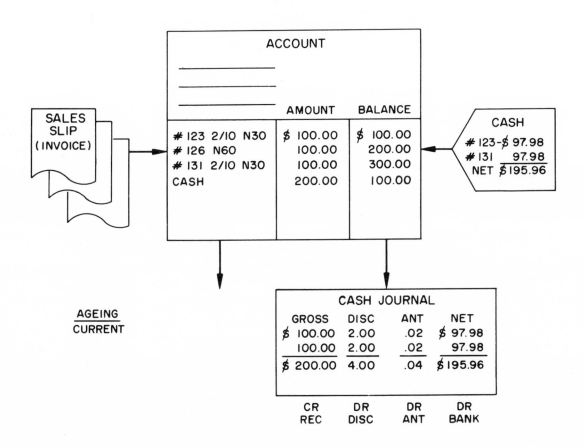

Exhibit 13-E
SYSTEM CONCEPTS: RETAIL vs. MANUFACTURING RECEIVABLES

check. (Personal checks are sometimes used to make payments for a corporation; third-party checks, etc.)

Typical entries in Cash Received Journal are shown in Figure 13-1.

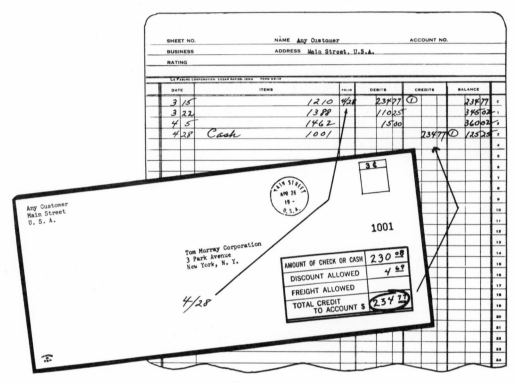

Figure 13-1
APPLYING CASH AND KEYING OFF PAYMENTS

Bank Deposit

After all checks are recorded in the journal, they are deposited in the bank.

One disadvantage of this plan is that frequently the checks cannot be deposited promptly, since they are retained temporarily for use in bookkeeping routines.

Credits to Customer Accounts

After the checks have been deposited, the Cash Received Journal is the source of credit-postings to receivables.

PLAN 2. REMITTANCE ENVELOPE PLAN

Many manufacturing and wholesale concerns customarily receive most of their cash by mail; either directly from the customer or by special collections made by their salesmen. Some well-known firms use the remittance envelope as the basic accounting document for substantiating cash received and discounts allowed; and for posting credits to receivables.

For applying cash the use of the envelope as an accounting document offers many advantages over the use of the check itself. If customer checks are the basis for entries in the Cash Received Journal, this journal then differs from all others in that the basic documents (the checks) *cannot be retained to substantiate the entries,* but are deposited in the bank and returned to the remitters eventually. (This interesting peculiarity of a typical Cash Received Journal has been widely ignored, yet it has a vital bearing on adequate audit procedures.) Experience indicates that the utilization of a suitable substitute such as the remittance envelope provides several major benefits in the cash-accounting system.

When comparing the procedures of one firm using the envelope plan with those of another firm, you will seldom find uniformity in all details of processing the envelopes and the checks. However, the basic principles will remain virtually the same. Listed below are some typical suggested procedures which will provide all necessary accounting records and positive internal control over cash.

Procedure

After the mail is received in the mailroom or in the office, all envelopes are opened, remittances removed and processed. Further instructions may be as follows:

1. Block-stamp the face of each envelope for later entry of cash, discount and total-credit amounts. (See Figure 13-2).

2. Sort all envelopes into alphabetical order, then *consecutively number* each one with a numbering machine. *Stamp the same control number in a corner of the check* removed from the envelope.

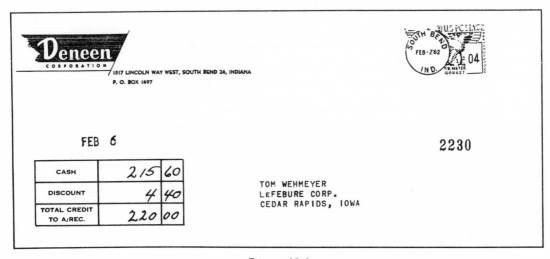

Figure 13-2
REMITTANCE ENVELOPE UTILIZED AS BASIC DOCUMENT
FOR CASH RECORDING PROCEDURES

3. Record the check amount as "cash" on the face of the envelope in the block area provided for this purpose.

(At this point, some firms require the separation of checks from envelopes; others leave them together until cash has been applied.)

4. Now match each envelope with the appropriate accounts receivable ledger card and

apply cash. Write the earned discount amount on the envelope. Later, record the total credit to accounts receivable on each envelope. Typical entries are illustrated by the envelope above.

5. Next, list all check amounts with an adding machine. Then list the pencil-written cash amounts appearing on the envelopes. Be sure the two totals agree. It is important to detect any discrepancy between a check amount and the cash amount written in pencil on the envelope.

Envelopes Are Source Documents

1. Use the envelopes for recording all entries in the Cash Received Journal.
2. Next, use the envelopes as posting documents for posting credits to accounts. The benefits of this procedure are itemized later.

Standard Cash Received Journal

The Cash Received Journal (see Figure 13-3) is one of the forms included in a general accounting plan developed several years ago by the author.

This journal provides columns on the left for three types of debits: cash, discounts and freight allowed. The credit side is also versatile in that provision is made for payments received on notes as well as payments on receivables. The "Cash Sales Clearing" column (explained subsequently) provides a means of bringing "cash sales" cash from the Sales Journal to the Cash Journal. Necessary columns are also included for recording bank deposits and cash adjustments.

The usual accounting instructions are pre-printed underneath each accounting column.

Proving Receivables Postings

As credits are posted daily from the envelopes to ledger cards, the accounts are set to one side in the tray. After posting is finished, an old and new balance proof run is made to verify accuracy of posted amounts and new account balances. The total developed by the proof run must agree with the accounts receivable credit column total in the journal.

Collections on Notes

Envelopes containing note payment checks are stamped "Notes Receivable." These envelopes are used for journal entries and for posting credits to note ledgers also. The proof of posting is the same as that used for proving receivable postings.

Record Retention Period

It is customary to retain the envelopes for at least three months for reference to postmarks, date received, cash-item control numbers, etc. Some accountants require retention of the envelopes until completion of a yearly audit.

General Instructions to Implement Envelope Plan

1. The customer's name is generally provided by the return address on the envelope. If the name is missing, write it on the envelope when the remittance is removed.

CR PAGE NO. 5

DATE	SOURCE NO.	CASH ON HAND	DISCOUNTS ALLOWED	FREIGHT ALLOWED	RECEIVED FROM	ACCOUNTS RECEIVABLE	NOTES RECEIVABLE	CASH SALES CLEARING	BANK A	BANK B	CASH OVER	CASH SHORT	DEBIT	A/C NO.	CREDIT
2/5/6	2228	7409	151		Barnes & Brown	7560									
	2229	9800	200		Charles C. Barton	10000									
	2230	21560	140		Denson Corp.	21000									
	2231	50000			Dudley Beaver		50000								
	2232	6250			Geo. Franklin	6250									
	2233	4500			Hugh Humphreys	4500									
	2234	18710			Lou Lanham Corp.		18710								
	2235	11761	244		Ed Malone	12205									
	2236	90000			Bob Roberts & Son	90000									
	2237	31909	651	1256	Tom Trainer & Son	33810									
	2238	5000			H. L. White Corp	5000									
	2239	14070						14070							
					Bank Deposit				1881 69			1000			
YESTERDAY'S MONTH-TO-DATE TOT		301,600				22,1052	35000	51725	3022 85		3000	2215			
TODAY'S TOTALS		1,859 69	4207	2070	DATE 2/5/6	1,093 25	68710	14070	1881 69		3000	1000			
NEW MONTH-TO-DATE TOTALS		40,4669	5393	3320		330,377	1,037 10	65798	4,904 54		3000	3215			
		DEBIT 2	DEBIT 801	DEBIT 820		CREDIT 6	CREDIT 7	CREDIT 78	DEBIT 3 CREDIT 2	DEBIT 8 CREDIT 2	DEBIT 2 CREDIT 707	DEBIT 804 CREDIT 2	DEBIT EACH		CREDIT EACH ACCOUNT

FORM NO.3

ORDER BY FORM NUMBER ABOVE
FROM
LITHO-FORM CORPORATION
21 WEST 9th STREET
NEW YORK 11, N.Y.

FOLD UNDER AT THE PERFORATION

Figure 13-3
STANDARD CASH RECEIVED JOURNAL

2. Transcribe, to the outside of the envelope, any identifying invoice numbers or other data appearing on the face of the remittance.

3. If the remittance is a voucher check with a remittance statement attached, remove the statement and staple it to the envelope. (This will assist the bookkeeper in applying cash.)

4. When a letter or a note accompanies a remittance, staple it to the back of the envelope.

Benefits of Envelope Plan

1. Since remittance checks are not used for applying cash or for bookkeeping purposes, they can be deposited promptly in the bank. This provides better internal control over cash.

2. The envelope provides the finest kind of document for reference. For example, cash-discount terms are usually based on payment within a stated period of time beginning with the invoice date. When a customer's remittance reflects an unauthorized discount, the postmark on the envelope may be valuable for reference. If the envelope shows date received, this plus the postmark provides evidence as to when the check was mailed and when it was received.

3. Initial cash control is established by the person who opens the mail and numbers the envelopes and the checks. IMPORTANT: This person must not have access to any cash fund in the office.

4. Recording the consecutive number on the envelope and the check is a suggested procedure and is not followed by some firms. However, the value of the numbering procedure is twofold:

   a. It sets up immediate numeric control over each cash remittance.
   b. It positively *identifies* the check if it later is returned by the bank for any reason. It is not always easy to identify the customer who received credit for a remittance when an item is returned for lack of funds, drawn on wrong bank, etc. The control number on the check enables the bookkeeper to trace the check to the numbered envelope, or to the numbered entry on the Cash Received Journal.

5. It saves the time required for writing cash receipts tickets for each item.

6. After the envelopes have been recorded in the Cash Received Journal, they may be stuffed into the accounts receivable tray binder in front of the ledger cards to be posted. This speeds the subsequent posting operation.

PLAN 3. COMBINED DEPOSIT SLIP AND CASH JOURNAL

Introduction

This plan is similar in many respects to the Remittance Envelope Plan. It is primarily applicable in firms which receive all, or nearly all, cash receipts by mail.

The practitioner will select this plan for one or more of the following reasons:

1. To obtain daily a detailed deposit slip in addition to a complete cash journal.

2. When it is desirable to assign some of the bookkeeping work to a person who normally performs duties other than bookkeeping, such as a switchboard operator or receptionist.

3. To obtain better internal control of cash. When this plan is used, the person who handles the incoming checks has no access to the receivables ledgers. The bookkeeper, in turn, never handles the checks.

4. This plan is suggested if branch operations require the preparation of several copies of a detailed cash journal.

DEPOSIT			DEPOSIT				
SECURITY NATIONAL BANK			URITY NATIONAL BANK				
DALLAS, TEXAS			DALLAS, TEXAS				
CREDIT THE ACCOUNT OF			DIT THE ACCOUNT OF				
CENTRAL CHEMICAL CO., INC.			RAL CHEMICAL CO., INC.				
DALLAS, TEXAS			DALLAS, TEXAS				
DATE _____			RECEIPTS JOURNAL				
CHECKS AS LISTED	AMOUNT		DISCOUNT	ACCTS. REC. CREDIT	MISC·L.		Cash Sales Cr.
TOTAL							

Figure 13-4
COMBINED BANK DEPOSIT—CASH JOURNAL FORM

Suggested Daily Procedures

1. The person assigned to processing cash receipts performs the initial step of removing each check from the envelope in which it was received. The check is temporarily paper-clipped to the top edge of the envelope.

2. Envelopes are now sorted into alphabetic order.

3. Each check is detached from its envelope and the amount is written on the face of the envelope.

4. All check amounts are listed on an adding machine and a total is obtained.

5. Then all pencil-written check amounts appearing on the face of the envelopes are added. The total obtained must balance with the total of the actual checks established as part of step four.

6. The envelopes are routed to the bookkeeper for applying cash against receivables ledgers. The bookkeeper determines the discount amount and total credit to accounts receivable for each remitter, as outlined for the Remittance Envelope Plan.

7. After the bookkeeper has applied cash and has written discount and accounts receivable credit amounts on all envelopes, they are returned to a typist for the final step.

8. The typist inserts the combined bank deposit and cash journal into the typewriter. The remitter's name is read from the return address shown on the envelope and typed on the form. Amounts are copied from the face of the envelope.

Cash Sales: Cash Sales may consist of checks and currency received for goods or services. Checks representing cash sales are typed separately on the bank-deposit form to prevent mixing them in with received-on-account items.

Currency received through cash-sales transactions is listed in total at the bottom of the daily bank-deposit form. The *total* of all cash sales is entered in the journal column "Cash Sales Credit" to offset the debit to the bank.

Miscellaneous: If an envelope does not bear a return address, the remitter's name should be copied from the check to the envelope when the latter is opened.

When the bookkeeper applies cash, it is, of course, necessary to compare the return-address name on the envelope with the account title on the receivable ledger card. In the event of a discrepancy between the two, the bookkeeper is required to write the correct account title on the envelope, as the envelopes are later used for typing names on the deposit-journal form. And, in turn, credits are eventually posted from the cash journal form to the accounts receivable ledgers.

PLAN 4. CASH RECEIPTS TICKETS USED FOR RECORDING AND POSTING CASH

This plan is particularly applicable for use by the type of business in which it is common practice for customers to come to the business premises in person to make payments.

Instructions

When this plan has been selected for a client, the instructions for the cashier, bookkeeper or office employee of the firm may read as follows:

1. Write serially numbered cash-receipts tickets in triplicate for each collection received. One copy is given to the customer as a receipt. This leaves two copies for uses which are detailed herein.

2. At the end of the business day, add the cash-receipts ticket amounts and balance the total against the cash on hand. Then all cash and checks may be deposited in the bank at once.

3. Now remove the duplicate cash-receipt forms from the bound receipt book or autographic register. These duplicates will suffice for bookkeeping; the triplicates are filed as a permanent office record for reference and audit.

4. Use the bookkeeping copies for applying cash. Write discount amounts on the face of each ticket. Later, add the discount amount and the cash amount together and write the total credit on each ticket.

5. Now record each cash ticket in numeric order in the Cash Received Journal.

6. Add all journal columns and balance the journal.

7. The next step is to post credits to customers' accounts from the serially numbered cash-receipts tickets. Do not post from entries in the cash journal.

8. Prove the amounts posted by the old and new balance proof method. The total posted to all accounts must equal the journal column total "Accounts Receivable Credits."

9. The sum of the entries in the journal column "Cash on Hand," adjusted by a cash over or short amount, is the amount that should be deposited in the bank each day.

Received-on-Account Cash

Administrators of trade receivables departments frown on received-on-account cash. Typically, the customer pays a round amount "on account." All unpaid invoices remain open on the customer record; the cash credit is a temporary offset. Eventually the customer is supposed to send in additional cash which, when added to the prior cash credit, will exactly settle one or more invoices which are due or past due.

There are two other situations which result in "on-account" cash being posted to the account. The first stems from the inability of the cash application bookkeeper to find one or more invoices referenced by the customer's remittance as being paid by the remittance. This situation occurs because of posting invoices to the wrong account at the time the sales were posted. The cash is taken in on account, and a search is made to locate the misposted invoices. Every effort is made to find and transfer the missing invoice amounts to the appropriate account—then the cash is keyed off against these items.

Also, there is the "debits-to-come" cash situation. This means that the check is received in payment of an invoice *before* the invoice itself has been processed through the sales or internal accounting departments; it has not yet been posted to the customer record. This type of received-on-account credit should be specially identified or marked, since the bookkeeper is responsible for keying off paid invoices subsequently when the invoice amounts are finally posted. To recap, the cash is received before the invoices are posted, but it must be applied, audited and controlled the same way as regular cash—as soon as possible.

To apply this "early cash" to open-item invoice amounts at a subsequent time requires special notations or forms and a follow-up procedure. That is, the details of the paid items may appear on the face of the check itself, or on a voucher apron. The bookkeeper should copy the paid item data to a memo form, or detach and keep the voucher apron. These documents provide the bookkeeper with a follow-up file, so that it is easy to apply the cash eventually, after the indicated invoice amounts have been posted to the account.

HOW TO AGE RECEIVABLES

There are two distinctly different methods for aging receivables, depending upon the basic receivables method of *balance control,* which is characteristic of retail receivables, or *item control* where terms are applied to each invoice.

Method for Retail Receivables

The total purchases for a calendar month are compared to the cash payment received in the following month. If the payment is less than the total net purchases of the prior month, the difference is aged as 30 days old.

The aging process calls for entering the account balance, then successively calculating each month's purchases and payments. The table of purchases and payments below illustrates the aging of the latest balance.

Month	Net Purchases	Cash Payments	Balance
April	$100	—	$100
May	60	75	85
June	72	50	107

Aging Schedule for Above Account

Current	30 Days Past Due	60 Days Past Due	Account Balance
$72	$10	$25	$107
	($60-50)	($100-75)	

One way to help identify each month's postings, when charges and credits are posted daily, is to change the color of the inked ribbon on the posting machine on the first day of each month:

April	Black ink
May	Blue ink
June	Green ink
July	Brown ink

Open Item Control

As prior chapters dealing with invoice terms have established, the application of terms to each invoice creates individual due dates for each invoice. Therefore, all purchases for a month cannot be aged as a group; it is necessary to age each unpaid invoice by comparing the date when the aging is being done with the long-term or final due date.

Invoice Date	Terms	Discount Due Date	Final Due Date
5/10	2/10 N60	5/20	7/09

If the bookkeepers are preparing an Aged Trial Balance as of July 31, the above item is placed in the category of 1 to 30 days *past due.*

Aging Is Easy with Mechanized Records

The aging of open items one at a time, by clerical personnel, is a slow and costly process. It involves the mental calculation of a due date for each open item—by noting the terms, then adding terms-days to the invoice date. When this preliminary step is followed by typing or writing the open item data on an Aged Trial Balance report, the overall time and work is apt to be substantial.

Experience has shown that one of the major benefits of mechanizing receivables records by the application of tab equipment or computers is that the Aged Trial Balance can be prepared rapidly by a machine, since the invoice records are in machine-readable form.

Summary

This chapter covered the types of receivables records, posting methods and methods for applying cash. The next chapter concentrates on receivables administration, and focuses on ways to protect and control this prime asset, customer receivables.

14

Receivables Administration and Control

Since there are eleven sources of profit dilution in accounts receivable, this prime asset should have the protection of continuous internal audit and control, coupled with knowledgeable supervision by management.

Members of management who are charged with financial administration are frequently aware that there is a "gray area" in receivables accounting. That is, the amount of cash deposited in the bank seldom matches the comparable volume of credit sales, even after making allowance for cash or trade discounts. This chapter concentrates on identifying the many sources of profit dilution which cause a reduction in cash received—and which in many instances represent a serious profit control problem. It tells how to report and control the primary sources of profit losses, such as remittance deductions, excess and unearned discounts taken, errors and differences.

Remittance Audit Is Imperative

Several potential sources of loss must be controlled through effective audit of remittances—accompanied by appropriate policies relative to the absorption of error amounts, unearned or excess discount amounts and small deductions taken by the customers.

Here is a list of the various reasons why the check amount may be considerably less than the sum of the gross invoice amounts paid by a remittance:

- Discount earned (according to invoice terms) and taken.
- Excess discount amount taken (error in discount amount).
- Discount not earned, but taken anyway.
- Anticipation earned and taken (early interest).
- Excess anticipation taken (error in interest amount).
- Unadjusted Deductions and claim amounts arbitrarily subtracted from the remittance by the customer.
- Remittance errors and differences in general.

165

Discounts Earned or Unearned

As part of the remittance audit procedures, the bookkeeper must determine whether the discount amount was earned or unearned—by applying terms to the invoice date or to an "as of" date included in the terms. If the bookkeeper finds that the customer deducted a cash discount, but the payment was not made soon enough to earn the discount, then the bookkeeper prepares an Unearned Discount Statement for mailing to the customer. The same type of notice is prepared when the customer deducted excess discount.

One of the important guidelines established by management and used in auditing remittances, is the amount of unearned or excess discount and remittance differences to be absorbed without billing the customer. Some firms set the maximum absorption amount at 50¢; others are more generous and are willing to absorb up to $5 or more.

Maximum Absorption Amount

Broad experience with computer audit of hundreds of thousands of remittances points to this urgent suggestion for financial management:

The amount selected and set by a policy decision as the maximum absorption amount should be carefully watched and reviewed occasionally.

There are several reasons for stressing the importance of the amount set up as the maximum absorption amount according to house policy:

- An absorption limit that is too generous is opening the door to substantial internal profit losses, since studies reveal that up to 17% of all checks have an adverse effect on the P & L account one way or another.
- If the amount is too small, this causes excessive paper work, clerical follow-up work and customer irritation—and collection of amounts billed may be very small in relation to the time and expense invested in the effort.

The significance of the amount selected as the maximum absorption amount can easily be realized upon consideration of the volume of paperwork and the total dollars involved in processing and auditing cash remittances in those firms that generate reasonably large volumes of invoices. For example, a firm that prepares about 1200 invoices daily will receive, on the average, about 500 checks per day. This check volume adds up to 11,000 per month or 132,000 per year. From the standpoint of dollar control, it is well to remember that practically the entire total amount of annual sales dollars flows through accounts receivable in those firms with no cash sales or retail outlets.

Disposition of Differences Report

The usual practice of allowing (or even encouraging) bookkeepers to add errors or differences to "discounts allowed" when processing cash, can be quite costly to a firm over a period of time. This practice makes it very easy for a bookkeeper always to turn in "balanced" remittance documents and cash journals—yet the so-called "discounts allowed" may include substantial sums made up of unearned and excess discounts taken, plus a considerable number of miscellaneous remittance errors and shortages.

A CASE HISTORY

To illustrate the point, consider the case of the factoring firm that took over a smaller firm which received about 300 checks per day—requiring the application of cash in the usual way to machine-posted customer ledger sheets. Trained auditors of the buying firm reviewed how cash had been applied by the bookkeepers of the smaller firm, and analyzed a couple of months' remittances. They found that the bookkeepers, as a group, had been concealing and absorbing approximately $2,000 per month (through the discount account) in legitimate charges and charge-backs to customers—not for any personal gain, but because it was easier and required less paper work to ignore these items!

This situation is not at all uncommon, and accentuates the need for supervisory management to be alert to the possibility of substantial sums being absorbed against profits routinely, and without management having an opportunity to review these losses.

One control method is to add special columns in the Cash Journal where unearned discounts taken, excess discount amounts and errors are shown separately from the discounts legitimately allowed. This would serve as a report of differences for management to review and make appropriate decisions as to the desired disposition of major amounts.

Anticipation Allowed

Firms in the soft goods trade allow customers to pay before the due date—established by the invoice terms—and deduct early interest. Such amounts should be carefully audited and controlled. Audits reveal that some customers date their checks several weeks before mailing them; yet, they deduct anticipation calculated from the check date to the invoice due date.

UNADJUSTED DEDUCTIONS

An "unadjusted deduction" originates when a customer makes an arbitrary deduction of an amount from a remittance for any one of many reasons. Such deductions are sometimes called "claims," possibly because many of them are caused by freight damage during shipment of the merchandise from the seller to the customer.

On a remittance voucher, the information provided for an unadjusted deduction makes it appear that the customer is using a credit invoice as part of the settlement for the indicated paid invoices. Only after looking at the ledger record—and finding that no such credit amount exists—can the deduction amount be properly identified as an unadjusted deduction or claim.

It is essential that deductions be properly set up, controlled and followed within a reasonable time—since such amounts frequently amount to as much as 4% of the total outstanding receivables! (The amount of capital tied up in such "receivables" was usually unknown until the advent of data processing equipment—which made it easy to analyze and break down the various types of open items which constitute a typical receivables file.)

Reasons for Deductions

Studies reveal that there are as many as 30 reasons why a customer may make a deduction from his remittance. Some of them are:
- Wrong price
- Wrong quantity billed
- Freight damage
- Freight allowance claimed by customer
- Sales tax deducted
- Parcel post allowance claimed
- Returned merchandise
- Shortage in shipment

- Advertising allowance
- Unknown

Management can benefit greatly from an occasional analysis of the reasons for deductions. So, one important suggestion for any firm is to prepare a list of major reasons, and assign a two-digit code number to each one. Give this list to the bookkeepers, so they can code each deduction set up.

Internal Paperwork

Each deduction requires that the bookkeeper prepare notice documents for internal processing of credit memos to cover deductions, and for eventual disposition. For example, a remittance accompanied by a documented deduction for freight damage is routed to the traffic department for follow up, investigation and disposition. A deduction for a freight allowance, or an advertising allowance is routed to the sales department for a decision.

If the customer claims that the wrong unit price has been applied to an item on an invoice, the deduction notice may go to the order department for checking.

Follow Up and Control

Unadjusted deductions pose a special problem in customer relations. They are temporary receivable items, but are not in the same category as past due invoices. For this reason, many firms assign specially-trained clerks to follow and control open deductions. These people are frequently called "adjusters" or "customer correspondents."

Adjusters work with internal company personnel to get deductions cleared by the issuance of appropriate credit memos. The majority of deductions are eventually allowed; therefore, most of them are cleared from the files by matching credit memos to them.

Controlling Deductions on Receivable Ledgers

The customer ledger sheet shown in Exhibit 14-A illustrates accounting control over deductions on receivables ledgers. The ledger shows a gross credit to accounts receivable of $155 posted in the credit column. The number key 1 indicates that this gross credit cleared both open-invoice amounts. However, the customer still owes $10 since this amount appears in the special "deductions" column, on the same line as the cash posting. (The check amount was actually for $141.90, since the customer earned a 2% discount on the paid items, or $3.10.)

This method of using a special ledger column for deductions is a very effective control technique. Note that the "reason code" is also shown. This provides a clue as to which department within the firm is supposed to take action on the deduction papers, and eventually issue a credit memo or provide information as to disposition of the $10 amount.

Automatic Disposition of Deductions

Systems analysts who have studied the entire deductions problem carefully have reached the conclusion that certain types of deductions, up to a maximum amount, should be charged off to an internal expense account at once. For example, if studies show that any freight claim of less than $5 costs far more than that amount to process a claim for recovery, then it may be a

CUSTOMER LEDGER

• Joseph Cataldo Co., Inc.
• 6634 Hillside Ave.
• Belmont Park, N. Y.

Old Balance	Date	Reference	Terms	Deductions		Debit		Credit		Balance
				Rsn No.	Amount					
	JUN 10 '6—	3448	2/10 EOM			55.00	1			55.00*
55.00	JUN 16 '6—	3715	2/10 EOM			100.00	1			155.00*
155.00	JUL 12 '6—	Cash		2	10.00			155.00	1	10.00*

Exhibit 14-A
USE OF SPECIAL LEDGER COLUMN FOR DEDUCTIONS

good idea to charge such customer deductions directly to freight expense. This avoids all the internal paperwork, and also eliminates the writing of credit memos which is costly.

Elimination of credit memos also avoids the possibility that the customer bookkeeper will deduct the same amount *again*. In many instances the customer bookkeeper writes a debit memo as authority for the initial deduction amount. When the supplier or manufacturer processes the paperwork caused by the deduction on the receiving end, and finally issues a credit memo, a copy of this credit memo may be routinely, but improperly, sent to the customer. Then, the customer's bookkeeper is very apt to use this credit as part payment of other invoices—resulting in a duplicate deduction.

A word of warning: Do not set up *one* amount as the maximum for automatic charge-off of deductions, and apply this maximum amount to all types of deductions. Lumping all deductions under one policy amount may be a very costly policy. Rather than to do this, management should make a very careful study of the more common reasons for deductions, apply estimated costs of processing such claims—and set up a variable list of charge-off amounts by *reason categories* to be followed by the bookkeepers when processing remittances.

Value of Reason Codes

Periodic tabulation of deductions set up by reason code can pay big dividends. Such a study may point to several hidden weaknesses in the internal operations of the firm, or it may point to needed changes in areas outside the firm. For example, one such study revealed very clearly that an extensive number of claims for damaged freight resulted from poor packaging of the products shipped. In another case, the finger pointed to a particular motor freight line which was damaging considerable merchandise through careless handling of the goods.

Such a study may show a large number of customer claims for freight *allowances* originating from certain sales territories. Investigation may well reveal that the salesmen are verbally offering freight allowances as a special incentive to the customer to place an order.

Eliminating Deductions from Receivables

It is the responsibility of the bookkeepers to clean off open deductions from the customer records. However, the paper work begins with the adjusters, who file copies of the Deduction Notice forms. Here are four time-tested procedures which serve both groups of clerical personnel effectively:

1. Accumulate copies of credit memos for one week, sort them into alphabetic order by customer name, and route them to the adjusters.

2. Adjusters match each credit memo to the corresponding Deduction Notice copy, to determine those now covered by a credit.

3. Adjusters write the credit memo date and number on the face of the Deduction Notice. Notice copies are routed to bookkeepers.

4. Bookkeepers find the posted credit memo on the ledger, and *key off* the credit memo against the open deduction amount.

If a credit only partially clears a deduction, the Accounts Receivable Supervisor should determine the disposition of the balance. The supervisor may decide to try to collect the balance from the customer—or prepare a journal voucher to charge off the remaining amount.

CREDIT MEMORANDUMS

It is a mistake for systems analysts to consider a credit memo as simply the reverse of an invoice. These documents have a built-in hidden potential for loss of profits. Further, they can point the way to major improvements in the operations of a firm.

I once analyzed 1,675 credit memos issued by a garment manufacturing firm. When I had completed the tabulation of REASONS why the credit memos had been issued, it was most interesting to realize that I had developed very valuable clues to many internal problems in the following departments:

- Order/invoicing department
- Warehouse and shipping departments
- Manufacturing and quality control

Without going near the manufacturing plant or the firm's office, it was easy to establish the existence of serious problems in the above departments, as evidenced by the large number of credits created for the following reasons:

- Wrong prices applied to goods
- Wrong quantities shipped
- Wrong colors and sizes shipped
- Goods shipped to wrong location
- Goods returned because they were streaked—dirty—oil spots—flaws, faded, etc.

Here are certain significant facts about credit memos not generally known:

- Most credit memos are not prepared until the corresponding invoice is past due.
- More than half of all credit memos written cover unadjusted deductions previously set up as part of the receivables records.
- A large percentage of credit memos representing a cross-section of businesses provides no direct identification of the applicable invoice.

Suggested Overall Policies for Memos

- When aging credits, apply credit amounts against the oldest open invoice or invoices. (Reason: Most credits are not prepared until the original invoice is past due.)
- Do not permit bookkeepers to arbitrarily offset a credit memo against an open invoice, *even though the credit memo may reference the invoice by number*. (Reason: The customer's bookkeeper has the option of using a credit at any time to settle any invoice or group of invoices. For example, a credit may make reference to a current invoice not yet due, but the bookkeeper in the customer firm may elect to use this credit to help pay one or more prior, *past due* invoices.
- Do not prepare a check for credits (which have created a credit balance in the customer's account)—and *then key off* the credit amount after the check is prepared, mailed and posted as a debit to the account. (Reason: The customer may use the credit while the check is in process. Then the firm has the problem of trying to recover the check amount from the customer.) If the credit manager has the urge to send cash to a customer to clear a credit balance, key off the credit items first—then prepare the check.

Application of Terms to Credit Memos

Failure to properly apply terms to credits is one of the 11 sources of profit dilution through receivables. How does failure to apply appropriate terms to credits create a source of profit loss? To answer this question let's analyze an actual situation that occurred in a large firm which manufactures and sells detergents. Here is the sequence of events:

- Customer orders and the manufacturer ships merchandise covered by an invoice for $1,000—subject to terms of 3%/30 days.
- Customer receives merchandise, remits net amount of $970 to supplier.
- Customer later returns all merchandise as unsuitable or damaged.
- Supplier issues a credit memo in the amount of $1,000—since it was the supplier's policy not to apply terms to credits.
- Customer requests a check in lieu of the open credit on the books; supplier sends a check for $1,000.

We see, then, how *it is possible to create a direct loss* of $30 in this instance *by not applying invoice terms to credits*.

Why Deduction Amounts Should Include Discount Percent

Since the majority of credits cover open deductions on receivable records, it follows that the applicable discount percentage should be recorded along with the deduction amount. Here is why:

- Customer pays a 3% $500 invoice with a check for $385 which was the net amount owing after subtracting a deduction of $100 and a discount of $15.
- Bookkeeper in the firm receiving the check sets up the $100 deduction on the customer's record—and marks the applicable deduction terms as "net." That is correct because the customer figured 3% discount on the *full $500 amount*—not on $500 less the deduction of $100. Marking the deduction amount "net" means that the credit

memo, when applied against the deduction, must NOT be subject to any terms other than net.

Suppose the credit comes through and shows terms of 3% 30 days, because the invoice to which it applies offered these terms. Since discount terms on a credit are the reverse of discount terms on an invoice, this means that the $100 credit memo amount is *reduced* by 3%, or $3. That is, the credit has a discounted face value of only $97. When it is applied to the $100 deduction, the customer still owes $3.

The examples above show how the application of invoice terms to credits affects profitability, and how such terms should also be applied to deductions set up in the receivables records.

Handling and Controlling "Equals"

One of the seldom-mentioned aspects of receivables administration is the systematic removal of offsetting equal debit and credit amounts from the records. It is obvious, from a review of statements found in offices of all types of firms, that many systems analysts do not properly provide procedures for cleaning off offsetting equal amounts—or supervisory personnel is very lax in this aspect of receivables administration. Many computer-prepared statements that go to business firms include a large number of debit and credit amounts—obvious offsets—still on the records after more than a year!

You have learned how to clear equal debit and credit amounts from the records systematically by applying credit memos against open deductions. The word "equal" does not mean that the amounts must be exactly the same; it means that the credit is intended to clear the debit entry from the records.

CREDIT AND COLLECTION FUNCTIONS

As was stated earlier in the first section of Chapter 13 on receivable methods and procedures, the primary purpose of maintaining customer records is to facilitate the credit approval and collection functions. All aspects of receivables operations and procedures should be designed to aid and assist these two prime functions.

Customer Statements

A customer statement is one type of collection device. When designing the customer ledger record, a decision should be made as to the type of customer statement that's to be prepared. Accounting machines, when applied to posting receivable records, can easily post all charges and credits to a ledger *and statement simultaneously.*

There are two distinct types of statements in wide use; a "full account" statement and an open item, "past due" statement. The full account statement provides a record of all debit and credit entries posted to the account, usually for a calendar month. It provides the customer with full details of account activity and shows all items which make up his account balance. This type of statement is particularly appropriate for retail receivables.

It is questionable whether firms that offer discount terms should send out a full account statement. In fact, experience tends to prove that an open-item, past due statement gets much better collection results.

Past Due Statement

A past due statement shows primarily open items that are past due, according to invoice terms. This focuses the customer's attention on invoices which are due and payable. Adding current invoices that are not yet due to such a statement dilutes its effectiveness as a collection tool.

Some firms also show all merchandise credits, as well as cash credits, on their past due statements. At American Management Association seminars, I have had the opportunity to discuss the advisability of showing merchandise credits on such statements, with many people who were holding various job titles, such as Credit Manager, Controller, Treasurer, Accounts Receivable Supervisor and others. The consensus of opinion resulting from such group discussions is that merchandise credits should be omitted, but cash credits should be shown. (Do not show "debits-to-come" cash, since this is a special problem.)

The reasoning behind the omission of merchandise credits is that it is the prerogative of the customer to use these credits to apply against the payment of *any* invoice or invoices, current or past due, and at any time.

Other Collection Forms

Some firms use a second copy of a past due statement as a follow-up or reminder form if the customer has not paid within a designated period of time, such as ten days or two weeks. Other firms switch to a collection letter approach if the original past due statement gets no results.

Notification of Past Due's Paid

It is important to include in any effective receivables system some method of halting collection activities when checks are received which *pay past due invoices*. One simple method is to provide the bookkeepers with copies of past due statements. As they apply cash, they pull the copy of the statement and use it to notify the collection section that these items have been paid.

This type of communication is especially important when the credit department maintains an "orders pending" file—orders which will not be approved for credit until the customer settles his past due items. When cash is received bringing the account to a current status, the credit department should quickly release these pending orders for shipment.

OTHER FACETS OF RECEIVABLES ADMINISTRATION

From a standpoint of financial control and receivables administration, do not overlook changes of terms and journal entries.

Changes of Terms

Requests for changes of terms may originate from the sales department, from credit men who have constant contact with customers, and from other sources. Such requests should not be treated lightly, since it is true that "time is money," especially whenever high interest rates are in effect. When the sales department readily accedes to a customer's request for sixty days additional time to pay an invoice for $5,000, the financial cost of such an accommodation is a minimum of $50.00, if figured at only 6%.

The credit manager should design a set of pre-numbered forms and distribute them to all parties who are in a position to request approval of a change of terms. The bookkeepers should have authority to change terms on a customer's ledger only if in possession of signed and approved Change of Terms forms. Further, a copy of such forms should be kept and the financial costs recapped and reported monthly to the chief financial executive of the firm—so that this source of profit dilution can be controlled effectively.

If a firm practices profit center accounting, the direct cost of all changes of terms for customers of each operating or selling division or subsidiary should be charged to that operating entity as an internal charge, with an offsetting credit to home office financial costs.

Journal Entries

The prime authority for removing from accounts receivable uncollectible deductions, disputed invoices and accounts to be charged to bad debts is a journal entry document. Most accountants agree that internal control dictates the use of pre-numbered, formal journal entry voucher forms for such entries.

When posting journal entry debits or credits to the accounts, the posting machine operator should show the source of the entry as a "JE"—and the number of the journal entry voucher.

SOURCES OF PROFIT DILUTION IN ACCOUNTS RECEIVABLE

In summary, planning an effective system for receivables administration and control should cover all of the following eleven sources of profit dilution:

1. Earned Discounts Taken
2. Unearned Discounts Taken and Allowed
3. Excess Discounts Taken and Allowed
4. Errors and Differences Absorbed
5. Unadjusted Deductions
6. Excess Anticipation Allowed (early interest)
7. Changes of Terms
8. Bad Debts
9. Late Payments
10. Failure to apply terms to Credits.
11. Interest Costs on Receivables Investment.

(All but two of these sources (item nos. 9 and 11) have already been discussed.)

Late payments are a financial cost, since the customer used the capital represented by the invoices for a period of time beyond the due date.

Interest costs on the average investment in receivables represent a very tangible financial expense. Executives charged with financial responsibilities should strive at all times to reduce the total amount invested in receivables without a corresponding reduction in the volume of profitable credit sales.

15

How to Organize and Perform a Systems Engagement

MECHANICS OF ORGANIZING AND CONTROLLING A SYSTEMS ASSIGNMENT

To establish an appropriate background for the material covered in this chapter, we will assume that you are an accounting practitioner in management services. You have recently presented a proposal to a client (possibly drawing on the suggestions and the material in Chapter 4) to make a basic review of his office systems and procedures—to be followed by a report and specific recommendations in regard to new equipment to be selected and installed.

During the presentation of your proposal, you followed the sales pointers found in Chapter 2 and Chapter 3 and carefully explained to the prospective client the many potential savings and benefits to be derived from the proposed assignment. He accepted the benefits and authorized your firm to proceed with the assignment, as outlined in your proposal.

You initially intended to handle the assignment yourself, but you now find that the required starting date conflicts with another major job, so you assign this job to an associate in your firm. He is ready to begin the job; he will be assisted by a junior staff man.

Organizing the work is the primary subject of the first section of this chapter; therefore, pertinent suggestions found in the remainder of this section are addressed to the consultant assigned to the project. It is understood that since you sold the job, you will participate from time to time as a supervisor.

Analyze the Assignment

Take a copy of the proposal which has been accepted by the client and place it in a 3-ring binder. Put a supply of pre-punched, ruled, composition note paper in the binder for work notes.

Read the proposal very carefully and determine:
- What is to be done.
- When it is to be done.
- What the end-results of the assignment are to be.

175

The latter is most important. Concentrate on that section of the proposal which defines the *purpose, scope and objectives* of the assignment accepted by the client. Once an assignment is well under way, it is easy for the consultant to become embroiled in details and actually lose sight of the "big picture" of what the client expects to be accomplished as a result of the assignment being performed.

Now, determine the number of working days allowed by the amount of the fee, if the assignment is a fixed fee arrangement. From the total fee, deduct the estimated value of the supervisor's time. Divide the remaining amount by your standard per diem rate (multiplied by the number of men on the job); the result is the number of *working days* which can be invested in the assignment without exceeding the budget.

Plan the Assignment

- Divide the assignment into logical work phases. Outline what has to be done to implement each work phase. Then, list the steps from the beginning to the end of the assignment. As stated above, the end-results must coincide with the purpose, scope and objectives of the job as documented by the proposal.
- Set up a manning table; decide which of the work phases you will handle, and assign the others to your staff man or men.
- Develop a rough time chart showing the allocation of working days to each major job phase. If necessary, convert the time chart to a graphic bar chart.
- Recheck the total number of days indicated on the time chart; the sum of the allowed days should not exceed the total man-days provided in the assignment budget.

Assign Responsibility

Ordinarily, each man on an assignment does a part of the following:
- Interviewing.
- Basic review of methods, procedures and clerical studies.
- Analysis of data gathered from review.
- Development of new forms, systems and procedures.
- Field research.
- Report writing.

Jobs may be split according to functions or departments. For example, one man might begin the basic review in the office where orders of all types are received and recorded. Another staff man might begin in the shipping department by observing warehouse stock picking procedures and by studying shipping forms and related procedures.

Establish Time Requirements

When establishing time requirements, keep in mind that time is required for:
- Interviews
- Rewriting memorandums of interviews
- Analysis of reports, statistics, procedures, forms, etc.
- Discussion of findings with client personnel and your own staff.
- Field Research.
- Check-backs for verification or clarification of information

Schedule Report Writing

Develop a time schedule for report writing, production and presentation.
Schedule necessary time for the following:
- Report outline
- Preparation of exhibits and charts
- Report writing
- Report typing in draft form
- Review of typed draft with team members
- Discussions for preselling
- Report presentation and changes
- Final report production

Keep on Schedule—and on "Target"

From time to time as the assignment proceeds, do the following:
- Check your progress against the objectives and the schedule prepared for the assignment.
- Check time and expenses against the budget.
- Send weekly time and progress reports to your associate or supervisor.
- Inform the client of progress on a periodic basis.
- Ask client for guidance, if the assignment is veering away from stated objectives because of unexpected developments during the basic review.

Internal Audit of Work Done

When a staff man or a team reports completion of an assignment, a partner or an associate who has been delegated to supervise the work of the field staff should carefully review all work that has been done . . . and check it against the proposal, step by step. This will provide insurance that the assignment actually covers all of the areas specified in the proposal, and that the assignment represents a completed job.

This review is a form of quality control which is essential for the consulting firm that is determined to gain and maintain a reputation for doing outstanding work. The man or men on an assignment frequently lose their objective outlook on the job—and they may even fail to achieve certain vital objectives of the assignment which the client understood would be done. Also, this review affords an opportunity for the partner or supervisor to establish a good relationship with the client—which will be of value when presenting to the client the final report, accompanied by an invoice.

The Final Report

The final report is a wrap-up of the assignment, and usually includes a written recap of the scope of the work done, the interviews held, how the work was done, departments or sections analyzed, and problems encountered. The final paragraphs include conclusions and recommendations; special exhibits may also be included.

Chapter 6 of this book covers report-writing. A key section of that chapter is titled, "How to

Gain Client Participation in Report Writing." This section stresses the importance of *never submitting a flawless final report to a client, which he has never seen.* The best procedure is to prepare a rough draft of the final report, then review it with the client and his staff in detail. Stress the fact that the report is in rough-draft format. Invite his participation; he should feel free to suggest any and all changes which will make the report more accurate or more acceptable.

PERFORMING AN OFFICE SYSTEMS REVIEW ASSIGNMENT

An assignment to review a client's office systems and procedures may cover a considerable number of work phases. The time and work required for the review will vary, depending upon the size of the firm under study, the number of people in each section or department and the scope and objectives of the assignment.

The *major steps* usually required to implement a basic review are:
- Conduct basic review, step by step.
- Determine management objectives for new system.
- Conduct interviews and document each one with written memorandums.
- Obtain data on paperwork volume and job assignments.
- Do field research on equipment, forms housing and other aspects of the new system which will be recommended in the final report.
- Outline tentative suggestions and recommendations; review them with other staff members.
- Prepare a rough draft of the report to be submitted to the client.
- Prepare special exhibits to be presented with your report.
- Prepare a list of benefits to be gained by the client if he puts your suggestions and recommendations into effect.

The Survey

A survey of office systems and procedures is sometimes called a "diagnostic review." It is the only sound basis for making the vital decisions and judgments involved in developing a new system and related procedures. Since it is the foundation for all conclusions and recommendations, the consultants should do a thorough job of obtaining and documenting all the key facts. In systems work, details are quite often very significant. During the survey, the consultant must uncover all of the exceptions and unusual problems in order to develop sound, practical solutions to be incorporated into a new system.

Preparation for Survey

A check list of work areas and functions to be covered, along with basic questions to be asked is quite helpful. If the consultant and his associates have performed a similar assignment at a prior time for another client, it is a good idea to review the working papers and reports to determine critical areas and special problems to research during the upcoming survey.

Where to Begin?

The question always arises, "Where should we start the survey?" One practical starting point is at the beginning of the paper flow. For example, in a systems assignment that involves order, billing and shipping, start with sales orders received in the office from any and all sources, such as outside salesmen, customers and brokers. Get samples of order forms with entries on them from the various sources; check into counter cash sales procedures if the firm operates such a facility.

Organize Working Notes

Throughout the survey phase of the assignment, take extensive and complete notes. Organize your notes by subject or function, and letter each page as follows:

> A—Procedures currently in use.
> B—Cost and volume figures developed as result of interviews.
> C—Questions to be Answered.
> D—Report Subjects.
> E—Things to do, departments to be covered.
> F—Why, and Why Not notes.
> *G through T:* Reserved for identifying individual departments or functions studied.
> X—Temporary notes; not a permanent part of the working papers.

Your working notes may be preceded by a couple of pages which provide basic client data, such as:
- List of client officers and key people and their titles.
- Organization chart.
- Plant locations and other pertinent data.

Interviews

A prime method of gathering necessary information on a project is interviewing key people. Interviews with members of top management should be aimed at developing management objectives for the new system. Take notes as to what the various owners or executives of the firm expect or would like to obtain from the new system.

Interviews with line management or experienced employees are usually for the purpose of gathering specified data and information for guidance in the subsequent systems development work. There is no adequate substitute for intensive spadework at the operating level. Talk to the people who are actually doing the work; ascertain their duties, and get their ideas as to needed changes and improvements. Only in this way will the practitioner find out what is actually being done, step by step, function by function. Sometimes these facts conflict in regard to what management *thinks* is being done; and also, the procedures now in existence may not agree with the contents of the procedure manual.

If the consultant depends solely on brief interviews with line management or top management for detailed, basic information, the results may be very incomplete or misleading.

The basic reason for this is that procedures in a firm are dynamic and constantly changing. New problems arise from time to time and new solutions are routinely developed to take care of them. Supervisory personnel may forget to mention very significant problems and exceptions which they have learned to accept as the normal routine.

A further point is that the practitioner or systems analyst will uncover significant information about the present system and procedures only by working with the older, more experienced people in a department. Here is why:

1. People doing the work from day to day are not in a position to readily distinguish between significant points and those that are routine or relatively insignificant.

2. These workers may fail to mention special problems which the systems analyst should know about. He will discover some of these problems only by exposure to the actual work as it is being done.

Use of Client's Staff

Be alert to special situations in which you may be justified in requesting that certain information be developed by a designated person or persons on the client's staff. For example, if you believe that a detailed analysis of a large group of credit memos will reveal data of value for your report and for the client, you may assign a consultant to do the work, or request the client to designate one of his employees to do it.

Even if the assignment is an open-end, per diem arrangement, it is an excellent approach to hold costs down, whenever possible, through proper utilization of client personnel on the assignment. A client does not appreciate paying per diem consulting rates for routine, clerical work that could easily be done by his people, if given the opportunity.

Solicit Ideas and Suggestions

A significant part of consulting work can be classified as "human relations." A successful consultant should be diplomatic, and he should know how to enlist the best possible cooperation from people at all levels.

Never disdain to listen to ideas or suggestions from anyone within the client firm. In many instances people at the operating level are able to offer very sound ideas based on their years of experience with the problem under review or study.

It is equally valuable to the alert consultant to uncover the details of *prior attempts* to reach a solution to a problem. This type of information may steer the consultant away from proudly proposing what seems to be a new approach, only to find out that it had been tried many years ago, with unsatisfactory results.

Another major reason for soliciting full participation whenever possible is that the new system and procedures will be readily accepted if they are developed as a team effort. People normally resist change; unless they have been consulted in advance, they are apt to take a negative view toward something new and different that has been introduced without warning or advance notice by "those outsiders."

Systems Design and Flow Charting

After the systems analyst has accumulated all the essential facts relating to management objectives, and about the present system and procedures, he then analyzes the accumulated data and begins to outline, in rough form, a new system.

One effective method of documenting the new procedures and testing for loose ends, is to *flow chart* the proposed procedures in detail. Flow charting should trace each copy of each form to its final destination; if a copy is left unaccounted for, then a flaw in the system is apparent.

Some clients expect that the existing procedures will be flow charted as one result of a survey or study. This may or may not be an essential part of a survey; it depends on what intended use is to be made of the flow charts.

After the systems designer is satisfied with the overall flow chart of the proposed new system, he begins to fill in the details around the system framework by designing the forms,

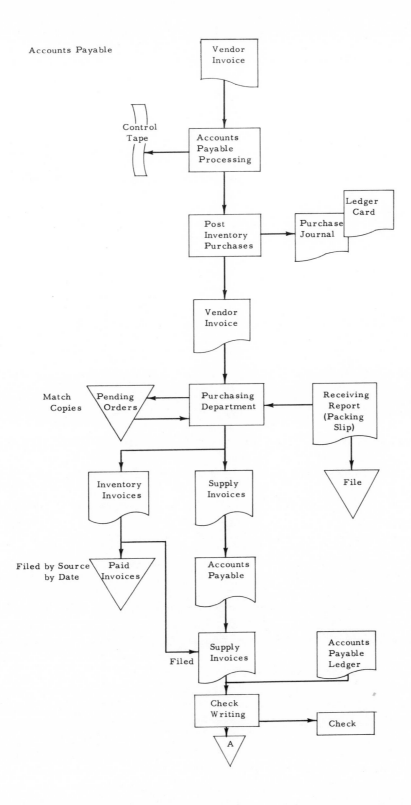

Figure 15-1
FLOW CHART OF ACCOUNTS PAYABLE PROCEDURES

determining the machine features necessary to mechanize the functions, and by doing field research.

Field Research

Even though a systems analyst may make every effort to keep informed about the latest available office equipment, the frequent releases of new equipment or new auxiliary devices make it very difficult to remain abreast of the many developments in the office equipment industry. Therefore, the analyst or consultant, before making any final decisions as to equipment, should spend enough time in the field researching recently announced equipment, prices and features to satisfy himself that he has selected the best equipment at the best price for the job.

Equipment salesmen are usually very cooperative and are eager to demonstrate their equipment, either in their showroom, or "on the job" in a user's office. Also, the more experienced salesmen will point out the weak points in competitive equipment, either openly or by indirection.

In summary, adequate field research is an important element of a system review assignment to assure selection of the right equipment for the client's applications.

Prepare Alternative Solutions

With today's wide-ranging choice of equipment, and the different known ways of handling the more commonly-found office applications, it may be unwise to plan and develop only one major systems approach for presentation to the client. There may be several practical objections to the particular approach which you believe to be the best method. If you are firmly committed to one particular method or approach, and have no alternatives in mind, you may be on a collision course with the client with no detours in sight. It is better to be flexible and develop alternative ways of doing the job. This not only gives the client more choices, but the end-results are apt to be better because thorough evaluation of the pros and cons of each approach may reveal that a combination of methods will produce the best results for the client.

Inside Assistance

It is essential for the client to assign a key person to a project involving the design and development of a new system and related procedures because of the need for continuing control and maintenance. Likewise, there are cogent reasons why the client should assign a representative of management from inside the firm to assist the consultant in a basic review assignment. This approach provides several benefits:

- The insider can save the time of the consultants by setting up necessary interviews and meetings.
- He can handle all introductions and inter-departmental clearances without undue loss of time.
- The total cost of the project may be reduced because the key person assists with research and secures necessary facts and figures in the absence of the consultants.
- The key person, because of his personal participation in all review steps, helps sell the suggestions and recommendations included in the final report to his management.

How to Conduct Interviews

Because of the nature of their work, consultants are essentially in the interviewing business. Developing skill in this art is essential to being a successful consultant. The purpose of this section is to provide ideas and suggestions for interviewing people at the line and staff management levels.

An interview is usually intended to accomplish one or more of the following purposes:
- Determine certain facts—interviewing a person to gather information.
- Inform—to tell the person being interviewed something.
- Motivate—to influence the person being interviewed in a positive manner.
- Appraise personnel—interviewing a person for the purpose of appraising his attitude, experience and aptitudes.

Results from interviews will be improved by following the suggestions listed below:

A. *Decide Why an Interview Is Necessary:* Do not waste time on interviews until you have a specific, worthwhile reason for one. Utilize interviews to:
- Obtain objective data and information.
- Determine opinions, attitudes and beliefs of an individual—to establish a better rapport with the individual.
- Obtain needed guidance from a key member of client's organization.
- Obtain advance reactions to forthcoming suggestions and recommendations.

B. *Make Thorough Preparation:*
- Define your interview objectives in advance.
- Prepare an interview outline in detail with numbered topics.
- Learn something in advance about the person to be interviewed.
- Make specific appointments at the convenience of the interviewee.
- Try to provide for privacy.
- Respect the opinions and suggestions of the interviewee; they may be based on many years' experience in the business or trade.

C. *Observe the Courtesies:*
- Be prompt.
- Remember that you are a guest in the interviewee's office.
- Relax but maintain your pose and dignity as a businessman.
- Reschedule the interview if unfavorable conditions arise.

Points for Effective Interviewing

Study the following pointers for effective interviewing:
- Make a good first impression. Explain why you are present, and what you want to accomplish. If the interviewee is not a member of management, offer reassurance as to any personal impact or effect of the interview.
- Avoid any impression of "talking down" to a person. Show that you respect his importance as an individual and his position with the firm. Ask for his full cooperation and assistance.
- Be careful about taking voluminous notes; do not use a tape recorder.
- Explain why you want the information before asking direct questions of a sensitive nature.

- Be a very good listener. The person being interviewed may touch on side subjects which may be of great interest to you in developing information for the assignment.
- Control the interview. If the interviewee changes the subject, tactfully return to the topics on your list by asking direct questions, or by asking for copies of reports and statistics discussed during the interview.
- Summarize the key points of your discussion before closing the interview. This gives the other person an opportunity to offer additional information, or to correct a mistaken impression.
- Listen carefully for closing remarks since the interviewee may at this time volunteer significant information which has been withheld until this point in the interview.

After the interview is terminated, date your notes and write the full name or names of the person or persons interviewed. You may want to type a summary of each interview for general documentation and to acquaint your supervisor with the results of each interview.

List of Things Not to Do

- Don't do all the talking
- Don't interrupt the interviewee when he is talking
- Don't act like a "know it all"
- Don't offer your opinions; gather facts.

What to Do

- Plan the interview
- Develop a rapport with the person being interviewed
- Encourage the interviewee to talk
- Do not be afraid of a period of silence when the interviewee is pondering over what to say next.
- Take notes in an unobtrusive manner.
- Be a good listener.
- Summarize the discussion and topics covered before terminating the interview.
- Leave the door open for a further discussion if the situation indicates the desirability of a later interview.

16

Characteristics of Today's Electronic Office Equipment

In recent years, office-equipment manufacturers have released a broad array of office machines designed for mechanization of practically all of the major functions and record-keeping operations that are found in a typical modern office. At an increasing rate, these new machines (frequently called "desk computers") have incorporated various features and capabilities taken from full-size electronic computers. Also, most of them can read machine-coded data from punched cards or paper tape, and can punch coded data into punched cards or paper tape.

These modern machines have spawned new terminology, such as "input" and "output." When stored information is read into the "memory" of the machine from an outside source, this is *input*. Likewise, when the machine transfers data from its internal memory to some type of outside storage or printing device, this is known as *output*.

The purpose of this chapter is to provide an analysis and explanation of the functions and characteristics of the more commonly-installed desk computers and similar devices, to assist the practitioner and his staff who engage in management services in the selection and installation of this new electronic equipment.

Definition of Desk Computer

A desk computer of the type described in this chapter is a small-scale, *operator-oriented* electronic computer which has evolved from prior conventional-type accounting or billing machines.

Two Basic Types of Desk Computers

Each manufacturer continually strives to produce a machine that operates efficiently with unique features in order to give his sales force a competitive edge over salesmen representing similar products. This leads to a constantly changing product line, with new features and equipment being released periodically.

Basically, however, there are only two different types of desk computers now on the market, each with its own features, capabilities and basic characteristics. One type has evolved around an electric typewriter base; the other is built around a full keyboard accounting machine. (Several different manufacturers are represented by both types.) Since the base machine for each type is so dissimilar to its countertype, the practitioner should review and evaluate the basic differences between them; and, determine the benefits or disadvantages of each in relation to the application on which it will be installed. The special information presented in this chapter will aid and assist in such evaluations.

As mentioned in the prior paragraph each machine should be studied and evaluated in light of the particular job to be done. It is a truism that each type fits certain applications better than the other; neither type has a clear-cut, absolute edge over the other for all applications.

Figure 16-1 shows the Friden Desk Computer and billing machine; it features an electric typewriter as the base machine.

Figure 16-1
FRIDEN DESK COMPUTER/BILLING MACHINE

Figure 16-2 shows the Burroughs accounting machine keyboard pictured at close range; the desk computers manufactured by Burroughs and the National Cash Register Company are built around an accounting machine base.

Figure 16-2
BURROUGHS ACCOUNTING MACHINE
(Some Desk Computers Are Built Around an Accounting Machine)

Common Characteristics

Even though there is little similarity in appearance, the two basic types of equipment share these features and characteristics:

1. The typewriter or accounting machine is the central printing unit for printed output.

2. The central processor is a solid state, electronic arithmetic control unit built inside the desk. This unit usually includes an electronic "memory" section, which has the ability to store instructions and/or data.

3. Electronic accumulators are built into the desk unit. (A desk computer built around an accounting machine can also provide up to 21 mechanical accumulators built inside the accounting machine itself.)

4. A limited number of repetitive instructions can be stored in punched cards, in paper tape, or stored in the electronic memory.

5. Unit forms such as ledger records are inserted and removed by the operator.

6. The operator maintains primary control over all machine operations, even though fixed, repetitive instructions may be stored internally in the machine.

7. *There are several ways to input information into the working memory of the machine:*

- Keyboard entry by operator.
- Paper tape read at an input "read" station.
- Punched card reader attached to the machine.
- Small disk drive.
- Magnetic striped ledger card.

8. *There are several types of stored output:*

- Printed forms or journals.
- Updated data carried in magnetic striped ledger card.
- Paper tape.
- Card punch attached to the machine.
- Small disk drive.

Desk Computers Represent Major Improvements

Today's desk computers represent many major improvements over ordinary accounting machines, or the electric typewriter billing machines in use in recent years, such as:

- *Rapid Arithmetic Operations:* Desk computers add and subtract and perform electronic multiplication and division at speeds expressed in "milliseconds." (A millisecond is 1/1000 of a second.)
- *Multiple Accumulators:* Because of the compactness of the electronic memory units built into the desk which stores numeric data in a binary coded decimal (BCD) format, some models of today's desk computers can store and accumulate up to 400 individual 10 or 12 digit totals.

This makes it possible to store control totals and develop extensive analysis figures as a by-product of an accounting or data-handling application.

- *Stored Instructions:* A pre-programmed set of instructions can now be stored in the machine's memory to operate the machine as automatically as possible, leaving the operator with the primary responsibility of handling the forms and entering variable data as the program calls for it.
- *Automatic Input/Output:* Desk computers may be equipped to *automatically read in* data stored in prepunched paper tapes, punched cards or edge-punched cards.

Furthermore, after the electronic computer component develops the updated balance or other data useful for later processing, it can be programmed to punch IBM cards or paper tape as *output*.

Another method of acceptable input or output is the use of ledger cards with magnetic stripes for data storage. This method of data storage is explained in considerable detail later (see Figure 16-3).

- *Logic Decisions:* Desk computers are able to make decisions to a limited extent. In common with their big brothers, the full-scale electronic computers, they are able to compare one set of data to another, then follow a chain of instructions based on the result of the comparison. The most common decision-making technique is based on a comparison of two specified data fields, which must be of the same length. To see how this works, examine the following table:

Contents of Data Field "A"	Contents of Data Field "B"	Result of Comparing "A" With "B"
$5,450	$6,600	Less Than
6,600	6,600	Equal To
6,601	6,600	Greater Than
6,602	6,600	Greater Than

These tests are based on a payroll job where the maximum amount of gross earnings taxable for FICA deductions is stored in the computer's memory as data field "B". The machine tests the year-to-date gross earnings for each employee (data field "A") against the stored maximum amount—and *makes a decision* about calculating and deducting FICA tax as a result of the comparison.

- *Printing Capability:* The printing mechanisms found in today's desk computers compared to predecessor models of accounting or billing machines have not changed very much. In fact, this is the weakest aspect of otherwise-capable equipment. Printing speeds have not been increased very much. However, Burroughs and National Cash Register now offer separate line printers as optional, auxiliary equipment with their top line of desk computers. This is definitely a step in the right direction to overcome this output bottleneck.

One major improvement is that a great deal of the typing and numeric printing is now done automatically, by means of codes read into memory from the various types of input devices.

METHODS OF STORING DATA

It is essential and fundamental for any systems designer to possess a thorough knowledge of methods for storing data in general, including the methods that full-scale computers utilize to store coded alphabetic and numeric data. Let's now explore each prime method of data storage, so that the systems-designer will know how and when to use each method to best advantage.

1. *Ledger Cards:* Ordinary posted ledger cards are one of the oldest and best-known methods for storing data. The characteristics of this type of data storage are:
- Information is stored in visible, printed form.
- Any interested person can refer at random to any ledger card.
- Does not provide a common language for communication with machines.
- Cannot automatically transfer information to other records or be read by data processing machines, other than photographic equipment.

2. *Ledger Card with Magnetic Stripes:* Several manufacturers of office equipment have released accounting machines, and desk computers which use magnetic tape data storage—in the form of narrow stripes on the back of the ledger card. (See Figure 16-3.)

The characteristics of this unique combination are:
- Provides visible printed information storage.
- Has random access capabilities.
- Stores customer name and address for automatic reading and typing.
- Stores account balances; automatically introduces the prior balances into the electronic memory unit for subsequent posting or processing.
- Provides for automatic alignment of ledger card for the next posting.

- Ledgers may be automatically passed through a Ledger Processor Unit which reads the data stored in the magnetic stripe; the data can then be printed or accumulated for trial balance purposes.

3. *IBM Punched Cards:* Punched cards have been in wide use for many decades. The characteristics and usage of punched cards are:

- Used primarily for bringing information into a data processing system, since the punched holes are machine-readable codes. Each card is limited to 80 coded characters of information.
- Unit cards sometimes represent a complete record, such as an accounts receivable invoice, or an inventory record.
- Punched cards are also used as output, for storing data to be used in subsequent machine processing.
- Can be interpreted across the top for easy, visual reading of coded information.
- Provides a form of random access, since one or more cards can be physically removed from a deck, changed and replaced—or referenced for visual information.

4. *Punched Paper Tape:* Paper tape came into use before the turn of the century. However, it was not used for data processing or data storage until the last 15 or 20 years. Its characteristics include:

- Used for input and output.
- Records can be of almost unlimited length.
- Provides no random access.
- Not convenient to store or handle.
- Unlike other input carriers, paper tape is awkward to fold, store or thread into reading heads.
- Most machine operators find it difficult to read and interpret the coded data punched into the tape.

5. *Edge-Punched Cards:* An edge-punched card is a unit record with coded data punched on one edge. The codes are usually identical to those found in paper tape. Characteristics:

- Not limited to 80 characters; the only limitation is the heighth of the record on the punching side.
- Combines coded, punched data in a card which may also contain posted or printed information for visual reference.
- Used primarily as input for billing machines.
- Size of the card varies according to the requirements of each application.

6. *Unit Card (Punched Card Size) with Full Surface Magnetic Coating:* The Monrobot Desk Computer, manufactured by Monroe International, Inc., features a unique data storage device—a card identical in size with the conventional punched card, but is not punched. It is fully coated on one side with a magnetic coating capable of storing information in coded format. Characteristics of the Data Storage Device are:

- A unit record.
- Stores up to 400 characters of data per card.
- Provides random access in that each record is available for individual selection.
- Used for data storage, primarily for input.
- Data stored on the coated surface is in the format of a common language; the information can be read into the memory of the desk computer, then put outside in a form acceptable to other machines.

7. *Registers or Accumulators:* One type of data storage is taken for granted; accumulating

NAME					ACCT. NO.		
ADDRESS					CREDIT RATING	CREDIT LIMIT	
DATE	FOLIO	DEBITS	✓	✓	CREDITS	BALANCE	
BALANCE BROUGHT FORWARD ⟶							

Figure 16-3
LEDGER CARD WITH MAGNETIC STRIPES

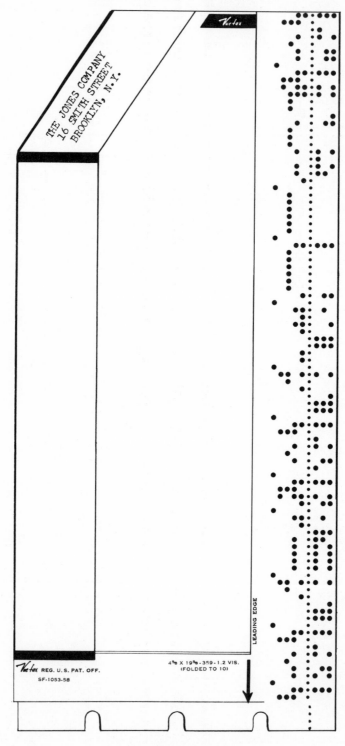

Figure 16-4
AN EDGE-PUNCHED CARD

quantity or dollar totals in mechanical or electronic counters or accumulators is a form of data storage. As mentioned before, some of the desk computers provide from 12 to 400 totals.

Other Methods of Data Storage

To complete this review of data storage devices and methods, let's cover two methods commonly found in connection with full-scale computers, but seldom used in conjunction with small desk computers.

1. *Magnetic Tape:* The standard reel of magnetic tape now widely used is ½" wide and 2,400 feet in length. The number of characters which can be stored in coded form per inch of tape varies from 200 per inch to 1600. Until recently, the standard packing of characters per inch was 556; recent developments in this field have increased the density to as much as 1600 per inch.

The speed of reading or writing information contained on magnetic tape is difficult to comprehend when the tape serves as input or output for a regular, full-scale electronic computer. Typical speeds range from 15,000 characters *per second* to 80,000 per second, or more.

Some of the more important characteristics of magnetic tape are:

- Used for storing large volumes of coded data.
- Serves as both input and output—for bringing stored data into the memory of a computer for processing and updating, and for storing information on the outside of the computer for subsequent use.
- Non-visible storage of information.
- No random access capabilities.
- Tape reels can be used repeatedly over a long period of time.
- Features strictly sequential storage of data or records.

2. *Random Access Disk Records*:

The first disk records for storage of information which could be retrieved upon call, or at random, resembled phonograph records. The cylindrical disks in use today are coated on both sides with a magnetic surface, similar to that used on the mylar tape which is the basis for reels of magnetic tape. One or more mechanical and electronic arms are positioned so that the read/write head (or heads) can access any part of the cylinder surface to "read" data into the computer—or "write" information from the computer to the coated surface.

The major characteristics of this type of auxiliary computer equipment are:

- Each cylinder surface is divided precisely into a certain number of tracks.
- Several thousand characters of numeric data or alphabetic information can be stored on each track.
- Each track is numbered, which is part of the address given to the machine when it is desired to find a particular record on the track.
- Features *direct access* to any desired record or records, without reading and passing other, unwanted records through the computer before accessing the desired record—as is necessary with magnetic tape files.
- Disk records are used interchangeably for both input and output.
- The disks for the IBM random access device are removable; this provides the ability to store large volumes of records "off-line"; that is, they are not connected with the computer until the job is ready to run again, at which time the disk packs are mounted on a hardware unit called the "disk drive."

Random access devices currently available are designed for use in conjunction with full-scale electronic computers, and are illustrated in the chapters dealing with such computers. However, it is quite probable that this data storage concept will soon be introduced as auxiliary equipment for the line of desk computers by one or more manufacturers of such equipment.

HOW DATA IS STORED IN CODED FORM

Today's designers of systems necessarily learn to work with punched cards and paper tape, since the general trend is increasingly toward office mechanization. Furthermore, as the cost of full-scale computers continues to decrease, more and more medium-sized firms are installing them. At the same time, many of the smaller firms are installing desk computers or equivalent equipment at an increasing rate.

Now, as you have seen in this chapter, the desk computers make full use of various means of automatic input of stored data, especially from paper tape, edge-punched cards and regular punched cards. Because of these developments, now is the time for the practitioner who engages in systems work to learn how to read coded data, and to learn how to work with these various inputs.

Paper tape was in existence for many decades before the electronic computer was invented. The "ticker tape," often seen inside a glass bowl in photographs of a typical stockbroker's office around the turn of the century, was a 5-channel paper tape. The 8-channel tape was developed in recent years to provide for a wider range of characters and internal checking of punched data.

5-Channel Paper Tape

As Figure 16-5 shows, the 5 channels or rows of holes provide for various combinations of punches which represent letters of the alphabet, numeric digits 0 through 9 and special functional characters.

Note that the representation of numeric data follows no pattern. The numeric value of 1 consists of a punch in channel 1 plus a punch in channels 2 and 5. An 8 is represented by punches in channels 2 and 3. Punches in channels 4 and 5 represents the value of 9, etc.

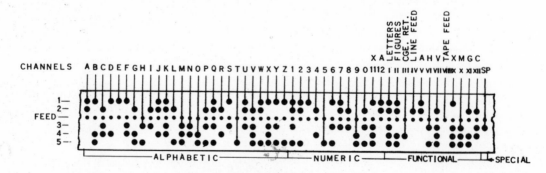

Figure 16-5
5-CHANNEL PAPER TAPE CODES

8-Channel Paper Tape

Numeric values in 8-channel tape follow a consistent pattern based on the binary coded decimal system used to store coded data in many electronic computers. (See Figure 16-6.)

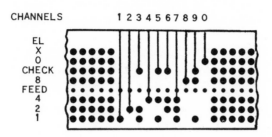

Figure 16-6 (Part 1)
HOW 8-CHANNEL PAPER TAPE REPRESENTS *NUMERIC* VALUES

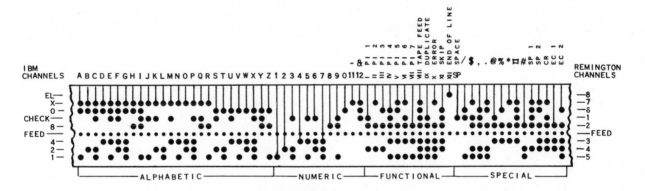

Figure 16-6 (Part 2)
8-CHANNEL PAPER TAPE PROVIDES FOR FOUR TYPES OF CODES:
ALPHABETIC, NUMERIC, FUNCTIONAL AND SPECIAL

Note that the four horizontal channels at the bottom of the tape have been assigned arbitrary values of 1-2-4-8. (The feed holes have no significance. These small holes are for the sprocket wheel which moves the tape.)

Note that the numeral 5 consists of punches which have values of 4 plus 1. Numeral 7 consists of punches which represent values of 4, 2 and 1, etc.

Chapter 26, the first of three chapters in the last part of this book which are devoted to full-scale, electronic computers, explains and illustrates how data is stored in "BCD" format. You will find that the code pattern in 8-channel paper tape is very similar to the computer BCD code.

Parity Check: The row of "check" holes requires explanation. The punches in the parity channel provide a method of checking on the metal punching device; this method is known as a "parity check." The equipment is geared to punch always an odd (or even) set of holes in each frame. For example, the tape in the illustration is odd-parity. If a punch die fails to work and the device punches an even number of holes, this sets up a warning signal in the subsequent tape reading operation.

Overpunches: The channels designated as "X" and "O" represent overpunches to represent letters of the alphabet and special characters.

Punched Cards

Nearly everyone in the systems field is familiar with IBM punched cards. The card shown in Figure 16-7 rounds out the illustration of how data is stored in coded form.

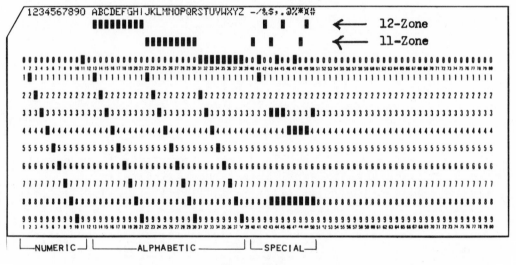

Figure 16-7

A REGULAR IBM PUNCHED CARD ILLUSTRATES THE USE OF OVERPUNCHES TO REPRESENT ALPHABETIC AND SPECIAL CHARACTERS

Note that the letters of the alphabet are represented by two sets of punches in the same card column: a regular numeric punch plus an "overpunch" found in the upper area of the card. The top area is known as the "12-zone" and the next lower area is the "11-zone" where "x-punches" appear.

Here is how these two zones, plus the zero row, are used to represent the letters of the alphabet:

Letters	Numeric Punches		Zone Punch
A–I	1–9	plus	12
J–R	1–9	plus	11
S–Z	2–9	plus	0

For example, the letter "A" is represented by a numeric 1 punch plus a 12-zone punch directly above it. The letter "I" consists of a 9 punch and the 12-zone punch, etc.

PROGRAMMED INSTRUCTIONS AND CONTROLS

Various methods have been employed over the years to store "instructions" for office equipment in order to assist the operator, wherever possible, in automatic operations and controls. The simplest version of machine controls is exemplified by the mechanical control bar found on the early posting machines.

This type of machine was usually set up for posting debits and credits in two different columns, and to accumulate one or more totals in "registers"—if the posting machine was equipped with mechanical counters or accumulators.

The mechanical control bar was equipped with special control arms which controlled the arithmetic functions of the machine as it moved from one carriage position to the next during the posting operation.

Other methods used to instruct or control office machines are:
1. Wired plugboards which provide electrical control over tabulating equipment.
2. Punched cards with coded instructions that are fed into the electronic memory of the machine before the job begins to instruct the computer in each operation, step by step.

(The concept of internally-stored instructions came into being with the advent of large-scale, electronic computers. This same concept has been introduced into various models of desk computers.)

3. Paper tape which contains punched instructions.

The paper tape may be read and the instructions stored for subsequent operations, or the paper tape may continue to "cycle" through the machine on those machines which do not feature extensive storage of instructions.

4. For full-scale computers, instructions are frequently stored on magnetic tape reels, referred to as the "library tape," or on disk drives. When the computer operator is ready to begin a particular job, he calls for the instructions for that job by number. The computer searches for the corresponding list of instructions, then reads them into the memory of the machine, ready to begin operations.

Significance of Program Controls

The primary point for the systems analyst to remember is that the method of storing instructions for the machine is significant in relation to the amount of *time required to change from one job to another*. Let's discuss this aspect of office equipment in more detail.

Before the advent of desk computers, the various makes of accounting machines were controlled by mechanical control bars. If a machine was set up for several major applications, an important feature to check on, when evaluating and selecting equipment for a client, was the ease of changing from one job application to the next. And, a machine demonstration in a sales showroom was sometimes misleading, because the equipment was preset before the prospects arrived. The knowledgeable practitioner would insist on seeing exactly what had to be done for a job changeover. The changeover procedures might consist of removing one or two control bars, finding and inserting replacement bars. Or, the procedure might be to turn a knob and change the forms guides.

	Old Bal.	Date	Ref. No.	Debit	Credit	New Bal.	2nd Old Bal.	PROOF
Crossfooter →	ADD		NA	ADD	SUBTRACT	SUB-TOTAL	SUBTRACT	TOTAL
Registers →	NA		NA	ADD 1	ADD 2	NA	NA	ADD 3

Figure 16-8

HOW THE POSTING MACHINE CONTROL BAR CONTROLLED ADDITION, SUBTRACTION
AND OTHER FUNCTIONS

Stored Instructions Versus External Storage

Control bars, plugboards and paper tape loops, cycling through a machine, all represent forms of externally-stored machine instructions and controls. By contrast, internally-stored instructions are those which are read into the electronic memory of a computer and stored for use during the machine operating run.

The fastest method of changing from one job to another is accomplished by stored instructions. Punched cards or paper tape containing the coded instructions are simply read into memory one time at high speed before starting a run; this erases prior instructions for the job just completed.

It is preferable to maintain instructions in punched cards because of the ease in making changes. With card decks the programmer can locate the card that contains the instruction to be deleted or changed, keypunch a new card or cards, and then manually insert the card or cards into the appropriate position in the deck.

Summary

Today's electronic office equipment is becoming increasingly automated, with several methods for data input and several types of output in machine-readable format. The small desk computers now resemble full scale computers by featuring solid state components, arithmetic and logic functions operating at millisecond speeds, and internally stored programs. A recently released machine by Friden, Inc. even specifies English-language programming. Its electronic memory is large enough to store a translator which interprets up to 38 English commands, and converts them to the equivalent machine language codes.

Any practitioner or analyst who learns to work with the broad line of office machines now available is actually qualifying himself for eventual entry into systems work on full scale computers—because of the many common features, especially the input and output devices To illustrate the point, at least two nationally known business machine companies have now released desk computers which feature full size central processors to operate the full capacity line printers and other auxiliary devices. This release exemplifies the trend of the small equipment configurations moving toward many of the capabilities of the larger computers.

17

Selection, Application and Installation of Office Equipment

EQUIPMENT SELECTION

The central purpose of this chapter is to offer guidelines on the selection, application and installation of office equipment. The management services practitioner or systems analyst is faced with a perplexing task in this endeavor because of the broad range of new equipment that has been developed by the office equipment manufacturers and released in recent years.

Until then, there were only two distinct types of office machines available to users. In the first category were mechanical billing and accounting machines. Unit record or tabulating equipment (utilizing punched cards for information processing) represented the second category.

Since the advent of computers, office machines increasingly reflect a "cross-breeding" of features and capabilities; that is, certain features have been transplanted from full-scale electronic computers to today's desk computers and electronic billing machines. Further, the input/output equipment initially designed for tabulating machines and computers has now been developed, in modified or original form, for use with the small desk computers.

Machine Productivity

Regardless of the many and varied claims for each make and model of office equipment being studied for application to a job, the primary gauge of the efficiency of office machines is the actual output of work per hour, expressed in meaningful units of production, such as:

- Number of completed checks per hour (payroll job).
- Number of entries posted per hour (accounts receivable or accounts payable).
- Number of invoices and the number of lines of billing per hour.
- Number of vendor checks per hour (accounts payable disbursements).

Factors Involved in Productivity

Many interrelated features and other factors govern or influence work output of office equipment in general, and desk computers in particular:
- "Overlapped" (multiple and concurrent) machine operations.
- Speed of carriage movement.
- Single-stroke printing versus "gang" or line-printing.
- Internal operating speed (executing programmed instructions).
- Construction of machine carriage (front-feed versus rear-feed) and related forms handling requirements.
- Availability of sufficient accumulators.
- Accessibility of forms to be inserted into the machine, plus forms housing equipment and forms handling.
- Automatic alignment of inserted forms versus manual alignment.
- Manual indexing of old balances versus automatic reading of old balances as the form enters the machine carriage.
- Error correction procedures.
- Skill and experience of system designer.
- Operator training, supervision and motivation factors.
- Quality of programming.
- Time required for job changes.

Overlapped Machine Operations

When the design of a machine permits or enables simultaneous operations or functions, productivity will be increased. For example, if the machine operator who is posting entries to ledger records is able to index the figures on the machine keyboard even though the machine is still printing one or more automatically-calculated balances, the overall posting work will be accomplished more rapidly.

When evaluating electronic office equipment, look for features such as reading in a punched card (or paper tape) at the same time the carriage is tabulating from one position to another. Also, if the machine can print or type while calculating and storing results internally, this feature obviously will increase work output per hour.

Achieving overlapped machine operations is frequently accomplished by special effort on the part of the systems designer, backed up by the skill and experience of the programmer. In summary, the ability to achieve overlapped machine operations is not necessarily a built-in mechanical or electronic feature; it may represent a combination of several things.

Printing Mechanisms

For several years the primary limitation of accounting machines, billing equipment and desk computers has been the relative slowness of the printing mechanism. When the first models of electronic desk computers were released, the printing speed was actually slower than that on a comparable mechanical accounting machine because of certain necessary internal operations and interlocks.

Only in recent years has this bottleneck been broken in two ways. First, the manufacturers have continued to increase the speed of all internal operations until arithmetic calculations and the execution of programmed instructions stored internally no longer slow down the speed of the printing device. Secondly, two manufacturers have now released specially-designed "line printers" as separate hardware units. These printers are able to print up to 132 characters on a single line (13.2 in. of printing spread across a page) at one time. Since the rated speed of these line printers is very respectable, the manufacturers of desk computers have, in effect, now brought some of the printing capability of full-scale computers to the small business firm.

When evaluating desk computers or similar equipment, the systems analyst or practitioner should note that there is a basic difference in the printing mechanisms built into the two types of desk computers discussed earlier. Type I, built around an electric typewriter, writes numeric data or alphabetic information one stroke at a time, including essential punctuation. Type II, built around an accounting machine, prints an account balance or a calculated product or quotient at one stroke. The type hammers are lined up in a row, and are able to print together, including punctuation, as a group. This is known as "gang" printing.

The printing speed of the typewriter devices, which depend on one type hammer at a time striking the paper, is constantly being increased. As a result, the machine equipped with gang printers may not be faster than the single-stroke typewriter device. One guideline in selecting the right machine for a job is to analyze the quantity and type of printed data required by the forms and reports to be produced on the machine. If the major applications are accounting-oriented and feature a substantial volume of the printing of subtotals, balances or other calculated results, the machine built around an accounting machine will probably produce the work faster than a typewriter-based machine. However, if the printing is predominantly alphabetic, with relatively little accounting data to be printed, a Type I machine may prove to be the most efficient unit for the job.

Speed of Carriage Movement

The speed with which the carriage moves is a factor in work output—on those machines which feature a moving carriage. If the carriage movement tends to restrict the work of the operator, then the output potential will obviously be reduced. Carriage movement may be greatly influenced by the speed (or lack of it) with which the machine executes internal instructions.

Internal Speeds

Until the advent of electronic arithmetic components, now an integral feature of billing machines and desk computers, multiplication was slow enough to visibly restrict or hold back the output of billing and accounting machines. Most desk computers now feature electronic addition, subtraction and multiplication; these functions are performed at impressive speeds, expressed in milliseconds.

All arithmetic functions performed by this type of equipment are based on electronic addition. Subtraction is performed by adding complementary figures; multiplication is repeated addition. Division is performed by repeated subtraction. This basic fact emphasizes the importance of high internal speeds; otherwise, multiplication or division would inevitably inhibit work output.

Programming

"Programming" refers to the act of writing the necessary instructions for the machine so that the desired results will be obtained, step by step, during the machine operation. An instruction consists of special codes or symbols, plus numeric and/or alphabetic characters, which represent a meaningful "instruction" to the machine.

Programming first came to the attention of the business world and the general public in connection with the advent of full scale electronic computers in the early 1960's. Publicity relating to this glamorous new equipment frequently mentioned the necessity for instructing the machine what to do, one step at a time; as a result the word "programmer" came into prominence.

Actually, programming office machines is not new. Even the first primitive posting machines (circa 1914) required programming in the sense that a mechanical control bar controlled certain functions of the machine as it moved from one carriage position to another during a posting operation.

When the automating of factories began in the 1950's users of the first automated machine tools found it necessary to plan each machine operation in great detail, then to program the machine to produce the desired results.

When punched-card equipment represented the latest developments in data-processing equipment, the word "programming" was seldom heard. Possibly the reason was that this equipment operated from electrical impulses transmitted through hubs in wired plugboards. Trained people in tab installations learned to wire the plugboards for each job, and never considered themselves as programmers.

Today's desk computers must be programmed; the instructions are stored internally in the same way that programs are stored in large, full-scale computers. In one respect programming a desk computer is more difficult than a full-scale computer because of the limited number of instructions which can be placed in the electronic memory of the machine. Also, the printing in each carriage position is controlled by a separate, mechanical program built into the basic unit itself.

Skill and Experience of Systems Designer

Machine output is not solely determined by basic characteristics, or special features built into the equipment. The overall machine set up, application design and machine programming exert considerable influence on productivity and output. One outstanding example of this fact is explained in considerable detail in the section of this chapter devoted to machine applications, wherein the feasibility of combining two or more jobs for one machine operation is questioned.

The systems designer should exercise great care when developing the system and procedures, if the objective is to obtain maximum output at lowest dollar cost. A specific example centers on form design: Suppose that a typical posting operation involves typing a name on a register which remains around the platen of an accounting machine throughout the journalizing or check-writing operation. Unless the systems designer has done his forms-design job well, it may be necessary to move the carriage into a special typing position in order to type the name on each line. On the other hand the systems designer may design the form in such a way that the typing is integrated smoothly into the machine operation with no loss of time.

Another example of form design is to set up a job in such a way that the machine operator can complete all entries into the machine before certain automatic functions begin. This makes it possible for the operator to pay attention to media for the next entry—while the machine is still making calculations, printing one or more balances, and returning the carriage for the next printing line.

By definition the systems design phase of a systems project is very important, because it is the veritable foundation for all programming work which follows. The programmer must implement the operation as designed by the systems analyst.

Forms Handling, Housing and Accessibility of Input Forms

Forms handling is a major consideration in estimating machine productivity whenever the application requires the selection, insertion and alignment of individual forms or records into the machine. (Note: One primary difference between desk computers and full-scale computers is that the former requires *intermittent operator intervention* and input as a job is being done. Full-scale computers operate from stored instructions, and print reports or lists of updated records on continuous forms which feed through the printer automatically and without the operator's attention.)

One very popular machine application—posting sales invoices to a customer ledger—will serve as an example to illustrate the point that the time required for forms handling may exceed the machine operating time very easily. Normal work standards in units of time required for posting invoice amounts to a ledger sheet on an ordinary front-feed accounting machine and for proving each posting are:

Locate, insert and align the form for posting—then return it to its position in the ledger tray		10 seconds	
Index and print the old balance	2 seconds		
Index and print invoice reference number ..	2 seconds		
Index and print the amount	2 seconds		
Automatic printing of new balance	1 second		
Prove the posting	3 seconds		
	10 seconds	10 seconds	
Total time for one posting entry		20 seconds	

The forms handling time shown above is 10 seconds for locating, inserting and aligning the form in the machine carriage, ready for the posting line. It also includes the time required to remove the form from the machine after the posting operation is completed and to return it to its position in the ledger binder or tray.

The time shown here may not be achieved in actual practice if the account activity rate is too low, or if the account ledgers are not properly indexed. A low activity rate requires a random search for each ledger card; this is a typical condition in commercial receivables if invoices are posted daily. Seldom will the sales activity for one day affect more than 10% of the total number of active customer accounts. By direct contrast, a daily posting run in a commercial bank where operators post checks and deposits to depositor's accounts may affect as many as 40% of the total number of accounts. The rule is that the speed of forms location increases as the percentage of active accounts increases since little additional time is required for forms location and handling.

Two Solutions for Low Activity

If an application features low activity, there are two ways to save operator time in locating forms:

- Match invoices to customer ledgers, remove the ledgers and route them to the machine operator, along with the media to be posted.
- Insert sufficient indexes in the trays or binders to divide the ledgers into small groups. Normal indexing may average 40/1, but indexing intended to speed random selection and return should provide one index sheet per 20 ledgers. "Heavy" indexing set up for jobs which require the utmost speed of forms location may feature one index sheet for each group of only 10 ledgers or records. (Example: Window posting of savings account ledgers in the savings department of a bank.)

Machine Carriages and Forms Handling

There are two basic types of machine carriages—"front-feed" and "rear-feed." This refers to the location of the unit form inserted relative to the rubber platen or cylinder against which the type bars strike when printing on the form in the carriage.

An ordinary typewriter has a rear-feed carriage; the typist must insert the sheet of paper or a form behind the platen, and roll it forward into typing position. By contrast, most accounting machines feature the front-feed carriage, which opens to receive the form which is inserted *in front of* the rubber platen or cylinder.

Even if several different machines under evaluation all have front-feed carriages, it is essential to examine the method of forms alignment and controls. Evaluate the ease of changing the rear-form guides. Look for features such as an automatic stop which limits or positions a form for the first printing line. All of these or similar features have an effect on operator productivity.

Automatic Forms Alignment

Any device which features automatic alignment of forms inserted into the machine carriage will increase output. If the operator is required to align a ledger (or a ledger and statement) manually, a significant amount of time is required for this preliminary step. One aligning device simply punches a small hole in the paper form as an entry is posted on the face of the form; this serves as a signal to the machine for aligning the form for any subsequent posting.

Magnetic stripes, bonded to ledger records or similar forms, provide for storing the posting line number electronically each time information is posted to the face of the record. When the form is inserted into the carriage of the desk computer for another posting, the machine automatically reads the data in the stripe, then advances the form instantly to the appropriate posting line. In addition, the old balance or several balances stored in the same stripe are brought into the electronic memory of the machine, ready for updating, with no effort on the part of the operator.

When the first machines with these unique features were released in 1955, the potential efficiency and posting speed were under-estimated. Actual installations quickly proved the value of automatic alignment and automatic indexing of prior balances; some firms found that capable operators could average five or six postings per minute, as compared to the usual two-and-one-half or three postings per minute on conventional accounting or posting machines.

Availability of Sufficient Accumulators

If a machine cannot accumulate all the desired totals as a by-product of the basic machine operation, considerable time may be lost through the additional handling of paper and recapping of amounts. Because of this, the systems analyst should make sure that the machine under consideration has the capability of accumulating and storing all essential control totals or desired breakdown totals. If the desired breakdowns require several hundred classifications and separate corresponding totals, it may be necessary to punch out distribution cards as a by-product of the basic machine operation. These cards are subsequently sorted and tabulated to obtain the desired expense totals, sales analysis breakdowns, or similar types of analysis figures.

Error Correction Procedures

Error correction procedures deserve close study and attention in evaluating equipment. Some machines of the type under discussion in this chapter include special features for error correction. Remember that the difficulty of error correction tends to increase in proportion to the number of automatic operations and functions performed by the accounting or billing machine or desk computer.

Operator Training, Supervision and Motivation

Machine output, where operator intervention is required, is dependent to a large extent on the operator's ability and desire to work. The operator should be thoroughly trained on the machine, and on each application that he is required to handle.

It is well known that supervision and motivation are important elements in personnel productivity and performance. If supervision is lax and there is no real incentive to work hard, the average machine operator will relax and adjust his output to that of the slowest operator in the group.

One element of motivation which costs little is recognition. This merely requires that accurate records of work output be kept for each person or machine operator. When clerical personnel or operators realize that their output is a matter of daily record, they tend to speed up and handle more work. If the supervisors then use this information for complimenting the good producers on a job well done—or use it as a basis for making recommendations for salary increases—it serves the purpose of motivating each person to do more work on a consistent basis.

Time Required for Job Changes

Special attention should be devoted to the time that's required for changing a machine from one job to another. One prominent manufacturer of office machines released a desk billing machine a few years ago which had great potential for billing and for related applications. However, installation experience revealed that considerable time was required to change the machine from one job to another. Equipment designed for multiple applications usually includes special features which facilitate changing from one application to another in a minimum of time.

APPLICATION GUIDELINES

Many different factors are usually involved in a successful installation of a desk computer. The known capabilities and basic features of the equipment are not the only criteria to be considered. Of equal or even greater importance is the easy accessibility to ledger records, edge-punched product description cards or other forms that have to be located, selected and inserted into the machine, as required. Physical housing of the records and how they are indexed may be of great significance from the standpoint of operator production. Even the type of chair in which the operator sits and the physical features of his work station are important.

There is a tendency on the part of equipment salesmen and systems designers to overload desk computers and billing machines. Often this is the user's fault, in that he may expect or demand too much from the equipment. For example, a desk computer may be able to handle a firm's billing work with no problem. However, if the receivables are to be posted at the same time, the posting process will slow down the billing operation. If the application also calls for updating individual inventory records at the same time, billing production may drop to a very low level.

Some office-equipment brochures feature "Automated Billing and Inventory Control." Others go even further to feature billing, and posting accounts receivable and inventory records as one continuous operation. Such brochures indicate that such a combination of jobs is logical and feasible. However, let's examine a few of the major problems involved in making such combination applications work satisfactorily.

Combined Billing and Inventory Control

Each product line on an invoice represents an issue from inventory—unless the firm makes some shipments directly from the factory. When inventory updating is combined with billing, the operation requires that all of the inventory records be *accessible* to the operator for a random search as the billing progresses. (The active inventory records cannot be pre-pulled since the same product may appear on several different invoices.)

Accessibility of records is just one of many important considerations involved in this combination application. Other pertinent questions which require carefully-developed answers might be:
- How many inventory ledgers are there in total?
- How many ledger trays or other housing units are required to store the inventory records? (If records are kept in ledger trays or binders, use the rule of thumb that a tray which provides easy access to each and every record in the tray should be no more than 20 in. to 22 in. in length, and will contain from 1,200 to 1,400 ledger records, including a reasonable density of indexes.)
- Can the total number of trays be made available to the operator in such a way that she can find and reach any one ledger record as it is required by a line on the invoice?
- Does the billing volume require more than one operator? If so, how will the operators obtain access at random to one set of inventory ledgers?
- If the records are within convenient reach as a group, does the indexing in the trays make it easy to find the specific record without undue lost time?

Even if the answers to the above questions indicate that combining inventory posting with billing is practical, it is possible that analysis of the inventory activity will point to a more efficient method, such as inventory updating as a separate, independent posting operation. Optional methods are detailed in a subsequent section of this chapter.

The 80-20 Story

Sales analysis figures representing a broad range of types and kinds of businesses show that frequently 80% or more of all sales are generated from relatively few products which, in number, may represent *20% or less* of the total number of different products sold.

If 80% of the inventory activity centers on a few products, the constant locating, inserting, posting and replacing of the same ledger records (or punched cards representing inventory) repeatedly, as the billing is done, may represent a considerable waste of the operator's time.

Posting Accounts Receivable with Invoicing

Brochures which recommend combining billing, inventory posting AND accounts receivable seldom mention what is to be gained from this optimum combining of related functions. One obvious benefit is that it eliminates a later listing of the invoice amounts—a step that's required if invoices are posted to receivables after the billing is completed. Now, since the time allowed by office work standards for listing a five-digit amount on an adding machine is only two seconds, no substantial case can be established for posting receivables as a by-product of the billing function.

However, utilizing the accounts receivable ledger to "head up" (type) the invoice with the correct customer name and address is a benefit worth considering. Ledgers which have magnetic stripes on the back of them may store the full customer name, address and *account number* in the stripe. When the ledger is inserted into the carriage adjacent to the invoice about to be prepared, the desk computer reads the pulses in the magnetic stripe, and automatically types the name and address on the invoice. Bringing the correct customer account number (stored in the stripe) into play is also a significant feature—if paper tape or punched cards are punched as output from the billing operation—for sales analysis purposes.

To determine the feasibility of combining receivables posting with billing, or with billing and inventory updating, the systems designer must determine the number of ledgers to be housed within convenient reach of the operator. If the number of receivables ledgers, when added to the inventory ledgers, increases the total number of ledger records to the point that it is not practical to place all of the ledgers within easy reach, consider the technique of pre-pulling a customer ledger to match each customer order.

There are other valid considerations which may lead to the overall conclusion that the benefits of combining receivables posting with billing do not outweigh the disadvantages:

- The machine must be equipped with a carriage sufficiently wide enough to accommodate the insertion of an invoice on one side and the accounts receivable ledger on the other side.
- Since the customer ledgers must be made available to the billing operator, they are unavailable for long periods of time to the remittance application clerks who apply and key-off cash. They are also unavailable during the time of billing for preparation of open-item, past due statements, and for posting cash credits or for trial-balance purposes.
- If the firm has more than one billing clerk, the receivables ledgers would have to be pre-pulled and distributed to the clerk, who would bill the corresponding order.
- Accounts receivable ledgers will not be readily available to credit men for checking credit on orders received.

(Some of the points listed above, such as applying cash by keying off paid items, apply to trade receivables which feature invoice terms, rather than to retail or consumer receivables. It is interesting to note that the brochures which picture receivables records and methods always show *retail* receivables and methods. Since there is little similarity between the required procedures for retail receivables as compared to trade receivables, the practitioner or systems analyst must develop his system very carefully if the client has trade receivables.)

Analyze and Evaluate Optional Methods

A practical and flexible method for updating inventory records as a separate operation is to produce punched cards as output during the billing operation. Program the billing machine to punch one card for each invoice line, including sales taxes, freight or parcel post, and one card for the invoice total.

Interpret the cards for visual readability, then sort them on a mechanical sorter into stock or part number sequence. All transactions for the day can be posted to each inventory ledger in several different ways:

- If inventory records are kept on ledger cards with magnetic stripes, the punched cards can be quickly sorted and utilized as input for updating the ledger balances.
- If inventory records are in the form of punched cards, the cards representing sales issues are used as input, and new inventory balance cards are punched as output and filed.

One benefit of planning optional methods is that, even if the combination of billing and inventory updating is put into practice at first, a substantial increase in volume may make it mandatory to revert to separate updating of inventory records at some time in the future.

Benefits of the Combined Applications Approach

The trained systems analyst learns to look on both sides of the coin when analyzing jobs and making decisions as to methods and procedures. In this instance, he recognizes that insertion of the inventory ledger for each product line on the order provides one major benefit; the part number and description is automatically read and typed on the invoice from the invisible data carried in the magnetic stripe on the back of the ledger record. This insures accuracy—if the operator selects and inserts the correct ledger sheet.

Use of Memo Description Files

Many firms set up one or more files of *product description cards* which have no connection with inventory control. These cards are filed in product number sequence and typically contain the following pre-punched or coded data:

- Manufacturer's catalogue number
- Product class (as determined for sales analysis purposes)
- Stock or part number
- Full product description for billing
- Warehouse location code

Sometimes these cards also include a standard unit cost and the latest unit selling price.

The cards described above are normally either edge-punched cards with paper tape codes punched along one edge, or regular IBM punched cards.

Use of coded description cards that have no connection with inventory records provide considerable flexibility. For example, if a supply of cards is prepared and placed in the trays or tubs, order clerks can pull a description card for each item on an order. This method of operation speeds billing since the machine operator is not required to find, insert and post matching inventory records for each order line.

This approach also solves the problem of a multiple-machine billing operation where the volume makes this essential. Since the description cards represent memo records, the trays or tubs may contain a supply of *duplicate cards* for those items which are so active that several machine operators need the description card for the same item at the same time. This, of course, is not possible if the input record is the actual inventory record.

Hold Investment to a Minimum

The suggested systems approach described above requires pre-pulling of description cards by order clerks. This illustrates a principle for the systems analyst to consider at all times on behalf of the client because of the large investment that's required to install electronic desk computers and billing machines.

The principle is to find ways and means of holding the investment in equipment to a minimum by utilizing auxiliary clerical procedures to speed up the work on the machines, wherever possible. In prior years, when posting and accounting or billing machines represented an investment of only $3,000 to $5,000, the use of clerical personnel to aid and assist machines represented in many instances an even trade-off. The entire situation is different now that electronic equipment of the type described in this chapter costs from $6,000 to $35,000 and up. An installation requiring two billing machines and one general-purpose electronic accounting machine or data processing equipment may easily represent an investment of $60,000 to $75,000 at purchase prices.

ESTIMATING EQUIPMENT PRODUCTION

When estimating equipment and personnel requirements for office applications, never assume that full-rated machine speed will be achieved by any operator. Machine-rated speeds should be downgraded from 20% to 35% or more.

For example, when estimating the output of punched card tabulating machines, the rule of thumb has been to discount the machine speeds by 20% to provide for make-ready, paper handling, card handling and other related tasks.

When accounting machines or desk computers are the primary work tool, a certain amount of time is lost because of inserting journals or register sheets faced with carbon (by use of carbon jackets), clearing the accumulators, changing control bars or panels, changing plugboards or feeding in instructions from punched cards.

As has been pointed out, the production to be obtained from an accounting machine or comparable equipment when constant operator intervention is required is frequently no faster than the paper handling will permit. The timing example provided for posting one entry to an accounts receivable ledger shows that the paper handling time *equalled* the machine time required for the posting. Thus, the total time for one posting indicates that the operator should post three records per minute, or 180 per hour. An experienced consultant will not utilize this optimum figure for estimating the number of machines and operators required for the job under study; he will reduce this by at least 15% and estimate production ranging from 145 to 160 entries per hour, depending on such factors as the legibility of the source documents, number of operator interruptions per hour, length of the ledger trays, density of indexing, etc.

Work Period

Suppose that a work day in an office begins at 9:00 A.M. and ends at 5:00 P.M. With 30 minutes off for lunch, this appears to be a 7½ hour work day. However, contemporary business practice allows two 15-minute coffee breaks per day. In addition, employees invent many types of "breaks" which reduce the available work time. Experience indicates that it may be unrealistic to expect more than 5½ to 6 actual work hours per day for clerical workers or office machine operators.

WORK STANDARDS FOR CLERICAL JOBS

American industry is recognized all over the world for its manufacturing efficiency and high productivity per employee. Factory management in the United States is keenly conscious of the value of automated equipment for increasing output per employee and reducing per-unit product costs.

A corollary and important step toward achieving production efficiency has been the continuing development and use of *work standards* over the years. To set up production standards industrial engineers carefully study each operation to be found on a manufacturing route sheet for each product, and establish a standard allowable time for each unit or batch of work output. This standard is subsequently used as the basis for daily, weekly and monthly production efficiency reports for foremen and top management.

These production reports are usually of the exception type. They report only deviations from the norm or standard. For example, such a report typically pinpoints the worker who failed to meet the standard output requirements, and also reports the operation number, the machine number and the cost center—for possible corrective action by line management.

Up to the present time these well-proven concepts of measuring productivity have not, to any large extent, been applied to office operations. All too often management regards the office as a necessary burden, and is reluctant to invest in more productive equipment, or to allocate the necessary time and attention to office routines and procedures to increase productivity.

A Changing Situation

In the past two decades the number of production employees in factories has been dropping, whereas the number of clerical and other employees required to support the production workers has risen dramatically. There are several reasons for this. As more and more automated equipment has been installed on the production lines the number of workers required has dropped—according to the U. S. Department of Commerce. However, the number of people involved in engineering, planning, research, production paperwork, maintenance and support activities has increased; the net result has been an overall increase in total factory employment.

Today's high clerical costs per office employee, plus the increasing number of people engaged in clerical work are gradually forcing management to adopt a more progressive attitude toward the office and its operation.

When each typist or file clerk is budgeted at $3,500 to $5,000 per year, and keypunch operators earn up to $6,000 per year, the economics of the office situation positively require increasing attention from management. As evidence of this, some firms are currently hiring systems engineers who are familiar with office routines to establish a clerical work standards program. This subject is covered in considerable detail on subsequent pages.

Clerical Productivity

Clerical productivity, or the lack of it, depends upon three elements:
- Training
- Supervision
- Motivation

Supervision and Training

Supervisors of office personnel seem to have lost the firm discipline and control that once was prevalent through the 1950's. Perhaps this is one result of continuing prosperity, plus an over abundance of available jobs—and fat profits which cause top management to be permissive toward a high-cost office operation.

Another reason may be rapid turnover of office personnel. This dilutes the training effort; the supervisor may not have the time nor the inclination to instruct each new employee thoroughly in the job functions.

Motivation

Office employees require special attention and appropriate motivation if top output is to be obtained from them. Most employees in an office are paid on an hourly basis. Since their earnings are not connected with work output units, there is a natural tendency for each employee in a group to produce no more work than any of the others. In fact, the group may censure an individual who works harder than the average person in the group.

Under such typical conditions the output of each worker tends to conform to that of the slowest or the laziest individual in the group.

Keeping accurate records on each employee is one form of motivation. The results of implementing this one simple control step have been phenomenal in some instances. For example, I have seen the output of an entire clerical department increase by as much as 25% overnight—after management announced that production records would henceforth be kept on each person in the department! Those workers with the right attitude and a desire to work actually welcome the opportunity to show what they can do. Others who are inclined to be lackadaisical and lazy realize that when records are kept, their failure to produce will be duly recorded.

Accurate records of productivity provide a solid basis for pay raises that are based on merit rather than on seniority, which rewards non-productive employees merely for being on the payroll for a long period of time.

Work Measurement and Work Standards

A few consulting firms specialize in work measurement of clerical employees. The concepts of clerical work measurement are very appealing to the businessman who is hard pressed to maintain adequate profit margins for his stockholders.

The key to devising standards for clerical work is to determine that volume of work which the clerk or office machine operator can be reasonably expected to produce within a stated period of time, such as one hour. The experts say that a standard should be established for *each person* in the work force, since the experience and capabilities of office personnel vary considerably.

A CASE HISTORY

A large firm in New York City had six women operating identical posting machines on a volume listing and posting operation. To develop reasonable performance standards for each operator, we first analyzed the operation from the viewpoint of machine speeds and maximum machine production per hour. For Job A, we concluded that a good operator could process about 200 invoices per hour. However, we did not establish this figure as an arbitrary standard for all operators.

We selected one operator who seemed to be average in experience and capability. We enlisted her cooperation in making various test runs; she handled about 175 invoices per hour. Now we had a starting point for establishing standards for the other operators, as follows:

1. The supervisor assembled invoices to be processed into batches of 175 documents, and assigned a batch to each operator. When the operator completed her batch, she promptly returned the work to the supervisor who recorded the start/stop time on a register sheet.

2. The supervisor now began to *vary* the number of invoices in each batch. For example, if he found that operator A could handle about 175 per hour initially, he assigned her 185 in the next batch. If operator B posted only 150 invoices in one hour, he assigned about 160 invoices to this operator for the next hour's work.

The basic objective was to determine a "reasonable-expectancy" (RE) volume for each individual operator—but to increase this figure from time to time to provide motivation for greater achievement.

Other Key Points

The supervisor should adjust the work volume assigned to each operator so that it represents approximately one hour's work. Example: If an operator finishes one batch of work one-tenth of an hour ahead of schedule, for the next batch he should give her 1.1 hour's work, according to *each operator's own standard*.

The supervisor retains full control over the work assignment—and has, in effect, the actual amount of work output reported to him or her each hour throughout the day.

Based on the recorded output of each person during the day, the supervisor plans the work for the next day.

During the hour in which a coffee break is taken, reduce the RE hour to .8 (as an example) to make allowance for the 10-minute coffee break.

The supervisor may be required to report to the department manager the following valuable data at the end of each day's work:

- Actual amount of work produced per person, and in total.
- Work standards, and deviations from the norm.
- Volume of work carried over to the next day.

Benefits

Work measurement provides the supervisor with full control over his section at all times, hour by hour. The supervisor is required to allocate the work for each hour of the day, and to plan the work ahead of time. He constantly maintains accurate production records for each employee and for the entire section.

He learns the capabilities of each person and continually watches deviations from the established standards.

In turn, the department manager is aware of the performance of the section on a daily basis, and of the work load being handled by the section.

All of this leads toward an increasingly efficient operation, and consequent reduction of personnel costs. It aids manpower planning and provides the best insurance for staying within expense budgets.

PRODUCTION STANDARDS FOR ROUTINE OFFICE JOBS

The February 1965 issue of the *Electrical Distributor* magazine included an article dealing with clerical and warehouse work standards. The article covered the value of establishing a clerical work standards program, and included detailed procedures for improving clerical methods.

The article also included a chart of production standards for any clerk performing any one of the normal, routine office jobs included in the list. Since this type of data representing an overall average, reasonable production standard may be of considerable interest and value to systems analysts, it is included here as Figure 17-1.

Physical Work Standards for Clerical Jobs

It is, of course, difficult to tell whether specific types of work in the office and warehouse are over-manned, without having some definite work standards with which to compare actual performances. A maximum attainable speed-per-minute or per-hour is not a fair standard for office machine production because, in a four-hour period or a half work day, the elements of fatigue, rest periods, insertion of papers, securing supplies, adjusting machines, and correcting errors all must be taken into account. It is futile to set standards that cannot be consistently maintained throughout a work day by the average experienced operator. Therefore, the figures given below are reasonable production standards, allowing for the modifying factors outlined above:

Office Work Standards

TYPEWRITER
Copying from a clean
  copy . . . . .30-35 words per minute
Typing from a recording
  cylinder . . . . .25-30 words per minute
Transcribing from Steno-
  typed notes . . . . .25 words per minute
Transcribing from short-
  hand notes . . . . .20 words per minute
Bill typing—continuous 30 form sets per hour

form machine . . . . . .(assuming five items per
                              form)
With mechanical dictation 3 times ordinary type-writer activity per day. Typical stenographer type-writer idle one-third of time.

ACCOUNTS RECEIVABLE BOOKKEEPING
  Machine . . . . .150 items posted per
                            hour (using collated
                            statement and ledger)
                            500 per day doing own
                            heading up and paper
                            assembly
                            180 remittances posted
                            per hour preparing the
                            ledger statement and
                            cash receipts journal
                            180 statements and re-
                            lated records per hour
Posting remittances to
  Cash Receipts book . .125 per hour
Posting remittances as
  credits in a/c Re-
  ceivable Ledger . . . . .100 per hour
Addition of net balances
  a/c Rec. Ledger . . . . .750 per hour

Calculating Machine
  Cost or price extensions

Physical Work Standards for Clerical Jobs—Continued

Semi-automatic machine ....165 per hour

Full automatic machine ....225 per hour

Key driven machine ..275 per hour

Division (two 6-figure numbers)

Semi-automatic machine ....105 per hour

Full automatic machine ....165 per hour

Adding Machine, Listing (avg. 5-digit figures) ..1800 times per hour

Check Protecting Machine Operation

Full automatic ....1200 checks per hour
Portable electric .... 500 checks per hour
Hand operated .... 400 checks per hour
(lower if continuous)

Office Typesetting Machine One 6" line per minute

Rotary-Type Printing Machine ....1500 copies per hour (hand-operated)

Rotary-Type Printing Machine ....2500 copies per hour (electrically operated)

Addressing Machines (from plates)

Small magazine ....3500 per hour
Large magazine ....6000 per hour

Mimeograph Machine ....1¼ minutes set-up time per stencil—100 copies per minute running time

Letter Sealing Machine ...100-200 per minute

Letter Opening Machine ...500 pieces per minute

Microfilm Record Machine .140 forms per minute

Photocopying Machine ...One copy—less than 3 minutes—120 copies per hour

SALES ANALYSIS
Entry of Sales Invoices in Sales Journal ....   60 per hour
Posting to Sales Analysis book by Commodities   125 per hour
Addition of Sales analysis details .....1000 per hour
Key punch operator holes punched per hour 6000

Accounts Payable—checks issued per operator per day 225

Payroll Checks ....100 checks and related records per hour. Job cost tickets—extended for payroll (Service Shop and Outside Service hourly rated employees) —500 per hour.

Clerical cost per payroll-check (Total) ....$ .65

Purchasing Dept. Cost per purchase order issued ..$3.75

Figure 17-1.

CHART OF PHYSICAL WORK STANDARDS FOR CLERICAL JOBS
(From the *Electrical Distributor*, February 1965)

Note that the figures given on the chart have been modified to allow for fatigue, rest periods, paper handling and error corrections.

RESPONSIBILITIES OF THE EQUIPMENT USER

The management services practitioner working in today's environment of data processing and increasingly complex equipment of all types should be prepared to guide his client as to the proper role to be played by the consultant, by the office-equipment representatives—and by the client himself. If the client does not understand the dangers of taking the wrong attitude and approach to a complete mechanized data-processing system for his business, he may well get into difficulties which may take years to overcome.

Who Should Assume Responsibility?

The key point is this: Who should be responsible for developing the new system, for programming it, and for installing electronic or data-processing equipment on office applications? A brochure distributed by a large manufacturer of accounting machines and desk computers to explain the features and benefits of a desk computer states: "Your X Company representative delivers your equipment completely programmed to your specific requirements. There is no need to concern yourself with programming costs."

No doubt this sounds very attractive to the prospective buyer. It implies that the equipment salesman is going to do all the systems design work, then program the machine to the buyer's requirements. There is an understandable desire and a tendency on the part of the buyer and even his outside consultant to "let George do the programming." (George is the salesman or technical representative of the machine manufacturer who is responsible for getting the equipment programmed and properly set up to do the job, as wanted by the buyer.)

However, a large body of experience, developed from data-processing and computer installations, clearly proves the fallacy and dangers of permitting outside specialists to develop and install a system for which all future changes and improvements will depend on the immediate availability of "George" or his counterpart. To permit these outsiders to do this is a very unsound approach and represents inexperience or wishful thinking on the part of business management.

To get the best results, and to control the installation during its entire existence, the user must participate fully in the systems project from the very beginning.

Appoint a Project Leader or Manager

A systems design project should always begin with a review of what is now being done, followed by a determination of management objectives for the proposed new system. This should be followed by the actual systems design and development work phases. In the early stages of the project, management of the business should select and appoint an experienced individual from within the firm as the project leader and coordinator.

This key individual should assume responsibility for the success of the project. He should guide and direct all phases of the systems and programming work. Representatives of the equipment manufacturer and the outside consultant should work closely with the project leader or manager at all times as a team. The project leader should receive adequate training in programming the machines so that eventually he will be able to direct and control the entire operation of the new system and equipment with no reliance on anyone outside the firm.

Benefits

The approach as described above offers many benefits to all concerned:
- The system is more apt to fit the needs and requirements of the business, since an experienced insider assumes responsibility for the success of the project.

- Users of output and reports of the new system are less apt to resist the necessary changes which usually accompany a new system and related procedures, because top management, by appointing a competent, experienced inside representative to the project, has shown convincing evidence of full commitment to the new system.
- Management will not find itself dependent upon individuals outside the firm's control for making future changes, improvements and for developing valuable new applications from time to time.
- The consultant will be able to do his job, then go on to other assignments without the contingent liability of being required to return and solve unexpected problems or defend the new system against the criticisms of disgruntled insiders.

18

Mechanization of Order Writing and Billing

In many offices the first jobs to be mechanized are the twin functions of writing internal shipping orders (and related documents) and billing. Every wholesaler, distributor or manufacturer must process customer orders and prepare invoices. As the volume of work increases, clerical costs rise accordingly; at some point, mechanization of the work becomes a feasible solution for reducing these costs. In addition, it may offer many valuable side benefits, such as sales analysis data for management information and guidance.

A Complex Systems Problem

It is easy to underestimate the difficulty of designing and installing a complete, efficient order/invoicing system. A successful system must take into account a wide variety of special problems, and it involves clerical procedures in many different departments of the business.

Some of the necessary control functions and record-keeping steps involved in processing an order, in preparing an invoice and in shipping the merchandise are as follows:

- Interpretation of the order and determination of precisely what products are being ordered.
- Application of correct unit selling prices.
- Determination of applicable discounts.
- Determination of availability of products sold, and their location in the warehouse.
- Acknowledgment of order to customer and salesman.
- Application of correct unit cost prices.
- Preparation of invoices.
- Recording back orders.
- Preparation of appropriate shipping documents.
- Controlling orders and shipments.
- Posting quantities sold to inventory records.
- Posting salesman's commission records.
- Posting accounts receivable records.
- Preparation of sales journal.

219

- Handling sales analysis and customer profitability records.
- Recording sales taxes.
- Preparation of production orders if the product is to be built for the customer.

Origin of Orders

Orders originate from a variety of sources. Customers may send orders through the mail, or telephone them directly to the supplier. If the supplier has outside salesmen calling on customers, the salesmen usually mail in orders each day or periodically. And, some firms receive orders directly from customers who come into the supplier's place of business to transact business.

Receipt of an order starts a long chain of steps and procedures that involves many different departments and functions of the business.

Processing Orders

Some firms find it practical to process the original order document as received from the customer or salesman; this saves the time and cost of transcribing the order to another form. However, this approach is frequently impractical or undesirable for a number of reasons:

- The order may be difficult to read; the product descriptions may be unclear or inadequate for correct interpretation by pricing clerks or the shipping department, and for invoice preparation.
- Internal procedures usually require that a number of special-purpose forms be prepared, such as shipping orders, a packing list, acknowledgment copies, and shipping documents.
- Customer letters or order documents frequently do not provide sufficient writing space for noting quantities shipped, quantities back-ordered, applicable discount, sales taxes, or other data.
- If products are not manufactured until an order is received, then it is necessary to write multiple-copy production orders for each order received.
- Certain copies are required to serve as internal control documents over orders in process.

Summary

In summary, orders are usually rewritten to:

- Provide accurate, uniform product descriptions and part numbers to the shipping department for stock picking—and for subsequent posting of issues to inventory records.
- Provide a neat, accurate packing list to accompany the shipment to the customer.
- Provide a complete set of shipping papers for the shipping department.
- Provide internal control over subsequent shipping/invoicing procedures.
- Prepare production control and planning documents for the manufacturing department.

Decision on Combined Forms

If a systems designer decides to transcribe all orders to a specially-designed set of forms, usually called a "Shipping Order" set, his next major decision is whether the invoice writing can be combined with the order-writing operation. Many factors, such as the total number of copies required and the status and reliability of inventory control records, enter into this important decision.

The number of copies required for one invoice may vary from as few as 4 or 5 for a simple invoice set to as many as 20 or 30 for a manufacturing firm which manufactures products to customer specifications. (The number of copies with variable data and the broad span of areas and functions covered by the order/shipping/invoicing procedures illustrate very clearly why an assignment involving these applications requires careful study and review of practically all major departments of the business.)

Since it is not feasible for many firms to combine the shipping order and invoice forms— for reasons covered in depth in subsequent sections of this chapter—the discussion in the remaining section of this chapter is based on the asumption that it is necessary to prepare two separate sets of forms.

Shipping Order Forms

A shipping order is an order to the shipping department to pick and assemble the merchandise as specified and described on the face of the order forms, then to pack and ship it to the customer.

A typical shipping order set consists of several copies, preferably pre-numbered by the printer:
- Original and duplicate shipping orders for the shipping department.
- Triplicate copy—filed and held in the office as the order register copy.
- Packing slip.
- Shipping documents (3 or more copies).
- Acknowledgment forms.

Since the shipping order is the basic document used subsequently for invoicing merchandise shipped, the form should include three quantity columns:
- Quantity ordered.
- Quantity shipped.
- Quantity Back-ordered.

Refer to Figure 18-1.

INVOICE NUMBER	INVOICE DATE	CUSTOMER NO.	CUST. ORDER NO.	SHIP VIA		
104732	4/16/64	1234321	XY4932A	BEST WAY		
QUANTITY ORDERED	QUANTITY SHIPPED	BACK ORDERED	PRICE	ITEM CODE	DESCRIPTION	NET AMOUNT
10	10		3.75	1216	HANDYMANS REPAIR KIT	
13	13		2.50	0472	10 OZ. CLAW HAMMER	
25	25		1.00	3094	BRASS CABINET CATCH	
60	48	12	.50	6597	MAPLE DRAWER PULL	
17		17	4.22	1481	9 INCH BLOCK PLANE	

Figure 18-1

CENTER SECTION OF A WELL-DESIGNED SHIPPING ORDER FORM;
ONE COPY BECOMES THE *PACKING LIST*

Shipping Documents

The preparation of shipping documents and control over shipments of all types represent a very important phase of an assignment involving order writing, shipping and invoicing. The various types of shipping documents are directly connected with the mode of transportation and are reviewed on subsequent pages.

There are five major ways to transport goods from the seller to a customer:

1. By rail freight
2. By motor freight carrier
3. By Railway Express
4. By parcel post
5. By local delivery

Regardless of how the goods are transported to the customer a complete and efficient office system will include ways to control merchandise shipments and will insure that an invoice is eventually prepared for each shipment. Such a system may well save the client many thousands of dollars annually in shipments of merchandise assembled and dispatched to the customers—but never invoiced!

Types of Shipping Documents

A different type of shipping document is prepared for each method of transportation:

Carrier	*Type of Document Prepared*
Railroad	Uniform Bill of Lading
Motor Freight Carrier	Uniform Bill of Lading
Railway Express	Railway Express Receipt
Parcel Post	Parcel Post Forms
Local Delivery	Delivery Receipt

Some firms use all four specified types or forms listed above, if they use the various methods of transport available to them. In this case the shipping clerks invariably have many different receipt pads, parcel post forms and a supply of bill of lading forms provided free of charge by *each carrier* who solicits the firm's freight business. These forms are seldom pre-numbered for control purposes.

How to Control Shipments

For appropriate and effective internal control over shipments, the situation just described must be corrected. The first thing to do is to order specially-printed, *pre-numbered* bill of lading forms, and discontinue the use of the forms provided by the various carriers. Next, reduce the various types of shipping documents to a minimum. For example, it is legally permissible in certain sections of the United States to *combine* the Railway Express receipts with the bills of lading—merely by adding the appropriate clause to the regular bill of lading forms.

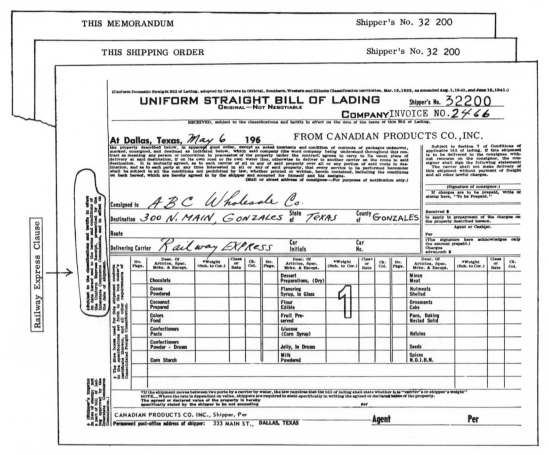

Figure 18-2
UBL FORMS WITH RAILWAY EXPRESS CLAUSE INCLUDED

The special clause reads as follows: "Subject to the classifications and tariffs in effect on date hereof and to the terms and conditions of the Uniform Express Receipt, prescribed by the Interstate Commerce Commission, and in effect on the date of shipment."

Another step toward reducing the number of different forms is to use the regular UBL forms for local deliveries.

The primary objective of the changes described here is to require the shipping clerk to prepare a uniform, *pre-numbered document* for every shipment of merchandise from the warehouse—regardless of the method of transport.

Subsequent Invoicing Procedures

After shipment one copy of the bill of lading is routed back to the office—attached to the original shipping order form. These two forms become the basis for invoicing. For control purposes, write the invoice number on the face of the bill of lading form and file it in uniform bill of lading (UBL) number sequence.

This provides positive assurance that each shipment will be properly invoiced because:

- Each bill of lading copy must be accounted for by number.
- Any bill of lading copy without an invoice number recorded on it starts a search for the corresponding invoice—which may uncover the fact that no invoice was prepared.

Should Shipping Forms Be Included in Order Set?

In most firms the product description used for orders and invoices bears little resemblance to the correct, legal product description prescribed by the Interstate Commerce Commission for the application of freight tariffs to calculate the amount of freight charges. For this reason, it is common to block the transcription of the product descriptions from the face of the shipping papers included in the order set.

One may wonder, then, why these shipping documents are included at all. The primary reason is to inscribe the "Ship To" name and address on the top part of the forms, as a by-product of preparing the order forms. This may seem to be a minor benefit, but experience has shown that this may eliminate a clerk who would otherwise be required in the shipping department to copy names and addresses from order forms to shipping forms.

INVOICING

The third function in the order/shipping/invoicing cycle is the preparation of an invoice to cover each shipment of merchandise. An invoice is a legal document which creates an obligation on the part of the buyer to pay to the seller the invoice amount.

Objectives of Billing

The objectives of an efficient, well-designed billing operation are:
- Prepare accurate, detailed invoices promptly.
- Provide documents for subsequent posting of accounts receivable, for sales analysis and for costing sales.
- Provide copies for posting inventory records.
- Provide data for posting salesmen's commission statements.
- Supply figures for accounting for sales taxes, freight charges, parcel post expense, etc.
- Provide records for follow-up and control over back orders.

Invoice Design

An invoice is composed of two major sections:
1. *Invoice Heading—contains the following information:*
   - Sold To—Customer name and address
   - Ship To—Name and address of the firm or individual who will receive the merchandise
   - Invoice date and number
   - Salesman's name or number
   - Invoice terms
   - How shipped
2. *Body of the Invoice—includes the following:*
   - Product numbers, descriptions, quantity ordered, quantity shipped, quantity back ordered, unit selling prices and the extended total of each item shipped.
   - Additional charges such as sales taxes, parcel post or freight charges.

"Sold To" and "Ship To"

When a firm sells to individual proprietorships, the "Sold To" and "Ship To" are usually one and the same. However, when products are sold to a large chain store operation, the "Sold To" name and address is the entity doing the buying and *paying* of invoices. The "Ship To" address may be one of several hundred stores in the chain. Sometimes the "Ship To" name and address is completely different because of centralized purchasing for subsidiary firms.

Special Instructions

Data in this upper portion of the invoice form includes:
1. "Ship via ABC Motor Carriers."
2. Customer order number, salesman name or number, invoice number and date, *terms* of payment, etc.

Product Data

Products are described in many different ways:
- Product Code
- Catalogue No.
- Product Description
- Part Numbers
- Colors, sizes, patterns, etc.

The body of the invoice should show the quantity ordered, quantity actually shipped—and the quantity *back ordered*.

Non-Merchandise Charges

If invoice terms require the buyer to pay the shipping charges, the invoice may include charges for parcel post, motor or rail freight, or local delivery charges. If the terms are "freight collect," then the common carrier bills the freight charges to the consignee.

Billing Procedures

Since billing usually requires multiplication of quantity shipped by the unit selling price, an order clerk makes the initial extensions and writes the amounts on the shipping order form. Later, the biller (usually, a typist unless the work has been mechanized) merely copies the data from the shipping order form to an invoice form.

Verification

Before the invoice is released for mailing, a verification clerk should make all extensions a second time in order to verify the invoice total. In theory, this internal checking of invoice extensions and the invoice total will detect all errors in calculations or additions. In practice, it does not.

In the 1940's, I installed a large number of billing machines in many types of business firms. At that time the Model 72 billing machine manufactured by the Burroughs Corporation was one of the best available mechanical billing machines. This machine multiplied the quantity by the indexed unit price, then *printed the result* properly pointed off. This proved to be far more accurate than the prevailing practice in manual billing methods of making all extensions twice. This was difficult to comprehend, until I realized that it was the human factor which defeated the theoretically efficient verification of all calculations. That is, the human eye, quite often, sees what IT EXPECTS TO SEE.

Here is an example to show how errors remain undetected under manual methods even where all extensions are made twice. The three lines shown below appear on an order form; the extensions were initially made by the order clerk:

6 Gadgets	2.20 EA	$13.20
350 Products	48.40 C	16.44
10 Widgets	5.00 EA	50.00
		$79.64

The extended amount on the second line represents the well-known decimal-point type of error. The correct extension is 164.40. The verification operation is supposed to uncover this by calculating the total amount for each invoice line, independently of the order clerk. Yet, this type of error may go undetected—simply because, "The human eye sees what it expects to see."

BASIC BILLING METHODS

In designing a mechanized billing operation, one of the major decisions which must be made is to use prebilling or postbilling.

Prebilling

"Prebilling" combines the order set and the invoice set; all forms are prepared with ONE WRITING.

The success of prebilling depends primarily upon two things:

1. A controlled inventory situation with accurate and current stock records maintained in or near the office.
2. A constantly-replenished source of goods for sale with nearly all back orders eliminated.

A situation which points to prebilling as being feasible may become more complicated if the seller adds parcel post or shipping charges to the pre-written invoice. It is usually difficult to estimate or calculate shipping charges before the merchandise is picked, packed, weighed and shipped. Therefore, shipping charges must be added to the invoice after it has been prepared. This tends to complicate internal procedures and accounts receivable accounting. Some firms have solved this problem by creating a separate accounts receivable invoice for the freight amount. Others simply add the shipping charges to the invoice in pencil, after the merchandise has been shipped.

One large wholesale paper supply house in New York City which uses a computer for billing and inventory control also utilizes the concept of prebilling. Experience has shown that this method of operation creates a surprising number of credit memos, since warehousemen find discrepancies between the "book records" kept on the computer files, and the actual stock situation in the warehouse. For example, if the computer indicates sufficient stock on hand to fill an order, it immediately prepares the complete invoice for the quantity ordered—if the computer inventory records indicate availability of the products ordered.

When the warehousemen subsequently find that the products are not actually on hand, they must so indicate on their shipping order copy. Since the goods have already been included on the invoice and are part of the invoice total, the invoice is mailed "as is," but this requires the preparation and issuance of a credit memo to the customer.

Use of the prebilling approach does not necessarily require that the inventory records be kept on a computer with random access capabilities; many companies in the past have done prebilling based on various methods of maintaining the inventory records. Several such methods are covered in the next few pages.

INVENTORY RECORDS

Inventory Records Posted Manually

Possibly the most widely used manually-posted inventory control system is the "Kardex" system, developed and marketed by Remington Rand. It consists of a metal cabinet with multiple trays which slide in and out of the cabinet. Each pull-out tray holds up to 100 inventory card records; the product number and description of each inventory item is visible to the posting clerk.

When this system is in use, the orders are routed to the inventory clerks for *immediate posting* of the quantity required to fill the order. Since this meets the prime requirement of a controlled inventory situation, prebilling is feasible where Kardex is in use.

Punched Cards Represent Inventory Records

Scores of wholesale grocery firms in the United States have installed a unique punched-card system, where the inventory quantity on hand is physically represented by a group of punched cards filed in indexed card tubs. Each card has pre-punched data in it, such as product number, full description, unit selling price—and the quantity that the unit record card represents. The function of these cards is to produce mechanically a combined invoice and order set—when the cards are processed through IBM punched-card machines along with a customer name and address master set of cards.

Under one approach, each punched card has a quantity value of 1. Thus, if an order calls for 6 cartons of cigarettes, an order clerk pulls 6 unit cards from the file to represent the order quantity.

Denominated Cards

In some prebilling installations using pre-punched inventory cards, the cards are "denominated." That is, the *quantity represented* by each unit record card varies in regard to the particular requirements of the installation. The quantity value of one card may be 1, 5, 10, 12, 24, 100, 144, etc. The quantity values usually follow a pattern which agrees with the quantities packed in the various cartons, boxes, packages or other types of containers. For example, if a popular product is packed 12 to a case, the punched cards will include a card with a quantity value of 12.

To fill an order where such a system is in use, the order clerk merely pulls from a file a combination of cards to represent the total quantity ordered. As an example, suppose the order calls for 16 of a certain product. The card puller will pull 3 cards representing the following quantities:

Card 1	Quantity value of	10
Card 2	" " of	5
Card 3	" " of	1
		16

These inventory cards may be pre-extended; the coded data includes the unit selling price and the extended total for the indicated quantity.

While this prebilling system has worked reasonably well in unique situations where the concept fits the billing situation, the disadvantages and related problems are obvious: If unit selling prices are changing periodically, the entire supply of pre-punched cards for many different products must be continually scrapped and replaced with corrected cards. If a firm carries many thousands of different products, a considerable amount of space will be required to store the punched cards representing inventory. Also, the quantity values in the available cards may not satisfy the puller's requirements for processing orders for variable quantities.

Review

In the majority of order writing and billing situations the full use of pre-punched inventory cards is not practical for many reasons, some of which are outlined below.

In many firms, including manufacturing enterprises, there are several selling price structures in use for certain sound reasons. Even if there is only one primary unit selling price structure, certain groups of accounts or special customers may be given special discounts on specific products, or on the entire invoice. Pre-punched inventory cards which include selling prices would not represent a feasible approach in either instance.

As mentioned before, if unit selling prices change rapidly, or if customer requirements cause the stocking of large quantities of many products, the use of pre-punched cards to represent the quantity on hand is not feasible.

However, there is a way to obtain the benefits of automatic product description from pre-punched cards, without using them to represent the actual inventory on hand.

Pre-punched Product Description Cards

In recent years, with the advent of billing equipment which accepts and reads cards or ledger-type forms with coded holes punched on one edge, increasing use has been made of pre-punched *product description* cards. The use of such cards for the automatic typing of repetitive data has no connection with inventory records. Their primary function is that of input to the billing machine—for automatic typing of the product number, the manufacturer's catalogue number, a complete and accurate description, the warehouse location number and other basic data.

How such cards are set up and used as part of the order-writing procedures was described in more detail in the preceding chapter dealing with electronic office equipment.

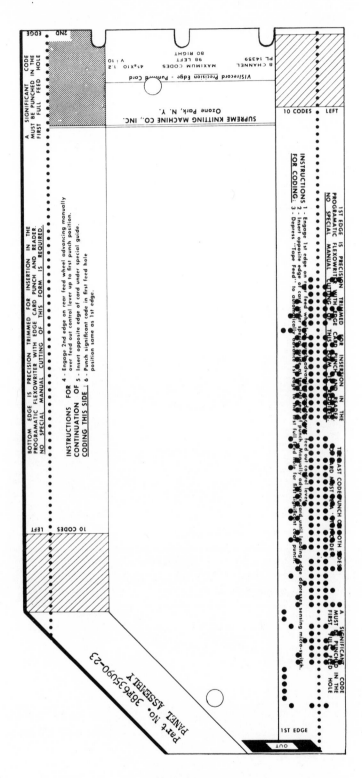

Figure 18-3
EDGE-PUNCHED PRODUCT DESCRIPTION CARD

Postbilling

The writing of an invoice set of forms after the shipping order has been completed and returned by the shipping department to the office is referred to as "postbilling."

Postbilling obviously requires considerable writing or typing where manual billing methods are used. Most of the information already on the shipping order form must be copied to the invoice, plus writing the extended line item amounts, adding taxes and shipping charges, and writing the invoice total. Even so, it offers one major advantage in that the various copies required for the wide variety of accounting functions and internal record-keeping can be prepared, since the forms required for shipping and order-filling were included in the shipping order set.

Postbilling has become much more palatable since the advent of billing machines which type automatically from data in paper tape or edge-punched cards. The Friden Flexowriter applied to order-writing is frequently the first step in an integrated, mechanized order/invoicing system.

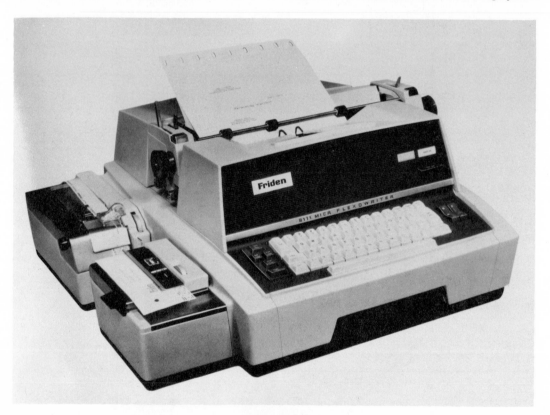

Figure 18-4
THE FRIDEN FLEXOWRITER

Order/Invoicing Procedures

- Working from the original customer order, the machine operator types a complete shipping order set, which may include the shipping documents, as well as the packing list.

As a by-product, the machine punches a paper tape as output. The operator tears off the strip of paper tape and attaches it to the order copy which is held in the office.

• When the office copy of the shipping order is returned to the office from the warehouse, the billing operation begins—after unit selling prices are entered on the order form. The operator at the billing machine (see Figure 18-4) inserts a set of invoice forms, and positions the order tape on the side of the machine for automatic reading. The machine reads the coded holes in the tape which causes the electric typewriter to transcribe the order data to the appropriate sections of the invoice at high speed.

When the operator positions the invoice to the body of the form, the machine types the quantity ordered, and then waits for the operator to type manually the quantity shipped and back-ordered. The machine starts the automatic typing again by typing the full product description contained in the order tape. The operator completes the line extension by entering the unit selling price on the machine keyboard.

Figure 18-5
FRIDEN BILLING MACHINE

Capturing Data for Subsequent Reports

A very significant optional by-product of a billing operation where this type of equipment is used is the punching of paper tape which contains coded data for each line on the invoice—

including the customer and salesman number. This tape is the source for sales analysis reports, customer profitability reports, sales commission statements and other reports as required.

SPECIAL SITUATIONS ENCOUNTERED IN ORDER/INVOICING PROCEDURES

We have already indicated that designing and installing a complete, efficient order/invoicing system may be a complex systems problem. This section documents some of the reasons why this is true.

Applying Selling Prices to Orders

Many business firms find it necessary to offer different selling prices or special discounts to various categories of customers. For example, contractors and governmental units may qualify for special prices. Yet, the price books or catalogues usually include only the selling prices offered to regular customers.

Line Discounts

Applying special trade discounts to the product line on an invoice is popular, because this practice eliminates the need for constantly changing price books or catalogues. However, this obviously increases the complexity of the order/billing procedures, since order clerks must apply the correct discount percentage to each product sold to special customers.

This also dictates the form design since it is customary to show the discount rate and the net extension. (See Figure 18-6.)

The systems analyst, when designing the invoice form, must consider the basis on which commissions are calculated, as well as bear in mind the multiplication capabilities of the billing equipment. If commissions are paid on the "gross profit" rather than on the "net selling" amount, the analyst may decide to widen the office copies of the invoice to show the unit cost, the total cost and the "gross profit" amount.

As the salesman receives his invoice copies all during the month, he can figure his total earnings from commissions based on gross profit. This also provides an incentive to the salesman to sell high profit merchandise to increase his commissions.

Prices Vary with Volume

Another price list may be required if management decides to favor the customers who buy in large quantities over those who buy smaller quantities. This concept is valid and is well recognized in the business world. Therefore, the order clerk who applies unit selling prices and special discounts may have to consider the quantity being sold, as well as the category of customer to whom the merchandise is being sold.

Credit Memos

The systems analyst should give special attention to the procedures for writing credit memos for returned merchandise. A credit memo is an invoice in reverse; the *same* invoice terms and special trade discounts should be applied to such documents as were applied to the invoice. If this is not handled properly, credit memos may be a source of hidden profit losses.

INVOICE

The Crossroads Paint Company
Hillside and 164th St.
Jamaica, N.Y.

SOLD
TO

● CENTRAL HOME IMPROVEMENTS CO.

● 1428 JAMAICA AVE.

● JAMAICA, NY

SHIP
TO

TERMS	CUSTOMER ORDER NO.	SHIP VIA	REPRESENTATIVE	INVOICE DATE	INVOICE NUMBER
N 30	4488	Pickup		12/02/68	2378

ITEM DESCRIPTION	QUANTITY ORDERED	QUANTITY SHIPPED	QUANTITY BACK ORDER	PRICE	PRODUCT CODE	DISCOUNT RATE	EXTENSION	TOTAL
09-600 RT FLOOR TILE	400	400		.08	15	15%	27.20	
04-312 GAL BA 300 PAINT	5	5		2.50			12.50	
12-333 GAL FB 10 PAINT	10	10		5.49	208	20%	42.92	
							$ 82.62	

Figure 18-6
INVOICE DESIGNED FOR TRADE DISCOUNTS ON INDIVIDUAL PRODUCTS SOLD

A further consideration is that merchandise shown on credit memos represents a *receipt* of goods back into the warehouse, and it must be properly recorded in the inventory records.

Unit costs should be applied to credit memos and the amount of commission on "gross profit" should be calculated. Exactly the same billing procedures apply here as for invoices. The only notable difference is that all figures are reversals for accounting purposes:

● The "net selling" amount is a debit to Returned Sales and a credit to accounts receivable.
● The cost amount is a credit to Cost of Goods Sold—and a debit to inventory.
● The commission amount is subtracted from commissions due the salesman.

Discounts on Invoices

Another method for reducing the selling price to favored customers is to deduct a discount percentage from the gross invoice amount. Sometimes this is done even though the line items were discounted on the face of the invoice. This practice creates a problem in reconciling sales totals as reported through sales analysis reports with net discounted sales. Since sales analysis totals are based on the selling amount for each product appearing on an invoice, and since the net sales are taken from the net invoice totals, the discount amount represents the balancing figure.

One way to maintain a balance is to apply the discount percentage applied to the entire invoice to each line item on the invoice. This procedure will, of course, slow down the billing substantially.

Direct Factory Orders

Shipments of merchandise directly to the customer from the factory should be handled as a special situation for several reasons. First, such sales have no effect on warehouse inventory. Secondly, freight charges billed by the factory to the distributor must be taken into consideration when preparing an invoice for the customer. Also, the selling prices may well be special prices not found in the usual price books or catalogues.

The problem of applying unit costs to each item on a direct factory shipment is often solved by referring to a copy of the Purchase Order sent to the manufacturer.

HOW TO DETERMINE UNIT COSTS

Applying accurate unit costs to goods sold may be done in many different ways. As a quick review of basic costing methods, the practitioner has a choice of four different costing methods:

Last In, First Out (LIFO)
First In, First Out (FIFO)
Average unit cost
Last invoice cost

If the planned procedures call for applying the unit cost automatically from data stored in the magnetic stripe of inventory ledgers, the first two methods cannot be used. However, either of the last two methods listed above will fit in with the concept of automatic call-in of unit cost when posting sales issues to inventory records.

Average Unit Cost

Desk computers or comparable data processing equipment applied to inventory accounting make it feasible to carry both quantity and total value for each inventory item. Since the actual cost value of each receipt of merchandise can be introduced into the posting operation along with the quantity received, the equipment can quickly calculate the new quantity on hand, plus the total dollar value; and it can calculate and print the *unit cost price* as well. At the same time it can store this data as part of the inventory record for later call-in for costing sales issues.

Receipt of Merchandise Before Invoice

One problem that is commonly encountered in connection with value accounting for inventory is the receipt of the merchandise before receiving the vendor's invoice. Here is a time-tested solution for this special situation: When designing the inventory system and procedures, provide for posting quantities received from a receiving report which shows quantity, but *no monetary value*.

Apply the average unit cost that is in effect before receipt of the new merchandise to the quantity received; the result is the temporary monetary value of the merchandise just received for posting to stock records.

When posting quantity and value to the inventory records, record the cost value on one copy of the receiving report. Route this copy back to the accounts payable department where it is held until the vendor's invoice is received. Once the invoice is received and audited, the accounts payable department prepares a "Change Report" form which makes cross-reference to the invoice, and provides a document for posting an *adjustment amount* to the inventory records.

The amount shown on the change report for each product received is the *value difference* (debit or credit) between the actual invoice amount and the value amount *already posted* to the corresponding inventory record. This adjustment posting changes the total value of the goods on hand, and requires re-calulating the average unit cost price for application to subsequent stock issues.

The new average unit cost is then applied to all subsequent issues, until another receiver and the corresponding invoice changes the cost price. See example below.

INVENTORY RECORD FOR PRODUCT # 16-AL 405

Date	Type of Document	RECEIVED Quantity	Value	Quantity Issued	Quantity on Hand	Total Value	Average Unit Cost	
5/10	Receiver & Invoice	60	180.00		60	180.00	$3.0000	
5/12	Sales Invoice			5	55	165.00	3.0000	
5/20	Sales Invoice			32	23	69.00	3.0000	
5/30	Sales Invoice			3	20	60.00	3.0000	
6/12	Receiving Report	40	120.00		60	180.00	3.0000	A
6/14	Sales Invoice			4	56	168.00	3.0000	B
6/17	CHANGE REPORT	—	24.00		56	192.00	3.4286	C

EXPLANATORY NOTES

Line A: 40 items were received with no invoice attached to the receiving report. The present average unit cost of $3.0000 was applied to this quantity received, which added $120 to the total value. The unit cost price, of course, remained the same as before.

Line B: A sale of 4 items was costed out at $3.0000 each.

Line C: When the Change Report was received from accounts payable, it indicated that the actual invoice value for the 40 items was $144, which is an increase of $24 over the value posted at the time of receipt.

Now, the total value of the items in stock is correct, and the new average unit cost of $3.4286 will be applied to subsequent issues.

HOW TO HANDLE BACK ORDERS

Back orders are a special problem because they represent goods sold in advance of availability of the merchandise. Failure to fill back orders in a reasonable length of time leads to poor customer relations, and an outright loss of sales. For these reasons, an efficient follow-up system is required; processing of back orders when goods are received in the warehouse should take priority over regular, current orders.

Analysis of Back-Order Problem

A sales order for a product which is not available and cannot be shipped becomes a "back order." The quantity on back order creates a definite requirement to obtain and ship the product ordered by the customer. Another view is that it is an obligation on the part of the seller, who offered the goods for sale to the buyer, to complete his part of the "contract" as soon as possible by shipping the goods ordered.

The basic requirement of a back-order situation is to set up a system and procedures that provide efficient follow-up on the status of individual products which appear in the back-order invoice file.

Usual Back-Order Procedure

Usual back-order procedure is to file a copy of each invoice which shows one or two more items as being on back order. As merchandise is received from time to time, a clerk scans all the back-order copies searching for those prior invoices which require shipment of stock items of the type just received into the warehouse or shipping department.

The back-order invoice copy becomes the basic document for originating the shipping and billing routines all over again. If there are several products on one back-order invoice copy, it is re-filed and held for further processing when additional items are received at some later date.

This procedure is very time-consuming. And, it is easy to lose profits by overlooking items previously ordered and now available for shipment.

A Suggested, Low-Cost Back-Order System

Since the foundation for a practical back-order system is reference to the status of individual inventory items on back order, an efficient solution will provide unit records for each product on back order.

The following procedures feature a manual approach.

From the back-order copy of an invoice, post the following data to an ordinary 3″ × 5″ cross-index file card:

1. Write the stock number and merchandise description on the top of the card.
2. Post the invoice number and quantity ordered to the card. (See Figure 18-7.)

Now file the invoice copy in a back-order file; file it in numeric sequence *by invoice number*. Place the file card in a box-type file *in stock-number sequence*.

Back-Order Follow-Up

When goods are received in the warehouse, a receiving report is prepared and sent to the office.

Working from each line on the receiving report, the clerk responsible for filling back orders removes from the file box the 3″ × 5″ cross-index card that bears the same stock number as shown on the receiving report. Since the card shows the numbered invoices on which this stock item was originally ordered, *it serves as an index* to the back-order invoice-file copies.

In this way the clerk locates and quickly removes the appropriate invoice-file copies. Now the recently received merchandise is applied against quantities back ordered by indicating the quantities to be shipped on each order. Later the back-order form is used to initiate the usual shipping and invoicing procedures, just as though a new order had been received.

The procedures just described are illustrated in Figure 18-8.

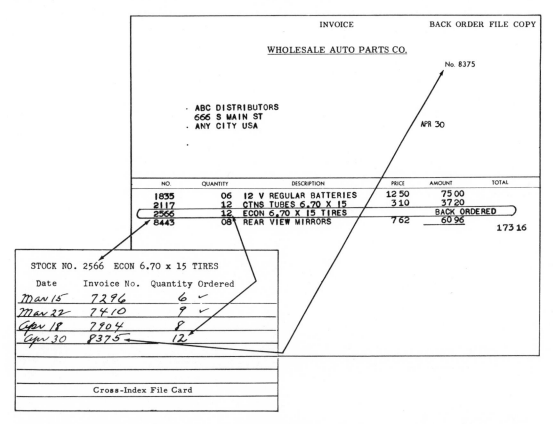

Figure 18-7
INVOICE NUMBER AND QUANTITY ORDERED ARE POSTED TO A CROSS-INDEX FILE CARD

Benefits of Proposed System

1. The back-order clerk does not have to study constantly all back-order file copies to apply goods received in the warehouse.

2. This system pinpoints goods on back order and makes it difficult to overlook an item.

3. The file card is a summary of all unfilled orders for each part number, stock number, or commodity on back order.

4. When goods are received, no time is lost in allocating them to existing orders for subsequent shipment and invoicing.

5. The number of posted lines on the file card indicates to the owner or buyer whether an item is on back order too often. When a card has been filled with postings, it should be reviewed to see if a larger quantity of the stock item should be carried in inventory to reduce the number of back orders.

6. Changing the color of the 3″ × 5″ cards periodically or coding them with numbers makes possible a quick check of the cards each week; for example, to detect overage back orders. In the event of a long-pending item on back order, it is important to notify the customer of the difficulties involved in filling the order and to request his indulgence on the delay.

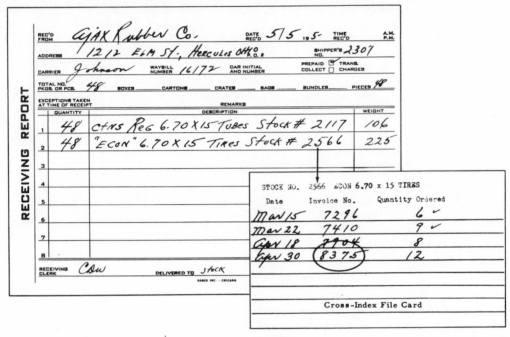

Figure 18-8

CROSS-INDEX CARD FOR EACH COMMODITY ON BACK ORDER
PIN-POINTS BACK ORDER INVOICES

Alternative Solutions

If a firm has tab or computer equipment, more sophisticated methods can be utilized for the back-order problem. However, the principle involved will remain the same; follow-up on each individual item whenever quantities appear on a receiving report and are posted to inventory records.

Even though the inventory record may indicate the total quantity currently on back order, a separate file is usually maintained, which provides the cross reference to specific invoice numbers as well as to customer names and addresses who are to receive the products when available.

HOW TO SAVE MONEY ON FREIGHT BILLS

Solicitors of the various motor freight lines and railroads customarily supply the shipper with pre-printed, standard bill of lading forms free of charge. As a result, a typical shipping department has pads of UBL forms scattered all over the office.

For internal control, each set of documents should be printed with consecutive numbers on them. This means that the shipper will pay a printer for forms which are not provided by the carriers. Yet, the shipper may be able to reduce his freight expense by a very considerable amount each year if the forms are properly designed, as the following facts outline.

The amount of freight charges on a shipment of merchandise depends upon three factors:

1. The weight of the goods hauled.
2. The distance the goods were hauled.

3. The ICC tariff classification of each item shipped—which includes how it is packaged.

Tariff classifications are very technical and complicated. The professionals in this field refer constantly to ICC manuals which list practically every product made by any company in the entire United States. This manual provides the correct, legal description for every commodity or product and the freight rate.

Factors Which Determine Rate

- The type of material of which the product is made is very important—wood, iron, steel, glass, aluminum, brass, copper, etc.
- The way in which the goods are crated or packaged has a bearing on establishing the correct rate to be applied. For example, a commodity which is shipped already assembled will usually take a higher rate than the same commodity shipped unassembled. This is called shipping it "knocked down." Presumably, the reason for the lower rate in the latter instance is that the unassembled commodity will require less space in the carrier's vehicle.

The type of package or container in which an item is shipped has some effect on the rate. A chemical shipped in a glass container will be subject to a higher rate than the same chemical contained in steel cans.

Rates Applied

A first-class rate is known as a "100% rate."
A second-class rate is 85% of the first-class rate.
A third-class rate is 70% of the first-class rate.
A fourth-class rate is 55% of the first-class rate.
A "double first-class" rate also exists; it is 200% of the first-class rate.

Savings through Correct Classification

A wholesale auto-parts distributor in the city of Dallas had been shipping auto parts of all types all over the Southwest for many years. His shipping clerk habitually described nearly all outgoing items as "Auto Parts." A study of the products and the correct, legal descriptions to apply revealed that the mere addition of three words, "Iron or Steel" behind the words "Auto Parts" would *save 15%* on all iron or steel parts shipped!

It was also found that when shipping rubber floor mats, 45% could be saved by describing them as "Rubber Floor Mats"—because a fourth-class rate (55% of first-class) would then apply.

The savings mentioned above are not unusual, and they are indicative of what usually can be done in almost any business.

How To Effect Savings on Freight Costs

By following the steps outlined below you can assist the client in controlling his freight shipments better—and save money on freight bills at the same time:

1. Prepare a list of those products which are shipped *most often*. Describe them, and note how they are packaged and what containers are used.

Figure A — Office Equipment Manufacturer Bill of Lading

DELIVERY CARRIER				CAR OR VEHICLE	
				INITIALS	NUMBER

NO. PACKAGES	DESCRIPTION OF ARTICLES, SPECIAL MARKS AND EXCEPTIONS	*WEIGHT (SUB. TO CORR.)	CLASS OR RATE	CHECK COLUMN	
	BOXES ADDING, BOOKKEEPING OR COMPUTING MACHINES OR PARTS				Subject to Section 7 of Conditions of Applicable Bill of Lading, if this shipment is to be delivered to the consignee without recourse on the consignor, the consignor shall sign the following statement:
	BOXES CASH REGISTERS OR PARTS				The carrier shall not make delivery of this shipment without payment of freight and all other lawful charges.
	BOXES MICROFILMING, INDEXING AND VIEWING MACHINES OR PARTS				
	BOXES ADDING MACHINE STANDS, I. S. (K. D.)				(Signature of Consignor)
	BOXES ADDING MACHINE PAPER, PLAIN				If charges are to be prepaid, write or stamp here, "To be Prepaid." PREPAID
	BOXES ADDING MACHINE PAPER, PLAIN; INTER-LEAVED OR BACKED WITH CARBON				Received $_____ to apply in prepayment of the charges on the property described hereon.
	BOXES, EMPTY WOODEN, RETURNED N. O. I.				
	A				Agent or Cashier Per_____ (The signature here acknowledges only the amount prepaid.) Charges Advanced:

Figure B — Food Manufacturer Bill of Lading

Consigned to

Destination — State of — County of

Route

Delivering Carrier — Car Initials — Car No.

Received $ to apply in prepayment of the charges on the property described hereon.

Agent or Cashier

Per

(The signature here acknowledges the amount prepaid.) Charges advanced: $

No. Pkgs.	Desc. Of Articles, Spec. Mrks. & Except.	*Weight (Sub. to Cor.)	Class or Rate	Ck. Col.	No. Pkgs.	Desc. Of Articles, Spec. Mrks. & Except.	*Weight (Sub. to Cor.)	Class or Rate	Ck. Col.	No. Pkgs.	Desc. Of Articles, Spec. Mrks. & Except.	*Weight (Sub. to Cor.)	Class or Rate
	Chocolate					Dessert Preparations, (Dry)					Mince Meat		
	Cocoa Powdered					Flavoring Syrup, in Glass					Nutmeats Shelled		
	Cocoanut Prepared					Flour Edible					Ornaments Cake		
	Colors Food					Fruit Pre-served					Pans, Baking Nested Solid		
	Confectioners Paste					Glucose (Corn Syrup)					Raisins		
	Confectioners Powder - Drums					Jelly, in Drums					Seeds		
	Corn Starch					Milk Powdered					Spices N.O.I.B.N.		

*If the shipment moves between two ports by a carrier by water, the law requires that the bill of lading shall state whether it is "carrier's or shipper's weight"

NOTE.—Where the rate is dependent on value, shippers are required to state specifically in writing the agreed or declared value of the property. The agreed or declared value of the property is hereby specifically stated by the shipper to be not exceeding _____ per _____

AMERICAN PRODUCTS CO. INC., Shipper, Per _____ B _____ Agent _____ Per _____

Permanent post-office address of shipper: 1501 LATIMER ST., DALLAS, TEXAS

Figure 18-9

TYPICAL BILL OF LADING DESCRIPTIONS USED BY AN OFFICE EQUIPMENT MANUFACTURER (A) AND A FOOD MANUFACTURER (B)

(A) Office Equipment Manufacturer

(B) Food Manufacturer

2. Take the list to the traffic manager of the client's most widely patronized motor-freight carrier. He will study each item on the list, and look up each commodity in his ICC tariff manual to select the *correct technical description* for each item. Note: The rating clerks in his firm must do this for every item on every freight bill anyway—but they have orders to apply the *highest possible rate* when the description of the commodity leaves doubt as to what it actually is, or how it is packaged.

3. After the correct, legal descriptions have been obtained call in the representative of a business-forms firm and order custom-printed bill of lading forms.

On the face of the forms, print the correct descriptions of those commodities which make up the bulk of most shipments. Leave blank spaces for other, less-popular commodities.

Include the Railway Express clause if allowed by local shipping regulations.

Instruct the printer to number each set of forms consecutively.

19

Accounts Payable Systems and Procedures (I)

Accounts payable accounting is an office function which deserves special and concentrated attention from the accounting practitioner or systems analyst for several reasons:

- It involves the disbursement of funds to vendors.
- Unpaid invoices represent current liabilities which affect the firm's working capital ratio.
- Prompt payment of invoices may produce substantial financial earnings through discounts taken.
- Accounts payable procedures supplement the purchasing, receiving, warehousing and inventory control functions of the business.

Criteria of a Payables System

An adequate accounts payable system will limit disbursements to cover only authentic, audited invoices representing goods or services actually received. The system should detect duplicate invoices previously paid, and provide positive means of signaling invoice-due dates to avoid loss of cash discounts. Also, the system should provide information to management for cash requirements forecasting.

Methods and Equipment

Accounts payable systems and procedures have progressed through the years from pen and ink methods through accounting machines and punched-card equipment to the present computer age. Now, many firms are computerizing both accounts receivable and accounts payable with excellent results. This chapter outlines specific systems and procedures for all of these methods, including the latest procedures for applying a full-scale digital computer to payables and check-writing.

Fundamentals of Payables Accounting

An approved and coded vendor's invoice represents an amount owed to a creditor. If the invoice is entered in the books of account before payment, it is credited to an accounts payable control account, then it is entered on a vendor's detail payables record.

There are several types of widely-used vendor records, ranging from accounts payable ledger sheets to voucher-check forms. (These are illustrated and discussed in a subsequent section of this chapter.)

For the distribution side of the accounting entry for a payables invoice, there are one or more debits to an asset or expense account. Statistical studies of payables invoices consistently reveal that in a merchandising or manufacturing firm the majority of the vendor invoices represent purchases or direct charges to inventories. In a retail, service or research firm most debits are to expense accounts.

Depending on the number of accounts on a firm's General Ledger Chart of Accounts, expense distribution may present a problem because of a large number of departments and detail expense accounts within each department which may be affected by any one invoice. This chapter presents several practical methods for expense distribution, regardless of the number of expense accounts on the chart of accounts.

PRELIMINARY PROCEDURES FOR ACCOUNTS PAYABLE

Many preliminary steps usually precede the formal recognition of a payables obligation of the buyer in favor of the seller. Receipt of a vendor's invoice by the buyer is the culmination of a flow of various documents between the two firms which began within the buying firm by some individual initiating a purchase requisition form.

Purchase Requisitions and Orders

A purchase-requisition form is used when a department head or some other individual initiates a request that goods, supplies or services be purchased. This request may be in the nature of a telephone call, a memorandum or a regular purchase-requisition form.

A purchase-requisition form is for internal office use and it resembles a regular purchase order. It usually is a simple form that provides space for entering quantity wanted, product description, reason for the requisition and the name of the person initiating the request.

When the requisition is received by the purchasing-department personnel, it becomes the basis for issuing a formal purchase order to a vendor to authorize shipment of the desired item or items.

Distribution of Purchase Order Copies

1. Original to vendor.
2. Duplicate is filed in numeric order for future reference.
3. Triplicate is filed alphabetically for later matching with vendor's invoice and with receiving report.

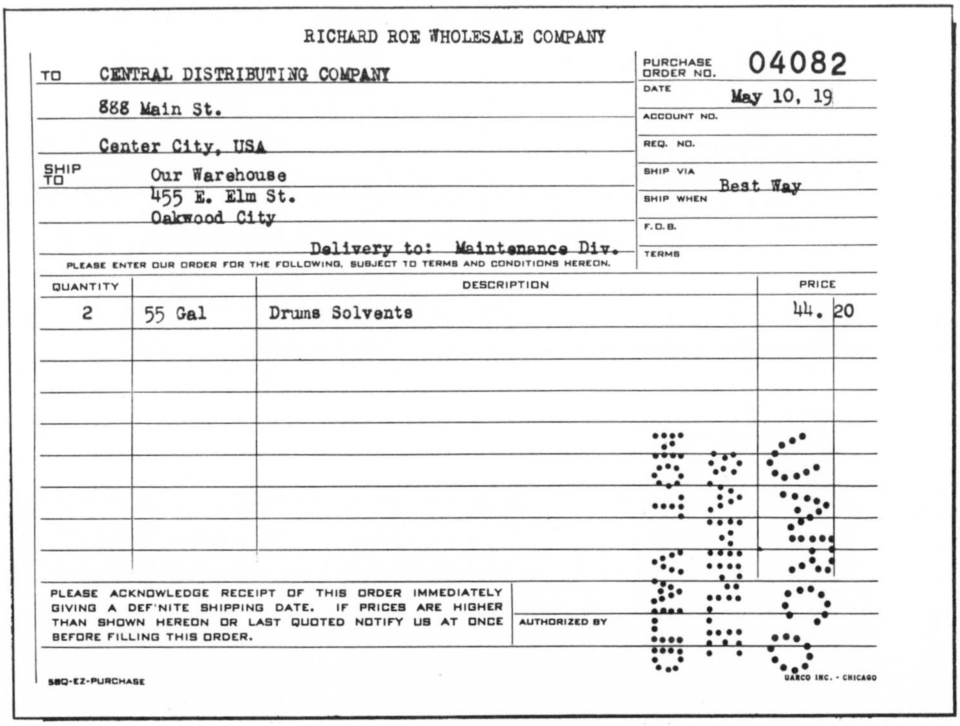

RICHARD ROE WHOLESALE COMPANY

TO CENTRAL DISTRIBUTING COMPANY
888 Main St.
Center City, USA

SHIP TO Our Warehouse
455 E. Elm St.
Oakwood City

Delivery to: Maintenance Div.

PURCHASE ORDER NO. 04082
DATE May 10, 19
ACCOUNT NO.
REQ. NO.
SHIP VIA Best Way
SHIP WHEN
F.O.B.
TERMS

PLEASE ENTER OUR ORDER FOR THE FOLLOWING, SUBJECT TO TERMS AND CONDITIONS HEREON.

QUANTITY		DESCRIPTION	PRICE
2	55 Gal	Drums Solvents	44. 20

PLEASE ACKNOWLEDGE RECEIPT OF THIS ORDER IMMEDIATELY GIVING A DEFINITE SHIPPING DATE. IF PRICES ARE HIGHER THAN SHOWN HEREON OR LAST QUOTED NOTIFY US AT ONCE BEFORE FILLING THIS ORDER.

AUTHORIZED BY

SBQ-EZ-PURCHASE

UARCO INC. - CHICAGO

Figure 19-1
A PURCHASE ORDER

4. At least one copy, preferably two, is sent to the receiving department. This copy shows who ordered, or wants, the materials listed on the form. This enables the receiving-department personnel to move the materials without delay, once received, to their ultimate destination within the company.

Receiving Department

A receiving-report form is a very important component in a control system for purchase and payment transactions. These forms are written by the men on the receiving docks who actually unload the trucks or freight cars. They record information as to the common carrier, make notes of damaged goods, count the boxes, cartons or containers actually received, etc.

Routed to Purchasing

The purchasing department receives a copy of the receiving report. A clerk matches the receiving report to the alphabetic copy of the purchase order which was originally filed for this purpose. Both documents are kept together until the supplier's invoice is received and matched to these two documents.

RECEIVING REPORT

REC'D FROM CENTRAL DISTRIBUTING COMPANY — DATE REC'D 5/17 19 — TIME REC'D — A.M. P.M.

ADDRESS 888 Main St., Center City — P. O. # 4082 — SHIPPER'S NO.

CARRIER Johnson Lines — WAYBILL NUMBER 66675 — CAR INITIAL AND NUMBER — PREPAID ☐ COLLECT ☐ TRANS. CHARGES

TOTAL NO. PKGS. OR PCS. 2 Drums BOXES ____ CARTONS ____ CRATES ____ BAGS ____ BUNDLES ____ PIECES ____

EXCEPTIONS TAKEN AT TIME OF RECEIPT None — REMARKS

	QUANTITY	DESCRIPTION	WEIGHT
1	2	55 Gal Drums Solvents	310
2			
3			
4			
5			
6			
7			
8			

RECEIVING CLERK CDW — DELIVERED TO Maintenance — No. 09667

UARCO INC. CHICAGO

Figure 19-2
A RECEIVING REPORT

Invoice Processing Routines

When the supplier's invoice is received, it is first matched to the filed receiving report and purchase-order copies. With all three documents now on hand, a control clerk does the following:

1. Compares quantities and unit prices on the invoice with those on the purchase order.
2. Checks terms and conditions on the invoice with the agreed-upon terms specified on the purchase order.
3. Compares receiving report with invoice to verify that all items billed were actually received—in good condition.
4. Staples all three documents together and routes them to other sections for auditing and coding for debit distribution.

Auditing Function

If the volume of accounts payable invoices is reasonably heavy, an audit clerk is usually assigned to process them. The audit clerk performs these steps:

1. Stamps a distribution block on the face of the invoice and determines the accounting distribution—if the audit clerk does the coding work also.* The clerk then writes account

* Department stores and other firms sometimes affix a special header form to the invoice to provide uniform areas for recording debit distribution amounts.

numbers and amounts in the block area and adds the distribution amounts to prove that the sum of the distributed amount equals the invoice amount.

2. Studies the invoice terms and writes the *due date* on the invoice. Also, the audit clerk circles the invoice date and number with a colored pencil. This saves time in subsequent processing steps; the location of this information varies considerably on invoices.

3. If discount terms are not consistent, the audit clerk calculates and writes the discount amount on each invoice. This saves time on subsequent payment procedures.

4. Calculates each line of the invoice to test accuracy of each extension.**

5. Adds amounts and verifies the accuracy of the invoice total.

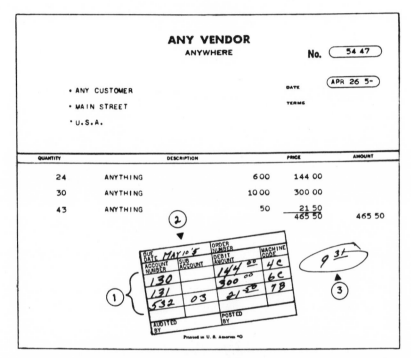

Figure 19-3
AN AUDITED, CODED VENDOR'S INVOICE

Flow Chart

The flow chart of accounts payable preliminary procedures shows graphically the many preliminary steps leading up to receipt of an invoice and the matching of documents prior to the auditing and coding procedures. (See Figure 19-4.)

** Calculating all extensions on vendor invoices may be unnecessary; an occasional test on invoices selected at random may well suffice. This is positively unnecessary if purchase orders are extended; a quick comparison of the invoice amount to the purchase order amount should indicate those which require further checking.

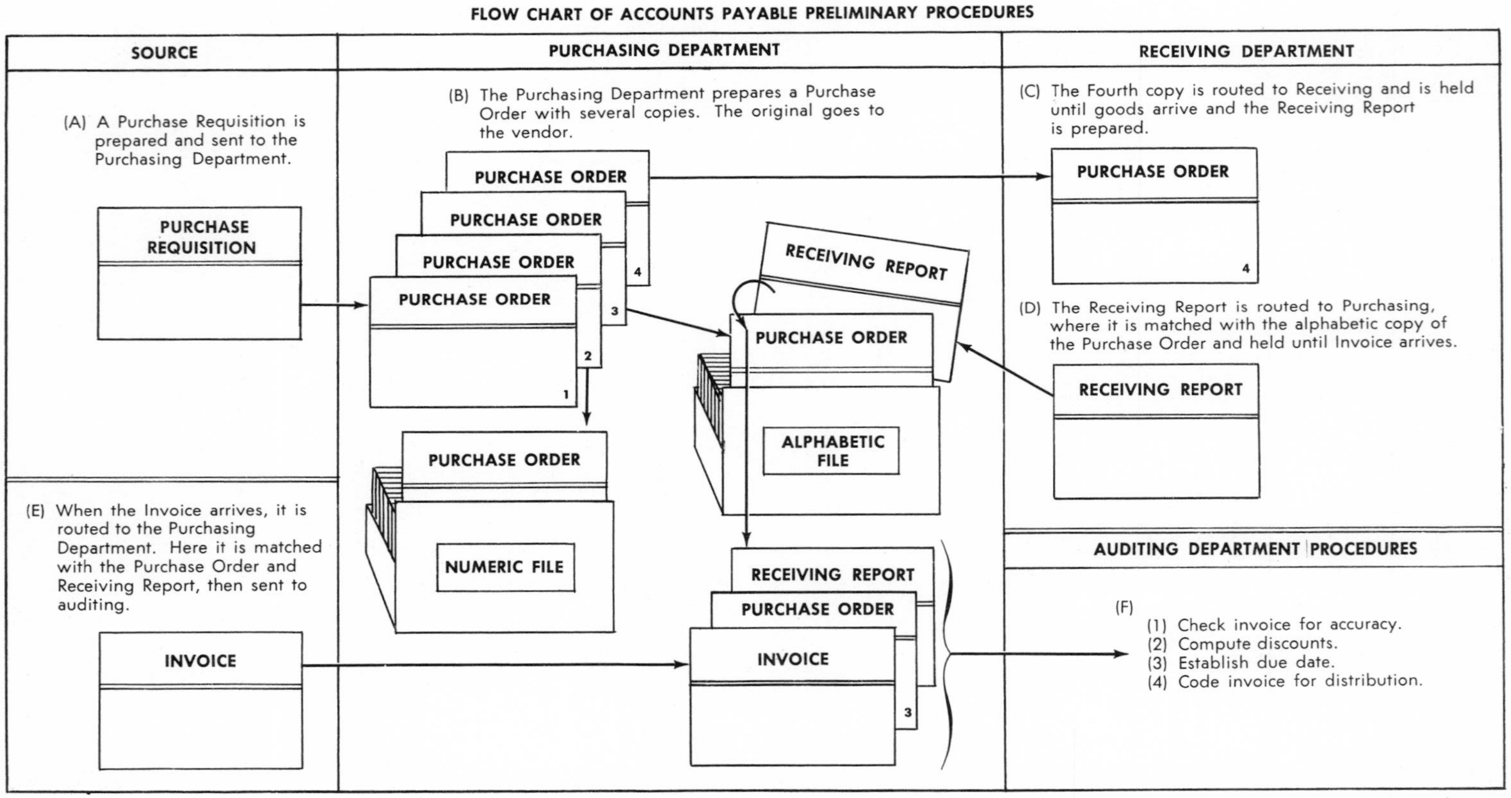

FLOW CHART OF ACCOUNTS PAYABLE PRELIMINARY PROCEDURES

SOURCE	PURCHASING DEPARTMENT	RECEIVING DEPARTMENT

(A) A Purchase Requisition is prepared and sent to the Purchasing Department.

(B) The Purchasing Department prepares a Purchase Order with several copies. The original goes to the vendor.

(C) The Fourth copy is routed to Receiving and is held until goods arrive and the Receiving Report is prepared.

(D) The Receiving Report is routed to Purchasing, where it is matched with the alphabetic copy of the Purchase Order and held until Invoice arrives.

(E) When the Invoice arrives, it is routed to the Purchasing Department. Here it is matched with the Purchase Order and Receiving Report, then sent to auditing.

AUDITING DEPARTMENT PROCEDURES

(F)
(1) Check invoice for accuracy.
(2) Compute discounts.
(3) Establish due date.
(4) Code invoice for distribution.

Figure 19-4

FLOW CHART OF ACCOUNTS PAYABLE PRELIMINARY PROCEDURES

METHODS AND PROCEDURES FOR RECORDING ACCOUNTS PAYABLE INVOICES

Choices of Methods

A broad array of equipment of all types is available for application to accounts payable processing. This makes it difficult to determine quickly the best approach and to select the best equipment, consistent with price and productivity potentials, for the job. For example, when the practitioner or systems analyst is contemplating a new system for the handling of accounts payable invoices, he is confronted with the following choices of methods and equipment:

- Post all records and journals with pen and ink.
- Use pegboards and specially-designed "one-write" forms with pen and ink entries.
- Post all vendor records and accounting journals—and write checks with an accounting machine.
- Apply tabulating equipment to the entire job, or merely use punched-cards for debit distribution.
- Install an accounting machine which is cable-connected to a keypunch.
- Design all procedures for application of an electronic computer which the client firm may have on the premises for many other jobs.

The number of choices listed above provides an indication of the difficulty of designing an efficient and practical accounts payable system for a client.

Since the purpose of this chapter is to provide quick reference to information about the various methods and equipment which can be installed for payables, this chapter is devoted to an explanation of each method, and includes illustrations of them.

Reference and Audit

Regardless of the method or equipment installed, the systems designer must not overlook the two basic requirements which a payables system must meet: *reference and audit*. If reference to paid or unpaid invoice is cumbersome, then the payables system may be rated as unsatisfactory.

Auditors frequently find accounts payable installations which fail to meet the fundamental requirements of reference and audit. However, with proper planning and a constant awareness of these two requirements, the systems designer can develop and install a very efficient and completely adequate payables system.

TWO BASIC PAYABLES METHODS

The systems designer is faced with a choice between two primary methods of processing payables invoices. These are:

1. The buildup method
2. The direct-payment method

The Buildup Method

The buildup method simply implies that incoming invoices are processed through the usual preliminary steps; then they are entered into the accounting records at once. That is, they are posted to some type of vendor records, then entered in books of original entry to reflect the debit side of the payables transaction.

Benefits of the buildup plan are as follows:

- There is no peak-load job of vouchering and distributing an accumulated volume of invoices at the time of payment.
- The books of account properly reflect the total accounts payable—and the expenses incurred or charges to purchases or inventory—before the invoices are actually paid.
- Management has the necessary figure facts for financial planning, since the records show the amount due each vendor and the total due by *invoice due dates*.

Direct-Payment Method

Under the direct-payment method, invoices are processed through the preliminary steps and possibly coded for later distribution; then they are merely filed for a period of time awaiting payment. Invoices are not posted to vendor records, nor are they taken into the books of account at the time they are received.

This method creates a peak-load of work at the time of payment, but it has the offsetting advantage of reducing the number of times that each invoice is handled. Also, it reduces the time required for the repeated posting of each invoice to a vendor ledger or voucher. And, the direct-payment method makes it possible to establish and post summary totals of expense or purchase debits—which saves time on the accounting function.

PEN AND INK METHODS

The use of conventional pen and ink methods usually involves only three basic forms: A Purchase Journal, a vendor ledger and a Cash Disbursements Journal. More often than not, vendor invoices are entered in the Purchase Journal when they are received and are subsequently posted to a vendor ledger.

Purchase Journal

A Purchase Journal is, of course, a book of original entry. The primary method of distributing invoice debits is by posting amounts in columns. The usual Purchase Journal makes limited provision for direct distribution to active accounts because the number of distribution columns which can be accommodated on the journal page is less than ten. Debits for accounts for which no column is provided must be entered in the "Sundry" or General Ledger column. If a large number of entries are posted in the sundry column, this causes lost time at month-end, since the entries for the various account numbers must be recapped and balanced before they are posted to appropriate General Ledger accounts.

There is a very satisfactory and simple method for increasing the number of columns available for direct distribution which has not been widely used. Addition of a fold-over flap to the distribution side of a Purchase Journal provides double the number of columns otherwise available. See Figure 19-5, taken from a complete General Accounting Plan that was developed by the author of this book.

As you can see, the additional columns on the top sheet are utilized for expense distribution; the distribution columns on the main page are assigned to a breakdown of *purchases* by departments. If the primary distribution consists of expense items, both pages could be dedicated to expense distribution.

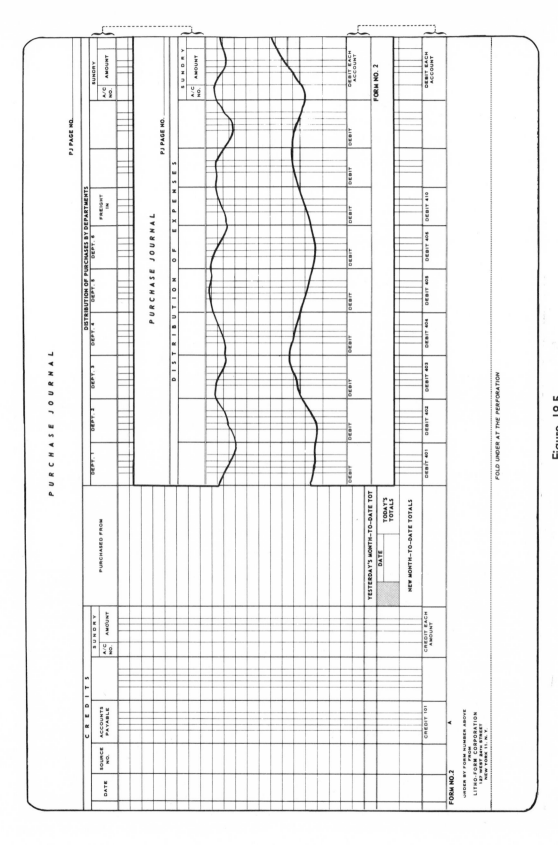

Figure 19-5
PURCHASE JOURNAL

Proper use of this added flap requires that all invoices first be entered on the main page, and distributed only if the columns on the main page are affected. If an invoice includes a distribution amount to be entered in a column on the top sheet, the invoice is turned sideways until all other invoices have been entered on the main page. Then, the bookkeeper refers once more to those invoices not completely distributed, and posts the amounts after bringing the top sheet down and *in front of* the main page.

Observe that both pages include a sundry column for miscellaneous distributions. The value of the additional columns provided by the fold-over flap is that they eliminate a large number of entries from appearing in the sundry column.

Vendor Ledger

After entry of all invoices in the Purchase Journal, the bookkeeper posts each invoice to some type of vendor record. The most commonly used form is a simple accounts payable ledger for each vendor. Invoices are posted individually as received; disbursements are posted when payments are made. The ledger balance represents unpaid invoices.

Voucher Envelope Plan for Payables

Many firms do not record vendor invoices in their accounting records when they are received. In keeping with this practice, a popular plan in use in automobile dealerships utilizes large envelopes (referred to as "voucher envelopes") to accumulate invoices from vendors until such time as the invoices are processed for payment. The envelopes serve the dual purposes of accounting *and filing*.

Typical Instructions: When the first invoice for the current period is received from a vendor, select a blank envelope and write the vendor's name and address on the top. Place all invoices received during the current accounting period inside the envelope. (These invoices have not yet been recorded in the Purchase Journal.) The invoices remain inside the envelope until a statement is received from the vendor in the month following the month of purchase.

When the statement is received, remove the invoices from the envelope and perform the following steps:

1. Check off each invoice against items shown on vendor's statement.

2. Write account numbers and amounts on each invoice for distribution purposes.

3. Now record each invoice on the face of the voucher envelope and distribute debits in columns provided.

4. Calculate cash discount on total of all invoice amounts if applicable. Write discount amount on the envelope for later use.

5. Envelopes are used as the basic document for entries in the Purchase Journal. The total owed each vendor is entered as a credit to accounts payable and appropriate debit distribution is made.

Disbursements: The envelopes are also the basis for writing disbursement checks. As the checks are written, the date and check number should be entered on the voucher form for later reference and audit.

The voucher envelopes with all paid invoices inside are now filed in alphabetic order.

Benefits of Envelope Plan

This plan provides a simple yet complete accounts payable accounting plan. It is very efficient even with a large volume of invoices flowing into an accounting department. It provides excellent reference and filing facilities both before and after payment. The filing of paid invoices has always been a problem because vendors' invoices vary in size and weight of paper. A voucher envelope provides one of the neatest invoice files available.

Optional Envelope Plan

An optional method eliminates the entering of each invoice on the face of the envelope. Instead the bookkeeper lists the amounts of all invoices received from a vendor and obtains a total. Next, distribution amounts are *summarized* by account number. The adding-machine tape is now the basis for writing account numbers and amounts on the envelope. The total of all invoices is entered in the credit column and also in the upper left-hand area of the envelope.

A typical adding-machine tape with summarized account-distribution figures appears adjacent to a sample coded invoice in Figure 19-6.

Both methods of recording invoices on the envelope are shown in Figure 19-7. The top group of figures, identified by the symbol "A" illustrate the entry of each invoice individually. The lower-line "B" shows the optional plan of entering summary amounts only.

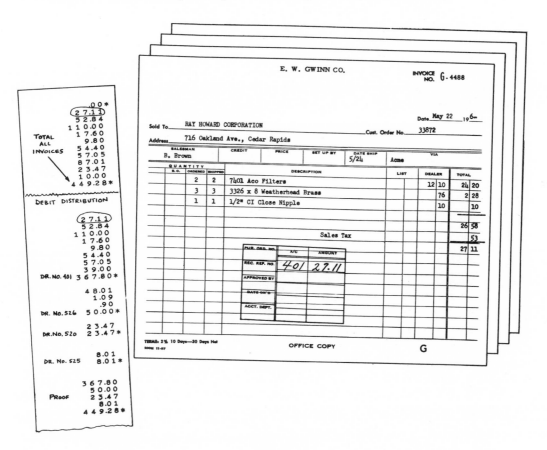

Figure 19-6
SUMMARIZING INVOICE DEBITS FOR DISTRIBUTION ON ENVELOPE

Disadvantages of Envelope Plans

1. A peak load of accounting work is inevitably created at a critical time in the accounting cycle.

2. Lost discounts may occur due to the filing of all invoices awaiting a vendor's statement.

3. Current accounting information as to daily purchases and expenses *is not* available.

4. It is difficult to estimate in advance the total financial requirements necessary to pay all current obligations accumulating in the files. (This may be solved simply by posting to a memo-control record the total of all invoices received daily and filed in the envelopes.)

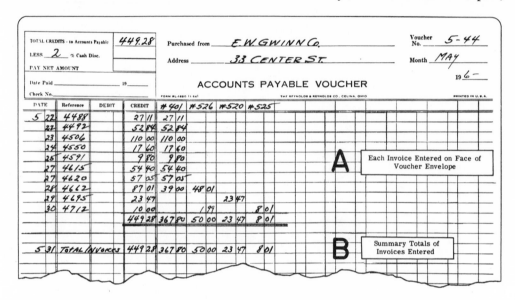

Figure 19-7
ACCOUNTS PAYABLE VOUCHER ENVELOPE

Cash Disbursements Journal

A typical pen and ink Cash Disbursements Journal provides the same number of columns for distribution of debits as are provided by the main page of the two-page Purchase Journal. If the majority of invoices are recorded in the Purchase Journal when received, then most of the payment debits will be recorded in the accounts payable column, with an occasional debit to notes payable.

Expense Distribution

Columns are provided for expense distribution in addition to the two primary debit columns for accounts payable and notes payable. Many checks represent direct disbursements for purchases or expense items. The nature of certain expense items makes it more convenient to pay them immediately rather than first enter them in the Purchase Journal for later payment.

Freight and traveling expenses are typical of expense items which are frequently paid immediately by check. Such amounts are entered in one of the seven distribution columns provided on the standard form.

These columns should be headed up for the seven most active accounts to eliminate as much month-end recapping as possible. Naturally, all occasional sundry entries will be entered in the "Sundry" column, which must be recapped later for account distribution.

Pegboard Accounting

The use of pegboards (writing boards) and specially-designed forms is a unique variation from pen and ink methods. The intent is to combine the posting of detail records with the entry into accounting journals. For example, several excellent plans make it possible to manually post charge sales to a collated customer ledger and statement while entering the amount on the Sales Journal.

On the disbursements side, special alignment and control over the forms enables a bookkeeper to post the check amount to a vendor ledger, complete the check itself and record the entry in the Cash Disbursements Journal—all with *one writing*.

The basic secret of any pegboard plan is that the writing board provides metal or plastic alignment pins which will position and hold checks, statements or ledgers in firm alignment with the next open writing line on the journal. Since the principle involved here (collation of related forms) is identical to that employed in accounting-machine methods, no special illustrations are provided.

THE DUE DATE PROBLEM

As discussed in prior chapters, trade invoices frequently bear terms and conditions, such as "2/10 N30" or "1/30 N31." The presence of "net" in the second option of each of these terms indicates that a cash discount is being offered if paid within the number of days stated in the first option. If the buyer does not pay within this period of time, then he (at least in theory) loses the discount privilege and must pay the full invoice amount—which, oddly enough, is referred to as the "net" amount.

Where a firm receives a substantial volume of invoices routinely and continually, the problem of assuring payment within the discount period may become rather acute.

Filing and Follow-up Methods

If accounting machines are applied to payables, one satisfactory method of controlling payables by due date is to post the incoming invoices to a prenumbered voucher form which is set up by *due date*. The posted invoices are filed alphabetically by vendor—or by due date within vendor name for later matching with the voucher at time of payment.

If invoice terms are interpreted literally, the accounts payable department will find it necessary to voucher and write checks every day, because of invoices which mature each day. Possibly, this can be avoided by a study of invoice terms, followed by making special arrangements with major vendors.

From the accounts receivable side of the accounting picture, it is interesting to note that most firms allow five days or longer as a grace period for customer remittances to be processed through the mail—and by the cash application clerks in the office of the vendor. Many firms allow a grace period of ten days or longer beyond the discount due date of the invoice. They

CASH DISBURSEMENTS JOURNAL

CD PAGE NO. ________

CREDITS							DEBITS		EXPENSES								
				SUNDRY												SUNDRY	
DATE	CHECK NO.	CHECK AMOUNT	DISCOUNTS EARNED	A/C NO.	AMOUNT	PAID TO	ACCOUNTS PAYABLE	NOTES PAYABLE								A/C NO.	AMOUNT
						YESTERDAY'S MONTH-TO-DATE TOT											
						DATE / TODAY'S TOTALS											
						NEW MONTH-TO-DATE TOTALS											
		CREDIT 3	CREDIT 701	CREDIT EACH ACCOUNT			DEBIT 101	DEBIT 102	DEBIT	DEBIT	DEBIT	DEBIT	DEBIT	DEBIT	DEBIT	DEBIT EACH ACCOUNT	

FORM NO. 4 A

ORDER BY FORM NUMBER ABOVE
FROM
LITHO-FORM CORPORATION
127 WEST 24TH STREET
NEW YORK 11, N. Y.

FOLD UNDER AT THE PERFORATION

Figure 19-8
CASH DISBURSEMENTS JOURNAL

will allow the discount if cash is received at any time within ten days after the discount due date. Because of this prevailing leniency in the enforcement of invoice terms, buying firms have been able to work out special arrangements with their vendors. For example:

Suppose that a firm is continually receiving invoices from a major source of supply all during the month. Since the invoice date changes each day, the discount due date may fall on any and all days of the month. Under these conditions, the buyer suggests to the seller that he would like to set up three payment dates during the month; he will pay on the 10th, 20th, and the 30th. Invoices covered by each payment date will be as follows:

> *10th:* Invoices due from the *6th* through the *15th*.
> *20th:* Invoices due from the *16th* to the *25th*.
> *30th:* Invoices due from the *26th* through the *5th* of the following month.

This is an equitable arrangement since the vendor will pay some invoices five days in advance of maturity, while others will be paid five days after maturity. Since many firms have a minimum grace period of at least five days, a variation on the above arrangement is simply to pay no invoices before maturity, but always at the next later payment date. This would mean that the invoices would be paid, on the average, on the basis of five days after maturity.

20

Accounts Payable Systems and Procedures (II)

ACCOUNTING MACHINE METHODS

Accounting machines have been widely applied to office applications for nearly thirty years. Certain types and models of today's desk computers with stored instructions and electronic features are an outgrowth of conventional accounting machines of prior years. As the trend toward mechanization of office functions continues, more and more machines will be applied to accounts payable.

This section of this chapter outlines payables methods and procedures developed for the efficient use of accounting machines, with some overlap into auxiliary punched-card methods.

The concept of combining several related operations into one has long been recognized as one of the major benefits derived from applying an accounting machine to record-keeping jobs. For example, a typical payables approach is to insert a Purchase Journal around the platen of the machine and align it for the first writing line. Then the machine operator inserts and aligns a vendor's ledger card or voucher check form for posting. At the same time the invoice number and amount are being printed on the vendor record, the same data prints on the Purchase Journal; control totals are also accumulated simultaneously.

Vendor Records

A majority of all mechanized payables systems employ the use of a multiple-copy voucher or voucher-check form as the basic vendor record. The voucher form is usually pre-numbered with a consecutive control number; the check number is not assigned until the check portion of the form is filled in at the time of writing checks.

When invoices are being entered in the Purchase Journal, the machine operator inserts the appropriate vendor's voucher for simultaneous entries. This represents a fast and simple operation, featuring automatic printing of the posting date, plus automatic calculation and printing of the latest balance due the vendor. (See Figure 20-1.)

259

1 | 2 | 3 | 4 | 5 | 6 | 7 | 8 | 9 | 10 | 11 | 12 | 13 | 14 | 15 | 16 | 17 | 18 | 19 | 20 | 21 | 22 | 23 | 24 | 25 | 26 | 27 | 28 | 29 | 30 | 31 | 5 38

DUE DATE TABS — DISC AMOUNT

DUE DATE May 10, 196- VOUCHER **No. 1234**

PAYABLE AT
THE FIRST NATIONAL BANK
ANYWHERE

DATE CHECK NO. DISCOUNT AMOUNT

$

PAY TO THE ORDER OF

- Any Vendor
- 2567 Poplar St.
- Anywhere, U. S. A.

NOT VALID

AUTHORIZED SIGNATURE

Printed in U. S. America

REMITTANCE VOUCHER
DETACH BEFORE DEPOSITING CHECK

VOUCHER **No. 1234**

DATE	REFERENCE		INVOICES	DEDUCTIONS	BALANCE
			BALANCE FORWARD		
APR 22'6-	12,34	2.32	13.75		13.75 •
APR 26'6-	12,34	2.65	75.10		88.85 •
APR 29'6-	12,34	2.98	33.21		122.06 •
MAY 3'6-	12,34	3.25	11.66		133.72 •
MAY 7'6-	12,34	3.71	135.00		268.72 •
←AUTOMATIC	←AUTOMATIC	←AUTOMATIC			←AUTOMATIC

WHEN CORRESPONDING WITH US IN REGARD TO THE ITEMS ON THIS REMITTANCE PLEASE REFER TO THE ABOVE VOUCHER NUMBER.

CHECK REGISTER COPY

This copy is placed in a post binder in Check Number order.

VOUCHER COPY

This copy is filed by Voucher Number. If paid invoices are to be attached to the Alphabetic copy, this copy is placed in a post binder at the time the voucher is assigned to a vendor.

ALPHABETIC COPY

This copy is filed alphabetically by vendor. The paid invoices may be attached to this copy if desired.

Figure 20-1
VOUCHER CHECK FORM

Number of Copies Required

The number of copies of the voucher-check form varies, depending upon the filing of paid invoices and whether a copy of the voucher is to be kept as a Check Register copy. For example, if paid invoices are to be attached and filed with the voucher copy (which is filed by *voucher number* for audit and reference), the alphabetic copy may be eliminated. However, this copy may be useful as a vendor cross-reference file, whenever it is necessary to find a specific invoice filed by voucher number.

The voucher-check form shown in Figure 20-1 is a four-part form. Note the due date tabs printed across the top edge of the form. When a voucher form is first headed up for a vendor at the time of vouchering and distributing one or more invoices, the due date of the item or items is marked; later, a colored metal tag or clasp may be placed on this date on the top of the voucher as a visual signal to trigger the check-writing procedures.

Remittance Advice

Some firms use a Remittance Advice form in lieu of a voucher-check form. The form design is identical with that of a voucher-check, but the top part is never filled in as the check. This requires that a separate check form be headed up with the vendor's name at time of payment.

A decision to utilize the Remittance Advice form usually stems from disbursing funds from a large number of different banks. Since a Remittance Advice does not refer to any specific bank, there is no need to make an advance decision as to which bank the funds for payment to the vendor will be drawn on.

Some accountants feel that use of the Remittance Advice form provides better internal control. Note that use of a voucher-check form for building up an accounts payable record for each vendor obviates the use of *pre-numbered checks*. If members of top management or the accountant are adamant about using pre-numbered checks, then the systems analyst would use Remittance Advice forms for a "build-up" method of recording vendor invoices as received. (See Figure 20-2.)

Vendor Ledgers

When a posting or accounting machine is utilized to post invoices and payments to a vendor ledger record, the invoices are usually posted in the *charge column;* check amounts appear in the credit column. Even though this method reverses the actual accounting situation, it is used for purposes of simplicity—to avoid developing and printing credit balances in the balance column. (It is easier for accounting-machine operators to index and handle debit balances than credit balances.) (See Figure 20-3.)

DEBIT DISTRIBUTION METHODS

In pen and ink accounting the primary method of debit distribution is columnar distribution. By contrast, the application of an accounting machine or desk computer to payables provides a broad choice of methods—depending upon the type and make of machine and

| 1 | 2 | 3 | 4 | 5 | 6 | 7 | 8 | 9 | 10 | 11 | 12 | 13 | 14 | 15 | 16 | 17 | 18 | 19 | 20 | 21 | 22 | 23 | 24 | 25 | 26 | 27 | 28 | 29 | 30 | 31 |

DUE DATE TABS

DUE DATE **May 10, 196-**   REMITTANCE ADVICE   **No. 1234**

- Any Vendor
- 2567 Poplar St.
- Anywhere, U. S. A.

WHEN CORRESPONDING WITH US IN REGARD   TO THE ITEMS ON THIS
REMITTANCE ADVICE, PLEASE REFER TO THIS NUMBER ➡ **No. 1234**

DATE	REFERENCE		INVOICES	DEDUCTIONS	BALANCE
			BALANCE FORWARD		
APR 22 6-	12,34	2.32	13.75		13.75 ●
APR 26 6-	12,34	2.65	75.10		88.85 ●
APR 29 6-	12,34	2.98	33.21		122.06 ●
MAY 3 6-	12,34	3.25	11.66		133.72 ●
MAY 7 6-	12,34	3.71	135.00		268.72 ●
↑AUTOMATIC	↑AUTOMATIC	↑AUTOMATIC			↑AUTOMATIC

Figure 20-2

SAMPLE REMITTANCE ADVICE

the total number of registers or accumulators available in the machine for storing distribution amounts.

The available choices of methods for distribution are:

- Columnar
- Register selection and accumulation of amounts in mechanical or electronic counters or registers
- Combination of columns and register selection
- Unit distribution ledgers
- Unit distribution tickets
- Punched-card output for sorting by account number.

Columnar Distribution

Distribution of debit amounts by listing and printing the amount in a designated column on a multi-column Purchase or Cash Disbursements Journal is a practical approach with an accounting machine. If the machine provides a separate total or accumulator for each major column, time is saved by eliminating the manual addition of each column which is necessary with pen and ink journals.

More than 3,000 automobile dealers in the United States have installed, in recent years, a mechanized accounting-machine plan (developed by the author), which features a two-step approach to posting detail records and journalizing. For example, contrary to all previous attempts to mechanize the complex accounting journals and other records found in auto-dealer accounting, this plan does NOT combine the posting of accounts receivable and the Parts and Service Sales Journal. As a result, the speed of journalizing on the machine is very impressive; the operator is not held back by finding, inserting, posting and removing customer ledger and statement forms. Time studies and actual installation experience proved that it is actually faster overall to handle these two operations separately, rather than to combine them.

This approach provided many other benefits. For example, no carbon is used at any time. When posting charge tickets (parts or repair orders) to customer records, the operator inserts an original ledger and statement side by side. An invoice number and amount is entered once on the ledger and *repeated automatically* on the statement. Further, these amounts print on the *back of the Sales Journal* (back side out), because the operator inserts the journal in the machine and places it around the platen before beginning the posting operation.

This provides proof of all debit amounts actually posted to customer accounts, plus the grand total posted. The method is a great assist to the internal auditor or accountant when checking out a difference between the accounts receivable trial-balance total and the General Ledger receivables control total.

This concept of separating journalizing from the posting of detail records is followed throughout the plan. Figure 20-4 which follows shows the proof and audit record of postings to detail customer accounts—printed on the back of the Cash Received Journal.

The illustration shows the customer statement, but not the ledger record. The entry shown on the journal and the statement is repeated automatically on the ledger record which was placed in the machine to the left of the statement.

Even if posting to detail records is combined with the journalizing function, the columnar method of distribution is very practical. Figure 20-6 shows vouchering combined with purchase distribution.

LEDGER

NAME   ANY VENDOR

ADDRESS Main Street

RATING U. S. A.

CREDIT LIMIT

DATE	REFERENCE	CHARGES	√	CREDITS	√	BALANCE
BALANCE FORWARDED						
MAR 10'5-	52.16	75.25				75.25 ●
MAR 18'5-	52.89	37.75				113.00 ●
APR 10'5-CS	6.82			113.00		.00 ●
APR 15'5-	53.34	234.77				234.77 ●
APR 26'5-	54.45	24.00				258.77 ●
APR 28'5-CS	10.01			234.77		24.00 ●

↑—AUTOMATIC   ↑—AUTOMATIC   ↑—AUTOMATIC

Figure 20-3
VENDOR LEDGER

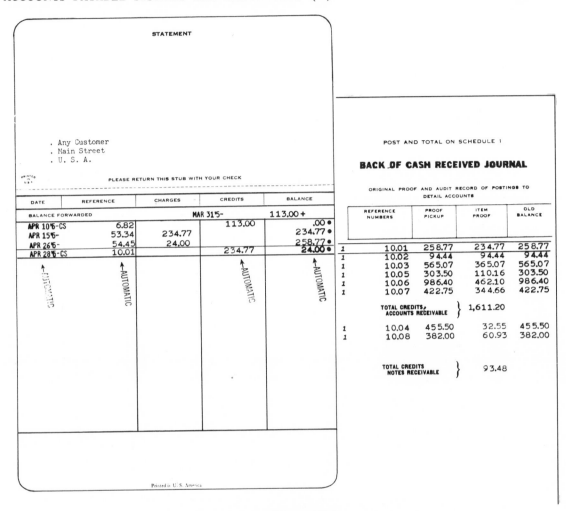

Figure 20-4
BACK OF CASH RECEIVED JOURNAL

Register Selection

"Register selection" refers to the entering and accumulation of debit amounts into machine registers or accumulators selected by the operator when vouchering and/or journalizing. A sound approach for using this method is to study the distribution account numbers found on coded invoices, and determine those which represent the majority of distributions.

Detailed surveys of accounts payable invoices in industrial plants reveal that from 55% to 85% of all vendor invoices are charged to no more than five or six distribution accounts! The active accounts are usually inventory accounts:

- Inventories of Raw Materials
- Inventories of Supplies
- Manufacturing Inventories—piece parts, subassemblies, etc.
- Freight In

Merely by assigning accumulators or "memory units" to these active accounts, the payables operator can handle distribution very rapidly and very easily—just by entering the distribution amount on the keyboard and depressing the selection key assigned to each major distribution account.

Amount	Register No.
88.40	3
110.55	9
1,250.00	1
994.60	3
50.00	4, etc.

The single digit to the right of the amount indicates the number of the accumulator into which the debit amount has been stored.

Figure 20-5 shows a Burroughs E 6000 Desk Computer with two rows of selector keys on

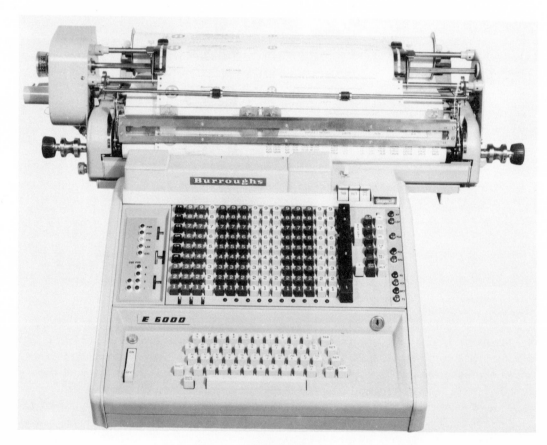

Figure 20-5
ILLUSTRATES SELECTION KEYS FOR 99 SEPARATE TOTALS
(Courtesy of Burroughs Corporation)

the left side of the keyboard; the selector keys are adjacent to the character keys. These keys provide access at random to any one of 99 accumulators. Since this type of equipment now provides such a large number of individually-selected accumulators, distribution exclusively by register selection is very feasible for many firms.

Combination of Distribution Methods

In some instances it may be desirable to combine columnar and register selection distribution methods. If an accounting machine applied to payables has a limited number of registers for accumulation of specified distribution amounts, the use of columns increases the total distribution capacity. If a high percentage of invoice debits can be distributed by the register selection method, then only a small number of entries would appear in the journal columns. (See Figure 20-6.)

PURCHASE JOURNAL

Date	Voucher No.	Invoice No.	Accounts Payable Credit	Inventory Debits Amount	Inventory Debits Code	EXPENSE 1	2	DISTRIBUTION 3	4	5	6
MAY 7'69	1,175	1,260	135.00					135.00			
MAY 7'69	1,290	4,456	288.40	270.00	04						
				18.40	09						
MAY 7'69	1,310	8,845	62.50			50.00	12.50				
MAY 7'69	2,345	12,119	557.35	550.00	03						
MAY 7'69	819	3,322	11,240.00	11,240.00	12				7.35		
MAY 7'69	3,666	1,877	88.30			88.30					
MAY 7'69	1,933	14,542	110.66					110.66			
MAY 7'69	1,500	5543	154.35	154.35	04						

Figure 20-6
COMBINING REGISTER SELECTION AND COLUMNAR DISTRIBUTION

Unit Distribution Ledgers

Thousands of accounting machine installations handling accounts payable have proven the practicality and the ease of distributing purchases and expenses by recording invoice data on *unit ledger records*. (See Figure 20-7.)

Unit ledger cards used for distribution are not the actual General Ledger accounts; they are the *source* of General Ledger postings at the end of the month. A unit ledger card serves the same purpose as a *column* in a Purchase Journal. The primary difference is that whereas the number of columns in a Purchase Journal is limited, the number of unit ledger cards which can be set up for distribution is almost unlimited.

Each time a detail entry is posted to a unit ledger record the machine extends and prints a new month-to-date expense balance. At month-end the accumulated balance for the current month is posted to the *corresponding General Ledger Account.* By ruling off the postings for the current month, the same unit card can be used again to record debit distributions for the coming month.

Miscellaneous debits: Occasionally an invoice debit involves an asset or a liability account. When this situation occurs the machine operator merely types the account title and number at the top of a blank unit ledger record—and posts the debit to the record. At month-end the balance on each unit ledger is routinely posted to the corresponding General Ledger Account.

The same unit ledger may be used subsequently for similar entries during following months by red-lining the balance figure at the end of each month, after posting the balance to the appropriate General Ledger Account.

The General Ledger

When an accounting machine is applied to payables records, it is feasible to set up the General Ledger itself on unit ledger cards for fast, accurate machine posting.

Entries from the following sources are posted to the appropriate unit General Ledger Account cards:

- Column totals from journals of original entry.
- Unit distribution ledger cards which have balances representing current month expense or purchases.
- Unit miscellaneous distribution ledgers; post each current month balance to the indicated asset or liability account.
- Grand totals of major distributions developed through assigned machine registers or accumulators.

When many different entries are posted to a General Ledger Account record, the machine carries forward a new, current month balance for income or expense accounts each time without disturbing or changing the year-to-date balance as of the end of the prior month. A new year-to-date balance is eventually calculated and printed automatically by the accounting machine—as a by-product of a trial balance operation. (See Figure 20-9.)

General Ledger Trial Balance

The trial balance operation as described and illustrated by Figure 20-9 accomplishes three things:

- A complete trial balance is obtained.
- The new, year-to-date balance is printed on each General Ledger Account.
- The current month expense or income is "red-lined" automatically.

The operator inserts the Trial Balance form in the carriage of the machine on the left side. Each unit General Ledger Account card is inserted one by one on the right side of the carriage. The operator reads the following data from the General Ledger card, and indexes on the keyboard successively:

- Account number
- Previous year-to-date balance
- Current month income or expense

The accounting machine then does the following things automatically:

- Calculates and prints the current trial-balance amount as a sub-total.

Unit Distribution Ledger

ACCOUNT NAME Delivery Expense

ACCOUNT NUMBER 630

DATE	SOURCE NUMBER	ACCOUNT NUMBER	DEBIT	CREDIT	CURRENT MONTH BALANCE	YEAR TO DATE BALANCE
BALANCE FORWARDED					APR 30 5-	382.55 *
MAY 3 5-PJ	8	6.30	12.75		12.75	
MAY 4 5-PJ	9	6.30	26.87		39.62	
MAY 5 5-PJ	10	6.30	10.00			
MAY 5 5-PJ	10	6.30	15.25		64.87	
MAY 6 5-PJ	12	6.30	17.58		82.45	

Figure 20-7
UNIT DISTRIBUTION LEDGER CARD

GENERAL LEDGER

Account Name Salaries- Other   Account Number 603

Date	Source Number	Account Number	Debit	Credit	Current Month Balance	Year to Date Balance
Balance Forwarded					APR 30'6–	5,412.75*
MAY 7'6–	22	6.03	375.50		375.50	
MAY 14'6–	28	6.03	410.25		785.75	
MAY 21'6–	32	6.03	387.10		1,172.85	
MAY 28'6–	37	6.03	382.05		1,554.90	
					MAY 31'6–	6,967.65*

AUTOMATIC   AUTOMATIC

Figure 20-8
UNIT GENERAL LEDGER CARD

- Moves to the General Ledger card and prints the end-of-month date underneath the current month income or expense in such a way that this effectively "red-lines" the account.
- Prints the new, year-to-date balance and returns to the trial balance form, ready for another line of printing.

Under this unique approach the Trial Balance form is not a carbon impression of each posting to the General Ledger record. The information prints first on the Trial Balance form, then repeats automatically on the General Ledger card.

Operating Ledgers for Manufacturing Accounting

In prior years, many accounting machines have been applied to the operating ledgers in manufacturing firms. Distribution of supplies and expense originating from vendor invoices and from journal vouchers may affect a wide range of accounts, since it is customary to set up a list of detail expense accounts for each department within a manufacturing entity.

The use of unit machine-posted ledger cards is a successful solution to the problem of random distribution caused by the fact that any invoice or internal journal entry may affect any detail account in any department.

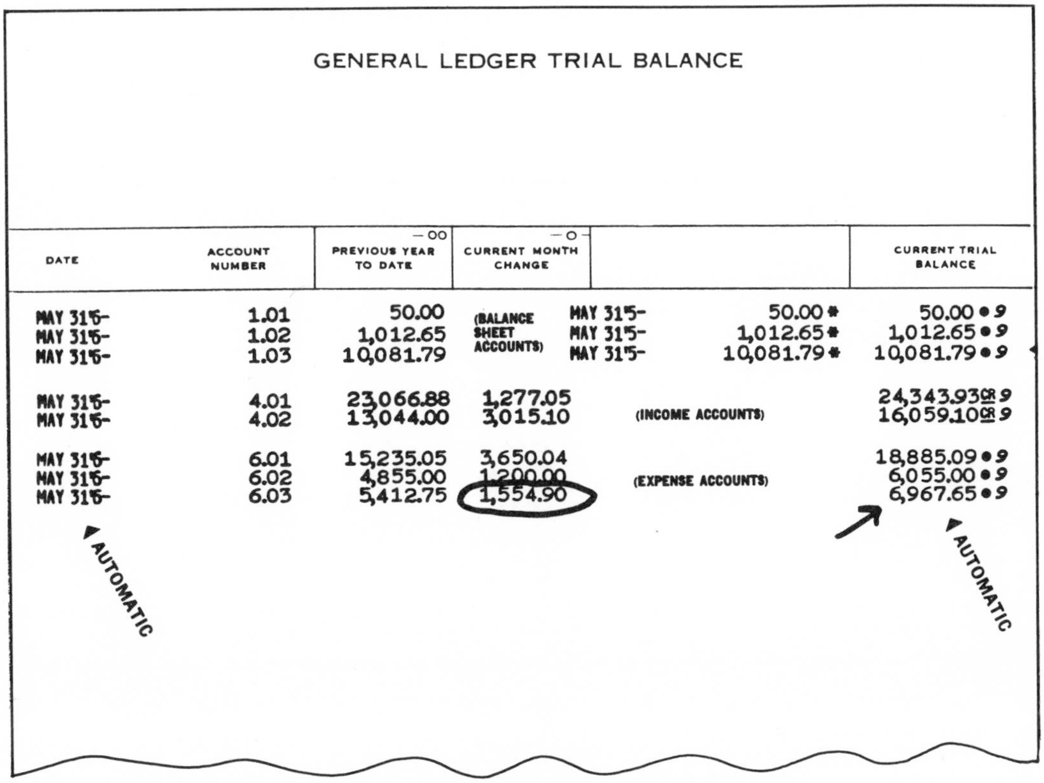

GENERAL LEDGER TRIAL BALANCE

DATE	ACCOUNT NUMBER	— OO PREVIOUS YEAR TO DATE	— O CURRENT MONTH CHANGE		CURRENT TRIAL BALANCE
MAY 31 5–	1.01	50.00	(BALANCE	MAY 31 5– 50.00 *	50.00 • 9
MAY 31 5–	1.02	1,012.65	SHEET	MAY 31 5– 1,012.65 *	1,012.65 • 9
MAY 31 5–	1.03	10,081.79	ACCOUNTS)	MAY 31 5– 10,081.79 *	10,081.79 • 9
MAY 31 5–	4.01	23,066.88	1,277.05		24,343.93 ⊂℞ 9
MAY 31 5–	4.02	13,044.00	3,015.10	(INCOME ACCOUNTS)	16,059.10 ⊂℞ 9
MAY 31 5–	6.01	15,235.05	3,650.04		18,885.09 • 9
MAY 31 5–	6.02	4,855.00	1,200.00	(EXPENSE ACCOUNTS)	6,055.00 • 9
MAY 31 5–	6.03	5,412.75	1,554.90		6,967.65 • 9

▲AUTOMATIC   ▲AUTOMATIC

Figure 20-9
GENERAL LEDGER TRIAL BALANCE

The operating expense ledger cards shown in Figure 20-10 accumulate charges for two different detail expenses in manufacturing division #3, and department #01. The sub-numbers .06 and .07 identify each detail expense account.

In the instance of operating expense ledgers maintained in a manufacturing accounting installation, quite often the unit ledgers are subsidiary to the General Ledger in that they represent the details; whereas, CONTROL ACCOUNTS ONLY are kept in the General Ledger. For example, the General Ledger may contain only one account for each manufacturing division which reflects the *total* of all expenses for the division. The details are found by referring to the operating expense ledgers as illustrated.

Note that these ledger cards include a year-to-date balance column. This balance provides the necessary data for monthly Profit and Loss Statements. As charges are posted to the operating ledger record during each month, the year-to-date balance remains unchanged. However, a new year-to-date balance is calculated and printed at month-end as a by-product of the trial balance operation. The procedure for doing this is the same as that for the General Ledger.

Departmental Control Totals

Another advantage of this procedure is that the machine can accumulate all of the current month expense until the operator inserts—as the last ledger—the Departmental Control Ledger.

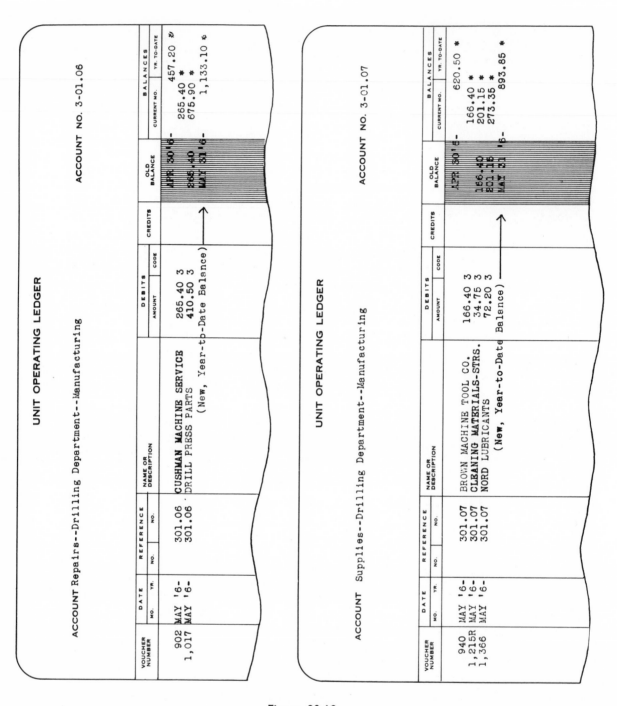

Figure 20-10
UNIT OPERATING LEDGER

After indexing the prior year-to-date control amount, the machine will automatically print the GRAND TOTAL of current month expense on the control ledger, then extend the latest year-to-date balance on the ledger.

Punched-Card Output for Debit Distribution

Many firms have, in recent years, installed accounting machines which are cable-connected to a "slave" keypunch machine. The purpose of this is to obtain punched debit distribution cards as a by-product of the basic vouchering operation.

This approach to the distribution problem is very practical and effective for those firms which have data-processing equipment, or which use the services of an outside data-processing service bureau.

The machine operation is very simple, since the operator simply lists the distribution account number and the amount, accompanied by the voucher or check number which identifies the source of the entry.

APPLYING A COMPUTER TO ACCOUNTS PAYABLE

For an application such as accounts payable, a computer should be considered merely as an advanced type of office machine for accomplishing the desired results. The reason is that the fundamental accounting requirements are the same regardless of the type of equipment applied to the job. However, the means of fulfilling the requirements are changed by the capabilities of the computer.

The procedures and the flow charts included in this chapter are based on the assumption that a firm has a full size, electronic computer with several magnetic tape input/output units on line, plus a card reader and printer. For simplicity in presenting the computer runs, punched cards are shown as the primary input for the updating runs. In actual practice, the systems design would probably call for reading in all data only once from the punched cards representing invoices and accounting distribution; the card data would be recorded on magnetic tape. This work tape would then be the primary source of input for all subsequent runs.

Preliminary Steps

Invoices received from vendors are first subjected to the usual preliminary auditing, coding and checking steps, as already outlined in this chapter. Then they are rough-sorted by letters of the alphabet for batching. The reason for this is that the vendor master file, kept on a reel of magnetic tape, is in alphabetic sequence since the vendor number bears a relationship to the vendor's name. If the vendor file is maintained on random access disks, it would not be necessary to pre-sort the invoices within each batch.

The payables control clerk groups about 50 invoices together, and assigns a consecutive batch number to the group. The next step is to add all invoice amounts in the batch, and write the batch total on a batch slip attached to the invoices.

Keypunching

The batched invoices are routed to the keypunch section for converting all data into coded form for later entry into the computer runs.

Step 1: Punch invoice details into a card, such as batch number, vendor number, invoice date and number, terms and amount.

Step 2: Punch *account number and amount* for each distribution appearing on the face of the coded invoice. Primary reference data includes batch number, vendor number and invoice number.

(Note: It is possible to punch accounting distribution information into the same card which contains invoice details for subsequent vouchering. For simplicity of explanation, the flow charts found on following pages show that separate cards were keypunched for accounting distribution.)

After the punched cards have been verified, they are routed to the Proof and Control group for processing by the computer.

Filing Invoices

The invoices are now returned to the accounts payable section for filing. They must be filed by *batch number* since this is the primary source number found in the account distribution records.

Computer Processing of Payables

The flow charts in Figure 20-11 show graphically each computer run required for processing payables. The runs are divided into daily, weekly and monthly runs. The run numbers as seen on the flow charts tie in with the run numbers explained in the following narrative:

Run 1: During the voucher register run, the computer adds today's vouchered invoices to an UNPAID FILE maintained for each vendor. As the computer prints the detail of each invoice on the voucher register, it should also apply terms to each invoice. A calendar stored in memory enables the computer to calculate both the *discount due date* and *final due date* which are stored on the updated vendor file as part of the data for each unpaid invoice.

This run, in effect, posts each invoice to a vendor payables record. It is not necessary to group invoices by common due dates since the computer can select invoices due for check-writing by testing the due date of each one at check-writing time.

Run 2: A companion run prints the Distribution Register for the same invoice batches which were vouchered, and writes the account distribution records on a special magnetic tape work file which is used at month-end for General Ledger accounting.

Check-Writing

Depending upon the payment policies of a firm, checks may be written every day for invoices due and payable on that day—or a compromise plan may be adopted to write checks weekly, or once each ten days.

The check-writing run writes voucher checks at high speed, complete with vendor name and address—and writes a new vendor file with *paid items deleted* from it.

During this run, the computer also copies all check data to a work tape for the subsequent printing of a check register. (See weekly run No. 1 on flow charts for a graphic illustration of this check-writing run.)

Check Register

While the computer is printing one line per check on a check register, it also adds today's paid items to a tape file of all items paid at prior times during the month. This special work

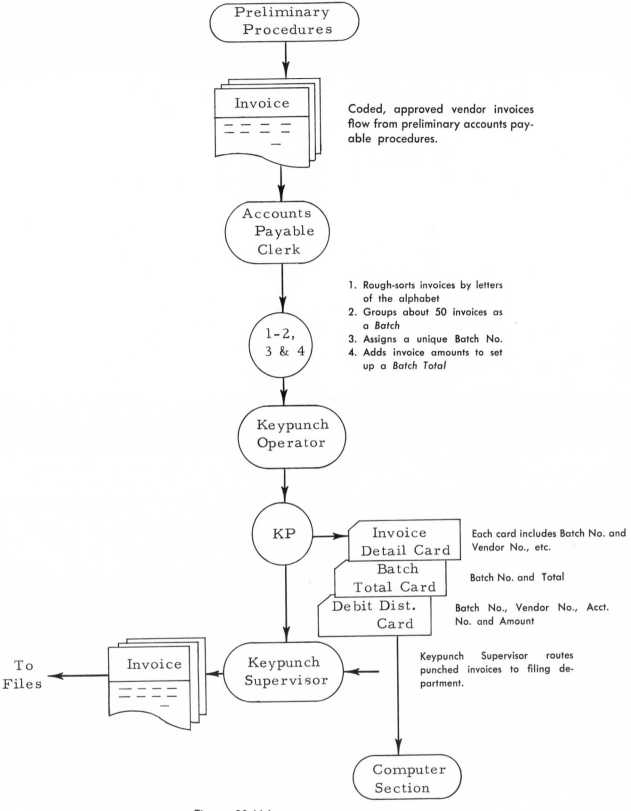

Preliminary Procedures

Invoice
— — — —
—

Coded, approved vendor invoices flow from preliminary accounts payable procedures.

Accounts Payable Clerk

1-2, 3 & 4

1. Rough-sorts invoices by letters of the alphabet
2. Groups about 50 invoices as a *Batch*
3. Assigns a unique Batch No.
4. Adds invoice amounts to set up a *Batch Total*

Keypunch Operator

KP

Invoice Detail Card

Each card includes Batch No. and Vendor No., etc.

Batch Total Card

Batch No. and Total

Debit Dist. Card

Batch No., Vendor No., Acct. No. and Amount

Keypunch Supervisor routes punched invoices to filing department.

To Files

Invoice
— — — —
—

Keypunch Supervisor

Computer Section

Figure 20-11A—

FLOW CHART OF ACCOUNTS PAYABLE PROCEDURES

I. Daily Computer Runs

Run 1: Prepare Voucher Register

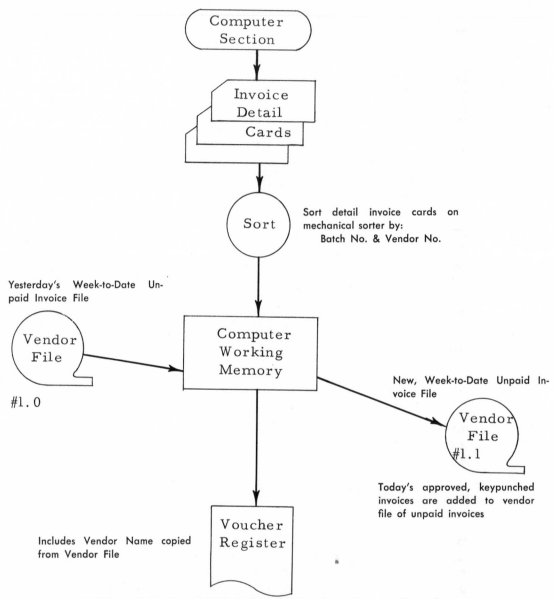

Sort detail invoice cards on mechanical sorter by:
Batch No. & Vendor No.

Yesterday's Week-to-Date Unpaid Invoice File

#1.0

New, Week-to-Date Unpaid Invoice File

Today's approved, keypunched invoices are added to vendor file of unpaid invoices

Includes Vendor Name copied from Vendor File

1. Computer applies invoice terms (found in each invoice detail card) to each invoice record as it passes through memory.
2. Computer calculates the discount Due Date and stores it on the invoice record, added to the Vendor File of unpaid invoices; see output file #1.1.

Figure 20-11B

FLOW CHART OF ACCOUNTS PAYABLE PROCEDURES (cont.)

I. Daily Computer Runs
Run 2: Print Distribution Register

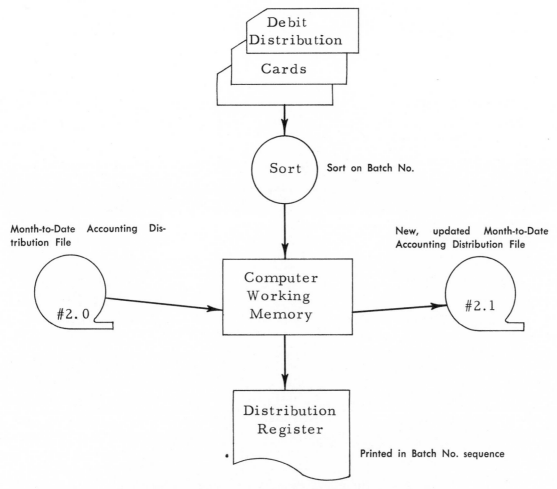

Total distribution debits for each batch must equal the
total invoices credited to accounts payable on the Voucher
Register.

Figure 20-11C—

FLOW CHART OF ACCOUNTS PAYABLE PROCEDURES (cont.)

Weekly Computer Runs
Run 1: Write Checks to Vendors for Invoices Now Due

File of unpaid invoices

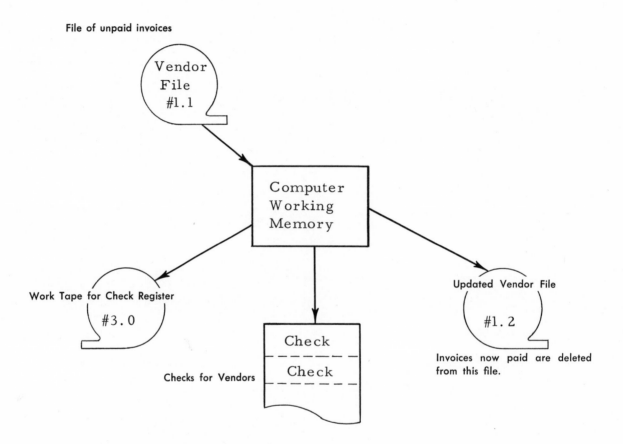

What the Computer Does:

1. Computer scans each unpaid invoice on the Vendor File #1.1.
2. When it finds an invoice due for payment (based on a comparison of the invoice due date and today's processing date) it prints the invoice date, number, amount and date due on the voucher check.
3. The computer addresses the check by copying the Vendor's Name and Address from the Vendor File #1.1.
4. At the same time it is printing the checks, the computer copies all paid items and check data to the special work tape #3.0.

Figure 20-11D
FLOW CHART OF ACCOUNTS PAYABLE PROCEDURES (cont.)

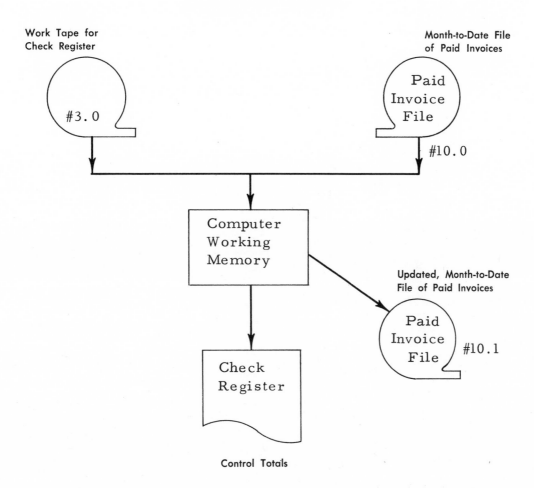

Weekly Computer Runs
Run 2: Print Check Register

What the Computer Does:
1. Writes the Check Register at high speed.
2. Copies all paid invoices extracted from the unpaid Vendor File at the time of check-writing, and writes the records on the Month-to-Date File of *paid* invoices.

Figure 20-11E
FLOW CHART OF ACCOUNTS PAYABLE PROCEDURES (cont.)

Monthly Computer Runs
Run I: Print Vendor Payment History Register

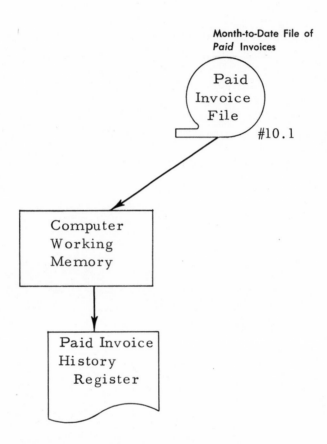

Printed in Vendor No. sequence for paid item references
(Invoice information always includes the original Batch No. where the
invoice is physically filed)

Other Month-End Runs

The Accounting Distribution File #2.1 (see page 3 of flow charts) is sorted
into account number sequence, then utilized to print a complete *Distribution
Register*.

The totals of all debits to inventory or expense accounts are posted to the
corresponding General Ledger accounts from the register.

Figure 20-11F
FLOW CHART OF ACCOUNTS PAYABLE PROCEDURES (cont.)

file makes it possible to print a "Vendor's Paid Invoice History Report" once each month for vendor reference.

Summary and Benefits

A key point is that the system outlined above eliminates the usual procedure of finding and matching invoices with voucher checks before the checks are reviewed and signed. The details on the voucher apron refer to the batch number, invoice date, number and amount. Invoices are handled a minimum number of times (after the usual preliminary checking steps) as they are batched, keypunched and filed immediately.

The system offers a number of benefits to the user. It provides for a relatively simple set of procedures and high-speed computer runs. Discounts are uniformly taken without undue paperwork and paper handling.

Increased use of funds may be obtained through centralized control over all disbursements. Better and more accurate debit accounting is obtained since a special, well trained group of people in the accounts payable section reviews all distribution codes, or applies the correct codes during the preliminary checking and review of invoices being processed to the batching clerk.

21

Job Cost Systems and Procedures

The management of many manufacturing plants operating today does not know actual production costs of products being manufactured and sold. Many firms have, through trial and error, established a selling-price schedule for each product which seems to provide an adequate operating profit. Due to a lack of cost figures on which to base sound pricing policies, such firms are especially vulnerable to competitive pressures and changing marketing conditions. It is increasingly essential for the accounting records of any plant classified wholly or partially as a "job shop" to provide a record of total costs on each job produced.

Guide to Planned Profits

Sales planning and forecasting is commonplace in business today. A corollary to such activities is the new management science of "planning for profits." This means that management establishes a total gross-profit goal for a period of time in the future. Then a sales quota is assigned to each major product line based on gross-profit contribution. This implies the availability of accurate cost data to obtain gross-profit figures on each product line. A recent case history will illustrate how planning for profits can improve the operating policies of a company.

A CASE HISTORY

Corporation "X" had been manufacturing and selling three distinctly different product lines for many years. This company knew its overall costs, but had never bothered to establish costs and profits on each of the three product lines. As part of the concept of "planning for profits," accurate cost figures were established on each product line for the first time. These figures indicated the following surprising facts:

	Product Line "A"	Line "B"	Line "C"
Percent of Gross Profit to Sales	27	42	45

For many years, this corporation had been pointing most of its selling time and promotional efforts towards increasing the sales of product line "A." Once the gross-profit percentages on all three product lines were known, management decided to make a major shift and emphasize product lines "B" and "C." One immediate action was to reduce the commission rate paid on product line "A" sales and increase the rates on the other, more profitable, products. Also, advertising coverage allotted to "B" and "C" products was increased.

Job Cost Figures Valuable for Bidding

Accurate cost figures are invaluable when bidding on large, potentially lucrative jobs. The firm that knows its costs can bid with confidence and know that if the bid is accepted, the result will be a profitable contract. While analyzing reasons for the business failure of several firms, a Bureau of Business Research recently uncovered an interesting fact. One firm had bid on scores of government contracts without a single award. Reason: The firm had no job-cost data, so it always bid high enough to be "safe"—with a resulting loss of the contract. A later examination of the records showed the firm could have bid low enough to obtain many awards at a good profit margin.

Three Elements of Job Cost

The origin of a job is the issuance of a production order to the plant which requires the production of a stated quantity of a designated product. And, when the initial manufacturing processes necessary to manufacture the product are begun, it then becomes essential to record and accumulate job costs.

Total job cost is comprised of three cost elements. These are:

1. Direct material costs.
2. Direct labor costs.
3. Overhead burden (expense) allocated to the job.

The remainder of this chapter provides comprehensive coverage of the first element of job cost listed above; i.e., direct material costs, with particular emphasis on the subject of material control. Our intent here is not to present accounting theory, but to outline specific procedures being used daily in actual, successful installations.

ACCOUNTING FOR AND CONTROLLING MATERIALS IN A MANUFACTURING PLANT

Securing accurate materials cost data and maintaining tight overall control of materials inventories are very important to the success of a manufacturing operation. As will be seen, the materials-control system exerts a definite influence on labor costs, particularly idle-time expense. Also, an adequate materials-control system, or lack of one, exerts an influence on customer good will in that it affects the fulfillment of delivery commitments to customers.

Materials-control procedures are necessarily related to the writing of production orders and are tied in with production-control procedures. To lay the groundwork for a complete coverage of detailed materials-control procedures, it is first necessary to review briefly the twin subjects of production orders and production control.

Production Orders

The document that authorizes the fabrication of a specified quantity of finished products in the plant is called a "Production Order."

A decision to build a designated quantity of a specified product (this decision precedes the writing of a production order) is based on one or all of the following factors:

1. *Sales Forecasts:* When the sales department issues a sales forecast, this may become the basis for a decision to manufacture a supply of standard products for filling future anticipated orders. To implement the forecast, a production order is written for the estimated quantity needed.

2. *Inventory Replenishment:* Inventory policies may require stock replenishment when the supply of standard products on hand reaches a predetermined stock level.

3. *Special Orders:* In plants which specialize in building products to customers' specifications, a production order is written for each "custom-building" order received and entered.

Production Control

Production control, in its broad sense, refers to controlling the flow and processes of manufacturing. In large manufacturing plants, production control covers the detailed, complicated scheduling of all machine and man-hours for weeks or months in advance of production. The Production Control Department correlates engineering and manufacturing changes, sets up production schedules, supervises the control of inventories, etc. In smaller plants, it is usually only necessary to notify plant supervisory personnel of pending production orders. They will route the various orders through the necessary departments and operations.

Inventory Control

One very important element of production control in small and medium-size plants is the maintenance and control of inventories. These are frequently classified and divided into several categories:

1. Raw Materials.

2. Manufactured or purchased parts.

3. Subassemblies. These may be defined as raw materials and parts which have been converted into a component of a finished product by applying manufacturing labor. Of course, many subassemblies are purchased from outside sources.

4. Supplies.

5. Finished Goods.

BENEFITS OF AN EFFICIENT INVENTORY CONTROL SYSTEM

Effective inventory management and well-planned procedures may provide the following benefits:

1. Automatic detection of impending stock shortages.

2. Permit maintenance of minimum quantities of inventory items without risk of production stoppages.

PART NO	DESCRIPTION		DRAWING NO	P.C.		OPER. SHEETS REV.
W54	Hi-Lo Metal Tray Binder		XB123			

Stand

SCHED START 6/2/6-
ORDER NO 8753
DATE OF ORDER 5/8/6-
QTY TO PRODUCE 50
NO. IN GRP | EST. COMP DATE

PAGE _____
OF _____

OPER	DEPT	WORK STATION	OPERATION	SET UP	RUN TIME / _____	JOB CLASS	MACHINE	TOOLS
1	3	4	FABRICATE	.5	5.0		Press Brake	
2	3	5	WELDING		5.0		Resist Welder	
3	5.	1	CLEANING		2.5			
4	7	2	PAINTING		2.5			
5	10	4	ASSEMBLE		13.33			
6	11	1	PACKING & SHIPPING		12.5			

ITEM	TOTAL PARTS REQUIRED	PARTS PER UNIT	STOCK LOCA-TION	PART NUMBER	DESCRIPTION	SUB LIST	NOTES
					See Separate Bill of Materials		

FORM NO. 4620-B

NUMERICAL FILE COPY

Figure 21-1
PRODUCTION ORDER FOR FINISHED PRODUCTS

3. Permit lowering of stock requirements and capital amounts invested in inventories, with a resulting decrease in financing costs.

4. Eliminate distorted book records of all parts or materials because of delay in posting incoming materials for lack of invoice value data.

5. Reduce record-handling and posting time.

6. Provide complete buying information and history without disturbing major stores-control records.

7. Provide accurate book records to serve as a check against unauthorized removal of inventory items from premises.

8. Furnish a complete history record of all transactions and usage to help eliminate over-buying and resulting obsolescence.

Materials Control Department

Every manufacturing plant, with the possible exception of very small plants, should maintain a Material Control Department. The major responsibility of such a department is to set up and keep adequate records on all materials, parts and subassemblies used in the manufacturing processes.

Ledger Design

Proper design of the materials-control ledger card (frequently referred to as a "stores" or stock record) is very important. The phrase "materials control" will be used frequently in subsequent discussions of records involved in this area of manufacturing activities.

A well-designed materials-control ledger card usually includes the following balance columns:

1. Quantity on Hand.
2. Total On Order (Memo Balance).
3. Total Quantity Available (Memo Balance).
4. Value of Quantity on Hand (Optional).

Form design may or may not provide space for unit cost data, depending upon the prevailing method for costing direct materials used in production. This will be discussed on subsequent pages. The form will also provide columns for date, posting reference data, recording quantities reserved, ordered, received and issued. (See Figure 21-2.)

Reservations and "Availability" of Materials

Since materials control is a vital part of overall production control, the Materials Control Department usually bears the responsibility for assuring that all necessary parts and materials *are avilable* when actually needed in manufacturing. It is very costly to idle an entire factory production group because of the lack of a few apparently insignificant parts or a quantity of raw materials. And, this may be commonplace in a shop serviced by a poorly operated Materials Control Department. We can now state that the word "control" means more than merely controlling stores on hand—it *refers to controlling and preventing future shortages* of materials at all times.

The problem of preventing future materials shortages begins with the writing of a production order. Since each production order requires the manufacture of a stated quantity of finished products, each order *demands the availability,* when needed, of definite quantities of raw materials, parts and other components necessary to produce finished products. However, there may be a time lag of days, weeks or months between the writing of the order and the start of actual production. This time lag obviously complicates the entire situation.

It is now very evident that the material-control ledger records, to prevent future shortages, *must reflect all manufacturing commitments* as they are incurred. This is accomplished by posting materials *requirements* (reservations) from a bill of materials. The procedural details are presented on subsequent pages in this chapter.

Available Balance

For reasons just outlined, the most important balance column on the material-control ledger card is the memo "available" balance. Posting quantities required for future manufacturing commitments immediately affects this balance, as will be seen. The quantity in this memo-

DATE	REFERENCE NO.	QUAN. RESERVED	QUAN. ORDERED	✓	QUAN. WANTED	QUAN. REC'D	VALUE OF RECEIVED		QUAN. ISSUED	UNPLANNED ISSUES	MONTH TO DATE	AVERAGE UNIT COST	QUANTITY ON HAND	VALUE OF ON HAND		TOTAL ON ORDER	AVAILABLE
MAY 5	BALANCE FOR WARD										20	1 45	300	435	00	-0-	70
MAY 8	PROD ORDER 2250	200	①														130 CR
MAY 10	PURCH ORDER 895		250	②												250	
MAY 25	REC. 664				250	240	384	00	③				1 52	540	819	00	-0-	110
MAY 26	B/M 1826									60	④	80		480			

STEEL LEGS — ARTICLE   Used with Unit No. W-5L, Hi-Lo Metal Tray Binder Stand — DESCRIPTION / SPECIFICATIONS   A 1260 — PART OR STOCK NO.   MAXIMUM _300_   MINIMUM _60_

MATERIAL CONTROL RECORD

Figure 21-2
MATERIAL CONTROL LEDGER CARD FOR HAND-POSTED SYSTEM

balance column indicates the "free" supply of parts or materials not yet committed or needed to fill existing production orders.

Because of the time lag between the writing of production orders and the start of actual production, quantity-on-hand data is relatively unimportant for preventing future shortages.

For example, it may be reassuring to know that we have on hand a quantity of 1,000 of a certain part, until a glance at the available balance indicates an overdrawn or danger condition due to committing 1,500 of these parts for future manufacturing requirements!

Manual Methods Versus Computer Methods

The principles of inventory control remain unchanged regardless of how the records are posted or updated. Note the similarity of the headings in the balance columns found on the *hand-posted* Material Control Record and the computer-posted record, Figure 21-3. The only difference is that the computer-posted record includes a running balance of quantity reserved; whereas, this was omitted for convenience from the hand-posted record.

PART NUMBER			DESCRIPTION OR MESSAGE	TRANSACTION				DATE RELEASED OR ISSUED	BALANCE		DATE REQUIRED	BALANCE	
PRIME	DASH	SUB.		AREA	PHASE	TYPE	NUMBER		ON HAND	ON ORDER		RESERVED	AVAILABLE
12669255	000		RESISTOR	5304	BEGIN	BALANCE	PLNR A	BUYER L	180	BUY			180
				5304		PURCH ORD	144445L	9 06 63		3000	9 23 63		3180
				40		RESRVATION	23218F	8 30 63			10 02 63	3000	180
					ENDING	BALANCE			180	3000		3000	180

Burroughs Corporation ELECTRODATA DIVISION — INQUIRY PLANNER A - ANDERSON — **INVENTORY ACTION SYSTEM** 9 06 63

Figure 21-3
MATERIAL CONTROL RECORD MAINTAINED ON A
LARGE-SCALE ELECTRONIC COMPUTER

Types of Stores Transactions

We will now examine the various types of transactions routinely posted to stores records and determine the effect of each transaction on the various balances provided on the ledger form shown in Figure 21-2.

1. *Reservations:* The quantity of each item needed to manufacture the total quantity of finished products specified by a Finished Goods Production Order is provided by a Bill of Materials. (See Figure 21-4.) The total quantity indicated for each item is posted to the corresponding materials ledger card as a *reservation.*

The posted quantity *decreases the available balance.* (See posting line identified by the numeral "1" on the form shown in Figure 21-2.)

2. *Orders:* Orders are documents written to replenish an item which is, or will be, in short supply. There are two kinds of orders:

a. Purchase orders are written and issued for parts or materials purchased from outside vendors.

b. Production orders are written for parts or subassemblies to be manufactured internally in the plant. This type of production order is sometimes referred to as a shop, or "parts," order to distinguish it from master production orders covering the manufacture of finished products.

Either type of order, when posted, merely increases the "Total On Order" balance. (In Figure 21-2, refer to posting line identified by the numeral "2.")

3. *Goods Received:* When materials are received in the stores room, a receiving report is prepared detailing all items received. This becomes the basic document for posting quantities received to materials-control records.

The quantity received affects the following balances:

(1) The "On Order" balance is decreased.

(2) The "Quantity on Hand" balance is increased.

(3) The "Available" balance is increased, since more items are now available for further manufacturing commitments.

(Some accountants prefer to increase the memo "Available" balance concurrently with posting a purchase or production order quantity in the "On Order" column of the stores record. Then, when the materials or parts are subsequently received, the "On Order" balance is decreased; "Quantity on Hand" is increased. The "Available" balance would remain unchanged.)

4. *Issues:* Parts or materials issued to plant personnel for production or maintenance purposes are posted as issues to stores records.

Posting of issues affects the following balances:

(1) Month-to-Date total of issues is increased.

(2) Quantity on Hand balance is decreased.

All four types of postings are illustrated in Figure 21-2.

OUTLINE OF A COMPLETE MATERIALS CONTROL SYSTEM

An investigation and a comparison of the methods used in many plants for controlling materials reveal invariably that no two plants use identical procedures in writing production orders and bills of materials. Also, the routing of copies varies considerably from plant to plant; the design and operation of the materials-control ledger varies; several methods of costing materials issued will be found, etc. However, certain basic principles have to be, and are, followed regardless of minor procedural differences.

Materials-control procedures may be very cumbersome, expensive and top-heavy unless full advantage is taken of the accumulated know-how of methods groups and individuals who have specialized in developing efficient, low-cost techniques at every step of the way.

The specific, detailed material-control plan which follows will adequately meet the requirements of many manufacturers. Many short-cuts have been incorporated into the plan to help reduce clerical costs wherever possible.

Bill of Materials

A plant which produces standard products should have on hand at all times a supply of bills of materials for *each finished product* manufactured intermittently. A bill of materials is a complete, detailed list of every part, subassembly and every item of raw materials needed to manufacture *one complete unit*.

Detailed engineering drawings are the original source for preparation of a bill of materials. The drawings itemize every part and each item of material needed to produce the finished product.

For "custom-built" products manufactured to customers' specifications, detailed engineering drawings and a list of materials are prepared for each order. Therefore, a bill of materials is available whether the plant builds standard products, or writes production orders for individual custom-built products. The form shown in Figure 21-1 provides space for detailing materials requirements on the face of the production order. This idea is especially applicable in plants specializing in custom-building small, simple products.

As stated before, the bill of materials is the *source document* for posting reservations to stores ledger cards.

To clarify the procedure for establishing the total quantity of each part, raw materials or subassemblies necessary for manufacturing a stated quantity of finished products, we will examine typical procedures in a metalworking job shop producing several types of office equipment, such as ledger tray binders, portable metal stands and related equipment.

TYPICAL MATERIAL CONTROL PROCEDURE

To begin our case history, let us assume that management makes a decision to build fifty metal stands for stock. These stands are called "Hi-Lo Metal Tray Binder Stands." The previously prepared bill of materials for this product lists all parts numbers, descriptions and *quantities needed to build one complete unit*. (See Figure 21-4.) To establish total requirements for manufacturing 50 units, it is necessary to multiply each quantity shown on the list of materials by 50. The result is written in the "Issues" column on the form because the total quantity needed will actually be issued later from inventory.

Subassemblies

The item "Locking Assembly Complete" on the list of materials in Figure 21-4 carries an "X" in front of the part number, followed by the word "breakdown" in the "Issued" column. The "X" designates a subassembly; a pre-assembled section of a finished product. For each subassembly there should be a bill of materials in the files; three copies of the "sub" bill of materials are removed from the files. Total parts requirements for making the specified quantity of subassemblies are calculated and written on these forms. The disposition and routing of these forms is the same as that explained below with regard to the copies of the master list of materials.

Procedure Instructions

A manual of instructions prepared by the practitioner for an installation may contain instructions to personnel in the Materials Control Department similar to those outlined below.

1. When a production order is received in the department, go to the files and remove three copies of the master bill of materials for the finished goods designated in the production order. (All bills of materials should be typed on carbon "masters" for quick reproduction on spirit-duplicating machines. In this way, a reserve supply of forms may be maintained in file cabinets for instant use.)

In this instance, remove the bill of materials for the "Hi-Lo Metal Tray Binder Stand" from the files.

2. Insert carbons between the three copies, then multiply quantity required per finished unit by the total quantity of finished products wanted. Write the results of the calculations in the "Issued" column on the form.

Disposition of Completed Copies

1. Route one set of forms to the Plant Supervisor. He will use them as a notification of future production requirements for planning purposes and as a check list of materials needed for producing the job.

BILL OF MATERIALS AND MATERIAL REQUISITION						
UNIT NAME Hi-Lo Metal Tray Binder Stand			PRODUCTION ORDER NO. *8753*			
DRAWING NO. XB123		UNIT PART NO. W54	PRODUCTION ORDER QUANTITY *50*			
DATE OF SPECIFICATIONS 8/1/6 -		TO CENTER OR DEPT. NO. 6				
DESCRIPTION OF PART	PART NO.	REQUIRED PER UNIT	ISSUED		▸	SHORT
Name Plate	A1255	1	*50*			
Stops	A1258	2	*100*			
Steel Legs	A1260	4	*200*			
Lock Nuts	A1261	8	*400*			
Angles	A1301	4	*200*			
2" thumb screws	A1305	2	*100*			
Screw Rods	A1307	2	*100*			
Adjusting Rod Bracket	A1340	2	*100*			
1/4-20 x 5/8 Bolts	B0012	4	*200*			
Large Nylon Bearing	B0015	4	*200*			
Casters & Sockets	B0121	4	*200*			
Locking Assembly Complete	XB0688	1	Breakdown			
Pivot Bolts	B0788	2	*100*			
Caster Bolts	B1155	8	*400*			
			☐ TO STORES ☐ TO PLANT FOREMAN ☐ TO MATERIAL CONTROL			

Figure 21-4

A COMPLETE BILL OF MATERIALS

2. Route one set of forms to the stock room. This copy now becomes a *material requisition*. All items listed on the requisition are removed from stock and placed to one side. When the production department actually needs the materials, then they will be issued.

In some plants, certain areas of the factory are "collection" points where plant people go to get all items needed for a specific job. Items removed from stock are placed here for this purpose.

3. Route one set of forms to the Materials Control Department for posting reservations to appropriate ledger cards.

Posting Reservations

Posting reservations from a bill of materials to materials-control ledger cards may present a problem if parts numbers on the bill of materials are listed in random sequence. This will reduce posting speed considerably. Here is one solution to the problem: When the master bill of materials is prepared from engineering drawings, list all parts numbers and material code numbers in ascending order, with the lowest numbers at the beginning of the list. This enables the posting clerk to begin posting at the front of a tray containing stock ledger cards bearing low-order parts numbers and work through the tray from front to back.

Posting Issues

As explained on the preceding page, one copy of a bill of materials is used as a material requisition. Stock-room clerks issue quantities indicated in the "Issue" column. Any deficient quantity is indicated in the "Short" column of the form.

Filled requisitions are routed to the Materials Control Department. Here, quantities issued are posted to materials cards. Again, the fact that stock numbers are listed in ascending sequence saves time in selecting and posting the records.

Unplanned issues are emergency issues not previously reserved for a production order. An unplanned issue quantity must *reduce the available balance,* and the quantity on hand balance.

Alternate Type of Material Requisition

Since the bill of materials is a carbon master suitable for reproduction of copies on spirit duplicating machines, an alternate type of requisition form may be produced if desired. Pre-shingled sheets of unit tickets may be fed through the duplicating machine; each line of information on the master bill of materials will be reproduced successively on the bottom edge of each unit ticket in the shingled set of tickets. Then each individual ticket is run through the machine again to pick up the information from the heading of the master form.

(The Part Requisition form illustrated in Figure 21-5 is a standard form used here primarily to show arrangement of shingled strips. In actual practice it would be necessary to design the requisition tickets to correspond to the exact format of the master bill of materials.)

After requisitions are filled in the stock room, unit tickets are routed to materials control for posting of quantities issued.

Summary Posting of Issues

Random posting usually results from multiple-line source documents. Posting one random entry at a time to individual ledger cards kept in several tray binders which may be scattered over a considerable area is very time-consuming. Use of unit tickets enables the posting clerk to accumulate all tickets pertaining to a particular stock ledger, then make *one summary posting* of issue quantities. To accomplish this, issue tickets are simply dropped in front of the respective ledger cards until the summary-posting operation begins. Then the tickets are removed from the ledger tray and quantities issued are summarized. A two-total accounting machine can be programmed to add all quantities on an adding-machine tape located to the

PART REQUISITION

FORM AO 6 1-51 90469 ® DITTOFORMS

PRECISION **ANALYSLIPS** SPACED ® — PRECISION SPACED DITTO ANALYSLIPS MANUFACTURED UNDER ONE OR MORE PATENTS SHOWN ON LABEL — ®

ORDER NO.	ASSEMBLY NO.	DRAWING NO.	AUTHORIZED BY	DATE	NO. OF PAGES	PAGE NO.
8753	TS 6679	XB 123	JBW			

DATE OF ORDER	ASSEMBLY DESCRIPTION					
MAY 8 6-	HI-LO METAL TRAY BINDER STAND					

QUANTITY						
50						

DATE WANTED						
JUN 2						

ASSEMBLY NO.	FILLED BY	DATE	RECEIVED BY	QUANTITY DELIVERED	UNIT COST	TOTAL COST

	QUANTITY REQUIRED	QUANTITY PER UNIT	PART NO.	DESCRIPTION	DELIVER TO DEPT.	
	50	1	A1255	NAME PLATE	2	
	100	2	A1258	STOPS	2	
	200	4	A1260	STEEL LEGS	2	
	400	8	A1261	LOCK NUTS	2	
	200	4	A1301	ANGLES	2	

Figure 21-5

PRE-SHINGLED SHEETS OF UNIT PART REQUISITIONS

left of the ledger card which has been positioned in the machine carriage for posting. The machine will automatically post total quantity issued, as one entry, to the ledger card.

Impending Shortages Automatically Detected

Material-control ledger-card design includes space for recording the minimum quantity established for the stock item. The minimum is determined by several factors: average monthly usage, length of time required to replenish stock when an order is placed, total investment in the item, etc.

The primary purpose of a minimum figure is to act as a signal for initiating replenishment procedures when the available quantity approaches the established minimum. This implies that the posting clerk will visually compare the minimum quantity with the new available balance after each reservation posting. Experience amply confirms the suspicion that posting clerks will not consistently compare the two figures as posting proceeds, thus causing costly production stoppages later when materials shortages suddenly appear. And, if a posting machine is used for posting stock ledgers, the minimum quantity must be indexed on the keyboard for every line of posting to enable the machine to compare the minimum with the available balance.

This comparison can be made entirely automatic, regardless of whether the records are posted manually or by machine, if the minimum quantity is posted once in the body of the form *as a reservation*. When this is done, the available balance will always reflect the minimum quantity, as it has now been reduced by that quantity. On subsequent postings of actual reservations, the necessity for writing a minus balance in the available-balance column will alert the posting clerk to an impending shortage. If a posting machine is applied to this job, it can be programmed to lock or automatically skip to a designated carriage position when the available balance is zero or a minus balance.

Either function serves as a definite warning to the operator to take action, such as offsetting the card in the tray, or flagging it for later attention. For example, Figure 21-6 illustrates a machine-posted material-control record. The minimum quantity of 182 has been posted once as a reservation on the top line of the form. When the available balance drops below zero (see posting lines identified by letter "R"), the machine signals the operator.

ITEM & DESCRIPTION: COILED WIRE SPRING, 3" x ½" **STOCK NUMBER:** 6819

SIGNAL TABS: BELOW MINIMUM | ON ORDER   MISCELLANEOUS TABS: A B C D

CODE	VENDOR	REMARKS	ITEM LOCATION
1	Johnson Wire Co., Cleveland, Ohio	(One month lead time)	Aisle E Rack 21 Bin 14
2	Industrial Spring Corp., Barston, Ohio		
3	Precision Steel Products., Winchester, Ohio		
4	Globe Manufacturing Co., Lynchburg, Ohio		

PURCHASING INFORMATION — NUMBER OF UNITS IN STANDARD PACKAGE: 144 | UNIT OF INVENTORY: each

MONTHLY USAGE

JAN	FEB	MAR	APR	MAY	JUN	JUL	AUG	SEPT	OCT	NOV	DEC	TOTAL ANNUAL USAGE	YEAR	AVERAGE MONTHLY USAGE
91	108	72	83	92	98	104	102	65	81	101	93	1090	'59	91
98	74	84	105										'60	
													'61	

MAXIMUM 379 — REORDER THIS QUANTITY WHEN AVAILABLE BALANCE DECLINES TO THIS QUANTITY: 288
MINIMUM (182) — 0

DATE – VENDOR – REFERENCE CODE	UNIT COST	ORDERED	RECEIVED	RESERVED	USED	TOTAL USED	ON ORDER	AVAILABLE	ON HAND
MAR 12'6- BALANCES FORWARDED				182		34		127	309
MAR 12'6-	1,703			22				105	
MAR 16'6-	1,817			19				86	
MAR 18'6-	2,041			17				69	
MAR 23'6-	1,703				22	56			287
MAR 24'6-	2,113			9	9	65		60	278
MAR 25'6-	1,817				19	84			259
APR 1'6-	2,191			23				37	
APR 5'6-	2,286			16				21	
APR 7'6-	2,041				17	17			242
APR 15'6-	2,404			14				7	
APR 16'6-	2,407			9	9	26		(R) 2	233
APR 17'6-	1, 807	288					288		
APR 22'6-	2,191				23	49			210
APR 24'6-	2,519			44				(R) 46	
APR 28'6-	2,286				16	65			194
APR 30'6-	2,684			40	40	105		(R) 86	154
MAY 3'6-	2,519				44	44			110
MAY 9'6-	2,774			21				(R) 107	
MAY 17'6-	2,804			32	32	76		(R) 139	78
MAY 18'6-	1, 11,603	33	288				0	149	366
MAY 27'6-	2,404				14	90			352

IF A QUANTITY APPEARS IN THIS SHADED BLOCK THE MINIMUM HAS BEEN RESERVED FROM AVAILABLE BALANCE

Minimum Posted

Figure 21-6
MACHINE-POSTED MATERIAL CONTROL LEDGER CARD
(Courtesy of Burroughs Corporation)

Re-Order Procedures

Offset, or flagged, ledger cards represent a definite signal to a group of people who work very closely with materials-control-department personnel. They may be called "buyers" in some plants; "ledgermen" or "expediters" in others. Their basic duty is to review all flagged accounts and initiate necessary steps for securing parts or materials in advance of production schedules requiring such items.

Traveling Requisition and Order Record

The expediters study the offset ledger cards, make a decision as to quantities needed, then write or type purchase requisitions. These documents, which are requests for written purchase orders covering specified materials, are sent to the purchasing department. (The procedures explained here apply to parts or materials purchased from outside sources.) Initiating purchase requisitions requires considerable writing or typing and errors occur in detailing part numbers and descriptions. One solution to this is to keep a "Traveling Requisition and Order Record" ledger card in the tray binder behind each stock-record card. This form shows item description materials code numbers and the part or stores number. It also shows all vendor information necessary for purchasing, plus a complete record of usage for several years. It reflects all previous orders, unit cost, names of vendors representing the source of supply, etc.

When this form is used, it is only necessary for the expediter to fill in the left side of the ledger card titled "Present Status of Stock Item." The quantity "short" is written in the column provided for this purpose. The card is then routed to purchasing. Purchasing selects a vendor and types a purchase order. The traveling requisition is then returned to the Materials Control Department.

Edge-Punched Requisitions

One of the more interesting developments in office machines in recent years is the automatic electric typing machine made by Friden, known as the "Flexowriter." Edge-punched cards are fed into the side of the machine which activates the typing keyboard and automatically controls the machine in many other ways.

The traveling requisition form illustrated by Figure 21-7 is an edge-punched card. The Flexowriter is first used for punching the coded holes across the bottom edge. These holes represent data such as item description, part number, material code numbers, etc.

Automatic Typing of Purchase Order

When this form, which also serves as an order record, is received in purchasing, a decision is made as to the vendor from whom the goods will be purchased. One or more edge-punched cards which contain the vendor's name and address, code number, etc., in coded form is then removed from a master file. By inserting a purchase order form into the carriage of the Flexowriter the purchase order will be typed automatically. This is done by inserting name-and-address cards, followed by order-record cards. The operator merely types the quantities wanted. This not only saves time; it assures accuracy in typing the extensive parts numbers and descriptions so essential when typing purchase orders.

Posting "On Order" Quantities

After the traveling requisition card is returned from purchasing to the Materials Control Department, it serves as the source document for posting "On Order" quantities to stores

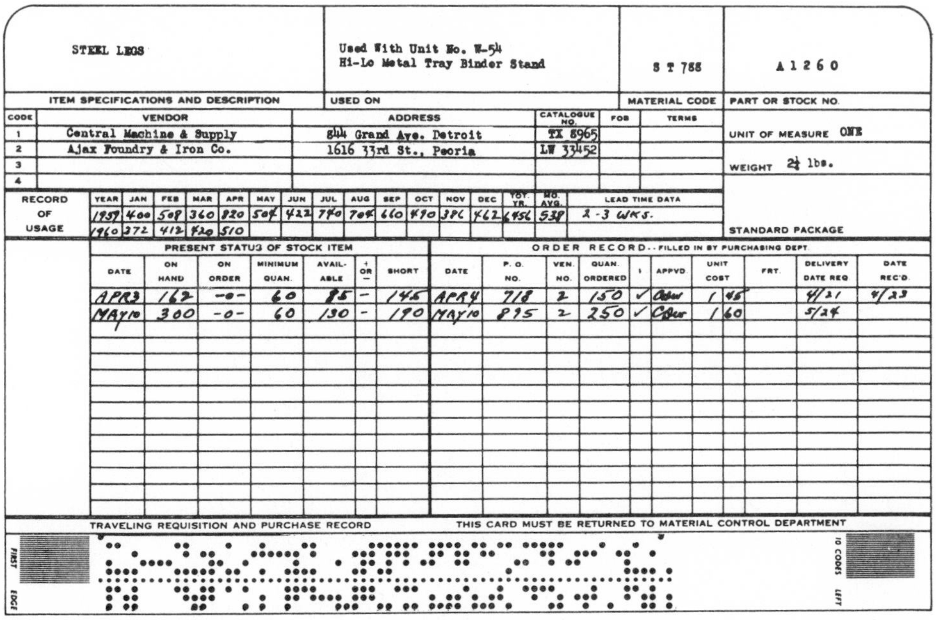

Figure 21-7
EDGE-PUNCHED TRAVELING REQUISITION AND ORDER RECORD

ledgers. This is the reason for the checkmark column found to the right of the "Quantity Ordered" column on the order-record ledger card.

Material Shortage Card

In some plants the expediters do not have ready access to stores ledgers because of physical location of the Materials Control Department, or because of space limitations. Flagging, or off-setting, ledger cards in the tray binders as signals for review would accomplish little. And, suppose that the use of a traveling requisition form is not under consideration for various reasons. Under these circumstances, how can we devise a method for providing the necessary information to the expediters?

Preparation of a Material Shortage Report form is a practical answer. (See Figure 21-8.)

When the accounting machine signals that the available balance on a card being posted requires review, the operator places a shortage card in the machine carriage. The machine then prints all quantity balance figures on the card to provide all necessary information for the expediter who reviews the shortage cards.

Computer Control over Reorders

When a computer posts a reserved quantity which changes the available balance to a negative value, the programmed instructions may cause the computer to produce a printed list of all inventory records which now require action by the *production planner*. (See Figure 21-9.)

The details of the inventory ledger for part #12669255 were printed by the computer because of the following events:

MATERIAL SHORTAGE No. S- 45273

RESERVE	ON ORDER	ON HAND	STATUS
525	0	0	(Red) 525

JUN 3   60-01-0211
DATE   MAT'L   CODE   NO.

ACTION TAKEN

☑   PURCHASE REQUISITION NO. *2466*

SHOP ORDER _____ QUANTITY _____

☐   TRANSFER NUMBER _____

SHOP ORDER _____ QUANTITY _____

☐   CHANGE ORDER POINT TO _____

☐ OTHER _____

REMARKS — _____

R L B.   6/5
FILLED IN BY   DATE

PL 4629—AP 1   EB 836

Figure 21-8
A TYPICAL MATERIAL SHORTAGE REPORT FORM

- The Bill of Materials for Job #23218F showed a requirement of 3,000 units of Part #12669255.
- When the computer posted this required amount to the part record, and subtracted the 3,000 from the available balance of 180, it created a *minus quantity balance of 2,820 (—).*

This caused the computer to do two things:

(1) Print the details of the part record for the planner to review.
(2) Punch an ACTION REQUISITION CARD for the planner to use subsequently to communicate a purchase request to the appropriate buyer in the purchasing department.

Automatic Ordering Status—Buy Item

The ACTION REQUISITION card for a "BUY" item is sent to the responsible planner in the same manner as for a "MAKE" item.

The ACTION REQ card is used by the planner to communicate a purchase requisition to the buyer responsible for the part.

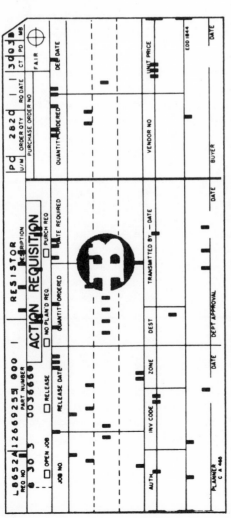

ACTION REQUISITION

RESISTOR

INVENTORY ACTION SYSTEM 8 30 63

Burroughs Corporation — ELECTRODATA DIVISION

INQUIRY   PLANNER   A - ANDERSON

PART NUMBER			DESCRIPTION OR MESSAGE	AREA	TRANSACTION			DATE RELEASED OR ISSUED	BALANCE		DATE REQUIRED	BALANCE	
PRIME	DASH	SUB			PHASE	TYPE	NUMBER		ON HAND	ON ORDER		RESERVED	AVAILABLE
12669255	000		RESISTOR	5304	BEGIN BALANCE	PLNR A	BUYER L		180				180
				40	RESRVATION	23218F	8 30 63				10 02 63	3000	2820 −
					ACTIONREQ	8652A	8 30 63			2820	10 02 63		0
					ENDINGBALANCE				180	2820		3000	0

The part record printout showing when the materials are to be used serves as a guide for the planner decisions covering the purchase material delivery schedules.

Figure 21-9

AUTOMATIC NOTIFICATION OF IMPENDING SHORTAGE

Computer Follow-up

When inventory records are maintained on a computer, many remarkable results can be obtained. For example, Figure 21-10 illustrates how the computer may be programmed to remind the planner of the open purchase requisition (issued by the computer for action) if he *fails* to take action within seven days.

When the planner fails to take action on the ACTION REQ within seven working days, an action message is printed as a reminder that a decision is required.

Burroughs Corporation								INVENTORY ACTION SYSTEM	
ELECTRODATA DIVISION			INQUIRY PLANNER A – ANDERSON						9 12 63
PART NUMBER			DESCRIPTION OR MESSAGE	TRANSACTION				DATE RELEASED OR ISSUED	BALANCE		DATE REQUIRED	BALANCE	
PRIME	DASH	SUB		AREA	PHASE	TYPE	NUMBER		ON HAND	ON ORDER		RESERVED	AVAILABLE
12669255	000		RESISTOR	5304	BEGIN BALANCE	PLNR A	BUYER L		180	BUY			180
				40		RESRVATION	23218F	8 30 63			10 02 63	3000	2820−
			NO OPEN ORDER ISSUED		ACTION REQ		8652A	8 30 63		2820	10 02 63		0
					ENDING BALANCE				180	2820		3000	0

Figure 21-10
COMPUTER FOLLOW-UP AND REMINDER NOTICE

Writing Shop Orders

When the planner or expediter notes that a part in short supply is manufactured in the plant, he writes a simple shop order to replenish the supply needed for future production. The expediter calculates the quantity of raw materials needed to build the desired quantity of parts, then he prepares the shop production order form (See Figure 21-11) in triplicate. The second copy goes to the plant supervisor for production planning. One copy is kept in the files.

The expediter also prepares a Material Requisition form for the necessary raw materials. This form is first used for posting quantities needed (requirements) to Raw Material stock ledgers, then routed to Stores for issuance.

Key to Smooth Operation

It is easy to see now that the key to an efficient, smooth-running production line is controlling the availability of all parts and materials needed for scheduled production.

An interesting case history involves a material-control installation for a very large manufacturer of hospital and physicians' equipment. This firm operated for many years without an adequate materials-control department or system. After installing a new system similar to the one described in this chapter, an official of the Shampaine Company of St. Louis described the many benefits as follows:

> "It is no longer necessary to lose time and production by shifting our production people from job to job because parts are not available.
>
> The foremen were stock boys under our old system. When the production line ran out of parts and the stores section was unable to supply the necessary items, the foremen searched the plant trying to find an adequate supply to keep production lines going.
>
> And, under the old system, many people were constantly requesting the stock clerks to

order materials for their various departments. With the inventory-control cards that we now use, we have a uniform ordering procedure. When the available balance and the minimum quantity factors indicate a danger condition, we take action before it is too late."

Benefits of Accounting Machines

Figure 21-2 shows manual postings; Figure 21-6 illustrates basically the same form, but one which is designed for machine posting. Accounting machines are widely used nationwide

```
┌─────────────────────────────────────────────────────┐
│ PO100 REV. 15M 12-53 NK                              │
│                   PRODUCTION ORDER                   │
│                                                      │
│  PART No._____  ORD N⁰   3451       │
│                                                      │
│  DESCRIPTION_____DEPT._____     │
│                                                      │
│  QUANTITY_____REFRIG_____VOLTS_____FREQ_____ │
│                                                 STR.  │
│  INLET:_____P.T_____SAE_____ODS_____THRU   │
│                                                 STR.  │
│  OUTLET:_____P.T_____SAE_____ODS_____THRU   │
│                                                      │
│  LGTH. CAP. TUBE_____TYPE REMOTE BULB_____ADAPTER__│
│                                                      │
│  EQUAL. PORT_____SUPERHEAT: SET_____MARK_____ │
│                                                      │
│  DELIVER TO_____REQ. BY_____   │
│                                                      │
│  INSTRUCTIONS_____   │
│  _____   │
│  _____   │
│  _____   │
│                                                      │
│  AUTHORIZED BY_____DATE ISSUED_____    │
│                                                      │
│  INSPECTED BY_____DEPT._____DATE_____    │
│  DELIVERED TO_____DEPT._____DATE_____    │
│  L-97 R                                              │
└─────────────────────────────────────────────────────┘
```

Figure 21-11
"SHOP" OR PARTS PRODUCTION ORDER

on stores records, job-cost accounting, and a host of other statistical and accounting jobs performed in manufacturing plants. An accounting machine, properly programmed and properly applied to inventory control can be a "blue chip" investment for the plant owner or owners. Here are some of the major benefits:

1. *Accuracy:* Machine records will always be more accurate than manually posted records simply because the machine eliminates many *decisions.* We have seen that the posting of each of four types of stores transactions affects two or more balances. Some balances increase; some decrease—and this action changes with the type of transaction being posted. This becomes very confusing to a bookkeeper with a pencil and an adding machine. Also, figures are frequently copied incorrectly when read from adding-machine tapes. By contrast, an accounting machine makes the decision to add or subtract and automatically figures and prints new quantity balances when the appropriate column or columns are reached!

2. *Speed:* A machine definitely makes it possible to increase posting production by a considerable margin. Dates and punctuation are automatically printed; columns for detail entries are automatically selected; addition and subtraction are automatically performed. New balances are figured and printed with no effort on the part of the bookkeeper.

3. *Reduces Clerical Costs:* Ample evidence proves that substantial salary savings are not only possible, but probable, when machines are applied to stores accounting and other jobs of this type. The following case histories furnish proof of this fact.

(1) The Westinghouse Meter Division installed one machine to handle nearly 8,000 stock accounts. The departmental supervisor has publicly stated that one machine performs up to 1,200 postings per day. Also, an overall savings of two people was accomplished. The former manual system required six "ledgermen" who did the posting, reviewing and ordering. With the machine, one operator performs all posting and three ledgermen do the reviewing and initiating of replenishment orders.

(2) The Binks Manufacturing Company of Chicago has gone on record as having installed two machines on ledger cards for each of 15,000 parts and inventory items, with a resulting saving of several people.

A machine should be considered as an office tool. It does not pay to handicap high-salaried bookkeepers by equipping them with pencils, ballpoint pens and adding machines when an accounting machine can accomplish so much. Plant management now recognizes that factory concepts of efficient utilization of new cost-cutting tools should be applied to office procedures to accomplish comparable cost reductions.

Machine Programming Considerations

When applying a machine to stock records, several basic decisions must be made in order to select the appropriate model with necessary features for a specific job. Figure 21-6 illustrates, for example, one basic plan which *changes only those balances affected by each posting.* A contrasting method is one which *carries forward all balances together,* on the same line, each and every time one or more of the balances changes.

A discussion of these two conflicting plans is in order. The first method has merit in that it speeds up all posting because of the fact that only active balance figures are indexed in the machine; those not affected are ignored. This, in turn, means that a lower-priced machine with fewer accumulators can be applied to the job. The posting work shown in Figure 21-6 can be done with a low-priced two-register machine.

One possible disadvantage of the first method is that the quantity balances indexed on the machine keyboard prior to posting a transaction are not proved or verified as part of the posting routine. If positive accuracy is one of the major objectives of mechanization, this plan may not be favored by management people.

The second method, as stated above, features carrying forward *all* balance figures for *all* postings. This provides the possibility of proving all old balance figures entered to start a line of posting—before any postings are made. Some firms select a four-balance ledger form for this primary reason. The four balances represent a mathematical equation. See illustration below.

Part No. 60-01-0211 ⅝-11NC-22X3
Balances

Reserved	On Order	On Hand	Available
525	0	0	(Red) 525 (—)
525	2,500	0	1,975
525	0	2,500	1,975
452	0	2,427	1,975

The mathematical equation is this: "On Order" quantity plus "On Hand" less quantity "Reserved" equals the "Available" Balance. When all four balances are indexed into the machine preparatory to posting a line representing a stores transaction, the figures indexed can be proved instantly by programming the machine to add and subtract the various balances and print two ciphers if all quantity balances are correctly read and indexed.

Old Balances Indexed

(Reserved)	(On Order)	(On Hand)	(Available)	PROOF
452+	0—	2,427—	1,975+	.00

Benefits of Computers Applied to Inventory Control

The benefits to be derived from the installation of a computer for processing business data are no longer available only to medium-sized or large firms. The rental and purchase prices have dropped continually over the years as the size of the equipment has been reduced; yet, the speed and efficiency of the equipment have *increased* at the same time. As a matter of fact, full-scale punched-card computers are currently available at monthly rentals which are approximately the same as for a complete installation of the small desk model computers and auxiliary data-processing equipment.

Application of a computer to inventory control in a manufacturing plant may represent an excellent investment for four primary reasons:

1. An efficient inventory control system makes it possible to reduce substantially the investment in parts, subassemblies and finished goods carried in stock.

2. The tremendous cost of unexpected work stoppages in the production areas almost mandates installation of equipment, systems and procedures to eliminate such occurrences.

3. The high cost of clerical employees, coupled with the large number usually required for production and inventory control, provides a potential for substantial cost savings when a computer is properly applied in these operational areas.

4. Accumulation of detailed and accurate job cost figures for bidding and estimating future jobs has a tremendous potential for future profit improvement.

MONETARY ACCOUNTING FOR STORES

In a great many stock-record installations found in manufacturing plants, no attempt is made to record the monetary value of goods in, out, or on hand; quantities only are recorded. This is especially true when a system of applying standard costs to manufactured goods is in use. A standard cost system eliminates the need for applying a unit cost price to quantities issued, since it is not necessary to calculate the total value of material released into production. Standard costs are discussed more in detail further on in this chapter.

Manufacturing plants that build variable, nonstandard products or those that specialize in making special products tailored to each customer's requirements or specifications—with each job different from the last one—should apply *actual current costs* to each production order. Therefore, an efficient, accurate materials-control system in a job shop requires the application of appropriate unit costs to each item or batch of items issued from stores. Unit cost per item is multiplied by the quantity issued and the result is written on the issue document. This document then serves for posting direct materials costs to the Job Cost Ledgers set up to accumulate actual costs for each production order in process in the plant.

Methods of Figuring Unit Cost

1. *Last Invoice Cost:* Some firms use "last invoice cost" as unit cost for current issues. This means that the unit cost applied to issues is determined from the last invoice received. Since the quantity on hand may represent several different batches of materials bought at varying prices, this method is not very accurate and leads to distorted cost and profit information. However, it does have the merit of simplicity of application.

2. *Average Unit Costs:* The average unit-cost method is very popular with accountants and is in wide use today. This method is illustrated by the following example:

Part No. 123-478

Description	Quantity	Unit Cost	Value
Quantity on Hand	10	$0.50	$ 5.00
Items Received in Stock Today	20	0.60	12.00
Balances	30		$17.00

The total quantity on hand (30) divided into the new total value on hand ($17.00) produces a result of $0.566, which is the new average unit cost. This figure will now be used for costing all subsequent issues until the receipt of another shipment of parts necessitates figuring the unit cost again.

Quantity and Value Balances

Stock-record forms in use in job shops nearly always show unit cost on the form for reasons explained above. As a corollary to this, the form usually provides a value balance in addition to the quantity balance. For every issue made from stock, the quantity on hand is reduced and the value of stock on hand is also reduced. Refer to skeleton example which follows.

Part No. 435-872

Date	Issues Quantity	Value	Unit Cost	Balances Quantity on Hand	Value on Hand
Oct 1			2.00	100	200.00
Oct 2	12—	24.00		88	176.00
Oct 3	10—	20.00		78	156.00

Extending the new value on hand each time an issue transaction is posted increases the overall clerical work and introduces the possibility of error into the value balances.

An analysis of the stores-accounting function indicates that it really is not necessary to extend a new value balance concurrently with posting of issue quantities. Eliminating an unnecessary posting is significant when we realize that the number of issue transactions far exceeds all others in stores-posting work.

The primary justification for updating the total value of stock on hand is the necessity for calculating a new average unit cost upon receipt of a new shipment of materials. For this reason, the timesaving procedures outlined below should be considered.

Suggested Procedures

As postings are made from receiving reports, the posting clerk offsets each posted stores ledger card in the tray binder for the next step of figuring new average unit costs. The design of the ledger card illustrated in Figure 21-2 provides for these procedures:

(1) Multiply quantity on hand (before receipt of new materials) by old average unit cost and write result in the value-balance column.

(2) Add the value of new materials received to previous value, then write new total in the value-balance column.

(3) Divide total quantity now on hand into the new total value to establish new average cost per unit. Write the quotient on the ledger card in the unit-cost column. Refer to the posting line designated by the numeral "3" in Figure 21-2.

(4) All subsequent issues will now be costed at this latest price until another shipment of goods is received.

It will not be essential to extend the value balance again until another shipment of materials is received and posted.

Materials Received Without an Invoice

Materials are frequently received prior to availability of the vendor's invoice. This may be due to delay in receiving the invoice, or due to the time required to process the incoming invoice through the mailroom and through purchasing and accounts payable procedures. To avoid the situation of overdrawn stock balances appearing on materials-control records, the material received may be entered immediately using the *present average unit price* for valuation of the new quantity received.

After all stock items are posted from the receiving report, it is filed awaiting arrival of the invoice. When the report is eventually matched with the invoice, the difference between the total value established by applying average unit price and the actual invoice value (which frequently includes freight charges) is then entered on an adjustment form sometimes called a "Change Report."

The Change Report is now used for posting the value difference, either debit or credit, in the appropriate column in the "received" section of the ledger card. This posting changes the total value of goods on hand and requires the computation of a new average unit price. This new unit cost is then applied to all subsequent issues of stock items until such time as receipt of another batch of materials creates a change in unit cost.

3. *The FIFO Method:* Unit cost may be applied to stores issued on the basis of "first in, first out." This means that the unit cost of the first batch of materials bought is used for all subsequent issues until that batch is exhausted. If another shipment of the same materials is received at a different cost, this batch is ignored (for costing purposes) until the first batch has been totally charged out of stores and into production or expense.

The principle involved in this method makes it mandatory to maintain a reducing batch-balance figure on the stores record, and in addition maintain a total quantity on hand balance.

During a business cycle of constantly rising materials prices, this method has the effect of tending to decrease the book figures on cost of goods manufactured which in turn increases gross profits on sales. Reason: the oldest costs (which are lower than current costs) are applied to stores issues, and in turn these figures appear as part of the lower cost of goods manufactured and sold. If prices are dropping, this method will have the opposite effect of increasing costs and decreasing profits.

4. *The LIFO Method:* The LIFO method applies unit cost to issues on the basis of "last in, first out." The unit cost applicable to the *most recent batch* of materials purchased is applied to all issues until that batch is exhausted. Then the unit cost for the shipment received prior to this is applied, etc.

Again, we see that it is necessary to maintain a reducing *batch-quantity balance,* and also update a total quantity on hand balance on the stores record.

During a business cycle of constantly rising materials prices, this method has the effect of increasing the cost of goods manufactured and sold, which reduces book profits. If prices are dropping, it will have the opposite effect on costs and profits.

Simplified Posting

When FIFO and LIFO are in use, we have established that the posting clerk must maintain two quantity balances—an individual batch balance and total quantity on hand regardless of batch. And, when an issue "straddles" two batches—that is, the quantity involved exhausts one batch and takes part of the next batch—the posting clerk must watch this and record two different unit costs on the issue document for cost-accounting purposes.

A properly programmed Stock Record Accounting Machine can save many hours of work on this type of posting and eliminate mental decisions and errors in figuring and writing new quantity balances. Accounting machines today have decision-making ability built into them. For example, if batch number one (FIFO plan) has a remaining balance of 20 parts, and an issue of 25 is posted, the machine will instantly recognize that the first batch is now exhausted and that the issue reaches into the second batch. Since this situation changes the posting procedure, it is necessary to warn the operator of this at once. The machine will do this by automatically skipping past the batch-quantity balance column. Then it will print the overdraft quantity and stop in a special column for the operator to index the quantity of the *next batch involved.* This is easier to understand by examining the sample postings shown in Figure 21-12.

Explanation of Figure 21-12.

The primary purpose of this exhibit is to illustrate the function of a specially designed form which will handle the problem of keeping various batches of materials separated for the purpose of applying correct unit costs to each materials issue document. In addition, this form provides an opportunity to review the various types of transactions necessary in accounting for materials, and the effect of each type of transaction on the three balances: "On Order," "Available," and "Quantity on Hand." Small line numbers appear in parentheses to the left of the quantity on hand. These numbers tie in with each line of explanation appearing below.

(1) The initial stock of brass rods consists of a quantity of 12,000. Since no reservations have been posted, all of these are available for future production.

(2) We now post the established minimum quantity of 5,000, which reduces the available balance to 7,000. Remember, the purpose of this posting is to reduce the available by the

Stores Item #34-445 Code 8467

DESCRIPTION 3/8" DIA XABT 12' BRASS ROD

ITEM NO. LOCATION

CODE 1 SUPPLIER

CODE 1

2

3

4

MAX. 20,000 MIN. 5,000

Date	Vendor Code	Ref. No.	Unit Cost	Quan. Ordered	✓	Quan. Rec'd: Wanted	Quan. Rec'd: Rec'd	Quan. Reserved	Quan. Issued	Total Issued	FIFO Batch Data: Remain. Bal.	FIFO Batch Data: New Batch Quan.	FIFO Batch Data: Over-Draft	Balances: On Order	Balances: Available	Balances: Quantity On Hand
Balances Forward																
Oct 2	Initial Stock		0.325				12,000				12,000			00	12,000	(1) 12,000
Oct 2	Min Reserved							5,000						00	7,000	(2) 12,000
Oct 5	Prod Ord	2,417						4,600						00	2,400	(3) 12,000
Oct 6	M Req	3,112							1,600	1,600	10,400			00	2,400	(4) 10,400
Oct 8	M Reg	3,190							8,000	9,600	2,400			00	2,400	(5) 2,400
Oct 9	Prod Ord	2,426						3,150						00	Red750	(6) 2,400
Oct 10	Purch Ord	1,522		10,000	✓									10,000	R 750	(7) 2,400
Oct 20	Rec Rep	6,610	0.364			10,000	9,750							00	9,000	(8) 12,150
Oct 21	M Reg	3,285							3,000	12,600	9,150	9,750	600	00	9,000	(9) 9,150

Explanation of FIFO Batch Data Columns
(Refer to last posting line.)

1. *Operator indexed FIFO batch balance of* 2,200
Before inserting stock ledger into machine carriage.
2. *Operator then posts an issue quantity of* 3,000
3. *This creates an overdraft in the machine which is automatically printed in red in OD column* 800
4. *The operator scans the "Quantity Received" column and lists the next batch quantity of* 9,750
5. *Now, the machine computes and prints the remaining FIFO balance of* . . 8,950

Figure 21-12
STORES LEDGER CARD WITH FIFO BATCH BALANCE COLUMN

minimum quantity; when the available balance drops to zero or below, the machine provides an *automatic warning* of an impending stock shortage—with no effort or decision required of the operator.

(3) A production order is posted which requires that 4,600 brass rods be reserved for future production. This reduces the free, available balance to 2,400.

(4) A quantity of 1,600 rods is issued. This affects the following balances:
   a. Increases total issued to date.
   b. Decreases the FIFO batch balance to 10,400.
   c. Decreases quantity on hand to 10,400.

(5) Another issue of 8,000 rods is made.

(6) Another production order is written which reserves 3,150 rods. This creates an *overdraft* in the available balance. The new available quantity of 750 prints in *red* and signals the operator, who offsets the stores ledger card to one side, or flags it for attention by the buyers or expediters.

(7) An expediter studies the situation, reviews the minimum and maximum figures, the lead time required to replenish the item, etc., then issues a purchase requisition for 10,000 rods. This causes a purchase order to be written; when it is posted, it increases the "On Order" balance and does not affect the other balances. (Some accountants prefer to update the available balance at once when an order is posted.)

(8) A receiving report is posted which indicates that 9,750 brass rods have been received. The purchase-order quantity of 10,000 is listed to reduce the "On Order" balance to zero. The quantity actually received (9,750) now increases the available balance to a plus figure of 9,000. The quantity on hand is also increased to 12,150.

The last line of posting illustrates another routine issue of materials.

Cost Breakdown

In a job shop, most issue documents provide space for writing the unit cost price adjacent to quantity issued. In the instance of the last line of posting shown on the stores record shown above, it is necessary to show a breakdown of the quantity issued in order to apply correct unit costs. In the illustration, the remaining batch of 2,400 units are priced at $0.325 each. The 600 units of the next batch (red figure copied from overdraft column) are priced at $0.364 each.

Temporary Valuation of Goods Received

When materials are received prior to receipt of the vendor's invoice, it may be desirable to establish a temporary valuation of the materials for stores-accounting purposes. The following procedures will accomplish this result without resorting to the use of average unit costs.

1. When a purchase order is written, purchasing types the unit price of each item ordered on the order. Route two extra copies of the purchase order to the receiving department.

2. Receiving-department personnel file these copies in alphabetic order awaiting arrival of materials ordered. When the shipment arrives, these copies are used as the *receiving report*.

3. Route both copies of the completed receiving report to a calculator operator who multiplies quantity actually received by the unit price (appearing on the purchase-order-receiving-report copies) and writes total value adjacent to each stores item received.

(Some practitioners may question this practice from the standpoint that additional clerical time is required for extending every item on all receiving reports. Actually there is no extra calculator time involved because this procedure eliminates the commonly accepted practice of extending the vendor's invoice, checking for errors in extensions and additions. If the total calculated and written on the receiving report copy is in agreement with the invoice total—

disregarding freight charges, if any, added to the invoice—then there is no necessity for recalculating the invoice.)

Disposition of Receiving Report Copies

One copy of the extended receiving report is routed to the Materials Control Department, where it is used for posting goods received, both quantity and value, to individual stock records.

One copy is sent to purchasing, where it is matched with the corresponding purchase-order copy and placed in a suspense file.

Accounts Payable Procedures

When the vendor's invoice for the materials is eventually received, it goes through normal accounts payable procedures. It is matched with the purchase-order copy and receiving report; all data on the three documents are studied and compared. Any variance between total value shown on invoice and value calculated and written on the receiving report at the time the materials were received is noted and recorded on a "Change Report" form. Variances are caused by a difference in unit price shown on purchase order and invoice; also by freight charges added to the invoice. It is quite common for shippers to prepay freight, but add the freight charge to the invoice rendered to the buyer. Freight is, of course, a legitimate part of the cost of materials received.

The Change Report is routed to the materials-control bookkeeper who posts the dollar value, plus or minus, in the value column of the stock ledger card. This changes the total value of materials on hand. In turn, this changes the unit cost previously calculated from the value shown on the receiving report.

How to Eliminate Random Posting

If several different parts numbers appear on a receiving report, purchase order, invoice, or other posting document, stuff the report in the ledger tray before posting begins. First, place it in front of the ledger card representing the *lowest-numbered* parts number appearing on the posting document. After posting this item, move the document ahead and drop it in front of the card for the next-highest parts or stock number. Continue to do this until all items have been posted.

The purpose of this procedure is to secure the timesaving benefits of summary posting of quantities from several documents to the same ledger card with one handling of the card—even though the posting media are multiple-line documents with each line representing a different stock number.

Summary

Systems and procedures outlined in this chapter cover many aspects of the multifaceted subject of monetary accounting for stores. This subject is given relatively scant attention in many texts dealing with cost accounting or other books on inventory control. Yet, failure to recognize and provide for such an obvious contingency as receiving materials into stock unaccompanied by the vendor's invoice can destroy, to a large extent, the accuracy and useful value of the stores records.

Several years ago the author had occasion to assist in the installation of twenty-two multiply-

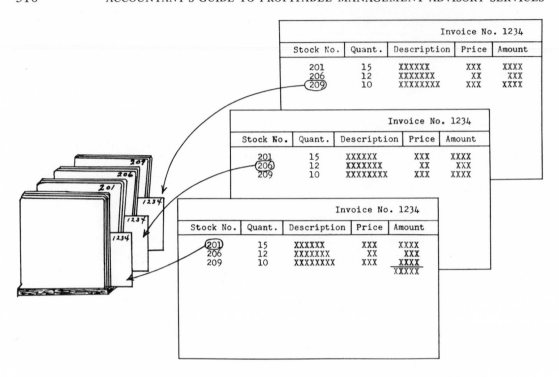

Figure 21-13
HOW TO ADVANCE A MULTIPLE-ITEM DOCUMENT PROGRESSIVELY FROM LOW TO HIGH-ORDER PART NUMBERS

ing-posting machines applied to the stores records of a very large aircraft manufacturer in Texas. Company policy required extension of quantity and value with posting of each issue ticket. Materials were *physically received* into stores several days before posting documents were available, because of the systems group's insistence that materials received must be posted only after receipt of vendor's invoice—in order to post correct value of materials coming into stores.

This policy resulted in organized confusion and a loss of integrity of the records. Newly received parts and materials were constantly being issued, resulting in book overdrafts in both quantity and value. Eventually, paperwork for posting receiving data would belatedly appear to correct the situation.

It is the policy of some firms not to create book overdrafts. Any materials requisition which causes an overdraft in quantity on hand is held until receiving reports are posted.

These examples point to the importance, from a systems viewpoint, of setting up practical procedures which will permit a smooth flow of data affecting the stores records to be posted currently, and which will provide accurate, timely information at all times.

22

Job Cost: Direct Labor

Cost-Gathering Procedures for Direct Labor Costs

Direct labor is a primary element of total job cost. This is the cost of all labor directly involved in completing a job.

Procedures vary widely for accumulating direct labor costs for each job passing through a plant, depending on the size of the manufacturing plant, the kind of products manufactured and cost information wanted. Comprehensive treatment of accounting for labor costs would fill an entire book. Many such specialized texts are already available. This text will not delve into this subject in great detail. The purpose of the material covered on succeeding pages, dealing with direct labor accounting, is to present a simple, efficient, definite set of forms and time-tested procedures which the practitioner, with complete assurance, can install in any small or medium-sized plant and obtain desired results at low cost.

Cost Data

Cost records in use in many factories are intended to provide only the total cost of labor expended on each job. However, management of some plants wants more information for better control of costs in various areas of operations. The following list of cost data accumulated may be regarded as fairly typical of a medium-sized plant:

a. Total labor cost for each job.
b. Labor cost of each operation performed.
c. Total labor cost by departments.
d. Total labor cost by work centers. (A work center is a group of related departments or functions.)

Labor cost-gathering procedures in a job shop start with the employee who does the work. It is necessary to prepare some type of job-cost record as the job moves through the various operations and work centers in the plant.

Two Major Objectives

Labor cost-accounting procedures in a job shop are usually set up to accomplish two important objectives. First, it is necessary to accumulate cost per job, possibly broken down by operations and/or work centers, etc. Second, for payroll-accounting purposes it is necessary to determine the employee's total earnings for each day and for the entire payroll period.

The first objective is easily realized if the job-cost record provides a unit ticket or unit record of some type for each job on which the employee worked. This unit record usually shows employee or badge number, job number, department or work-center number, time worked, etc. The big benefit of unit tickets is that they can be quickly sorted by job number for posting to cost records. Then they can be easily sorted by further breakdowns for additional cost data.

Some type of labor-summary record will accomplish the second objective. The top part of the Daily Job Cost Card, shown in Figure 22-1, which is a *summary* of all work done on a work shift, is designed for imprinting the employee's name and number from an addressing plate or stencil to identify the summary ticket. The four perforated stubs comprising the lower section provide unit tickets for each of four different jobs or operations.

Use of Job Cost Summary Ticket

The top part of the form shown in Figure 22-1 may be used for recording time in and out as the employee enters and leaves the plant for each workshift. The difference between these readings provides total recorded elapsed time worked on each shift. This in turn controls the sum of all hours recorded on the individual job-cost tickets attached to the summary.

As the worker begins a new job or a new operation on the same job, he writes his employee or badge number on a ticket, plus the appropriate job and operation numbers. He then takes the job-report form to a time clock which prints "time-on" in the column titled "Time Clock Record" on the left side of the job-cost form. Upon completion of the job or operation, "time-off" is recorded on the edge of the form.

Recording of time on and off is under the supervision of a foreman, a timekeeper, or some person acting in a supervisory capacity. This person assigns jobs, checks equipment setups and makes sure that materials or parts are available and ready for production. The supervisor's prime duty is to maintain an even flow of production throughout the work period. He also authorizes any overtime work required to complete an operation or a job.

At the end of the shift, job-cost cards are collected and routed to the Payroll Department for calculating elapsed time, job costs and earnings.

PAYROLL AND COST DEPARTMENT PROCEDURES

Payroll-department personnel figure elapsed time for each job or operation performed. It is the practice in some plants to use quarter-hour fractions when figuring elapsed time. Some use exact hours and minutes. Time-clocks are now available which are calibrated in tenths of hours. When these are in use, time is figured in six-minute intervals. Some plants have installed clocks which print in 1/100ths of hours. With these, the exact elapsed time may be used, or the nearest one-tenth fraction. Some time-clocks are set for Naval time; i.e., the hours run from one through twenty-four. This simplifies figuring elapsed time.

Name		Employee No.	Date
			Daily Job Cost Card

Time Clock Record	Hours Worked		Rate	Amount		Total Earned Today
OFF	Reg.					
ON	O.T. or Prem.					
OFF						
ON	Other				$	
OFF	Employee No.	Work Center	Op. No.	Job. No.		

ON	Hours Worked		Rate	Amount		Total Job Cost
OFF	Reg.					
ON	O.T. or Prem.					
OFF						
ON	Other				$	
OFF	Employee No.	Work Center	Op. No.	Job. No.		

ON	Hours Worked		Rate	Amount		Total Job Cost
OFF	Reg.					
ON	O.T. or Prem.					
OFF						
ON	Other				$	
OFF	Employee No.	Work Center	Op. No.	Job. No.		

ON	Hours Worked		Rate	Amount		Total Job Cost
OFF	Reg.					
ON	O.T. or Prem.					
OFF						
ON	Other				$	
OFF	Employee No.	Work Center	Op. No.	Job. No.		

ON	Hours Worked		Rate	Amount		Total Job Cost
OFF	Reg.					
ON	O.T. or Prem.					
OFF						
ON	Other				$	

Figure 22-1
EMPLOYEE'S DAILY JOB COST FORM

Regardless of the type of time-clock in use, each job-cost ticket is costed by multiplying elapsed time by the applicable rate, and the result is written on the ticket.

Balancing Hours Worked

One benefit of the suggested form is that it is a self-balancing form. The sum of all hours and fractions of hours recorded on the perforated job-cost stubs must balance with *total elapsed time* figured and entered on the daily summary ticket—before stubs are detached from the summary. Also, the sum of all labor-cost *amounts* charged to each job or operation must balance to the *total gross pay* calculated for the employee and written on the daily-summary form.

Components of Daily Time Record

After hours and money on job tickets balance with the totals shown on the summary ticket, job tickets are separated from the summary and routed to cost accounting.

The summary ticket is filed in a folder for each employee and becomes the basis for figuring gross earnings for the pay period. At the end of the payroll period, totals for regular and overtime hours and earnings are established by recapping accumulated daily-time summaries. These figures are then used for figuring and writing the payroll.

The cost of posting daily-wage-accrual records for each employee does not seem to be justified in view of the simplicity provided by merely accumulating daily summaries as outlined above. And, recapping of hours and earnings for payroll purposes is easily done by the application of key-driven calculators to the job.

Two-Part Form Suggested

One experienced CPA practitioner strongly recommends that the Employee's Daily Job Cost form be a two-part carbon-set form. This offers these benefits:

1. Second copy shows *all* time clock "in" and "out" records. (Sometimes an employee will punch out at noon on the individual job ticket, but fail to punch out on the top summary ticket.)

2. Job tickets may be detached, sorted and set up for job-cost postings without waiting for proofing before detaching.

3. Daily summaries, taken from original copies of the job-cost form, may be attached to paycheck or placed in pay envelope (since a copy is retained) to substantiate gross earnings calculated and paid.

Job-Cost Ledgers

When job tickets are received in the cost-accounting department, they are sorted by job number. This is facilitated by the fact that labor costs for only one job appear on each unit ticket.

Labor-cost tickets are now posted to job-cost ledger cards. One card is set up for each production order written. A properly designed card provides for periodic posting of labor and materials costs as the job moves through various operations and work centers. (See Figure 22-2.)

The detail-cost ledger remains "open" for additional postings as long as the batch of prod-

JOB COST LEDGER

CUSTOMER NAME OR JOB DESCRIPTION.

PRODUCTION ORDER NO.

DATE	REFERENCE	DIRECT LABOR		DIRECT MATERIALS	OVERHEAD BURDEN	BALANCES-TO-DATE				TOTAL ALL JOB COSTS
		HOURS	AMOUNT			DIRECT LABOR		DIRECT MATERIALS	OVERHEAD BURDEN	
						HOURS	AMOUNT			

SUMMARY OF JOB COSTS

	DIRECT LABOR		DIRECT MATERIALS	OVERHEAD BURDEN	TOTAL COSTS
	HOURS	AMOUNT			
ACTUAL COSTS					
ESTIMATED OR STANDARD .					
VARIANCE					

DATE STARTED ____________

DATE FINISHED ____________

OTHER DATA ____________

Figure 22-2
SUGGESTED JOB COST LEDGER CARD

ucts specified by the production order remains incomplete. When finished products eventually move from the manufacturing section to finished goods or parts inventory, then the job-cost ledger card is closed. At this point, the summary of job costs appearing at the bottom of the form becomes valuable. Space is provided for a comparison between actual and estimated costs for each of the three elements of job cost.

Note that both hours and money data appear under the caption "Direct Labor" on the ledger card. Also, the operation number may be posted in the reference column if information as to hours and cost of each labor operation is desired. The availability of such data makes possible detailed analysis of jobs which exceed the original cost estimates by a significant margin. Such a record is invaluable as a guide for future cost estimates on similar jobs.

Figure 22-3 illustrates a machine-posted job-cost ledger. Each time labor costs are posted, the machine extends a new balance of direct labor hours expended on the job to date, in addition to monetary value.

Stores requisitions are summarized in advance of posting on the accounting machine, and the total value is posted as one entry. This procedure is not always desirable; it may be better for job-analysis purposes if each issue document is posted separately in conjunction with a requisition number. If so, this form should be redesigned with a reference column adjacent to the column reserved for posting value of materials issued.

Note that "burden" charges (manufacturing overhead expense)—discussed on subsequent pages in this chapter—are added as one entry when the job is completed.

Work-In-Process Account

An individual job-cost ledger card, as illustrated in Figures 22-2 and 22-3, represents each job in process in the plant. A General Ledger account, "Work-In-Process" is the overall control account for these records. This account reflects at all times total labor, materials and overhead costs charged to *all jobs* in process.

In actual practice, separate work-in-process accounts are frequently set up for each of the elements of job cost—labor, materials and overhead. For example, after job tickets have been posted to job-cost ledger cards, labor costs represented by the tickets are summarized and posted as one summary entry to a "Work-In-Process—Direct Labor" *control account.*

Idle Time Reporting

Machinery occasionally breaks down; parts or materials may not arrive promptly when scheduled. Since time lost due to such occurrences is not the worker's fault, idle time is credited to the worker by creating a job ticket for idle time. Later, the payroll department calculates the value of lost time and charges an appropriate expense account in lieu of a job-cost record.

An alternate plan requires the employee to prepare a lost time report when idle time is encountered. These reports are supervised by the foreman. Management will accumulate these reports and file them by departments or work centers. The reports provide a basis for study to see what can be done to eliminate down-time in the future. Perhaps a major overhaul of certain equipment is indicated, or complete replacement may be desirable if breakdowns are a common occurrence.

Controlling Production Work Flow

A modern production control technique in effect today in many plants utilizes the telephone to control the flow of work in all departments of a plant. When a worker starts an operation required by a job schedule, the foreman calls a work control center and reports: "Number 279 has started operation number one on production order number 8753." A control clerk in the control center heads up a job control form with the production order number and time-stamps it. When the operation is completed, this information is telephoned to the control center, where it is recorded on the job-control flow sheet. In this way, the job-control sheet shows work completed and work-in-process for all phases of a production order. It also shows quantities involved in the various operations and *actual location,* at all times, of all parts, materials or subassemblies proceeding through various, specified manufacturing processes.

COST RECORD   ORDER NUMBER 8,765.

Form 787-R

DATE	REFERENCE	LABOR IN PROCESS			MATERIAL IN PROCESS	
		HOURS	AMOUNT	BALANCE	AMOUNT	BALANCE
JUN 3'6-	6	16.2	32.40			
JUN 3'6-	8	10.6	19.08	26.8 51.48 *		
JUN 3'6-	M/R				88.10	88.10 *
JUN 4'6-	8	12.5	26.25			
JUN 4'6-	10	22.3	53.52			
JUN 4'6-	12	6.1	15.25	67.7 146.50 *		
JUN 4'6-	M/R				204.60	292.70 *

	MATERIAL	LABOR	BURDEN	TOTAL COST
ACTUAL				
STANDARD				
VARIANCE				

Figure 22-3
MACHINE-POSTED JOB COST LEDGER WITH DIRECT LABOR HOURS-TO-DATE
PRINTED WITH MONEY BALANCE

OVERTIME OR PREMIUM PAY CONSIDERATIONS

Original Concept of Overtime Pay

When the Wage and Hour law was originally passed by Congress, it established a forty-hour week as a standard or "regular" workweek for employees engaged in certain activities covered by the law. It applied particularly to employees engaged in manufacturing products sold in interstate commerce.

Under the provisions of this law, if an employee worked more than forty hours in one week, then the law required that overtime be paid at a rate equal to the regular rate plus 50% for the excess hours over forty. For example:

> Total hours worked: 44.
> Hours at regular rate: 40.
> Hours at overtime rate: 4.

Suppose an employee's regular rate of pay is $1.50 and he works a total of fourty-four hours. His earnings are calculated as follows:

> 40 hours @ $1.50   per hour equals $60.00 Regular Earnings.
> 4 hours @ $2.25* per hours equals   9.00 Overtime Earnings.
>
> Gross Earnings $69.00

New Concept of Overtime

As the years went by, it was realized that a different method of figuring overtime is not only simpler—it will save money on Workmen's Compensation Insurance premiums.

This new method for calculating overtime is shown below.

> Total hours worked: 44.
> Regular rate per hour: $1.50
>   44 hours @ $1.50 equals $66.00 Regular Earnings.
>   2 hours @ $1.50 equals   3.00 Overtime Earnings
>
>   Gross Earnings $69.00

Total hours worked (frequently called "elapsed time".) are multiplied by the regular rate; then one-half of the excess hours over forty are multiplied by regular rate. Results of this calculation is the *premium pay* for working overtime.

This method saves time in figuring earnings. It will also result in lower premiums for those firms required by law to carry Workmen's Compensation Insurance.

Calculating Daily Earnings

When calculating daily earnings, the same principle should be used for calculating overtime premium pay. For example, consider the case of the employee who works nine hours in one day, and whose regular rate of pay is $2.50 per hour.

---

* The regular rate of pay is $1.50 per hour, $1.50 plus 50% or 75¢ equals $2.25 per hour.

9 hours @ $2.50 equals	$22.50 Regular Earnings.
½ hour* @ $2.50 equals	1.25 Overtime Earnings.
Gross Earnings	$23.75

Allocating Overtime Pay

Management policy dictates disposition of overtime premium pay on cost-accounting records. The problem becomes evident when we consider the situation caused by a production worker who works a total of nine hours on a shift, and works on four different jobs during that time. Here are the usual, accepted optional choices for recording premium pay:

1. *Pro-rate overtime pay* and charge all four jobs with a proportionate amount of overtime costs.

2. Charge overtime premium pay to a manufacturing expense account, considered to be an indirect overhead expense.

3. Charge overtime pay to the last job on which the operator worked.

The first method is rarely used because of clerical work required to pro-rate overtime premium to various jobs worked on. The second method is in widespread use because of its basic fairness and simplicity. The third method is also widely applied, due to the theory that overtime work must be authorized by a supervisor or foreman, and that the reason for the authorized overtime is the necessity for completing the last job.

APPLICATION OF STANDARD COSTS TO JOB COST ACCOUNTING

When a group of materials-control ledger cards obtained from a number of varying installations is assembled and studied, you will find that some of the cards show no unit cost data at all. The reason is that many firms use "standard costs" in their job cost accounting.

Standard Costs Defined

Standard costs are those nonvariable costs applied to materials, labor and overhead on a standard, recurring basis during the current-accounting period. By contrast, actual costs are variable because prices of materials vary from one purchase to the next, and the amount of time required for repetitive labor operations varies from one job to the next. This time variance, of course, changes the overall cost of labor operations even though the rate of pay may not change.

The purpose of a standard-cost system is to simplify and reduce clerical costs involved in job-cost routines. Briefly, the cost-accounting department performs the initial work of establishing standards for each product manufactured in the plant. Standards are set up for each and every labor operation, and for a standard amount of materials to be used. Once these standards are established, each product manufactured from then on is costed simply by applying pre-established standard-cost figures.

Establishing Standards

1. *Labor Cost Standards:* Time studies are made on every operation requiring direct labor to produce one finished product. A standard length of time is determined for each operation.

---

* One-half of the excess hours over eight.

A standard labor rate per hour or per piece is applied and a total labor cost is established.

The sum of all labor costs involved in each operation, or to produce the required number of pieces, is the total standard direct labor cost for one completed unit.

2. *Direct Material Standard Costs:* The bill of materials lists every bolt, nut, screw and subassemblies needed to build one unit. Cost accountants apply unit costs to each item of material. (If the item is purchased from outside sources, the unit cost may be based on previous invoice costs, or average unit cost established over a period of time. For parts manufactured in the plant, job-cost records provide unit-cost data.)

By applying unit cost to each item listed on the bill of materials, a total cost of all materials needed to manufacture one completed unit is obtained. Once this is developed, this total cost figure is applied to all subsequent units manufactured, until such time as it becomes necessary to refigure and update all cost data.

Variances From Standard

Naturally, standard costs applied to jobs going through the plant are never the same as actual costs. However, this does not pose any difficult accounting problems for the following reasons:

Labor Variances: Actual labor costs are maintained in total anyway and are obtained as part of payroll accounting. Direct labor costs, applied on a standard basis, eventually appear in the General Ledger Payroll account as a credit. Gross earnings of all employees appear as a charge to the payroll account. After salaries and wages representing overhead expense have been removed from the payroll account by journal entry, the remainder represents the variance (over or under) between *actual* direct labor costs and *standard* labor costs.

Materials Variance: Actual costs of materials used will appear when physical inventories are taken and the actual value of remaining inventories on hand is established. Now, as part of journal entries written periodically to reflect standard value of all items used in the manufacturing processes, book inventories have been reduced by standard values and a balance on hand per books is available. When the actual value of remaining inventories on hand is compared with this amount, direct materials variance will be known.

In some plants, direct material costs are posted to job-cost records for an immediate comparison with standard quantities and values pre-established for materials.

Where to Apply Standard Costs

A standard-cost system is primarily applicable to firms which continually manufacture quantities of standard products. Manufacturers who specialize in custom jobs (Building products to customer specifications)—with nearly every new job different from the last one—may find the application of standard costs very difficult. Also, preparation for a standard-cost system requires a considerable investment in time and motion studies, and analysis and determination of standard material costs for each product.

23

Overhead Expense and Absorption Costing

The two preceding chapters covered two of the three elements of job cost:
1. Direct Materials costs.
2. Direct Labor costs.

The third element of cost which enters into the total cost of a manufactured product is overhead expense, frequently referred to as "manufacturing expense" or "overhead burden." The word "overhead" refers to the fact that manufacturing expenses cannot be directly identified with a specific job moving through the plant. Therefore, they are considered to be "indirect" elements of job cost.

Two Distinct Types of Expenses

There are two distinct types of manufacturing expenses:

1. Those which are incurred directly by production activities—and which *vary in direct relation* to the ebb and flow of production in the manufacturing departments.

2. Those which have little, if any, relation to production, and which represent the cost of *being in business.*

Examples of expenses connected directly with production activities are:
- Direct Materials used.
- Direct Labor costs.
- Factory Supplies.
- Repairs and Maintenance.
- Indirect Labor.
- Process Steam.

Examples of the second type of manufacturing expense, which represents the costs of *being in business,* or *being ready to do business* are:
- Property taxes
- Fire and casualty insurance
- Heat and light
- Telephone connection charges

321

- Depreciation on buildings
- Executive salaries

Note that these expenses are related to *time*—and have no connection with production operations. For this reason they are frequently called "fixed" or "period" expenses.

Absorption Costing

Possibly beginning with the very successful W. B. Lawrence book, *Cost Accounting* (published by Prentice-Hall in 1925), practically all texts selected for use in teaching cost accounting in our colleges and universities present the concept of "absorption costing." Under absorption costing all manufacturing expenses, regardless of type, must be "absorbed" into production costs by charging an allocated share of expense to each production job moving through the plant. The inventory value of the finished product is the sum of the direct labor and direct materials costs, plus the allocated manufacturing costs and expenses.

This costing method has the effect of capitalizing ALL MANUFACTURING EXPENSES— since these expenses are included in the cost of the manufactured product charged to Finished Goods Inventory when the job order is completed. As a result of converting expenses to an asset, direct costs and absorbed plant expenses do not appear on a Profit and Loss Statement until the products manufactured are finally sold, shipped and invoiced.

Accounting entries which reflect the flow of costs are:

1. DR. Finished Goods Inventory   x,xxx.xx

     CR. Work in Process—Direct Labor   xxx.xx
     CR. Work in Process—Direct Materials   xxx.xx
     CR. Work in Process—Manufacturing Expense   xxx.xx

     Summary of completed production orders.

2. Cost of Goods Sold   x,xxx.xx

     CR. Finished Goods Inventory   x,xxx.xx
    Cost of goods sold and shipped

Applying Overhead Expense to Jobs

Even a cursory examination of the origin and nature of manufacturing overhead expenses reveals the difficulties of allocating the various types of expense to jobs in process so that each job will bear its fair share of such expense. By definition general manufacturing expense cannot be directly identified with specific production jobs being worked on in the production departments. This makes it necessary to select an arbitrary but appropriate base for allocating part of the total overhead expense to each job sharing in the manufacturing support services and facilities.

Now, if only one production job engaged all manufacturing facilities for an entire year, there would be no allocation problem since all overhead expenses would apply to that job. However, a typical job shop will process several hundred different production orders per month—through various operations ranging from those requiring the work of only one or two men for a few hours, to those requiring the labor of scores of men for several days or weeks. This makes it essential to establish some means of distributing indirect expense to each job on an equitable basis.

Cecil Gillespie, author of *Cost Accounting and Control* (Prentice-Hall, 1957), states: "The purposes of cost accounting might be defeated if expense is not applied equitably to the cost sheets. Equitable costing would mean that no production order should be penalized by expense application to the undue advantage of some other production order, and similarly that no product would be penalized to the undue advantage of some other product.

"Consider, first, the use of cost accounting in the measurement of performance, and, second, the use of product costs as a factor in setting selling prices. A production order charged with too small a factory expense application might appear to represent a satisfactory performance in the factory, whereas the performance was unsatisfactory, and ought to be investigated.

"Similarly, a product overcosted by the cost man may become a product overpriced by the sales department influenced by such reported cost. Although it is true that the sales manager does not necessarily set his selling prices with direct reference to the costs in his factory, he may be influenced by them and inadvertently price one of his products out of the market because of a 'high cost.'"

Bases for Applying Manufacturing Expense

There are several accepted bases for distributing manufacturing expense to jobs in process:

1. Units of Finished Products
2. Direct Materials Cost
3. Direct Labor Cost
4. Direct Labor Hours
5. Machine Hours

Unit Product as Base

If a plant manufactures a variety of products, and certain products undergo special processes or operations in a variable number of departments, the unit method of expense allocation is not practical. A common base must be selected so that overhead expense can be applied equitably to products of all types, regardless of variable operations in different cost centers.

Direct Materials Cost

Applying overhead expense on the basis of direct materials cost is seldom encountered. The basic reason is that a great many manufacturing expenses are incurred by the passage of time—supervision, rent, taxes, casualty insurance, depreciation, etc. For this method to be equitable, there should be more of a direct relationship between the cost value of materials used and the amount of time required in the manufacturing processes.

Direct Labor Cost

Highly variable wage rates found in a typical factory make this base generally unsuitable. This method may be utilized only if manufacturing expenses are placed on a strict, departmentalized basis—and only if all production workers in the same department receive approximately the same hourly rate of pay.

Direct Labor Hours

Surveys indicate that direct labor hours are the most commonly-used base for distribution of overhead expense. Direct labor is a common denominator found in all manufacturing operations, and varies in accordance with the number of pieces to be produced and the complexity of the job.

Use of direct labor hours as the base for expense allocation requires accurate job cost records which show the total number of man-hours expended on each job, preferably by department.

Machine Hours

If most production work is performed primarily by high speed, automated machines, then a machine-hour base may be preferable to the man-hour base. For example, one plant in New York manufacturing metal lamp bases utilizes specially-designed machines for every operation. One operator controls as many as three machines operating simultaneously. Under these circumstances it is very logical to use machine hours as the base for loading overhead expense to jobs in process.

Determining the Hourly Burden Rate

After the plant cost accountant has selected the base best suited for equitable distribution of overhead expense, other requirements must be met for the effective application of absorption costing. Thus:

- Budgets must be prepared, preferably for each factory department, which represent an informed estimate of the overhead expense for the coming year.
- Production estimates must be prepared as to the planned use of the manufacturing facilities in each department. For example, if direct labor hours offer the most equitable base for distributing overhead expense to job orders, the cost accountant needs to know in advance the estimated total number of these hours—in order to determine the *hourly departmental burden rate* for costing each job, starting the first day of the new manufacturing year.

Departmental Budgets

Preparation of departmental budgets first requires segregation of all manufacturing expenses by department. This procedure requires that various bases be selected for allocation or proration of the total manufacturing expenses of various types to each production department.

The word "department" refers to a group of workers or machines assembled as a production center, and doing similar work.

Distribution Bases

Manufacturing expense may be prorated to the various operating departments on a variety of bases, depending on the nature of each expense. The following abbreviated chart will illustrate this.

Overhead Expense Item	*Basis for Departmental Proration*
Rent and Taxes	
Depreciation and Repairs on Factory Buildings	Square Footage in the Department.
Fire Insurance Premiums on Buildings	
Heat and Light Expense	
Plant Superintendent's Salary	Charged to department on basis of number of employees in the department.
Wages of Service Departments— Toolroom, Hospital, Cafeteria, etc.	
Workmen's Compensation Insurance	Charged as a percentage of earnings of all employees in the department.
State Unemployment Taxes	
Federal Insurance Contributions	

As the above chart shows, a logical base is selected, depending on the type of expense, for distribution of each category of overhead expense.

By distributing expense to various operating departments, application of overhead costs to jobs in process can be much more accurate than by applying rates based on plant-wide operations. Also, by maintaining records on over-and-under applied expenses by *departments,* management can localize major discrepancies, analyze the figures and determine reasons for the discrepancies.

Any technique which facilitates departmental expense control will help improve overall operations.

Hourly Burden Rate

After all manufacturing expenses have been allocated to production and service departments, it is then necessary to allocate the expense of service and support departments *to production departments.* Examples of "service and support" departments are the cafeteria, medical and first-aid department, tool design, research and development, and many others not engaged in direct production work.

After the basic task of establishing the estimated expense budget for the coming year has been completed, a corollary effort is made to estimate the total number of direct labor man-hours which will be expended in each production department—assuming that this is the base which has been selected for application of overhead expense.

When these two factors have been established, the hourly burden rate can then be calculated by dividing the estimated man-hours into the budgeted total departmental expense. For example: If Department A has 10 men on the production line who will work 20,000 hours in the coming year, and the budgeted departmental overhead expense is $40,000, then the cost accountant will load departmental overhead expense onto each production job at the rate of $2 for each direct labor hour expended in this department.

If a job passes through four different production departments, it will be necessary to apply four different burden rates to the work done in each department.

Over-and-Under Applied Burden

When overhead expense is added to a job cost sheet, the amount is credited to a contra account, "Applied Manufacturing Expense." See accounting entry below.

DR. Work in Process—Overhead Expense   x,xxx.xx
    CR. Applied Manufacturing Expense   x,xxx.xx
    To record the total of overhead expense added to job
      cost records.

Because of the ebb and flow of manufacturing operations, it is not unusual for the total Applied Manufacturing Expense to differ by a substantial amount from the total of *actual,* recorded manufacturing expense for a calendar month, and for the year to date. The difference, debit or credit, represents *under-or-over applied burden.*

Example:

Actual Manufacturing Expense (Dept. I) for June	$35,000.00
Applied Manufacturing Expense (Dept. I)	42,000.00 —
Over-Applied Burden (Credit)	$ 7,000.00

This credit amount is carried to the Profit and Loss Statement for the month of June and becomes a part of the reported profits. Likewise, if the actual manufacturing expense exceeds the applied expense, the remaining debit amount appears on the Profit and Loss Statement. This method of handling over-and-under absorbed burden is a very significant aspect of absorption costing, and is discussed again in the next chapter on direct costing.

Accountants traditionally associate the earning of profits by selling merchandise. Here, we see a credit to profits created simply by the over-utilization of the manufacturing facilities. Because of this aspect of absorption costing, reported profits may vary sharply in relation to sales; subsequent illustrations prove this point.

CASES AGAINST ABSORPTION COSTING

Accounting records of any type are not generally kept merely for the sake of accumulating accounting data. And, a cost accounting system must be a vehicle for providing management with timely, accurate information for controlling expenses and for use in its vital decision-making functions.

Broad experience in the handling of reports produced with absorption costing has caused many accountants and consultants to become disenchanted with this method of cost accounting. Specific reasons for this disenchantment are given in the remainder of this chapter.

Case No. 1: Absorption Costing Produces Illogical Operating Statements

As long as actual plant production remains reasonably close to the average, estimated production levels, profits reported under absorption costing will be accurate from the standpoint that actual manufacturing expenses were neither over-absorbed nor under-absorbed by production. As a result, no significant debit or credit amount will be carried to the Profit and Loss Statement.

However, during periods of peak production or slack production, the figures reported to top management may be very confusing and very difficult for the industrial cost accountant to explain to members of management. Consider the actual case history of the "Able Manufacturing Company" located in the Rio Grande Valley of Texas: This firm manufactures metal cans used by the many canning plants that are situated in the area which grows tremendous quantities of vegetables ready for harvesting in the early spring.

In the canning business it is necessary to manufacture a very large quantity of cans of all sizes, well in advance of the crop-harvesting season, in order to supply the necessary products to the canneries when they need them.

The cost accountant, working closely with management of the Able Manufacturing Company, has established the following estimates for the production year which begins January 1st.

Sales per month				$150,000
Cost of Sales:				
Direct Labor			40,000	
Direct Material			20,000	
Manufacturing Expenses:				
Variable Expense	40%	16,000		
Fixed Expense	60%	24,000	40,000	
Total Cost of Sales				100,000—
Gross Profit from manufacturing				$ 50,000

Accounting records for prior years show that selling expense averages about 10% of sales; general and administrative expenses are expected to approximate the same percentage of sales.

Using the basic data above, let's see how some drastic changes in the production level affect operating reports prepared for management.

During the month of January the plant works 30% over the planned average production level in order to build an inventory of cans for the coming season. This creates the following accounting entries:

DR. Inventory on Hand	130,000	
CR. Direct Labor		52,000
CR. Direct Materials		26,000
CR. Manufacturing Expense Applied		52,000

Manufacturing Expense Applied consisted of these two elements:

Variable Expense:	40% of direct labor	$20,800
Fixed Expense:	60% of direct labor	31,200
Total applied expense		$52,000

During the month of January the actual fixed manufacturing expenses were $24,000. Now, let's examine a simple Profit and Loss Statement prepared from the foregoing figures.

Sales		$150,000
Cost of Sales		100,000 —
Gross Profit		50,000
Volume Variance		7,200*
		57,200
Less Other Expenses:		
Selling Expense	15,000	
General and Administrative	15,000	30,000 —
NET PROFIT		$27,200 (18.1% of sales)

During the month of February production drops to a level which is 30% *less* than estimated normal monthly plant production. However, the actual sales remain *exactly the same.*

Sales		$150,000
Cost of Sales		100,000 —
Gross Profit		50,000
Volume Variance (DR)		7,200 —
		42,800
Less Other Expenses:		
Selling Expense	15,000	
General and Administrative	15,000	30,000 —
NET PROFIT		$ 12,800 (8.5% of sales)

In this instance the volume variance amount is a debit, caused by the under-application or under-absorption of manufacturing fixed expenses. Actual fixed expense for the month was again $24,000, but the cost accountant applied only $17,200 to production since it was 30% below the norm.

When the president of the company received the February Profit and Loss Statement he called the cost accountant and requested an explanation of the figures. He could not understand why reported profits dropped from $27,200 to $12,800—when sales and cost of sales were *identical* for the first two months of the year.

Another Illustration

One practical way to test a concept or a new idea is to apply radical extremes to it to see what would happen. Let's do this with absorption costing:

Suppose that February sales were *zero,* but production ran 200% of normal in order to build a huge inventory for sales of future months. Production and inventory figures for the month were as follows:

---

* The "volume variance" credit originated from the fact that the cost accountant loaded the manufactured products with fixed manufacturing expenses of $31,200; actual expenses for the month were $24,000; the over-absorbed amount appears on this statement *as an addition to profits.*

DR. Inventory on Hand (February production) $200,000

CR. Direct Labor		80,000
CR. Direct Materials		40,000
CR. *Applied Manufacturing Expense*		80,000
Variable Expense	40%	$32,000
Fixed Expense	60%	48,000

Suppose that actual manufacturing expense was $48,000 for the month. Since applied manufacturing expense (both types) was $80,000, this created a volume variance on the books of *$32,000 credit.*

Working with these figures, the cost accountant now prepares his Profit and Loss Statement to present to management:

Sales		$ 0.00
Cost of Sales		0.00
Gross Profit		0.00
Volume Variance (Credit)		32,000
Less Other Expenses:		
Selling	7,500*	
General and Administrative	15,000	22,500—
NET PROFIT		$ 9,500

When studying the monthly operating statement, management sees that sales were zero for the month, yet there was an earned profit of $9,500! No wonder non-accounting executives cannot understand nor accept the validity of figures submitted to them when absorption costing is the method used for cost accounting and reporting.

Case No. 2: Changes in Levels of Finished Goods Inventories Distort Reported Profits

Under absorption costing all costs and all overhead expenses are absorbed by products manufactured and moved into inventories. These costs and expenses never appear in operating reports until the goods are eventually sold and shipped to customers. When shipped and invoiced, the cost of goods sold appear on the current month's profit and loss statement.

This has the effect of deferring costs until goods are sold. This aspect of absorption costing may cause distortions of future management reports, in addition to producing illogical accounting results for current reports.

To illustrate this point, let's assume that the canning plant operates for the first six months of the year at a pace which is *30% above* the norm. The accounting records indicate that this would create an *over-absorbed variance* of $8,000 per month because of overloading fixed expenses into production. (Variable expenses increase in proportion to production volume increases—otherwise, a 30% increase in direct labor hours worked would have caused the over-absorption of $12,000.)

The over-absorbed variance credit will be *reported as profit* each month during this hypothesized six-month period. Do not forget that the cost value of the products being manufac-

* (Even though sales in this example were zero, there was a certain amont of fixed selling expense for the month.)

tured is increased by a corresponding $8,000 per month. The net result is to *capitalize* fixed expense for future periods of time. This overloading of expense will not appear as a charge to income *until the goods are sold*. This means that if production, after the six-month period, drops back to normal and stays there—every single Profit and Loss Statement which reflects the sale of goods manufactured during the period of high production *will exhibit incorrect figures!* That is, the cost of goods sold will be $8,000 higher than actual, therefore reported profits will be proportionately less.

To recap the situation: During the period of high production, the cost accountant reported additional "profits" to management caused by the over-absorption of fixed expense. When these reported goods sold were eventually sold, the cost figures caused the Profit and Loss Statement to show a corresponding loss of profits through *increased cost of sales*.

Case No. 3: Unitizing Expense

When overhead expense is charged to units of production this procedure has the effect of "unitizing" expense. If 100 adding machines are built as a job lot, and $1,200 is charged to this production order as its share of factory overhead, then each *production unit* has been charged with $12.

This procedure is well accepted in practice and seems to be logical—until you remember that fixed or period expenses have no relation to production volume. To illustrate this point conclusively, consider the hypothetical case of a rented manufacturing plant in which only one product will be built—commercial scales for grocery stores. Management has signed a 10-year lease on the land and buildings at a rental cost of $30,000 per year. Assuming for a moment that rent is the primary factory overhead item to be allocated to each scale built, let's see what effect *volume variances* have on per-unit costs.

Situation No. 1: Business is excellent the first year. The plant builds and sells 10,000 scales. In addition to prime costs, each scale is charged with its prorata share of rent expense, which is $3.

Situation No. 2: Business is terrible the second year because of a new electronic competitive scale which has entered the marketing picture. Only 1,000 scales are built this year—but the rent remains at $30,000 which must be absorbed by production. Under these circumstances each scale is charged with $30 as its share of the rental expense.

Consider the significance of this sharp increase from the standpoint of accounting information and subsequent management reports. Suppose that the unit selling price is $200 and the prime cost of each scale has remained unchanged during the two years at $100.

| | *Unit Costs and % to Sales* | | | |
	First Year	% to Sales	Second Year	% to Sales
Direct Labor	$60.00		$60.00	
Direct Materials	40.00		40.00	
Prime Cost	100.00	50%	100.00	50%
Add: Manufacturing Expense	3.00		30.00	
Total UNIT COST	$103.00	51.5%	$130.00	65%

Conclusion: Since fixed expenses such as rent do not vary with production, unit costs *increase* as productive volume *decreases*—and unit costs *decrease* as volume *increases*.

Since absorption costing requires that fixed expenses be included in the manufacturing overhead expense allocated to each job, this forces the cost accountant to relate a fixed type of expense to a highly volatile vehicle—constantly changing units of production. Furthermore, this confuses management at all levels, because of the illogical reports generated from the cost figures. For example, at a time when sales are increasing, cost accountants report to their management that unit costs are *dropping,* profit is *increasing*—it appears that the selling price can be reduced, if necessary, to meet competition. On the other hand, when sales and production are constantly decreasing, the accountants report that unit costs are INCREASING—possibly the selling price should be increased to maintain the required margin of profit—but this step would generate a further drop in sales, which would then further increase unit costs, and so on.

This illustrates only one of the many perplexing problems caused by the faithful and unquestioning application of the well-known principles of absorption costing for determining product costs and for making management decisions based on reported costs and profits.

Unitizing "Direct" Overhead Expense

For comparison purposes, let's now examine the effect of variable overhead expenses on unit costs. Referring again to the scale that is being manufactured—suppose that certain component parts of this precision instrument go through extensive grinding and polishing operations. A cost study shows that it costs $1.00 for the materials used to grind and polish the parts for each scale. Such materials are classed as factory supplies, an indirect expense.

Situation No. 1: 10,000 scales are built the first year. Polishing materials used that year cost roughly $10,000; the unit cost per scale was $1.00.

Situation No. 2: Only 1,000 scales are built the second year. The records show that the total cost of grinding and polishing materials drops to roughly $1,000. Note that the *unit cost per scale remains at $1* even though production has dropped 90%.

Responsibility Accounting

Another indictment of absorption costing is that it confuses the problem of placing responsibility for poor, overall performance. Since the method mixes fixed or period costs with production costs, the key man in each department or cost center assumes no personal responsibility for costs which are out of line. He is quick to point out that he has no control over supervisory salaries, rent, taxes, depreciation, research and development, plus all the many other types of fixed expense—yet "his" costs include these uncontrollable and ever-increasing cost elements.

Profit Planning and Control

A growing trend in contemporary management practices is profit planning and control. This requires accurate accounting figures as to the marginal profit contribution of each product that is manufactured and sold. Marginal profit is that amount remaining after deducting the direct costs of manufacturing (including *variable* overhead expense) from the selling price. Fixed expenses are covered only by generating enough marginal profit from products manufactured and sold to pay the costs of being in business. Any additional profit is net profit.

Since accounting figure facts reported under absorption costing include fixed expenses of all types, management finds it very difficult to make clear-cut decisions as to product profitability and profit contribution.

Summary

Since absorption costing fails to meet the needs of modern management, the next step is to search for a better cost system which will provide accurate, meaningful accounting figure facts to be used as the basis for many vital management decisions. The next chapter explains the concepts behind a controversial new cost-accounting system known as "Direct Costing," or "Direct Standard Costing." This system is now in wide use as a replacement for absorption costing. It is considered to be an effective tool for modern management planning and cost control.

24

Direct Costing: A Tool for Modern Management

Anyone interested in the modern costing accounting system known as "Direct Costing" can find a wealth of excellent material on the subject. Available are several books, bulletins published by the American Management Association, pamphlets issued by management consultants who are active in the cost accounting field, National Association of Accountants bulletins, and copies of speeches, etc.

To assemble and present the material appearing in this chapter, my functions were to research, analyze and evaluate the available material, select and edit paragraphs and pages presenting the key concepts and related illustrations, then to select the appropriate places in the chapter where this authoritative information would be of greatest value to the reader.

While assembling and editing this material, I was fortunate to be associated with the management consulting firm Wright Associates, 522 Fifth Avenue, New York City. Wilmer Wright, formerly a Senior Partner with Stevenson, Jordan and Harrison, was one of the pioneers in the development of today's direct costing concepts and special management reports for profit planning and control. He and his highly-experienced cost engineers have installed direct cost systems in scores of manufacturing plants in recent years; many of these firms are found on the "Fortune 500" list of top American corporations.

Much of the information included in this chapter came from Mr. Wright's vast knowledge and experience in this challenging and fast-changing field of modern cost accounting, and related systems and procedures.

Two other major sources of valuable data on the subject were:

1. *Management Bulletin #54:* "Direct Costing: A Look at Its Strength and Weaknesses," published by the American Management Association.
2. Booklet written by James J. Hickey, CPA: *Direct Costing—An Invaluable Management Tool,* published by Kevmar Publications, Stratford, Conn.

Members of top management in hundreds of firms today, backed up by a large group of industrial cost and public accountants have reached the conclusion that absorption costing has been fully tried and tested—and has failed to satisfy the myriad needs of modern management, operating in a complex and highly competitive business environment.

Management Requirements from a Modern Cost System

It is literally true that accounting figure facts are the steering wheel of a business. And, cost figures, utilized in various ways, are the basis for the following management functions:
- Profit planning and performance evaluations.
- Identifying profitable products and allocating plant facilities to increase profits.
- Determination of the profit contribution of each major product or product line.
- Planning marketing, advertising and promotion campaigns.
- Determination of appropriate selling prices.
- Make or buy decisions.
- Allocation of responsibility for expense control and labor performance to key men.
- Determination of Breakeven Points.
- Preparation of realistic cost estimates for competitive bids.
- Determining the effects on production costs of increased labor costs during labor/management wage negotiations.
- Costing inter-plant transfers of manufactured products.

For the vital decision-making function of management, financial and operating statements must be provided which present realistic, accurate figure facts in such a way that management can grasp their significance at once.

The Industrial Cost Accountant

The industrial cost accountant is a member of a growing profession whose function and role in the contemporary business environment has become increasingly important. As a key member of the management team he is not content to merely accumulate cost figures for the sake of staying busy. He should be the leader in setting up modern cost systems to provide operating management and sales management with essential cost data.

As Ray E. Longenecker says, writing in the *American Management Bulletin #54,* "The major concern of the industrial accountant is profit determination and emphasis in reports on those factors which generate profit. A business profits only when its income exceeds the cost required to generate that income, and so it follows that the elements of cost and their impact on profit must be thoroughly understood in all decision-making levels of management from shop foreman to Company President."

Since absorption costing frequently places the cost accountant in the awkward position of attempting to explain and defend illogical, perplexing reports generated from cost records kept on the absorption basis, the new concept of "direct costing" should be welcomed by all progressive, dedicated industrial cost accountants.

What Is Direct Costing?

Direct costing is a method of cost accounting which capitalizes only those manufacturing expenses incurred directly by production activities. Fixed or period expenses are *kept out of* inventory values, are accumulated according to the rules of responsibility accounting—and are presented on the monthly Profit and Loss Statement along with selling, general and administrative expenses as a reduction of gross profit.

Direct costing, then, is an accounting and reporting system which *separates* expenses which vary with production volume from those that do not.

Another characteristic of direct costing is that fixed expenses are not unitized. Since these expenses are not loaded onto each unit of production, it avoids reporting to management that unit costs are rising because of falling production, or dropping because of increased production activity.

The concept of direct costing is deceptively simple; its implications and benefits to management are myriad and merit considerable thought and study by all members of the management team.

Direct Standard Costing

When labor, material and overhead cost standards are established and utilized in connection with a direct cost system, the combined concepts are then referred to as "direct standard costing."

Growth of Direct Costing

Wilmer Wright cites in his book the increasing acceptance of direct costing in recent years:
"The growth of direct costing has been dramatic. In 1953, a research committee of the National Association of Accountants found only 17 companies using it. In 1959 another NAA research committee found that 197 had adopted it. In 1961, *Business Week* estimated that 250 companies had converted."

There are many sound reasons for this dramatic growth. To quote Mr. Wright once more: "Emphasis in accounting theory and practice has shifted from the balance sheet to the income statement. External financial reports designed to meet the needs of creditors have given way to reports designed for investors and managers. Internal financial reports have become more and more the tools for planning and decision-making rather than historical records for post mortems. This swing to management accounting has resulted in the dramatic growth of a system of accounting called "direct costing."

Three Reasons for Growth

There are three primary reasons for this growth. First, direct costing provides a better measure of period income than does either prime or absorption costing. Second, direct costing eliminates the fuzziness of conventional accounting by presenting accounting and financial reports in the form required for decision making. And, third, direct costing provides better control through a more clear-cut application of responsibility accounting.

PREPARATION FOR DIRECT COSTING

The fundamental requirement of direct costing is the clear-cut separation of direct costs of all types from fixed or period expenses. Therefore, it is based on a specially-prepared Chart of Accounts which facilitates the reporting of fixed expenses on the monthly Profit and Loss Statement. These expenses never find their way into work-in-process costs.

A typical list of expense accounts for a small job shop firm appears below.

Fixed or Period Expense

Superintendence
Fire Insurance
Heat and Light
Property Taxes
Rent
Depreciation of Machinery
Building Maintenance
Depreciation of Factory Buildings
Clerical Wages—Factory Office
Office Stationery and Supplies
Miscellaneous Expense

Variable or Direct Expense

Indirect Labor
Machinery Repairs
Fuel
Power and Water
Telephone
Compensation Insurance
Factory Supplies
Uniforms or Apron Service
Payroll Taxes
Idle Time
Small Tools Expense
Material
Direct Labor
Patterns
Testing New Dies
Undistributed Freight In

One of the basic tests for classifying an account is to ask this question: "Was an expenditure incurred because the products now in inventory *were produced*?" If the answer is "No," then the expense belongs in the fixed category.

Converting an "actual cost" system from an absorption costing basis to a direct cost system requires the complete elimination of all period costs from the cost accumulation of each cost center. The job tickets or charge documents formerly utilized to report direct labor and direct materials costs can be used with the new system with no changes. To repeat what has been said before, it is the overhead manufacturing expenses which must be carefully separated into two types:

1. Direct overhead expenses which obviously vary with production.
2. Fixed or period expenses not affected by production activity.

Those expenses classified as "direct" are charged to the product in the usual way. For example, the cost of fringe benefits and payroll taxes on direct labor are allocated to each job worked on, using direct labor hours or cost as the base.

Mixed Accounts

By their very nature some expense accounts are mixed. That is, part of the expense may be fixed, and part of it may vary in accordance with production. For example, suppose that one employee operating a motorized materials conveyor inside the plant can support the production activity until the production rate reaches 70% of total capacity. At this point, an additional machine and operator are required.

The usual procedure for such accounts is to set up a budget sheet which provides for separating the expense into the two categories of fixed and variable. However, operating reports obtained from direct costing indicate that this precise separation of expense is not truly significant unless the amounts of money involved are very substantial. Therefore, authorities on direct costing suggest that the cost accountants, who classify accounts and set up budget sheets, concentrate on "balancing" the situation by placing certain minor mixed accounts in the fixed category and others in the variable or direct category.

The Income Statement

The Profit and Loss Statement shown in Figure 24-1 illustrates the simplicity of reporting operating results to management where the figures are obtained from a direct costing system.

Profit Contribution

As the statement shows, only direct costs and expenses are subtracted from net sales to determine how much profit remains to pay for the fixed expenses—the cost of being in business, ready to produce and sell goods.

This figure is labeled "Profit Contribution," which becomes especially significant when income statements similar to this one are prepared for various product lines.

P/V Ratio

Divide the Profit Contribution amount into net sales; the result is the "P/V Ratio," which is the percentage of profit to net sales. In Figure 24-1 the P/V ratio is 22.0%.

Breakeven Point

A clear-cut separation of direct and period costs as provided by direct costing makes it possible to determine easily a significant guideline for management—the "breakeven point."

Divide the total period expense by the P/V Ratio; the result is the sales volume necessary to *break even*. Any sales figure below this amount will result in a loss from operations. Since overhead costs have been increasing at an alarming rate in recent years, top management now is keenly interested in knowing the breakeven point.

This concept led to the development of "Profit/Volume Breakeven Charts." See Figure 24-2.

Determining Product Profitability

Management is periodically faced with difficult decisions as to which products to drop, or which products to promote. The basic objective of such decisions, of course, is to optimize profits. The basis for such decisions is product profitability. Now, because of the very nature of absorption costing, cost figures obtained from absorption costing hinder, rather than assist in such determinations.

An example of this is taken from W. A. Thorn's article in the May, 1965 issue of the

Figure 24-1
THE PROFIT AND LOSS STATEMENT

THE INCOME STATEMENT
(Modernized with Direct Costing)
A.B.C. MANUFACTURING COMPANY

NET SALES		$5,500,000
DIRECT COST OF SALES:		
Material	$2,400,000	
Direct Labor	840,000	
Direct Manufacturing Expense	600,000	
Sales Commissions	450,000	
Total Direct Cost of Sales		$4,290,000
PROFIT CONTRIBUTION		$1,210,000
P/V Ratio (% of Net Sales)		22.0%
PERIOD EXPENSE:		
Manufacturing Period Expense	$ 350,000	
Selling and Advertising Period Expense	300,000	
Administrative Expense	400,000	
Total Period Expense		$1,050,000
OPERATING PROFIT		$ 160,000
Margin of Safety (% of Profit Contribution)		13.2%
NOTE: Breakeven Point		

$$\$1,050,000 \div .22 = \$4,773,000$$

WRIGHT ASSOCIATES

Footnotes

1. Sales commissions appear under the caption of "Direct Cost of Sales" because this expense varies directly with sales volume.

2. Direct manufacturing expense was capitalized at the time of production, and became part of the value of the product in Finished Goods Inventory.

3. When the product was sold, one element in the Cost of Sales was direct manufacturing expense, as shown in the statement.

4. All period or fixed expenses appear under the caption "Period Expense"—along with Selling and Advertising Period Expenses.

Furniture Design and Manufacturing magazine, "Does Your Cost System Need Overhauling?" (Mr. Thorn is an associate of Wright Associates.)

"When variable and fixed costs are combined, such as in an actual cost system, or absorption standard cost system, some truly misleading figures may result. For example, management is always interested in knowing which product to promote. If fixed costs are included in product costs, and you use as a guide "Gross Profit Per Cent on Sales Price," you will arrive at the conclusion that Product A is the item to promote because it produces a 30% return on sales price, compared to 20% on Product B.

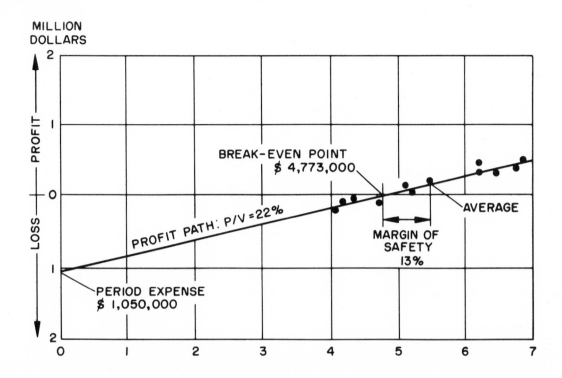

MONTH	SALES MILLIONS OF DOLLARS	OPERATING PROFIT	MONTH	SALES MILLIONS OF DOLLARS	OPERATING PROFIT
JANUARY	$ 5,250	$ 50	JULY	$ 5,500	$ 200
FEBRUARY	4,750	(100)	AUGUST	6,250	450
MARCH	4,200	(100)	SEPTEMBER	6,500	300
APRIL	4,100	(200)	OCTOBER	6,900	500
MAY	4,350	(50)	NOVEMBER	6,800	400
JUNE	5,150	150	DECEMBER	6,250	320
			AVERAGE	5,500	160

Figure 24-2
THE PROFIT/VOLUME BREAKEVEN CHART

Which Product Should We Promote?
Absorption Cost System

	Product A	Product B
Sales Price	$1.00	$1.00
Manufacturing Cost:		
Variable & Fixed	.70	.80
Gross Profit	.30	.20
% on Sales Price	30%	20%

"However, in a direct standard cost system we keep variable and fixed expense separated, and subtract from the product sales price only the variable expense to find out how much of the sales dollar will remain to pay off fixed expense and contribute toward profit. This figure is called profit contribution. Divide this by the sales price and we find the P/V Ratio, which represents the portion remaining in each sales dollar after paying for variable costs. In the example, Product A develops a 60% P/V ratio, or 60% remaining. Product B shows 70% remaining. Therefore, if the cost department had advised sales to promote Product A, they would have been incorrect, as Product B is more profitable to sell! *Profit contribution is the key to the decision.*"

Which Product Should We Promote?
Direct Cost System

		Product A		Product B
Sales Price		$1.00		$1.00
Manufacturing Cost:				
Variable	.40	.40	.30	.30
Fixed	.30	—	.50	—
Profit Contribution		.60		.70
P/V Ratio		60%		70%

WHY DIRECT-COSTING IS TAILOR-MADE FOR DECISION-MAKING

An article which appeared in the January, 1968 issue of *Furniture Design and Manufacturing* magazine titled, "Costing for Profits"—written by a Senior Consultant named Joseph Cataldo of Wright Associates—includes an excellent example of how a direct cost system aids management in making key decisions:

"Let us examine a direct cost system and the reasons why it is 'tailor-made' for quick decision-making. First, it is important to understand the basic concept of direct costing. Direct costing starts with the premise that certain costs will be incurred regardless of production or sales, and other costs are *directly related* to production or sales. The former are called fixed or period costs and include such expenses as rent, depreciation, supplies, supervision and executive salaries. Direct costs are made up of direct labor, raw materials, and certain manufacturing expenses incurred because of production and sales commissions. A direct cost system segregates period and variable costs and *maintains* this segregation throughout all accounting records and reports.

"Why is this important? Perhaps it can best be illustrated by example.

"Instead of a furniture manufacturer, we take the case of a *furniture dealer* who carries three product lines which he *purchases* from manufacturers. Since he receives invoices and pays accordingly, there is absolutely no question as to the direct cost to him of each product line. The dealer establishes a selling price for each product with the resulting gross profits.

	Product A	*Product B*	*Product C*
Unit Selling Price	$1,000	$700	$1,500
Unit Purchase Price	400	400	1,000
Unit Gross Profit	$ 600	$300	$ 500

"If he sold *100* units of each product, his profit and loss statement would appear as shown in Exhibit 24-A.

Exhibit 24-A
PROFIT AND LOSS STATEMENT (Direct Costing)

	Total	*Product A*	*Product B*	*Product C*
Sales	$320,000	$100,000	$70,000	$150,000
Cost of Sales	180,000	40,000	40,000	100,000
Profit Contribution Per Unit	$140,000	$ 60,000	$30,000	$ 50,000
Less: Sales Commission	23,500	7,500	6,000	10,000
Profit Contribution	$116,500	$ 52,500	$24,000	$ 40,000
Fixed Expenses	50,000—			
General & Admin. Exp.	34,500—			
Net Profit	$ 32,000			

"At this point, it would be easy for him to determine what the effect on profit would be under any combination of changed circumstances. For example, if the selling price of Product C were $1,600 instead of $1,500, the profit contribution of Product C would be $50,000. (Sales would have increased by $10,000 while costs would have remained the same.) Or if he sold 120 units of Product A and 80 of Product C, his sales would have fallen to $310,000 but his net profit would have increased to $34,500. The operating expenses are fixed and would have remained the same ($84,500) *regardless* of the quantities sold.

"Here is how the data can help in the decision-making process:

"If government fiscal action leads to reduced sales, the furniture dealer can easily determine that he can lower the selling price on Product A, and possibly Product C, while trying to hold the price on Product B.

"Recognizing the value of such data, why do manufacturers complicate their accounting system so they are not in a position to make the same type decisions which are so vital?

"Let us see what would happen to the dealer's decision-making ability if he applied the *theory of absorption costing* to his business. He estimates that during the coming period he will purchase 80 of Product A, 120 of Product B, and 120 of Product C. He allocates fixed expenses to each product based on the display area occupied by each in his showroom and arrives at the following allocation percentages:

Product A   50%
Product B   20%
Product C   30%

"He has fixed store operating expenses of $50,000, which are allocated to each product:

	Expenses	Estimated Purchases	Overhead Unit Allocation
Product A	$25,000	$ 80	$312
Product B	10,000	120	83
Product C	15,000	120	125
	$50,000	$320	

"Exhibit 24-B shows what his profit and loss statement might look like based on the fact that he actually sold 100 units of each product.

Exhibit 24-B
PROFIT AND LOSS STATEMENT (Absorption Costing)

	Total	Product A	Product B	Product C
Sales	$320,000	$100,000	$70,000	$150,000
*Cost of Sales	232,000	71,200	48,300	112,500
Gross Profit	$ 88,000	$ 28,800	$21,700	$ 37,500
% Gross Profit to Sales		28.8	31.0	25.0
Add: Overabsorbed Fixed Expenses	2,000			
Gross Profit	$ 90,000			
Selling, General and Administrative	58,000			
Net Profit	$ 32,000			

* Purchase Price per unit plus expense allocation per unit multiplied by the number of units sold.

"Now the dealer is confronted with data that tells him Product C is the one where a price reduction can best be made. In reality, every time he sells a unit of Product C, it makes a profit contribution of only $400 as against a profit contribution of $525 by Product A. At the same time, the gross profit percentage shown under the absorption cost method is *highest* for Product B which is making a profit contribution of only $240; *lowest* of any of the lines.[1]

"Readers of FD&M would most likely agree that it would be foolish for the dealer to keep his books on an absorption cost basis."

[1] Total profit contribution of each product (Exhibit 24-A) divided by 100 units sold equals profit contribution per unit of each product.

OTHER ASPECTS AND BENEFITS OF DIRECT COSTING

There seems to be little doubt that this new cost accounting system offers many benefits of great value in today's fast-moving, competitive business world. Leading proponents of direct costing attribute dozens of benefits to its use; some of the more outstanding ones are listed as follows:

1. Direct Costing Is Valuable for Short-Term Decisions

"Direct costing is of great value for fast, day-to-day decisions. Fixed overhead costs are not unitized; the inverse effect of rising or falling volume is kept out of cost figures. The actual, direct cost and profit contribution for each product is known."—Wilmer Wright.

2. Making Pricing Decisions

"In any pricing situation it is the proper function of the accountant to present to operating management the profit results of various alternatives. No matter whether the problem is simple or complex, direct costing provides the best basis for both short and long-range decision-making. Eliminating volume variances achieves a clear cut separation of sales and manufacturing responsibilities and provides objective measurement of the quality of pricing decisions.

"With a standard direct costing system, period costs are allocated to products or product groups as part of the profit planning operation at least once a year. However, they are allocated *in total* for the planned volume and sales mix. They are never unitized. It is the unitizing of period costs that makes absorption costs confusing to operating managers because these unit costs are valid only with the assumed volume and mix. By showing the allocation in total, along with the forecasted volume and mix, this confusion is avoided. Operating management can see clearly the true inter-relation of prices, costs and volume." (*Pricing for Profit with Direct Standard Costs*—Wilmer Wright.)

3. Fixed or Period Costs Subjected to Closer Control

"Those who advocate direct costing point out appropriately that by this method fixed or period costs may be subjected to even closer scrutiny and control than under the more conventional system which encourages allocating and unitizing of fixed costs. It is surely true that cost accumulations which are kept intact, rather than being 'piece-mealed' throughout the departmental accounts, may be dealt with more readily." (Lee Brummet, *AMA Bulletin #54.*)

4. Decision-Making Aided by Direct Costing

"The direct costing approach provides a completely understandable insight into cost elements and their behavior characteristics, thereby permitting soundly conceived decisions. Some of the problem areas which require incisive analysis before sound decisions can be made include the following: Cost control, expansion and deletion of product lines, new product additions, make-or-buy alternatives, sales assortment or mix, productivity improvements, pricing, and so on. Before a decision can be made regarding any of the problems arising in these areas, data must be available in such a form that the *issues are not obscured.*

"The very nature of direct costing sets up the statistical records, as well as the data related to future expectations, in a manner which facilitates sound analysis. This is so because direct costing recognizes the basic distinction between those costs relating directly to units produced and those costs relating to a period of time." (Ray E. Longenecker, *AMA Bulletin #54.*)

5. Responsibility Accounting

"Control can be effective only when exercised by people who have authority to make decisions affecting the costs for which they are responsible. The very first requirement of direct costing is a careful segregation and analysis of costs in the various cost centers identifiable with supervision in one form or another." (Ray E. Longenecker, *AMA Bulletin #54.*)

6. Inventory Valuation

"Inventory valuation is really not a valuation process but one of *cost deferral*. Direct costs are the only costs incidental to the production of goods and are, therefore, the only costs to be included in inventories. Other manufacturing costs are simply costs of maintaining a readiness to produce. Those who favor direct costing point out, further, that net income may be generated ONLY BY SALES TRANSACTIONS and that the deferral of fixed costs has no place in the process of income measurement." (Lee Brummet, *AMA Bulletin #54.*)

Summary

Only a few of the many benefits to be derived from the installation of a direct cost system have been outlined in this chapter. One major benefit of increasing importance is that the system provides clear-cut figure facts on direct product costs, marginal profit contribution figures, profit/volume ratios and breakeven analyses. Experience with direct costing has shown that even line management can quickly calculate and determine the effects of various potential changes, such as projected hourly wage increases, the use of substitute materials at variable cost prices, and other alternatives. And, if a wide variety of data covering many alternative product costs and selling prices is required, the various figures can be fed into a computer which will make extensive profit/volume projections for various volumes and product mixes.

It can truly be said that direct costing lends itself to a completely integrated management-reporting system; it is an ideal tool for the modern concept of profit planning and expense control.

25

General Ledger Control Over Production Costs

On previous pages, we have explained how individual job-cost tickets are prepared by each employee who works on any phase of a job. These tickets show time worked, rate and total labor cost. And, as part of the daily plant procedures, these tickets are routed eventually to the cost-acounting department. Here, they are posted to individual-job ledger cards in accordance with the job number appearing on the work tickets.

We also stressed that detailed job-cost records are controlled by General Ledger Work-in-Process accounts. Because of the importance of such control accounts, we will now review typical procedures and entries affecting these accounts.

Direct Labor Work-in-Process Account

The total of all direct labor tickets is charged to a General Ledger account called "Work-in-Process—Direct Labor." The balance in this account represents the total value of all labor that has been expended on all jobs which are in various stages of completion in all the production departments and work centers in the entire plant.

When labor costs are charged in total to a work-in-process account, an offsetting credit entry is made to a "payroll" account. More about this later.

Factory Payroll Account

At the end of a pay period, the time-clock cards or daily time summaries are used for figuring total gross earnings for each factory employee preparatory to writing the factory payroll.

After the payroll is written, the sum of all gross earnings is available by reference to the payroll summary, or Payroll Check Register Journal. Total gross earnings are charged to the General Ledger Payroll account.

DISTRIBUTION OF PAYROLL AND OTHER INTERNAL CHARGES

Journal Vouchers

It is customary in manufacturing accounting to distribute internal charges to various operating departments by means of special journal entry documents called "Journal Vouchers."

Many expense items, such as rent, utilities, insurance, depreciation, property taxes, etc., are prorated to production departments on some selected basis—square feet of floor space, number of workers in each department, direct labor hours, total departmental payroll, etc.

In a similar manner, the payroll is analyzed and entries are made to charge salaries and wages to the departments that should bear the expense. Note: The phrase "salaries and wages" refers only to supervisory personnel and wages of employees not directly engaged in working on production jobs. (Maintenance and general repair crews, janitors and others.)

Examples

1. Foremen's salaries are charged to their respective departmental salary expense accounts.
2. The plant superintendent's salary is prorated and charged to all departments on some equitable basis, such as the number of employees in each department.
3. Wages of janitors, repairmen and night watchmen are prorated and charged to various departments served (Indirect Labor Account).
4. All job-cost tickets for idle time are summarized and charged to idle-time expense for each department.

Credits to Payroll Account

When the distribution of all charges for indirect labor is determined and entries made on journal vouchers, the offsetting credit is to the payroll account. Amounts debited to the work-in-process account for direct labor are also credited to the payroll account.

The payroll account should now have a zero balance. It is merely a temporary account which is charged with all labor costs until such time as appropriate work-in-process and departmental expense accounts can be debited.

DIRECT MATERIALS COSTS

Stores Issues

We have seen that a material requisition or issue ticket is the authority for all parts or materials issued. Each issue document indicates the job number to be charged. Bookkeepers in the materials-control department post the issue quantity to stock ledger cards and apply unit costs to the issue document. Later, cost-accounting personnel multiply quantity issued by unit price and write the total cost on issue tickets.

Routed to Job Cost Section

Issue tickets now go to the job-cost section of the cost department. Here, they are sorted by job number and posted to job-cost ledger cards. In addition, the total value of all materials is *summarized* from the documents and posted to a work-in-process (materials) control account.

Materials Work-in-Process Account

One of the primary control accounts in a typical factory operating ledger is the "Work-in-Process—Direct Materials" account. The balance in this account represents the total value of all materials issued to production for jobs not yet completed. Inventories on hand, of course, are reduced by the total value of all materials issued and charged to work-in-process.

CHARGING OVERHEAD EXPENSES TO PRODUCTION JOBS

As discussed in detail on previous pages, overhead expense is one component of job cost. Several examples of this type of expense have been enumerated. Since it is desirable for job-cost ledgers to accurately reflect total costs for each job in process, it is usually considered essential to allocate a portion of overhead costs to each job in process. This is done by accountants in the cost department, who periodically analyze the status of each job in process and calculate applicable overhead on a predetermined basis.

Posting Overhead Burden

Cost-department bookkeepers then post overhead amounts to each job-cost ledger card and develop, as a by-product, a grand total of all amounts posted to individual account cards.

Overhead Expense Control Account

The grand total of all overhead burden amounts posted to individual job-cost ledger cards is then charged to a control account, "Work-in-Process—Overhead." When this is done, an account known as "Applied Manufacturing Expense" is credited.

"Over and Under" Applied Overhead

It should be clearly understood that the "applied manufacturing expense" account balance represents an *offset* to actual manufacturing expense. "Applied manufacturing expense" means that we have taken that much of actual *manufacturing expense* and transferred it to *job cost*.

At the end of an accounting period, a grand total of actual expense incurred in operating the factory is obtained from the operating-expense records. In theory, every penny of expense should have been charged to production during this period. In actual practice, it will not work out this way. If the total credited to applied manufacturing expense *exceeds* the total actual manufacturing expense, then burden has been *overapplied*. If the total credited is less than the actual total of manufacturing expense, then burden has been *underapplied*.

COST FLOW IN A MANUFACTURING PLANT

Journal-voucher entries record the transfer of costs from one phase of the production cycle to the next phase. The cycle starts with application of direct labor to raw materials, parts and subassemblies and ends when finished goods are delivered to the storerooms.

Here are the successive journal entries:

1. As direct labor is expended on a production order going through the various operations in the plant, job-cost time-tickets show hours and labor costs. These are summarized by the following entry:

DR.	Work-in-Process—Direct Labor	$xxxx.xx	
CR.	Payroll account		$xxxx.xx

To charge direct labor costs to work-in-process.

2. As raw materials, parts and subassemblies are issued for use in making or assembling finished products, material requisitions record the quantity, unit cost and total cost of everything issued. Materials costs are recapped and the following summary entry is made:

DR.	Work-in-Process—Direct Materials	$xxxx.xx	
CR.	Inventory on Hand—Raw Materials		$ xxx.xx
CR.	Inventory on Hand—Parts		xxx.xx
CR.	Inventory on Hand—Subassemblies		xxx.xx

To charge work-in-process account with cost of materials issued.

3. Overhead burden is prorated and applied periodically to various jobs in process. Then the following entry is made to reflect total overhead applied:

DR.	Work-in-Process—Overhead Burden	$xxxx.xx	
CR.	Applied Manufacturing Expense		$ xxx.xx

To record overhead charged to jobs in process.

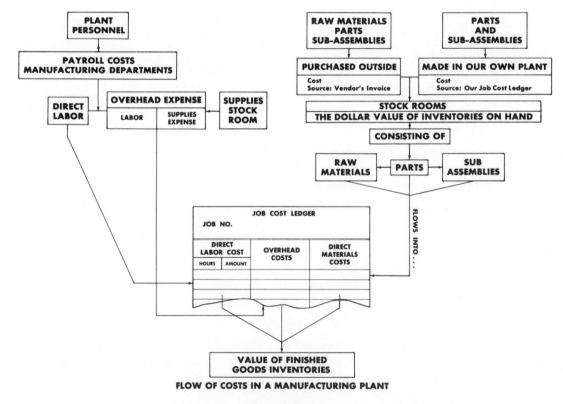

FLOW OF COSTS IN A MANUFACTURING PLANT

Figure 25-1
FLOW CHART OF MANUFACTURING COSTS

4. When production orders are completed, total production costs are transferred to Finished Goods on Hand Inventory by this summary entry:

DR.	Finished Goods Inventory	$xxxx.xx	
CR.	Work-in-Process—Direct Labor		$ xxx.xx
CR.	Work-in-Process—Direct Materials		xxx.xx
CR.	Work-in-Process—Overhead Burden		xxx.xx

To record the completion of jobs in process and the transfer of total job costs to Finished Goods Inventory.

5. When finished goods are sold from stock, the sales invoices are costed * and inventory on hand is reduced by the total cost:

DR.	Cost of Sales—Finished Goods	$xxxx.xx	
CR.	Finished Goods Inventory		$xxxx.xx

To record cost of goods sold to customers.

Summary

General Ledger work-in-process accounts are control accounts for all individual job cost records. Each of these account balances represents the total expended for each element of job cost for all jobs still in process.

Cost flow in a job-shop manufacturing plant follows a very definite pattern. A good cost system provides a logical, step-by-step process for recording all labor, materials and overhead chargeable to production.

The flow of costs is charted by Figure 25-1.

* The job-cost ledger record for each production order involving finished goods produced for shelf inventory, or for special orders, provides *unit-cost data* which makes it easy to cost sales invoices.

26

Electronic Computers

The electronic computer was a scientific curiosity confined to one or two universities until it invaded the business world in the early 1950's. The first computer for processing business data (as compared to scientific calculations) was the Univac machine installed by General Electric in 1954 in Louisville, Kentucky. This initial computer installation for processing payrolls received great publicity; the eyes of the business world were upon the systems planners and the programmers assigned the responsibility of making it work successfully. As with nearly all pioneering ventures, they encountered many unique problems, but the computer was finally installed as planned.

Very few additional installations in business offices were made; progress toward automation was slow until the big breakthrough in 1959. The International Business Machines Corp. announced the small, relatively low-priced IBM 1401 computer for business data processing. IBM obtained more than 4,000 orders from the initial release of this machine. The release was comparable to Henry Ford announcing the first Model T automobile which was priced to fit the pocketbook of the common working man.

One reason for the amazing acceptance of the 1401 computer was that IBM had built up over a period of many years approximately 32,000 punched-card tabulating machine installations in the nation. The IBM 1401 was designed as a card-processor computer and was immediately accepted by users of tab machines.

The number of actual computer installations in the business world continued to be small until about 1961, when the first 1401 machines began to be installed in the field in increasing numbers. From that time until the present the number of computers on order and in use has continually expanded at an amazing rate.

One important factor which has contributed to the rapid expansion of the number of installations is that computer manufacturers have actively engaged in a price-performance race. Each year has seen releases of new equipment and new input/output devices—each computer being smaller and faster than its predecessors and lower in price. Today, firms with as few as 100 employees may well be able to afford a small, full-scale computer for their data processing. This fact points up the basic reason why today's practitioner should become fully informed about computers and their application to business applications. More and more clients in businesses of all sizes will look to him for professional advice about the installation of a computer on their premises—or about the use of an outside service bureau.

Basic Objective

This is the first of three chapters devoted to electronic computers. The information presented in this section of this book is not intended to qualify the average practitioner as a technical expert in data-processing hardware and techniques. Rather, the objective is to provide essential, basic guidelines, facts and information on a broad basis to which the practitioner can refer before discussing a proposed computer installation with a client.

To supplement the information presented in this book it is suggested that the practitioner begin to build a reference library on computers, consisting of the following:

- Brochures and manuals obtained from computer manufacturers, exhibits and trade shows.
- Articles in trade magazines which describe actual installations.
- Informative material provided by the educational division of computer manufacturers, especially for consultants and other professional people.

Computer Definition

The word "computer" is applied to many different types of office machines. The noun can properly be applied to almost any device which performs arithmetic calculations, including the small electronic machines which are about the same size as an adding machine, but which perform addition, subtraction, multiplication and division at electronic speeds. However, the United States Government defines a computer as a machine which stores the operating instructions internally. By this definition, desk computers of small size are properly called "computers."

Operator-Oriented Computers

Today's "desk" computers are operator-oriented. They are about the overall size of a regular office desk, since the basic machine is either an accounting machine or an electric typewriter. The base machine is surrounded with electronic controls and circuitry, input/output devices and has a memory for storing instructions.

A common characteristic of most desk computers is that *operator intervention* is an integral part of the machine's operation. An operator is required to scan posting media to select that data which is to be posted or introduced into the machine. In addition, the operator manually inserts unit ledger records, voucher checks or other documents into the machine carriage and positions forms for printing.

Full-Scale Computers

When is a computer not considered a desk computer, but a full-scale computer? This question becomes increasingly pertinent as the trend toward smaller and smaller *full-scale* computers continues.

One distinguishable characteristic of a full-scale computer is that the machine operates entirely unattended—with no operator intervention while it is running a job. The computer executes the stored instructions entirely automatically and controls all input or output devices by itself until the job is completed.

Tabulating equipment was in wide use for many years before computers were introduced to the business world. These machines did not operate from stored instructions; they were controlled from electrical impulses wired through a plugboard. To change jobs the tab operator changed the plugboard, or moved the necessary wires to obtain different results. It is a common sight in large tab-machine installations to see many different plugboards on racks, each one wired for a different job.

Most of the early full-scale electronic computers utilized plugboards for certain control functions. However, these were soon made obsolete by the concept of storing all instructions internally in the computer's memory. Practically all of today's computers are stored program machines.

Programmed Instructions

The services of a new group of professional people have come into great demand as a result of the computer age. These professionals are known as "programmers;" they analyze jobs to be put on the computer and write instructions which direct the computer in its automatic operations.

This sounds very mysterious and unique until one reflects upon the fact that every practitioner has written instructions at one time or another for the guidance of posting-machine operators, for clerks entering sales or cash in journals, for billing clerks and others.

To understand the basic characteristic of instructions for a computer, let's analyze the instructions you would write if you attempted to instruct a moron or a mechanical robot in the use of a desk calculating machine on a payroll job. Suppose that we have a Friden or a Monroe calculator with two keyboards; one keyboard is for regular addition and subtraction, plus a small keyboard for multiplication and division. Also, let's assume that we have unit time cards representing the time worked for each employee.

Your written instructions would read as follows:

1. Sit down in front of the calculator; face the machine.
2. Place the employee time cards on the table to the left of the calculator.
3. Grasp pencil in right hand, with the lead point facing down.
4. Locate the hours worked which appear on the time card for the first employee.
5. Index the hours (and fractions of hours expressed in tenths) worked on the regular keyboard.
6. Index the rate per hour on the multiplying keyboard.
7. Depress the "Multiply" motor bar.
8. Point off answer appearing in upper dials by moving the point off slide 3 positions to the left.
9. Write answer from the dials to the time card; write amount earned in the "Gross Pay" square.
10. Turn first time card face down on the table.
11. Proceed with same instructions on next time card, etc.

A programmer, in effect, writes detailed instructions for a mechanical robot. He analyzes the job and the results to be obtained. He constructs block diagrams to represent each step or the logic behind each operation of the computer. Finally, working from his block diagrams, he writes each instruction in a coded format which the computer can handle.

Symbolic Versus Machine Instructions

Programmers write instructions or statements in a symbolic or generalized format. These symbolic instructions or statements are converted into actual, coded machine instructions either by an "assembler" program, or a "compiler" program. These programs consist of pre-written, complex instruction sets provided as a package by the computer manufacturer for the explicit purpose of coverting the programmer's "language" into coded instructions that are meaningful to the computer.

When the source instructions are converted to a machine code, the deck of punched cards generated by the computer when assembling or compiling is known as the "object" deck. After this deck is available, computer runs are made by loading the object deck into the memory of the computer before starting the operation. The machine stores each instruction in a designated location in memory; when the processing of data coming into the computer begins, the computer reads and executes each instruction until end of job is reached.

Changing Jobs

When a job is completed, and instructions for the next job are loaded into memory, the new instructions replace those which were stored for the first job. This explains the tremendous flexibility of stored program computers; the ease of changing jobs is impressive. For example, it may require only 15 to 30 seconds to read-in and store all instructions for a complex run.

INPUT AND OUTPUT DEVICES

If the computer memory is packed with instructions, how does the computer process large volumes of data? The answer is found in the use of input and output devices, plus the fact that records are stored *outside* the computer in the form of decks of punched cards, reels of magnetic tape, or they are stored on disks or on magnetic cards found in random access devices.

Types of Input Devices

Devices which can transmit data from the outside of the computer to the internal core memory are:
- Punch card reader
- Paper tape reader
- Magnetic tape unit
- Random access device
- Console typewriter
- Optical character readers

Types of Output Devices

- Line printer
- Card punch
- Magnetic tape unit
- Paper tape punch
- Random access components
- Console typewriter

The various input and output devices which are an integral part of a business computer system such as the one pictured in Figure 26-1 control the overall operating speed of the

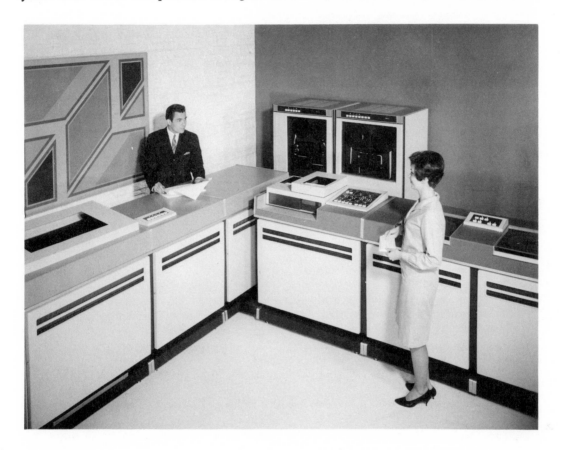

Figure 26-1
BUSINESS COMPUTER
(Courtesy of National Cash Register Co.)

computer. The reason is that most computers which handle business data are input or output-bound. That is, the internal functioning speed of the computer is many times greater than the fastest input or output device.

How Data Is Processed

The programmer or the assembler or compiler program allocates certain areas or sections of memory as "working" areas. A working area is large enough to store the data read in from one or more punched cards or magnetic tape records for processing. (The card reader or magnetic tape handling unit is the input device which brings the information into memory.)

After data has been read into the computer, it then executes the instructions which operate on the input data. For output records, it moves data or generates answers and stores them in an *output work area* which has been reserved for this purpose.

There may be a work area for each type of output, such as printing, punching or writing information onto a reel of magnetic tape. These work areas are illustrated in the following figure which shows a representation of the memory of a computer.

Suppose the magnetic core memory has a capacity of 12,000 characters for storage. The programmer reserved 80 characters in top area for card input; another 80 characters in lower right-hand corner were reserved for card output. For printing information, he reserved 132 characters in lower left-hand corner of the memory box for formatting one print line at a time.

The primary point to grasp is that the computer operates on only a few records at a time, but at high speed. To illustrate this point, consider how a computer posts sales invoices to a customer receivables file maintained on one or more reels of magnetic tape.

How a Computer Posts Receivables

Suppose an accounts receivable file for computer processing contains the unpaid items for 20,000 customers. All items for one customer are grouped together; each record includes the same unique account number which identifies the customer.

To post today's transactions of 2,000 invoices, the computer does the following:

1. Reads the account number found in the first invoice on today's transactions tape located on an input tape unit.

2. Reads the account number of the first customer record on the customer master file (file of open receivable records). This reel of tape is on another tape handler acting as an input unit.

3. Compare the two numbers in memory; if they are equal the computer proceeds to "post" the new invoices to the customer's account:

   a. First, it writes all open items for the customer from the input master file to a new output tape.

   b. It then adds today's invoice or invoices by writing it on the new output tape, following the records copied from the input tape.

   c. Computes and writes the new account balance in a special record, which is the last record of the customer's file.

   d. Stores in a memory work area the invoice amounts posted, plus accumulating the updated account balance in a trial balance accumulator.

A significant characteristic of a magnetic tape file is that the entire contents of the original tape must be copied onto a new tape in order to add new transactions, or to delete certain records when processing cash amounts against customers' accounts. This requirement would seem to be very time consuming, but the read/write speeds of magnetic tape are constantly increasing.

Data Representation

A computer which converts ordinary data to Binary Coded Decimal (BCD) format changes numbers, letters and symbols to an arbitrary internal representation utilizing magnetic cores or bits in a pattern. Seven magnetic bits, including a check or parity bit are required to represent one letter, symbol or number. (See Figure 26-3.)

To interpret the stored value for each of the eight vertical frames of bits shown in the diagram, visualize the solid dots as light bulbs which have been turned on by an electrical impulse. (An impulse magnetizes the bit which is made of iron oxide.) Each bit in the hori-

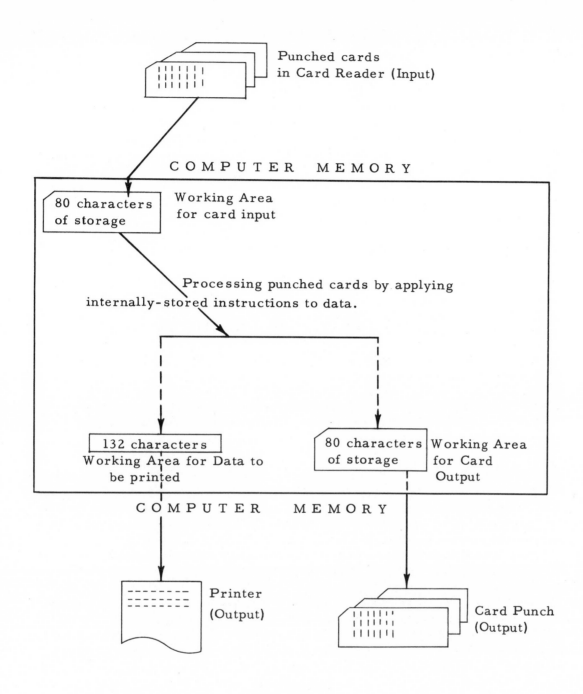

Figure 26-2
ILLUSTRATING CONCEPT OF WORKING AREAS OF MEMORY RESERVED
FOR INPUT AND OUTPUT

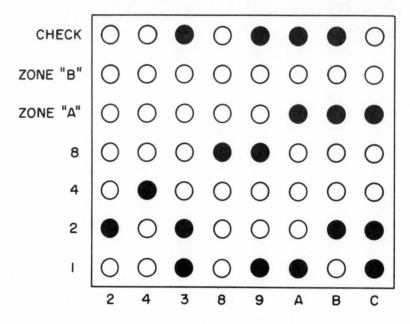

Figure 26-3
HOW A COMPUTER REPRESENTS DATA INTERNALLY
The Solid Dots Shown Above Are Bits Which Are Magnetized;
They Are "Turned On."

zontal row at the bottom of the grid has a value of 1 when magnetized. Each bit in the second horizontal row has a value of 2. Each bit in the third row has a value of 4. And the next row of bits represents the value of 8. Then, consider the next two rows. Even though these are identified as Zone A and Zone B, they do not represent the letters A or B. They are part of a pattern which may represent various letters of the alphabet, or special symbols.

To understand how these bits are utilized to represent letters of the alphabet, consider how punched-card equipment represents alphabetic characters. A common punched card has 10 horizontal rows, beginning with 0 and ending with 9, which represent numeric positions for each of 80 card columns. Alphabetic capability is obtained when the equipment reads the rectangular holes punched in the UPPER positions at the top of the card. The uppermost punching area is designated as "Zone 12." Holes in the next lower blank area are identified as "Zone 11" punches.

Now, in order to represent the letter "A," a hole in the upper 12 zone and a hole in the numeric "1" position are punched in the *same* card column. The letter "B" is represented by a 12-zone punch over the numeral 2. This pattern provides for all letters from A through I. For letters J through R, holes in Zone 11 are combined with punches in the 1 thru 9 numeric positions. For S thru Z, punches in the upper zero position are combined with numeric punches 2 thru 9.

Data Storage

Contrary to popular impression large arrays of data are usually not stored inside computers. Groups of related records which constitute a "file" are stored outside the computer, and are brought into the computer memory only for processing and updating.

There are several ways of storing data outside the computer:
- Punched-card decks (called "files" or "data sets")
- Magnetic tapes
- Random access disk files

Files of Punched Cards

A punched card which provides for 80 columns of alphabetic or numeric characters in each card is probably the best-known method of storing data in coded form. Punched cards have been in use since 1890 when the first tab installation was made at the United States Bureau of the Census in Washington, D. C.

Many thousands of individual transactions may be represented by decks of punched cards. For example, an open-item accounts receivable file may consist of a punched card for each invoice, placed in indexed card tubs for the bookkeepers for applying cash. The total number of cards for this application may range from a few hundred to hundreds of thousands in a large firm.

Magnetic Tapes

A very reliable and time-tested method of storing data in machine-readable coded format for a computer utilizes reels of magnetic tape. Today's computer tapes are only ½ inch in width, and are up to 2,400 feet in length. Information is stored on a coated surface of magnetic oxide material in a pattern similar to that illustrated for the computer memory. See Figure 26-4.

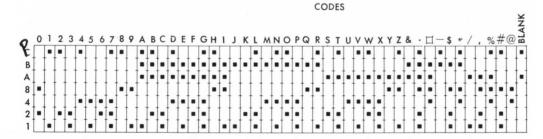

CODES

NOTE:
    The letters "A" and "B" shown on the left side of the tape codes do not represent alpha characters; they refer to zone positions A and B on the tape. To represent the actual letter "A," one bit in zone position A, one in zone position B, plus a bit in the numeric 1 channel are required; see example above.

    Letters J through R require only one B zone bit; letters S through Z require only A zone bits—in addition to the usual 1 through 9 numeric bits.

Figure 26-4
HOW DATA IS STORED ON MAGNETIC TAPE

The number of vertical rows of bits which can be packed into one inch horizontally on the tape is known as the "density" of the tape. Some of the first tapes that were used in computers stored only 200 characters per inch; today's tapes commonly pack 556, 800 or even 1,600 characters per inch.

Tape Speed

Read/write speeds for magnetic tapes are based on the number of characters (numbers, letters or symbols) which can be *read* (input) or *written* (output). The rated speed is expressed in terms of thousands of characters per second. For example, if the technical specifications of a tape-handling unit specify a transfer rate of "50K," this means that the tape unit can bring information inside the computer at the rate of 50,000 characters per second—or that it can write new data on an output tape at the same rate.

The rated speed is the product of multiplying the packing density by the speed of moving the characters past a fixed read/write head. See illustrations below.

	Model 1	Model 2	Model 3
Density, number of characters per horizontal inch of tape	200	556	556
Multiplied by tape movement speed, inches per second	× 75	× 75	× 90
Equals the "Transfer" rate expressed in seconds	15,000	41,667	50,000

Parity or Check Bit

If tapes are designed as "even-parity" tapes, this means that each and every character found on the tape will be represented by an even number of bits in each vertical frame. This is accomplished by the computer which tests the number of iron-oxide bits required to represent a character; if the number magnetized is odd, it turns on the parity or check bit. This is an internal checking device, and serves no other purpose.

Concept of Bytes

Illustrations of the bit structure found on prior pages show that only four bits are required to represent one numeric digit, since any numeral from 0 through 9 can be represented by various combinations of the values of 1, 2, 4 and 8. No single digit requires more than three bits, such as 7. (Bits 4, 2 and 1 combine to represent the value of 7.)

Computers introduced in 1964 were the first to feature a new pattern of 9 bits in each vertical frame—called a "byte"—for data representation. This format enables the computer to offer double storage capacity for numeric data, plus doubling the transfer rate for tape units when reading numeric digits. This is accomplished by storing two numeric values in one vertical array of nine bits. However, only one alphabetic character or symbol may be stored in one frame, since the zone bits are required as part of the character or symbol representation.

Magnetic Tape Reliability and Cost

Magnetic tapes have now been widely used for nearly a decade. They are extremely reliable as a means of data storage in machine-readable format and the cost per character stored is very low.

For example, the cost of a reel of magnetic tape 2,400 feet long ranges from $28 to $43. If the packing density is 556 characters per inch, one reel of tape has a potential storage capacity of about 16 million characters. If the packing density is 800 characters per inch the theoretical capacity increases to about 23 million characters. And, these impressive figures are based on the former 7-channel bit configuration, not on the new byte structure which potentially doubles the storage of numeric data.

However, no tape will, in actual practice, be fully packed with data from end to end because of the need for leaving "inter-record gaps." When the computer writes one or more records on tape, it leave a blank space up to ¾″ in width before it writes more information representing another record, or a block of records. This gap stops tape reading when information is being read into the computer memory from a reel of magnetic tape. It is known as the inter-record gap, or "IRG." The amount of space on a tape reserved for inter-record gaps varies considerably in direct relation to the overall length of the records or blocks of records written on the tape:

- If card images of 80 characters each are written on tape, each followed by an IRG, then only 1/7th of the tape would be used to store actual card data.
- On the other hand, suppose the programmer decides to write instructions which require the read-in of seven punched cards at a time for processing as a block. The instructions are applied to seven cards at a time, and moves the information for all seven cards to one output area. Then, if all seven cards are written out on tape as *one continuous block of information,* the computer would write 560 characters (7 ×80) on 1″ of tape, followed by an IRG of ¾″.

Tape Libraries

Part of the planning for a computer installation involves setting up a tape library and appropriate records to control the use of the tape files. This is extremely important for records protection.

Each time that changes are made to the master file, the entire tape filed is copied to a new reel of tape. It is commonplace for tapes to be used repeatedly over a period of time for many different runs; prior information stored on a tape is erased as new information is copied or written on it.

Suppose the computer erases a customer master file of 10,000 accounts with open items which add up to several million dollars, either because of an internal malfunction, or because the console operator mounted the wrong reel of tape on a tape-handling unit? This can happen despite the "locking rings" which the operator must insert inside the hub of a reel of tape before the computer is enabled to write on that particular tape.

For security and protection against such a disaster, users have long followed the principle of keeping "backup" tapes. The procedure utilizes the "grandfather, father and son" concept:

- When the customer master file is copied today to another reel of tape—because of new transactions added to the file—keep the original in the tape library, properly labeled.
- When the new master file is copied to still another tape tomorrow, keep it in the library also.

Since the original tape has now been copied twice, there are three tapes in existence. At this point it is permissible to use the original tape as a work tape, since it has been replaced by two other tapes.

Buildup of Tape Reels

The buildup of the number of tape reels which represent backup or current master files may be quite rapid. It is not unusual to find 100 to 400 reels of tape in the library of a firm with only 10 or 12 different applications being handled on a magnetic tape computer.

Further Precautions

Additional precautions against the loss of valuable files will be practiced by prudent men who recognize the potential danger of erasing vital records. For the purpose of describing typical precautionary steps, let's examine the procedures to protect an accounts receivable file; the same precautions would apply to files of any type.

1. When the Aged Trial Balance printout is prepared at month-end from the latest customer master file, label and store the tape (or tapes, if more than one) for one month.

2. Keep all input media (punched cards, paper tape or magnetic tapes) fed into the computer as transactions each day—for possible re-entry into the machine if necessary.

The availability of the customer master file which was current at the first of the month plus all original transactions makes it easy for the computer user to reconstruct the master file on a day-by-day basis if all current and backup master files have been lost because of a fire or some other internal problem.

Some firms store the month-end master file in a specially-designed, fire-protection safe, or make arrangements to store valuable master files in bank vaults.

SEQUENTIAL PROCESSING

Records stored on magnetic tape are always in sequential order. If the records for 10,000 customers are kept on one tape reel, the account number for the first customer will be the lowest number; the account number for the last customer on the tape file will be the highest number for the group.

Transactions processed against the tape file are first sorted into sequential order to match the sequence of accounts on the master file. Processing sequential records against sequential files is logically referred to as "sequential processing." The next section of this chapter covers random access devices, which feature random processing of selected records in a file.

RANDOM ACCESS DEVICES AND TECHNIQUES

The first computer featuring random access to any desired on-line record was released by IBM in the late 1950's. This was the 305 Ramac. More than 1,000 of these machines were installed before an improved, faster version designated as the 1405 disk storage unit was released.

Records in this unit were stored on the surfaces of magnetic disks which closely resembled phonograph records stacked vertically in a large cabinet. This model had the capacity for storing 10 million alpha or numeric characters of data on 25 disks organized into fixed-length record formats.

Purpose of a Random Access Device

The purpose of any random access device is to make it possible to seek out *one selected record* from a file of many thousands, then to extract data from that record, or to update it—without affecting any other record.

This process required a method of "addressing" the desired record. The 1405 disk device (see Figure 26-5) accomplished this by a combination of numbers which made up the address:

Unit Number	(2 modules of disks to select from)
Disk Face Number	(25 disks with 50 disk surfaces)
Track Number	(200 concentric tracks on each disk surface)
Sector Number	(Each track consisted of five sectors; each sector provided storage for 200 characters of data)

Access Arm

The 1405 unit featured an access arm mechanism which moved up to the specified disk surface, and then moved out and over the disk surface until it was positioned over the selected track. Once it was in position it would read or write information on the track designated by the address number.

The Address

Five digits of the address found at the beginning of each data record recorded on the track represented the disk face number, track and sector numbers. For example, the inventory record for part number 15,447 may have been assigned address number *24,353* which indicated the following:

24 (Disk Face No.)
35 (Track No. on the disk surface)
3 (Sector No. within the track)

Data Storage

Data and records stored on disks represent *outside data storage;* that is, they are not in the computer memory until processing instructions cause the data to be accessed and read into memory.

Fixed Length Records

The first random access devices featured fixed-length records. As shown in Figure 26-5, each track of the 1405 unit was divided into five sections of 200 characters each. If a record required more than 200 characters, but less than 400, then two sectors were assigned to store one record.

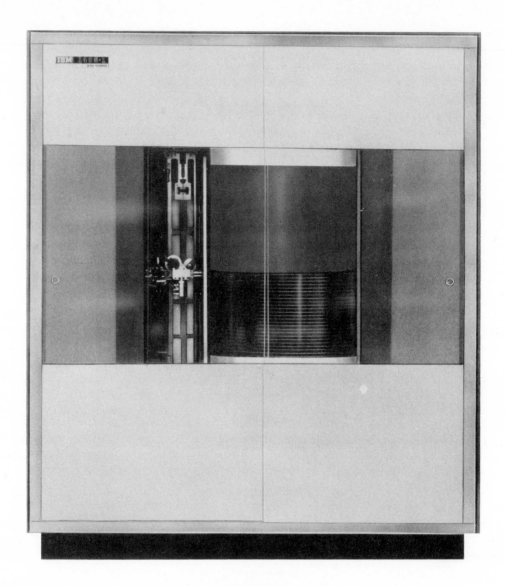

Figure 26-5
1405 DISK STORAGE UNIT

Disk Packs

Recent equipment releases have changed random access capabilities and potentials to a considerable extent. The release of "disk packs" by IBM has made it possible to store records not in constant use "off-line" in the library until needed. (By contrast, the 1405 disks were always connected directly to the computer, and all of the data stored on the disks was available for instant access at any moment.)

The disk pack consists of a set of five disks which are removable when a computer run is completed.

The ability to insert and remove disk packs means that the total quantity of data which can

Figure 26-6
1316 DISK PACKS

be stored on this type of random access device is unlimited. However, the reservoir of data available "on-line" for instant, random access by the computer is limited to the *number of disk pack read/write units connected to the computer's central processor.*

Card Storage Devices

Mylar cards coated with magnetic material are another type of random access device. These cards are numbered, contain a specified number of tracks; each track can store a large volume of data.

When the "seek" instruction identifies a specific card containing the desired record, the random access device selects the coated card from a mass of cards, then moves it to a read/write head which does the reading or writing in the same way that the access arm of the 1405 accesses data stored on the various disk surfaces.

The mylar card units offered by the Honeywell Corporation as a random access device for their computers offer large storage capacity, and reasonably fast access speeds at lower cost than comparable disk storage devices.

Several years ago National Cash Register Company introduced a random access device featuring coated cards suspended from rotating rods. It is known as "CRAM": *C*ard *R*andom *A*ccess *M*emory. When a seek instruction designates a specific card, the card drops from the suspension rods down to a rotating drum. After the card wraps around the drum, it is in position for the read/write heads to read the information stored on the face of the card in definite track areas. (See Figure 26-7.)

Variable Length Records

Random access equipment now provides for variable length records within the confines of a track. It is no longer necessary to fit a record within a prescribed, fixed area that is bound by indelible addresses. This technique of variable length records has greatly expanded the application of random access equipment to business applications.

Relative Costs and Other Considerations

Random access concepts have considerable basic appeal to businessmen, to systems analysts, programmers and others who work in the data-processing field. However, this basic appeal and the potential benefits of random access capabilities should be weighed against the relatively

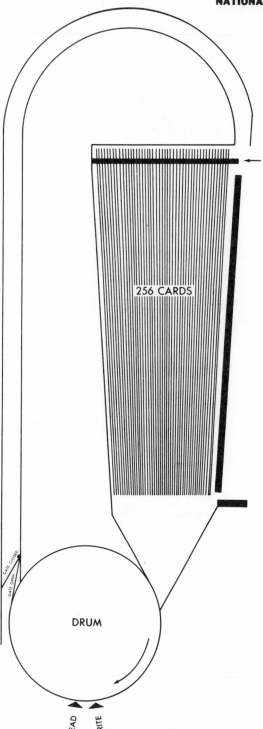

A deck of 256 magnetic cards hang from 8 electronically controlled rods. The rods can be positioned to drop any one of the uniquely notched magnetic cards.

Once dropped from the rods, the magnetic card wraps around a revolving drum. The card rotates over 7 write-read heads that permit reading or recording data at the rate of 100,000 characters or 150,000 digits per second.

Upon completion of the reading and recording, the gate to the raceway opens and the card is automatically returned to the rods through a tunnel of moving air.

Figure 26-7
CARD RANDOM ACCESS DEVICE

high costs and other major problems inherent in the application of random access equipment to many applications.

Since the practitioner, who represents management and counsels top management, should be fully aware of the costs and hidden problems behind the application and use of random access devices, the next few pages provide an outline of what is involved in the use of this type of auxiliary computer equipment.

1. *Cost of Data Storage:* The cost of storing data in a random access device is much greater than the cost of storing comparable volumes of data on reels of magnetic tape. For example, when comparing disk packs with magnetic tape, the disks represent the high side of a 25-to-1 cost ratio. Remember that a reel of tape costs only $43 or less to store 14 million characters or more.

By direct contrast, a disk pack costs up to $595 when purchased, and now stores a maximum of 7 million characters. Calculations as to the cost of storing each 1,000 characters will prove the asserted 25/1 ratio in favor of magnetic tape.

2. *Investment in Library Files:* This comparitive cost ratio becomes a serious consideration when a firm goes all out for disk pack applications—and has no magnetic tape units for writing backup information on tapes. If the same conservative concepts of storing backup files in the library are followed as recommended for magnetic tape, the overall cost of the disk packs will quickly represent a very large investment.

3. *Complexity of Programming:* Programming for a random access application is usually much more critical than comparable programming where magnetic tape is utilized. File organization, indexing techniques and other aspects of random access require considerable experience and skill at the programming level.

4. *Higher Monthly Rentals:* When a random access device is part of a computer configuration, the total monthly rental rate is usually increased by an amount greater than the rental cost of the random access unit or units because:

    a. Programming techniques associated with random access may require a larger core memory than would otherwise be required.

    b. Magnetic tape units may still be required, in addition to the random access equipment, for certain applications involving massive files where sequential processing is acceptable or even preferred.

5. *Overall Operating Speed:* Many random access devices have proven to be rather slow in actual operation, contrary to the user's expectations. Some of the reasons for this will be of interest to the practitioner:

(1) *Finding the Address*

Unless the indelible address number on the disk surface where the record is stored (Part # 12,417 in the inventory file will serve as an illustration—which is 1 of 30,000 parts carried in inventory) is the *same* as the number assigned to the record itself, the computer must go through certain preliminary steps *before it can access the record.*

    a. *Generated numbers:* One commonly-used technique applies a formula to the record (Part # 12,417) and develops the address number which the computer then refers to in order to determine if this area of the disk actually contains the data for this inventory item. If not, the address is provided here as a chaining address. This means that the computer must try again at another address, in another area of the disk surface.

    b. *Index method:* Another technique involves an internal search of a table to find the address where the designated part number record is stored.

(2) *Access Time*

The time required to bring a read/write head to the track specified in the address, or to position a coated mylar card for reading, may range from 75 to 800 milliseconds. 800 milli-seconds is 8/10ths of a second; this is tremendously slow in comparison with the speeds of other computer components which bring data in or out of the computer.

If the computer must make two or three accesses to complete the processing of most records, the total time required for volume operations becomes a significant operating factor.

Random access devices developed by Burroughs and several other computer manufacturers in recent years feature a permanently-positioned read/write head *over each track*. (See Figure 26-8). This completely eliminates the access or seek time; all that remains before a specific record can be found is the latency time, which is explained next.

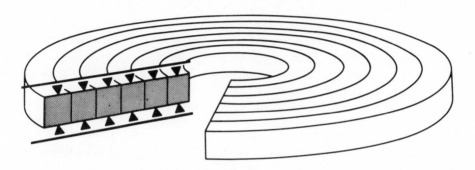

Figure 26-8
RANDOM ACCESS DEVICE FEATURING PERMANENTLY POSITIONED
READ/WRITE HEAD
"Seek" Time Is Completely Eliminated When the Random Access Device
Permanently Positions a Read/Write Head *Over Each Track.*

(3) *Latency Time*

Suppose that the rotational speed of a disk is such that 40 milliseconds are required for each full turn of the disk. Data is stored at various intervals along each track on the disk surface. This means that in order to access one specific record on the track, from 1 to 39 milliseconds will be required—depending upon the location of the record in relation to the access arm at the moment the seek instruction is initiated.

With the data given above the "average latency time" is 20 milliseconds. This must be added to the average access time when estimating random access speeds.

(4) *Chaining*

If a fixed-length area is allocated to each record, or group of records, and the volume of data posted exceeds the allocated area, then the information must be recorded in another area of the disk or coated card storage device. The address of the remote location where the additional "overflow" information is stored is written back in the "home" position. Now, this requires the computer to make one or more additional accesses when processing the record located in the home position, since it must continue to the remote location to complete the read or write operation.

Benefits of Random Access Techniques

Random access devices are becoming more and more popular for special applications of many types. If airline reservations had not been computerized, utilizing random access techniques to the utmost, today's passenger traffic would be nearly impossible to handle under former manual methods.

As corporations continue to centralize order entry, inventory control, invoicing and many other functions, random access capabilities play an increasingly significant part in the overall operations.

Business and Scientific Computers

All of the early computers were geared toward solving scientific and mathematical problems. This meant that great emphasis was placed by the design engineers on internal speed. Input and output speeds were very slow, but were deemed adequate for scientific applications.

Then the trend began for design engineers to develop faster and faster input and output devices which would make it possible to process large volumes of business data. The first breakthrough in this area came when a printer was developed which could print about 400 lines per minute. Since most business data processed results in printed reports of one type or another, this was a significant advance in the art of data processing. (The early computers utilized the tabulating machine as a printer, which was limited to 150 lines of print per minute.)

Scientific computers also featured such aids as "floating point." This referred to the problem of pointing off answers when problems that involved multiplication and division were processed by the computer. If the point off was handled through special programming, the entire run was slowed down considerably. If the equipment included a special electronic assembly to automatically point off all answers, the results were obtained much more quickly and with little or no programming effort.

Recent Trend

Today's computers represent a blend of the two requirements to a very large extent. For example, today's business-oriented computer features high internal speed and high-speed input/output components. The floating-point feature may be built into the central processor as standard, or it is offered as an optional feature.

Opportunities for Practitioners

The full-scale electronic computer is forcing rapid changes in business operations and management techniques. Computers are being installed in increasing numbers in the business community; the availability of experienced personnel to support them is not increasing proportionately.

There will be an increasing requirement for public practitioners and their staffs to become more and more involved in the entire business situation—ranging from initial fact-finding and guidance to management before a decision is made to install a computer, to planning the installation.

27

Planning a Computer Installation

Preparation and planning for a future computer installation covers a wide range of work phases which may extend over a long period of time. The situation obviously will vary from one firm to another, depending upon the extent to which the firm has installed data-processing equipment in prior years. For example, if tabulating equipment has been in use for some time before planning for an electronic computer begins, then the keypunch department will already be in existence. Also, unique numbers will already have been assigned to "units" which constitute a mechanized file, such as:

- Accounts Payable: Vendors are already numbered.
- Accounts Receivable: Customers have been assigned unique numbers.
- Payroll: Employees are identified by payroll number.

By contrast, if a firm moves directly from accounting machine methods to planning for a full-scale computer, it is necessary to include such preparatory steps as selecting a numbering system for each major file to be mechanized. For example, the system selected for customers may be different from that selected for accounts payable. In turn, the numbering plan for employees may vary from either the receivables or the payables numbering plan. And, after the basic numbering scheme has been selected, it is necessary to assign a number to each unit in the file at the time the conversion begins.

It will also be necessary to plan and set up an input department to translate information appearing visually on documents to a coded form that is acceptable to the computer. This requires the installation of keypunch machines, or special input machines which punch paper tape or punched cards—possibly as a by-product of some accounting or record-keeping function.

Work Phases Involved in a Computer Installation

The following work phases are usually involved in a properly planned computer installation, assuming that a firm is changing from manual methods to a computer operation:

371

1. Conduct a basic review and document management objectives for the proposed new system.

2. Perform systems planning and systems development work, thoroughly and in detail.

3. Write, test and "debug" all computer programs.

4. Plan and prepare the physical site for the computer.

5. Plan and set up all support departments or sections, including input and account coding.

6. Select the basic numbering system for major applications such as accounts receivable or accounts payable. Assign numbers to the original list of names for subsequent computer processing.

7. Order input equipment and all auxiliary gear, such as forms bursters, decollators, etc.

8. Plan the conversion steps for converting existing files to the new computer files.

The Basic Review

The prime objective of the preliminary, basic review is to determine procedures and policies currently in use, and to uncover all exceptions and unusual problems. A secondary objective may be to develop interim improvements which may save the firm time or money during the planning and preparatory periods.

The basic review should be conducted on the working level, not solely by means of conferences with management or department heads. Thus, in some instances the department head will tell the reviewer how the work is supposed to be done according to the procedure manual; the people doing the work may be doing things quite differently. Also, an experienced department head tends to forget the important exceptions; the reviewer will obtain a much better "feel" for the work being done from personal observation or participation.

The reviewer should take copious notes, organized by subject matter. These notes will become invaluable during the systems development phase of the project.

Documenting Management Objectives

Before systems planning can begin in earnest a systems analyst or consultant should interview members of top management to determine their objectives for the new computer system. The interviewer should be prepared to make suggestions in regard to special reports which may be useful to each member of management. However, the primary purpose of the interviews should be to obtain the ideas and suggestions of the management team.

Typed memos should be prepared after each interview to document the decisions that have been reached and the stated objectives of the new system; these memos should become part of the systems documentation.

Systems Development Work

The phrase, "systems development work," used in connection with developing data-processing systems covers a broad spectrum of planning and work phases of many types. It is the foundation for a practical, profitable computer operation on any application or for any complete computer system.

Systems development work covers all of the following work phases:

- Conduct meetings and conferences with future users of the proposed system, and determine company policies to be applied to various phases of the system.

- Determine the data content of each report, establish the overall list of reports that is wanted and establish the frequency with which the reports will be prepared.
- Prepare a master list of transactions that must be processed by the various programs which constitute the new system; assign a transaction number to each transaction.
- Design and draw all forms and reports to computer printer scale; test each form or report with sample entries.
- Draw unit work-flow diagrams which represent computer runs.
- Draw the format for each punched card which will be input to the computer, or which will be punched out by the computer.
- Write detailed specifications and description for each computer run.
- Determine the data fields for each magnetic tape file (or disk file) read into the computer, or written out by the computer.
- Prepare a master systems planning and installation schedule; assign target dates for the beginning and completion of each action or work phase included in the master plan.
- Write procedures for all manual steps or functions which are necessary adjuncts to the computer system.

Project Manager

As outlined previously the key member of the systems team is the Project Manager. His duties are to guide, coordinate and supervise the entire systems development project, including the programming, the installation planning and the preliminary and final conversion phases.

The Project Manager should be a highly experienced, competent member of the client's present management team. He should know the firm's policies, procedures and overall objectives in great detail. This person does not necessarily have to know or understand computers; the primary requirement is that he or she knows the job or jobs to be handled by the computer.

Bringing in an individual from outside the business and assigning the responsibility for the new computer system to this individual is not recommended. As mentioned above, the supervision and control of the project should be vested in a trusted, experienced person selected from within the firm.

The remaining members of the systems staff assigned to the systems development work may be systems analysts or others with the necessary background of training and experience in systems or data processing.

Planning Committee

Regardless of the skill and experience of the systems staff, it is desirable to appoint a Planning Committee to aid and assist the staff. Members of this committee should be selected from the various departments which will be prime users of the outputs of the new computer system.

Systems developed in an ivory-tower atmosphere by a systems staff, without consultations with the prospective users of the new system, will invariably meet with great resistance when finally ready. Also, any systems staff that works alone may overlook vital considerations, or omit information of potential value to the users.

The way to win the cooperation of key people is to consult with them and solicit their assistance in designing the new system. If the new system includes their ideas and suggestions, this assures its success when the new system is completed and is in use.

Systems Documentation

Since systems planning is the foundation for subsequent programming, systems documentation is of extreme importance. It is the primary material used by the programmers for implementing the desired results and objectives of the new system.

There are many facets to systems documentation:

- Forms and reports drawn to computer printer scale.
- Format sheets for punched cards which are read into the computer, or which are punched out of the computer.
- Format sheets for records to be stored on magnetic tape, or on random access devices.
- Work-flow diagrams representing each computer run.
- Narrative description of the purpose and functions of each computer run.
- Written procedures for clerical support functions.
- List of transaction numbers active in each run, etc.

Value of Systems Documentation

Thorough, detailed systems planning and documentation actually reduces overall costs in several ways. It speeds programming, and reduces the hours of machine time required for testing and debugging. Extensive re-programming, changes, and delays resulting from changes are largely eliminated.

ALL ABOUT PROGRAMMING

A prior chapter described briefly what is meant by an "instruction" to a computer. The act of writing a list of instructions to enable a computer to operate without human intervention is generally thought to be "programming." Further, this function is viewed as being a mysterious, technical procedure that is understood only by practitioners of the art of programming. For these reasons this section concentrates on explaining programming in considerable detail to enable the practitioner to acquire an understanding and perspective on this essential aspect of data-processing installations.

Basic Tasks in Programming

Programming covers a great deal more than merely writing instructions. The list of basic tasks to be performed in writing a program is presented below. This list was taken from the book, *Management Standards for Data Processing,* by Richard H. Brandon, who now owns his own firm in New York City, and who specializes in performing programming services for clients. This book outlines formal methods for organizing the data-processing department. It also provides guidelines for setting up performance standards for systems analysts and programmings—which have been badly needed for several years.

The Brandon book lists some 22 basic tasks which must be performed to write, test and document one computer program:

1. Read the job specifications manual (prepared by the systems group).
2. Review the program functions.
3. Analyze the layouts provided by the systems analysts.

4. Review the program flowchart.
5. Develop a macro-block diagram (illustrated in this chapter).
6. Assign block letters to distinct segments.
7. Develop micro-block diagrams for each of the segments. (This refers to detail block diagramming.)
8. Review the macro and micro-block diagrams.
9. Translate the program logic into symbolic language.
10. Develop coding for the item layouts.*
11. Add the necessary standard subroutines.
12. Desk check the translation.
13. After keypunching and necessary EAM checking, validate the preliminary listing.
14. Prepare the required test data.
15. Assemble the program.
16. Test the program.
17. Perform a production test with data supplied by the analyst.
18. Assist in performance of a systems test.
19. Prepare the program documentation.
20. Assist in conversion.
21. Update the block diagrams to include all corrections.
22. Turn the program over to operations.
* This one step is the one usually associated with "programming."

Some of these many tasks are time-consuming; others can be completed in a short time. One interesting section in Richard Brandon's book explains how each program can be analyzed and rated in advance of programming—and how performance standards established for the programs can be assigned to each programmer.

Performance Standards

We recommend that Brandon's book be used as the guide for establishing standards for any computer installation. To control the programming effort, the Data Processing Manager and the Project Manager, working with the practitioner, should establish the total number of man-days for each computer run before the programming begins. Then, this team should select one of the progress forms illustrated in the book to record actual programming work accomplished each week until completion of the program.

Brandon also explains the value of standardizing on symbols used by the programmer in the basic flow charting work, so that all programmers on the staff may follow a common pattern when indicating symbolic operations or functions. The systems analyst/programmer assigned to a new installation by the computer manufacturer should be requested to establish the standard symbols for his equipment.

Program Documentation

A major requirement of a well-organized programming department is that all programs be thoroughly documented by the programmers. As changes are made in the programs from time to time the documentation must also be changed. Adequate documentation saves time when changes are necessary—and provides protection to management for the investment in the program library.

Even with good documentation it is quite difficult for a maintenance programmer to understand and interpret the logic of the original programmer. Should the documentation be lacking or inadequate, it may save time if the new programmer rewrites the entire program, rather than try to patch the existing program.

Documentation of programs consists of the following:

- *System block diagram*
  This is an overview of the program logic using graphic EDP symbols.
- *Input and Output Formats*
  These format sheets show the details of data stored in punched cards, on magnetic tape or on magnetic disks.
- *Logic Narrative*
  Details the logic or algorithm of a program.
- *Program Narrative*
  The program objectives and functions are explained in narrative format.
- *Detail Flow Chart*
  The detail flow charts present the complete logic of the program.
- *Source Instruction List*
  A printout showing the symbolic statements prepared by the programmer.
- *Object Instruction List*
  A printout showing the actual machine language codes which are its instructions.
- *Sample Printouts—Reports, forms, etc.*
  Actual sample of any printing done by a program.
- *Operation Sheet*
  Prepared for the computer console operator. Provides the necessary set up and run instructions for executing the program. Usually includes a list of "Halts," and what the operator is supposed to do if the machine halts.

THE EVOLUTION OF PROGRAMMING

In the early days of the computer era, instructions were written slowly and carefully in the actual machine code; this was known as "absolute" programming. The programmer had to determine each operation to be performed, then he had to interpret and write the instruction in terms of numbers and/or letters which were meaningful to the computer.

In addition, the programmer had to keep track of and assign the actual memory location to each instruction. When the programmer later made corrections or changes which required adding one or more additional instructions, he had to go back and change the memory location addresses for scores, or even hundreds, of prior instructions.

These early programmers necessarily learned the internal workings of the computer very thoroughly. They became proficient at internal timings and understood thoroughly the technical details of the computer hardware. In effect, a completed program represented a hard-won triumph of man over machine; it was a laboriously-constructed, hand-crafted product.

It quickly became apparent that programming required far too much time, and the dollar investment in a large library of completed programs usually represented huge sums of money.

Assemblers

The next step up from writing programs in actual machine code was the development of "assemblers." An assembler program is a pre-written set of special instructions, which are provided by the specialists who are hired by the computer manufacturer to aid and assist the programming function of all users.

To use an assembler, the programmer writes instructions in a symbolic language rather than in machine language. For example, when writing payroll instructions the programmer may write SUBT FICA, GROSS PAY: rather than the machine equivalent expressed as ? 018,029. The symbol ? means *subtract;* 018 represents *FICA* and 029 means *GROSS PAY*.

The symbolic instructions are keypunched and fed into the computer behind the assembler package of pre-written special instructions. The assembler *translates and converts* the programmer's symbolic instructions rapidly into actual machine code.

Probably the greatest single benefit from the assembler process is that the programmer is freed from keeping track of and assigning memory addresses for his instructions, since the assembler program automatically assigns all memory locations. If major changes are required in a program, it is simply re-assembled; during this process the locations of the instructions are reassigned by the computer itself.

While the use of assemblers increased the rate at which programs could be produced, something was still lacking. An assembler produces only one machine instruction for each symbolic instruction written by the programmer. A step forward would be to write one symbolic instruction and let the computer generate and write many machine instructions.

This was first accomplished through the use of "macro" instructions included in assemblers. "Macro" instructions were worked in with input and output functions which were standardized. For example, the instruction "Get" might generate scores of specific, detailed instructions all tied in with the function of bringing into working memory one logical record for processing. Macro instructions are in wide use today, and save programmers countless thousands of hours of time which was previously required before these standard instructions came into wide use.

High-Level Languages

High-level languages represent an extension of the original "macro" concept in that one instruction produces *many* instructions in machine language. In a high-level language all the symbolic instructions may be considered to be the equivalent of macros. The programmer is, therefore, free to express his problem in a generalized and relatively unrestricted mode; the "compiler" takes over and does the detail work of writing the actual machine instructions at high speeds. Before explaining what a compiler is, let's trace the history of the development of the so-called high-level programming languages.

The development of high-level languages dates back to 1959. At that time the United States Department of Defense was the world's largest user of computers. The Department owned or leased hundreds of computers of many different makes, sizes and models. The budget required for programming support was almost equal to the budget for the computer hardware itself. Each machine had its own requirements as to the programming language which could be used; programs were not interchangeable with computers of other makes, nor with computers *made by the same manufacturer*. Practically all programs written in those days were strictly *machine-dependent*.

Pressure originating from the Department of Defense brought about the organization of a special industry committee composed of representatives of the Department, other government agencies, large computer users and representatives of the computer manufacturers. The stated purpose of the committee was to develop a uniform, standard programming language which could be run on almost any medium to large-scale computer, regardless of its make or model.

Another purpose was to divorce the programmer from concerning himself with the inner workings and intricacies of the computer, and to enable him to concentrate on solving the problem to be put on the computer.

Out of this organized, concentrated effort came today's high-level programming languages based on the concept of "compilers." A compiler is a very complex, sophisticated set of programs provided free of charge by the computer manufacturer to each user of his equipment. It enables the programmer to describe a problem in generalized, broad statements or in algebraic formulas. The computer, because of the power of the compiler stored in its memory, is able to analyze and interpret the formulas or statements fed into it—and then it *actually writes its own detailed instructions in machine code at very high speed!*

During the years of extensive trial and error which preceded the development of more modern compilers, many languages were developed, tested or used on all types and sizes of computers. The three languages which have been selected by the official committee set up for that purpose, or which are in wide use in the computer field, are ALGOL, FORTRAN and COBOL.

ALGOL and FORTRAN Compilers

ALGOL and FORTRAN were developed so that the engineer or scientist could express his mathematical problems in conventional algebraic formulas, following only a few rules and restrictions. When these formulas are keypunched and fed into the machine, the computer interprets the algebraic notations and equations and converts them into machine instructions for solving the problem. Some of our leading engineering universities now train students how to write formulas and problems in either of these two languages in roughly ten hours of classroom instruction.

The COBOL Language

COBOL stands for *Common Business Oriented Language*. It is the high-level programming language in wide use today for programming business problems for computers. The programmer writes his instructions in ordinary English language sentences called "statements." The statements are usually based on block diagrams which represent what the machine must do, in a general way, to solve the problem. These statements include notations in English. (See Figure 27-1.) Sometimes the notations in the block diagrams are identical with the instructions subsequently written on the formal coding sheets.

COBOL statements as written by the programmer mean nothing to the computer in their original state. The statements must be fed into the machine for interpretation by the COBOL compiler.

One may consider a compiler as the equivalent of a large and complicated dictionary residing temporarily in the computer memory during the act of compiling (interpreting and constructing) a program. When the computer digests a COBOL statement read into the memory from a punched card, it refers to its dictionary to analyze and select the equivalent machine instruction, or an entire group of instructions. The output of this process is referred to as "object instructions," which are written out on magnetic tape or on disk files, or which are punched out in the form of a deck of punched cards.

This process is truly "automatic programming." To witness the compiling function in operation is an amazing experience for the person who has a basic understanding of what is actually being accomplished. Until you see a fast compiler in action it is difficult to believe that the computer can read into memory several hundred source-language statements each minute—and convert these generalized statements into its own machine language at tremendous speed!

Sample of COBOL Block Diagrams

Since the future of business data programming seems to be increasingly tied to the COBOL language, the following example of how block diagramming is combined with COBOL-type notations will be of interest.

Explanation of Sample Problem

The sample problem shown in block diagram format in Figure 27-1 illustrates how a simple payroll problem might be diagrammed for COBOL.

Problem Specifications:
1. There are two classes of employees, salaried and hourly.
2. There is a fixed 25% deduction for withholding taxes, plus 2.5% deduction for Social Security taxes. The maximum deduction for Social Security is $374.40 per year.
3. There is only one other deduction for Blue Cross insurance. If the employee is the only member of his family covered, the deduction is $1. If the entire family is covered the deduction is $3.

The PL/1 Language

"PL/1" stands for Program Language One. It is a new high-level language developed by IBM which succeeds in combining the best features of scientific programming languages with commercial languages such as COBOL. Therefore, it is a dual-purpose language.

The early users of PL/1 are very enthusiastic about it and are now investing huge sums of money in programs written in this new language. This represents quite an important decision on the part of each of the PL/1 users since software costs are frequently about the same as hardware costs.

Benefits of Utilizing High-Level Languages

The use of these high-level languages is rapidly increasing. Some of the major benefits to the computer user are:

1. The programmer does not find it necessary to learn the inside operation of the computer hardware.
2. The programmer concentrates on solving the problem rather than on worrying about computer timings, index registers, and other intricacies of a highly technical nature.
3. The programmer writes fewer instructions in less time—and with less special training.
4. When COBOL is used the program instructions and documentation are intelligible to all concerned, since the problem is clearly expressed in English-language statements.
5. Use of PL/1, COBOL or FORTRAN makes it easier to train in-house personnel for the programming staff.

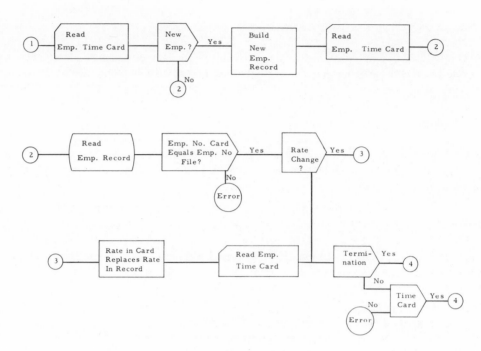

Figure 27-1
COBOL BLOCK DIAGRAMS (Page 1)

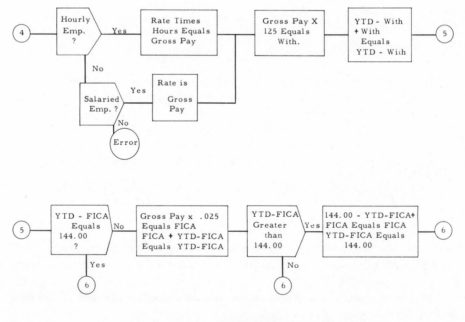

Figure 27-1
COBOL BLOCK DIAGRAMS (Page 2)

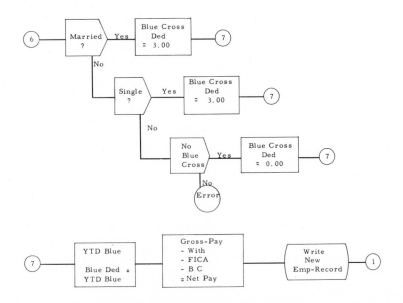

Figure 27-1
COBOL BLOCK DIAGRAMS (Page 3)

GUIDELINES FOR CONVERSION

The conversion and subsequent transfer of records and files which have been kept manually for many years or decades to the computer is a problem of considerable magnitude. Conversion requires and deserves very careful planning. There are two distinct phases of conversion planning; preliminary and final.

Three Methods of Handling Conversion

Three major approaches to the conversion problem have been used in different firms:

1. Operating two different systems for a period of time; the old system and the new computer system—with part of the documents received daily being routed to each for a period of time.

2. Running two complete systems in parallel, each handling the same data and each under full accounting control.

3. Full cutover, as rapidly as feasible, from the old system to the new computer system, with complete abandonment of the old records at once.

Maintaining Two Systems

Accounts receivable is the type of application which appears to lend itself to starting a new system on a specified date and to posting all sales to the new system—while routing checks to the former customer ledgers until such time as all open trade receivables items on the ledgers have been paid or cleared off.

Theoretically, this is a sound approach to avoid the problem of transferring thousands of open, unpaid invoices and other types of open items to the new computer file. The case history which follows, however, indicates some of the problems encountered in actual practice.

A CASE HISTORY

In 1963, the systems team in a firm with about 20,000 receivables accounts decided not to convert open items on the ledger records to the new computer system. Analysis of invoice terms revealed that the average invoice was due in 60 days. It seemed to be a reasonable approach to continue to apply checks to the old ledgers until all open items were finally paid or cleared off through application of credit memos.

A concomitant idea was to post all new sales to the new computer customer records, starting on a Monday morning. This meant that two independent receivables systems would be in operation, but hopefully for no more than three or four months.

In actual practice, the old system continued to function for about eight months, and it caused many internal problems:

- The posting machines and operators and the cash application clerks continued to function as an entity for eight months. This was added budget expense, and required needed floor space.
- Credits received daily affected both sets of records. The unadjusted deduction covered by the credit memo was sometimes found on the old ledgers—sometimes on the computer records.
- Credits against open invoices also might affect both sets of records.
- Remittances at first were primarily applied to open items on the old customer ledgers. In a short time, however, some remittances paid items on the new computer files; some had to be "split" between the two sets of records. This quickly led to many balancing and control problems, and clerical costs.

No Dual System

Hindsight indicated that it was a mistake to maintain dual staffs and two systems on a "split" basis over a period of time. The alternative to this method, or to running two complete systems in parallel, processing all transactions by each system, and one balancing against the other is the "instant cutover" method. This requires the conversion of large numbers of open items in a short time period. But this method, too, can be very troublesome unless properly planned and controlled. One way to convert is to use the "inventory" method of building up files of keypunched cards representing current sales transactions.

Inventory Method

This requirement brought about the concept of the "inventory method" for converting records of any type from a manual system to a computer system. Simply stated, this method requires the gradual *accumulation of punched and verified cards*—one card for each transaction or item—from a starting period to the day of final conversion.

Final conversion is then accomplished by matching ledger sheets to the file of open-item punched cards—and selecting only those cards which represent open, unpaid items on the ledgers (referring to a receivables conversion).

Requirements of Inventory Method

This method requires considerable advance or preliminary planning:

1. Accounts must be numbered several months before the date selected for final conversion.

2. The input department must be set up, staffed and trained several months before the final conversion date.

3. All transactions or items must be numbered, keypunched, verified and processed through the computer during the preliminary period—and the transactions must also be handled manually in the usual way.

In effect, this method requires two staffs for a period of time, but the benefits to be derived are worth the time and expense. For example, this method makes it possible to train account coders and input personnel on actual work before the new system is fully operative. It provides a source of actual transactions in volume to the programmers for *testing* all computer programs in great detail.

This method of converting large files has been applied successfully to the conversion of inventory records, as well as to accounts receivable applications.

SPECIAL MESSAGE FOR TOP MANAGEMENT

The initial installation of an electronic computer is a critical, major step for a firm of any size. It has even greater potential impact on the medium-sized or small firm which is converting from manual or bookkeeping machine methods to data-processing methods for the first time.

It is the duty and the responsibility of the management services practitioner to indoctrinate top management in his client firm with the appropriate concepts that are so necessary for success in this venture. Several of these concepts are:

- Computer applications generally cross the usual departmental boundary lines; the systems staff and the Project Manager must have the authority to study procedures and operations in any and all departments. This authority can only stem from top management.
- Management should make it very clear to employees at all levels that the proposed computer installation has its full backing and authority.
- Top management should participate in the systems planning to the extent of approving all major policy decisions.
- One key officer of the firm should be designated as the liaison man for the project; the Project Manager should report directly to him.

Summary

To summarize these points, several common denominators are usually found in computer installations which are an outstanding success. These common denominators are:

- Top management fully participated in the project.
- Top management gave the systems team full authority to investigate all aspects of the business regardless of boundary lines.

- Top management placed its full weight and authority behind the project and supported it at all times.

What Not to Do

1. Do not set up a systems staff composed of systems analysts and programmers who have been brought in from outside the firm—and turn the job over to them because they are "experts" in data processing. Control should be vested in the Project Manager who is an experienced person within the firm.

2. Management should not abdicate its responsibility by taking a hands-off attitude toward the computer project.

3. Do not restrict the results to be obtained from the computer system by limiting the systems group's access to ideas and information so essential for a complete, integrated computer installation.

28

Major Considerations in a Proposed Computer Installation

Section I. Cost Elements

There are two distinct types of cost involved in a computer installation; "start up" or one-time preparatory costs, followed by operating costs after the installation is functioning. This chapter outlines the nature of these costs and provides guidelines regarding the potential investment which is required for the preparatory phase of a data-processing installation.

This data and background information will enable the practitioner to advise his client as to financial requirements and personnel staffing; planning can then move ahead on a realistic basis if the objectives and benefits of a computer installation outweigh the anticipated costs.

START UP COSTS

Systems Development Work and Programming

The previous chapter outlined the many different work phases involved in the systems development work, after completion of the basic review. The programming phase is then implemented. The total time that is required for this depends upon the number of programs to be written and tested, the skill and experience of the programmers, the thoroughness of the systems development work—and the number of programmers sharing the work load.

Salary Ranges: Salaries for systems analysts cover a broad range from $10,000 to $15,000 per year, or more. Likewise, programmers of business computers are paid from $7,200 to $15,000 per year, depending on their background and experience in the field.

Typical Staffing Requirements and Budget Costs

In a medium-sized firm two systems analysts would be considered to be a minimum staff to handle the systems development work for the various projects decided upon by top manage-

385

ment. Two or three programmers would represent a minimum team for this important and continuing phase of a computer installation.

To estimate annual budget requirements, suppose the staff of specialists required to implement an electronic computer installation consists of two systems analysts and three programmers of average experience and skill. The budget for a staff of this size may easily range between $50,000 and $65,000 annually.

Conversion Costs

Conversion costs represent preparatory costs; included in this cost category are the expenses of setting up support departments and operating them before the new system is actually ready for the computer.

Several methods of converting records from the manual system to computer files have already been discussed. Any method selected involves considerable cost for these reasons:

1. The account coding and input departments are set up and begin to function one or more months before the conversion is made. This is necessary to provide actual transactions in volume to the programmers for testing and perfecting all programs written for the new application.

2. During the testing period, or while running parallel systems for a period of time, the firm is paying rental for the computer before the new system becomes operative. At the same time a temporary staff has been hired to operate the new support departments—while the old system is still functioning as usual.

3. Also, it may be necessary to hire temporary personnel for some of the initial work of keypunching name and address cards for master files, or part number and description cards for inventory files, for setting up the account numbering system, for converting open items to punched cards, or for carrying out other phases of conversion.

The conversion problem is one that requires long and careful planning; the costs associated with this one phase of the new computer system may be substantial.

Computer Environment Requirements and Costs

Providing the appropriate operating environment for a full-scale electronic computer may represent a substantial one-time investment. The total investment in the site preparation will vary considerably from one installation to another, depending upon many factors:

- Size of the computer room.
- Location with reference to a prime source of electric power.
- Capacity and type of air conditioning to be installed.
- Number and size of offices adjacent to or surrounding the computer room.
- Total number of computer components to be installed.
- Type of floor and ceiling to be installed.
- Type of data storage to be utilized by the computer.

The type of data storage has a direct effect on site costs. For example, if most data is to be stored in punched-card files, the environmental requirements are less exacting and less costly than those for a computer utilizing magnetic tape or disk packs for data files.

Some additional facts and details about environmental requirements include:

- The computer room must be air conditioned and properly humidified.
- The atmosphere in the computer room should be kept relatively free of dust particles. Magnetic tape or random access disks with specially coated surfaces may function poorly if dust is present in excess quantities in the surrounding air.

- Electrical power which meets computer operating requirements must be brought to the vicinity of the computer room.
- A special type of raised floor is frequently included in site specifications, because of the many large electrical cables which connect all of the peripheral hardware (input/output units) to the central computer-processor. Also, certain types of air-conditioning systems use the raised floor for circulation of air in the room.

If magnetic tapes are utilized for information storage, the computer room should be large enough to house the tape library. That is, all of the reels of magnetic tape which are used in the system should be kept in the same environment as the computer itself. This is desirable because the magnetic tape requires humidity and dust control to protect the information stored magnetically on the surface of the tape.

Supply and Work Room

A supply and work room adjacent to the computer is a desirable adjunct to any installation. Large quantities of forms are consumed by a computer printer; many thousands of punched cards will also be used in most installations. These supplies should be stored in a location which is convenient to the computer operators.

Another consideration is that the work room will probably contain several auxiliary devices, such as:

- Forms bursting equipment
- Forms carbon paper deleaver unit
- Mechanical card sorter
- Punched-card interpreter

Space for Field Engineer

Servicing and maintaining an electronic computer requires certain supplies and electronic test gear, such as circuit testing equipment. The Field Engineer (assigned to the installation by the computer manufacturer) will store on the premises spare parts, extra modules of control circuitry and special tools. He should be provided with a small metal file cabinet, a small desk and a chair. A room about ten feet square is usually adequate.

Guidelines for Site Costs

It is not possible to estimate the one-time costs involved in providing the proper physical environment without first establishing certain basic facts—which vary considerably with each individual computer installation.

To summarize, the factors which determine the total cost are the size of the computer room, the location of the prime power source in relation to the location of the computer room, the type and total capacity of the air-conditioning system, the type of flooring and ceiling selected, the size of offices or supply rooms associated with the computer room, etc.

Summary of One-Time or Start-Up Costs

To summarize, the major start-up costs of a computer installation are:

- Systems Development Work
- Programming, Testing and Debugging
- Computer Site Preparation

- Supply and Work Room
- Conversion Costs

The magnitude of these preparatory costs was evidenced by a recent report to a client who had requested that a management consulting firm conduct a computer feasibility study for his business. The final report to the client included this estimate on preparatory costs:

"We estimate that the initial investment in systems work, programming, setting up and staffing new departments, plus conversions costs will range from $100,000 to $125,000."

OPERATING COSTS

The cost elements which make up the total operating costs are:
- Computer rental
- Maintenance of programs and writing new programs
- Console operators
- Salaries of coding department personnel
- Salaries of keypunch machine operators
- Operators of auxiliary equipment
- Proof and Control group
- Forms and Supplies
- Power
- Library personnel

Computer Rental

Invariably, a businessman with no prior experience with data processing considers the monthly computer rental as being the "cost" of a computer installation. Reference to the above list reveals that the monthly rental is only the *base cost*.

Program Maintenance

There is a widespread belief often expressed thus: "We won't need programmers on our payroll after the initial group of programs are written, tested and installed." This is completely contrary to all experience in the data-processing field.

One or more programmers will always be required to maintain programs because of the inevitable changes which are a continuing part of every business operation. Also, it is usual practice for various members of management to request changes in reports, or to request new reports. Both of these facts explain why one or more programmers in a typical data-processing installation is kept busy maintaining old programs and writing new ones.

One guideline which has emerged over the years as a result of studying the continuing costs of existing computer installations is that the cost of maintaining existing programs and concurrently writing new programs frequently amounts to *50% of the monthly computer rental*.

Console Operator Salaries

Even though a computer is designed to function without operator intervention and at high speed after a run begins, a considerable amount of work has to be done in getting the machine ready to function properly. The trained console operator must refer to instructions in run books, and mount all necessary tape files. He loads the printer with the appropriate forms. He inserts cards into the card reader and/or card punch. He loads the programmed instructions into the memory of the computer. After these steps have been taken, the operator then starts the computer run.

A minimum of two people should be trained for this essential function because of sickness, vacation or running multiple shifts at month-end. If the computer is operated two shifts per day, then three or four operators should be trained.

The salaries of these console operators are, of course, one element in the total operating cost of the installation.

Control Group

A successful computer installation requires a proof and control group. This group is comparable to a quality control section in a manufacturing plant. The group receives all input batches, such as boxes of punched cards, and records the batch totals prepared by clerks who processed the original documents, such as customer invoices.

The control clerks record batch totals on spread sheets, route the punched cards or other input into the computer room, then wait for initial test runs (known as "edit" runs) to reveal any problems, such as invalid customer numbers, wrong dates, cards improperly punched, missing information in the input media, etc.

Basically, the control group's responsibility is to correct any and all problems revealed by computer test runs so that the runs can be successfully completed. Completed runs are routed back from inside the computer room to the control group for review, checking and final balancing.

Operators of Auxiliary Gear

A typical computer installation is supported by a variety of auxiliary equipment:

1. *Forms Burster:* This mechanical device separates continuous, perforated forms into unit sets of forms.

2. *Carbon Deleaver:* This device removes inter-leaved carbon paper sheets from sets of collated forms.

3. *Card Sorter:* Some installations include a mechanical card sorter to sort large volumes of punched cards either before or after the computer runs.

4. *Interpreter:* This device prints the information represented by the holes in the cards across the top edge of the card for visual reference.

When determining or estimating operating costs, the salaries of the operators of all auxiliary equipment may be a significant cost element. However, a few firms have found it feasible to utilize members of the proof and control group from time to time as operators of the auxiliary equipment. Feasibility of doing this should be determined only after a careful study has been made of the work volumes and the situation in each installation.

Forms and Supplies

Computers have the capacity for turning out impressive stacks of printed forms. The cost of forms may develop into a sizeable budget item, unless the systems planners limit most printed output to exception-type reports.

Also, the volume of punched cards utilized for input and/or output may be such that the amount involved is substantial.

Power

Many computer installations operate from 16 to 20 clock hours per day. The monthly power bill may be a factor worth considering when developing estimated operating costs.

Library Personnel

Maintenance of large numbers of tape reels or disk packs and the related records may require a full-time librarian. This person is charged with the responsibility of maintaining records which control the usage of each reel of tape—which should be numbered. The librarian issues tape reels or disk packs as required by each computer run. When the computer runs are completed, the console operator removes the tape reels or disk packs from the handling units and returns them to the library. The librarian then labels each tape, enters the information in the appropriate records, and stores the files in a bin.

Some firms operate with no librarian; this responsibility is added to the duties of the console operator. A medium to large-scale computer installation requires the services of a full-time librarian; it is a very important, supporting function.

Section II. New Departments Required

A full-scale computer installation in a firm which has had no prior data processing installation of any type requires that three new operating departments be set up and staffed. These are:

- The keypunching or input department.
- The account coding section or department.
- Proof and control group.

THE INPUT DEPARTMENT

The word "input" refers to the conversion of numerals, characters or symbols into a coded form which is understandable and acceptable to the computer. For example, a punched card contains up to 80 punches which represent Arabic numerals, symbols or letters of the alphabet. The computer can "read" and accept data in this coded format. After the data has been transferred inside the computer from the punched card, the data is acted upon in accordance with programmed instructions.

Keypunching

The most widely used device for card punching is the IBM keypunch machine. It punches holes into 80-column cards, one column at a time. The operator reads information from a source document (such as an invoice) and depresses keys on the keyboard which causes the holes to be punched into the card. To translate a sales invoice to a punched card for accounts receivable accounting, the keypunch operator would read and punch the following basic information:

> Customer account number
> Invoice date
> Invoice number
> Sales or Territory number

Invoice terms

Amount

When the punching of the card is completed, the machine moves the card into a stacking hopper and the operator proceeds with punching a card for the next invoice.

Key Verification

Keypunching is subject to many different types of errors. For this reason, another group of machine operators work from the same basic document as the keypunch operators—and "key verify" all or part of the information read and punched initially by these operators. The verifier operator places the punched cards into the input hopper of her machine, then feeds the first card into position. As she depresses keys which correspond to her interpretation of the data appearing on the face of the input document, a metal device searches the card for a hole which corresponds to the value of the key depressed. If the data punched by the verifier operator does not agree, digit by digit, with that punched by the first machine operator, a red light flashes on the verifier machine. At the same time the card column is notched to indicate the location of the error.

Production Objectives

Standards set up for a typical keypunch department seldom call for punching more than 8,000 card columns per hour per operator. Expressed in terms of unit punched cards, a typical operator would produce only 110 invoice cards per hour, if each card representing an invoice required punching 70 columns of data. (Punching alphabetic information is usually slower.)

In estimating average keypunch production, management should not use more than 5½ hours per day of actual work time.

Using the well-known criteria outlined above, it is possible to estimate rather accurately the number of keypunch and key verify operators for staffing a projected keypunch department, based on the volume of paperwork to be processed for the computer.

Salaries

Keypunch and key verification operators require extensive training to obtain satisfactory production. The salaries of these operators have risen steadily in response to the ever-increasing demand for their skills.

The hourly cost of operator and supervisory salaries, fringe benefits, machine rental, floor space, etc., in a major metropolitan area today ranges from $3.50 to $4.50 per hour.

Other Input Methods

Experience has conclusively indicated that the keypunch department is quite often a major bottleneck in the data processing schedules. It is an unglamorous manual operation, yet it is an essential, preliminary step to obtain the benefits of data processing.

To offer alternatives to keypunching, manufacturers of adding and accounting machines released special input machines as early as 1956. These machines punch paper tape as a by-product of listing digits on the keyboard of the machine, or as a by-product of an essential accounting operation. The holes punched in paper tape by such equipment represent coded data which is acceptable to the computer—if the installation includes a paper tape reader.

Currently there are two types of devices which will convert paper tape to other types of input:

1. The IBM paper tape to punched-card converter resembles a keypunch machine. It reads the strips of paper tape, and punches standard 80-column cards, one column at a time.

2. Mohawk Data Sciences has released a "keytape" machine which has a keyboard identical to that of a keypunch machine. However, data keyed in is first stored in an 80-character buffer. When the operator signals the end of one entry, the machine transfers the contents of the buffer to a reel of magnetic tape. Upon completion of a batch of input, the reel of magnetic tape is conveyed to the computer room in lieu of boxes of punched cards. One version of this new device is able to convert paper tape into characters on magnetic tape at high speed. This obviates the need for a paper tape reader attached to the computer.

Types of Input Equipment

There are five types of input equipment currently available:

1. Electric typewriters which type and punch numeric and alphabetic information.

2. Adding machines which add, print and punch—or print special characters readable by optical scanners.

3. Accounting machines which add, print and punch—and also perform normal posting functions simultaneously if required.

4. Cash registers which record sales transactions and produce paper tape output at the same time.

5. Cathode ray tube data display units—which resemble television screens—are now considered as one type of input device since a small keyboard is an integral component of the CRT unit.

Benefits of Input Machines

Depending upon their specific application, input machines which add, print and punch offer many tangible benefits and potential cost reductions over the use of keypunch machines. For example:

- Input equipment utilizing an accounting machine as the base unit is considerably more accurate than keypunching. And, a typical operator can outproduce a keypunch operator from 50% to 75%.
- The equipment can produce a printed proof sheet and control totals as the data is read, listed on the keyboard and punched into paper tape—or put into punched cards through a slave keypunch hookup.
- The machine may be set up to provide line-proof for each document, such as a sales invoice which is being broken down into product sales amounts for sales analysis.

Product #15	$33.20
Product #32	16.80
Product #50	25.00
Invoice Total	$75.00

If the sum of the distribution amount does not equal the invoice total, the input machine can be programmed to warn the operator that a difference exists.

1. Data for the computer may be captured as a by-product of an essential, preliminary accounting routine or batch-listing operation.

2. Many errors are detected and corrected before the work gets to the computer room.

3. Faster input and fewer errors improve the overall utilization and scheduling of the computer itself.

Figure 28-1

INPUT MACHINE: ACCOUNTING MACHINE WITH PAPER TAPE OUTPUT

Production Potential

It is not unusual to find output equipment of the accounting-machine type producing from 12,000 to 14,000 card columns per hour, while proving the work at the same time. Also, the operator may be producing hard-copy records or checks at the same time. One accounts payable installation using this type of equipment in a large drug company home office serves as an outstanding example of what can be done: The operator lists freight bills on the apron of a voucher check, then writes the check and a voucher register on the machine. It is cable-connected to a slave keypunch to obtain distribution of freight expense as a by-product. The operator routinely produces 30 to 40 checks per hour, representing more than 260 freight bills; the cards being punched without any operator attention represent a card-punching production of roughly 14,000 card columns per hour!

And, the accuracy of such equipment is phenomenal. In many installations all verification is eliminated, except proving of the dollar amounts which the input machine does routinely.

In summary, input machines are usually more productive than are keypunches; they provide better proof and control—and substantially reduce input costs.

COMPUTER PROOF AND CONTROL SECTION

Another new department which is essential for efficient computer operation and control is sometimes overlooked when the installation is in the planning stages. The proof and control section requires one or more persons to perform a variety of functions, ranging from control of all input coming to the computer for processing, to proving all runs and sorting forms for distribution.

Proof and Control

Original documents accompanied by the paper tape or punched cards are routed from the input department to the control group for processing. Here, the control clerk records control totals which are set up for each batch of documents. That is, a pre-list adding-machine tape listing the item amounts for each batch is required for a computer operation—just as it is necessary for proof purposes when accounting machines are used.

The control clerk routes the input media into the computer room for processing. After the run is made the console operator sends the printed journals or registers—which usually show the batch total as the last line on the printed sheets—back to the proof and control section.

Initial computer runs which process raw data for later updating of valuable files are called "edit" runs. The program tests the input data in every conceivable way for errors or omissions. When an invalid account number is found, for example, the computer printer prints the item with a message, "invalid number." Or, it may find missing data or erroneous dates in the input material. It is the duty of the proof and control group to study these invalid entries—and do whatever is necessary to get them corrected. The group makes changes in the control totals where necessary, and sends the corrected material back to the computer room again.

THE ACCOUNT CODING DEPARTMENT

The language of computers is numbers. All files and records to be processed by a computer are numbered as part of the preliminary steps when preparing for a computer installation. After the basic numbering system is set up and unique numbers have been assigned to customers, vendors, stockholders, employees, etc., it is necessary to *code* all incoming transactions before the paperwork is passed to the input department for keypunching.

Quite often not enough time or thought is given to the numbering system selected for the new system. Account coding is a basic ingredient of the systems foundation; selecting the best account numbering system is not as simple as it may seem. For these reasons, the last chapter in this book explains the three basic numbering plans, and the advantages and disadvantages of each plan.

Account Coding

After a numbering system has been selected and installed, the chore of assigning a number to each document that is to be processed by the computer is known as "account coding." It is tedious, slow and costly—yet it is undeniably a vital part of the total data-processing system.

Coding Files

A variety of files are being used by various firms as the basis for the daily coding task. A popular system uses interpreted decks of punched cards for reference when coding invoices. There are several disadvantages to using punched-card files for random lookup. The cards are all the same height, and have a tendency to pack. Interpreted cards packed together in a reference file are not easily visible; the coder must finger the cards to separate them in order to read the data across the top edge.

A better type of unit card file is available from the office-equipment firms that manufacture "visible" equipment. When unit cards or cardboard strips are prepared, showing customer name, address and account number (for receivables coding), and placed in metal files which have vertical sections rotating on a base, all the names in a section are visible as the operator rotates the file and opens a section for random search. This visibility feature is very desirable in a coding function, since only a small percentage of the accounts will be active at any one time—which necessitates finding one name at a time out of a large number of names.

An optional method places the unit cards in an electric, rotating file which rotates a bin of card trays in a circular arc, similar to the Ferris wheel operation.

Printed Lists

A successful approach to the coding problem is one that provides printed lists to the coders. Since the customer master file is maintained on the computer for accounts receivable purposes, the name and address sections of each customer's account on the master file may be utilized to print a complete directory of customers in alphabetical order. The printed directory is then separated into sections, grouped by certain letters of the alphabet, and made available to the various coders.

If a firm has several subsidiaries or sales divisions, a better solution is to print customer lists *for each division*. Since the invoices or orders are probably received in batches from billing points in each division, the coders can assign account numbers to each document by reference to the appropriate division customer directory.

Adding new customer names to the lists is a problem, but it can be solved very easily. One method of solving this problem is to maintain the customer list for each division on a magnetic tape file, and reprint the customer directory periodically so that new names will be included in the latest list.

Another method is to use the punched cards which were utilized to introduce the new customer's name and address into the computer posting run—for coding reference on a temporary basis. These interpreted cards are routed to the coders who file them adjacent to the printed list for auxiliary reference when necessary. When the new printed directory is made available to them, the coders destroy the interpreted cards.

Section III. Other Aspects of a Computer Installation
NEGOTIATING WITH COMPUTER MANUFACTURERS

The purchase or rental of a typical, full-scale computer configuration involves equipment with a value of several hundred thousand dollars. There are many important points which should be negotiated and resolved in writing before an order for a computer is signed.

Negotiations on the points listed in subsequent paragraphs are possible because the computer industry is highly competitive. Several major manufacturers have huge investments in plant and equipment, and in a sales and service organization. They are willing to accommodate the requirements of a prospective buyer, if the requests are reasonable and are negotiated in advance of placing the order.

Systems and Programming Assistance

Even though a firm should not permit outside people to do all of the programming (since the firm would subsequently have no one on the scene to administer and maintain the programs), it is desirable to get the computer manufacturer to assign at least one trained person to assist with the systems design and the subsequent programming work.

The firm which is buying the computer should review and hire one or several programmers for its own staff. The systems analyst/programmer who is assigned to the project by the manufacturer usually guides the other programmers, conducts on-the-job training and performs a liaison function between the user and the manufacturer's support groups.

Through negotiation it is sometimes possible to persuade the computer manufacturer to assign two or more programmers to the project—if time is short and more personnel is needed for a reasonable period of time.

Program Testing Time

The amount of computer time provided for testing programs is a vital consideration and should be clearly established in writing before an order is placed. Programming a major application may begin several months or years before delivery of the computer to the user. Yet, it is necessary to test each program thoroughly with sample data before the program can be considered ready for actual operation. This requires the availability of computer hardware with similar features and about the same memory size as the equipment on order.

The total required testing time is unpredictable; it may run into hundreds of hours—depending upon the complexity of the runs, the skill and experience of the programmers, the thoroughness of the basic systems work and the total number of programs to be tested.

Standard computer sales contracts provide for a very limited number of hours that are to be made available to the user free of charge. A typical contract provides from 30 to 40 hours. Any testing time over the stated number of hours is chargeable at various hourly rates. Since the hourly rate on a medium-scale magnetic tape computer may run as high as $65, this emphasizes the importance of negotiating for as much testing time as possible in the purchase contract or rental agreement.

Training

All computer manufacturers provide various training facilities for their users and prospective users. Even so, it is a good idea to discuss the various training programs to be made available to company executives and to the programmers in some detail before placing the order.

Software Programs

"Software" refers to pre-written "packaged" programs to be supplied without charge by the manufacturer. For example, if the firm ordering the computer now has a tab installation, the computer manufacturer should provide a "report generator" software package to assist in converting tab runs to computer runs.

If the firm ordering the computer has decided to write all programs in COBOL the manufacturer will necessarily provide a very complex software package known as the "COBOL Compiler."

Backup Arrangements

Any computer may periodically break down, and be out of action for a period of hours, or days. The prudent businessman will look to the sales representative of the computer manufacturer to assist in making backup arrangements to cushion the problem when the hardware is inoperative. Backup hardware may be made available at the local office of the manufacturer—or arrangements may be made to utilize equipment of another firm located in the area.

Parallel Runs

Some firms have made arrangements to use backup equipment for parallel runs—to thoroughly compare and test the new programs by operating the old system and the new system at the same time, over a period of weeks or months. This procedure creates many problems, and is not generally recommended.

If parallel runs are required, it is much more satisfactory to wait until the computer on order is actually installed on your client's own premises.

COMMON FALLACIES FOUND IN COMPUTER PROPOSALS

The practitioner can render a valuable service to his client by pointing out certain common fallacies usually found in a computer proposal. The word "proposal" as used here includes those proposals which are presented by outside computer sales representatives and those prepared by an internal staff or a group who propose that a major application be added to an existing computer operation.

This section explains what some of these fallacies are and tells how the practitioner can advise the client and steer him away from a major commitment based on incorrect assumptions and theoretical savings.

Personnel and Salary Savings

It is common practice to justify a computer installation—or adding a major application to an existing computer operation—by estimating that a stated number of people will be eliminated from the payroll because of computer speed or other capabilities.

Audits and reviews of hundreds of existing computer installations show that, in nearly every instance, the number of people actually replaced by automation has been much less than planned. A concomitant result has been that salary savings were over-estimated.

Even if the planned personnel cuts have materialized, certain compensating costs were generally overlooked or under-estimated:

1. A computer installation requires a new staff of specialists who earn higher salaries than the personnel eventually replaced.

2. The salary costs of the personnel in the many new departments or functions set up to support the computer installation may represent a very substantial budget item:

- Account Coding
- Input department
- Proof and control group
- Machine console operators
- Librarian

Under-Estimating Programming Time and Costs

Programming computer runs is a very technical and exacting task. One authoritative book on the subject written by Richard Brandon lists as many as 22 different steps followed by the programmer to write and test one computer run.

It is well known in the data-processing field that the actual time required for programming nearly always exceeds the estimated time. One possible reason for this is that relatively few people in supervisory positions in data processing know how to establish and use standards for programming performance. Very few installations utilize job-status reports prepared weekly which assist in keeping the programming work on schedule.

Time Estimates for Computer Runs

Time estimates for computer runs are usually under-estimated. Several factors tend to invalidate such estimates.

First, the rated speeds of input and output devices are usually greater than achievable speeds. There are several reasons why this is true. One reason, which is comprehensible to the layman, is that a computer operates at a speed no faster than the *slowest output unit*. As an illustration, consider the computer run which prints one line and punches one card per line. Now, the printer may be rated at 900 lines per minute, but if the card punch speed is only 200 cards per minute, the printer necessarily slows down to 200 lines per minute.

Set Up and Tear Down Time

Management may be surprised to find that, in a short period of time after a new computer has been installed, it is necessary to operate the machine a second shift each day. This happens partly because of the time required to prepare for making each computer run. As a rule of thumb, few computers are in operation for more than 70% of the total available clock time on any shift. Log books show that the time lost because of setting up each run, and subsequently changing to another job, ranges from 30% to 48% of clock time.

Internal Housekeeping

It has been aptly said that, in some installations, the computer is "its own best customer." This refers to the amount of time required to compile or assemble new programs, or existing programs which are being modified. Briefly, this means that the programmer's instruction cards are fed into the machine which then proceeds to interpret and convert the symbolic instructions to machine code for subsequent computer runs.

This type of internal operation requires considerable computer time in a medium to large-scale installation. This internal housekeeping is one reason why a second shift may be instituted sooner than expected.

Benefits of a Computer

The facts outlined in this section seem to be negative because they point to increases in salary costs, or a potential second shift when the computer is loaded with a number of major jobs. However, the purpose of including them is not to be negative, but to acquaint you with the cost factors apt to be present in a computer installation.

On the positive side, the realizable benefits of a properly planned computer installation may far outweigh the costs and all other potential disadvantages of automation.

Through up-to-the-minute data and reports, top management can operate the business more efficiently. It can make decisions as to alternative courses of action in order to increase the profitability of the business. In fact, the practice of scientific management is just beginning.

Computers are being utilized more and more for simulation of management problems. One illustration of the value of this unique function is outlined as follows:

A firm with nine marketing divisions selling products nationwide had nine warehouses and twelve manufacturing plants in various locations around the nation. A specially-written computer program which included all known distribution cost factors simulated day-to-day operations over a period of time. Cost information developed and printed for management indicated that it would be far more profitable to close five of the warehouses plus three manufacturing plants, and consolidate manufacturing and marketing operations in certain areas.

A computer installation provides the ability to handle greatly increased volume without comparable increases in office salaries. The stock brokerage business provides a case in point. Since 1960, the volume of trades handled daily has increased 400% or more in some brokerage houses. Those houses that have installed computers in recent years have been reasonably able to cope with such huge volume increases as these—and have reduced the cost per transaction at the same time.

DO'S AND DON'TS LEARNED FROM EXPERIENCE

1. Don't Turn the Project Over to Outsiders

Neither the systems development work nor the programming should be done solely by outsiders. Both aspects of a computer installation should be kept firmly under the control of people representing the firm. It is frequently desirable for experienced outsiders to *participate* in either, or both, the systems work and programming. However, they should act in an advisory or staff capacity to the Project Manager who is a knowledgeable employee of the firm.

2. Advise Management of Its Responsibilities

Since computers are complex and very technical devices, some owners or managers have the tendency to "let George do it." This can be a monumental and costly mistake. In the past, this attitude has frequently meant that the firm hired a couple of young programmers from the outside world, then turned the project over to them since they were the "outside experts."

A result is that the outsiders are forced into establishing company policy—their version is written into the programs and procedures, yet they may not have the experience or background for making such key decisions. It is unfair to the programmers or to the systems analysts to be maneuvered into such a situation.

Leading observers and experts in the data-processing field state emphatically that *any computer installation which does not enjoy the full and continuing backing and support of top management will accomplish poor or mediocre results.*

3. Don't Force Programmers to Make Key Decisions

The systems group which does the systems-development work should outline the entire system in great detail before the programming of it begins. One segment of the documentation behind the system is policy decisions and procedures which must be integrated into the computer runs. It is not the function of the programmers to fill in the gaps caused by incomplete systems work.

4. Consult with Department Heads

The systems group should consult at all times with experienced department heads or supervisors who will eventually be the "users" of the computer output. Key men in each department should be appointed to the planning committee, which meets with the systems group, to discuss all aspects of the proposed new computer system. Their ideas and suggestions should be earnestly solicited and implemented where feasible.

5. Avoid Crash Projects

Never place a firm order for a computer with a *firm delivery date,* then start the systems-development work and programming. The systems work and the programming should be carefully estimated, then increased by a safety factor of 25%. Only then should the computer manufacturer be given a tentative delivery date for the equipment.

Failure to observe this rule has cost many firms large sums of money, because the computer was delivered on schedule—but the programs were not ready for operation. Do not forget that computer rentals begin as soon as the machine is delivered, tested and pronounced "ready" by the field engineers employed by the computer manufacturer.

THINGS TO TELL YOUR CLIENT

1. Consider Alternative Methods

Before your client orders a computer, he should consider alternative methods and relative costs.

A basic review of what is currently being done in his plant or office may reveal possibilities for major improvements without a computer. A careful study of small desk computers and more conventional office equipment may indicate that the job can be done with this type of equipment—at far lower cost than by entering into a full-fledged electronic computer installation.

2. Computers Are not "Cure-Alls"

Computers are not a remedy for all business ills; in fact, some installations have caused serious business disruption and problems of great magnitude.

Computer feasibility studies and basic reviews sometimes reveal very clearly that the basic organization and existing procedures of a firm are in such bad shape that it is not feasible to develop and install a computer system—until the existing management structure, policies and procedures are thoroughly overhauled and improved.

3. Keeping up with the "Jones Company"

Avoid ordering a computer just because "it is the thing to do."

4. Avoid Under-Estimating Computer Costs

It has been clearly emphasized that the monthly rental for the equipment is only one of many costs involved in a computer installation. One of the functions of the public practitioner is to acquaint the client with the many other costs which must be considered before making a firm decision to proceed with a computer installation.

29

Account Coding

In recent years, the rapid advent of a host of new data-processing machines of all types, advances in punched-card techniques, and releases of punched-paper tape and electronic computers have caused considerable stir and confusion among systems and procedures groups, public practitioners attempting to keep up with the parade, and also among the potential buyers of such wares of the office-equipment industry. Now, in addition to the many problems encountered in properly applying such new equipment to office or factory clerical operations, we find, when such equipment is installed, that it is necessary to *number* customers, vendors, shareholders, employees, et al. Reason: *Numbers are the basic language* of high-speed sorters, collators, tabulators, computers and other automation equipment. If we want to utilize the speed, accuracy and other capabilities of such units, we must convert all account titles and names into numbers. Numbers represent a language which the machines are capable of reading and interpreting.

As a result of the rapid adoption by business of such machines, many unprepared practitioners suddenly found clients looking to them for help and advice in selecting the appropriate numbering system for a specific application. In addition, some found themselves faced with the necessity of studying, understanding and recommending one of several complicated mathematical methods for figuring "check digits," which are, indeed, a vital part of a good numbering system, as will be explained subsequently in this chapter.

A common mistake shared by some public accountants and corporation methodsmen has been to take the casual approach to the entire numbering problem. Apparently their thinking has been, quite frequently, something like this: "Assigning numbers to customers or vendors surely must be a simple matter—we will merely start numbering at 0001 and assign numbers in sequence until all names on the list are numbered. On second thought, we must provide for new customers' or vendors' names to be added to the list in the future. So, we will leave a gap of five or ten numbers when assigning numbers to existing names; this will provide plenty of numbers for squeezing in new accounts in the future. This numbering is really a simple project after all."

This line of thinking, plus an almost complete lack of knowledge of the subject, has led many firms into very difficult and costly situations. For example, a bank in Iowa numbered its checking accounts in such a way as to maintain perpetually (hopefully) an exact alphabetic and numeric relationship. At the time of numbering the customer list, a gap of 1,024 numbers was left between each number assigned to a customer on the list. This seemed to be, most assuredly, a generous provision for future account growth. However, the system began to bog down within eighteen months.

A large department store in New York State adopted punched cards for their sales audit and receivables operation in 1957. This naturally made it necessary to number all customers. A "simultaneous alphanumeric gap" plan was selected as the one best suited to their requirements. A specific gap of 512 was selected. Within six months after the initial numbering of all customers, the plan had to be discarded and a new attempt made toward solving the numbering problem. This experience was very costly and frustrating to top management. On subsequent pages, reasons for the system failures mentioned above will be discussed and explained.

Definition

Account coding is the science of selecting and assigning account numbers to specified account lists. A list may consist of customer names, vendors, shareholders, employees, or others. Assigning code numbers to General Ledger accounts is also a form of account coding.

Purpose of This Chapter

The purpose of this chapter is to equip the busy practitioner or systems analyst with the necessary background knowledge for analyzing the operating characteristics, benefits and disadvantages of the three basic account-coding plans which have come into wide use simultaneously with the expanding number of punched-card accounting and data-processing installations in recent years.

Variations in name lists to be coded, plus variables in equipment used and final reports to be prepared—all these considerations preclude outlining a complete "prepackaged" account-coding plan which would solve all problems for all firms. And, it is essential that the numbering system adopted by a commercial firm be compatible with the requirements of present equipment in use plus providing for future growth of data volume and possible use later of more advanced data-processing systems.

For all these reasons, this text material is intended to help the practitioner to carefully analyze the overall problem in each instance, devise necessary auxiliary codes, select a check-digit formula which will operate best with the equipment in use, and, finally, to recommend a complete coding plan which will best meet a client's specific requirements.

Benefits of Account Coding

We recognize that the most compelling reason for coding accounts is the increasing application of computers, punched-card equipment, and data-processing machines applied to a wide array of statistical, accounting and record-keeping jobs found both in the office and in the factory. However, there are other benefits to be gained from account coding, which point to the fact that many firms would be well-advised to investigate the potential benefits of numbering—even though the use of punched cards or other sophisticated equipment is not contemplated immediately. Some of these benefits are:

1. *Numbers Provide Positive Account Identification:* Quite often we find, when studying customer or vendor lists, numerous duplications and similarities in both individual names and

firm titles. This makes proper identification of charges or credits by name or title alone difficult or unreliable.

A recent study published by the Social Security Board revealed that there are only 970,000 surnames in use in the United States today. These names are shared by the entire population of more than 175,000,000 people. Seventy thousand of these names are of the rare variety and apply to only a few people, relatively; only 900,000 last names remain to be shared by all the other people in this nation. The study also revealed how a small list of given names is shared by an amazing number of people. For example, the given name of "John" now belongs to one man out of twenty-eight! One woman out of thirty-two is named "Mary."

Repetition among titles of business firms is also quite prevalent. This is prevalent enough that some firms have found it necessary to divide their vendor lists into geographic areas before assigning account numbers in order to minimize the possibility of crediting incoming invoices to the wrong vendor.

2. *Documents Can Be Sorted and Filed Faster Numerically:* A substantial reduction in overall paper-handling time can be accomplished by the use of account numbers. It is far easier to teach clerks to sort or arrange documents by number than to attempt to teach them the rules of alphabetizing.

3. *Posting Time Can Be Saved by Use of Numbers:* Some banks and commercial firms have been able to increase the efficiency of their posting up to 46%—using conventional posting machines—by numbering their accounts and all posting documents! In addition, various proof methods may be utilized which make it easy to prove that each document was posted to the correct account. This is very difficult to accomplish with alphabetic posting methods.

4. *Facilitates Machine Operations:* Assigning account numbers to customers or vendors makes it possible to sort, at high speed, punched cards representing source documents. It is possible to sort punched cards on a mechanical sorter alphabetically by the last name of an account. However, most laymen do not realize how greatly this increases sorting time over the use of numbers for sorting.

Here are the reasons for this:

(1) If fifteen card columns are allotted to keypunching customer or vendor name, the sorter operator must sort on all fifteen columns, one at a time. By comparison, a five-digit account number would provide for up to 99,999 names and would require a maximum of five sorts.

A further illustration involves a recent service-bureau job which required product colors to be alphabetically keypunched into the cards in lieu of use of code numbers to designate colors and color combinations. Even though there was a maximum of only 100 different color combinations, the sorter operator found it necessary to sort on eight-card columns to get the spelled-out colors into correct alphabetic sequence.

(2) In addition to the increased number of columns required for alphabetic sorting, the operator must pass all cards through the sorter *twice* for each card column. The reason for this is that a combination of two punches in the same card column represent each letter of the alphabet. For example, letter "A" is signaled by an overpunch in the top part of the card (the "12" zone) plus a "1" punch in the body of the card. The letter "B" consists of a "12" overpunch plus a "2" in the body of the card, etc.

Since there are two punches in each card column, then, all cards must pass through the sorter twice for each column. On the first pass, for example, a zone switch is thrown to select the overpunches. Then, on the second pass, sorting is done on the numbered punches in the body of the cards. Now, if the operator fails to return the zone switch to the "off" position before starting the second sort, all cards get out of sequence and all prior sorting time is lost.

Numbers are also necessary for *merging* decks of cards together to produce updated master records.

Numbers are necessary for high-speed *writing* of voucher checks on tabulators. Numbers are necessary for rapid *preparation* of sales reports showing a breakdown of product sales by customers. Numbers facilitate the *tabulating* of purchases from vendors for stated periods of time.

Computers are now being applied to the huge volume of transactions involved in maintaining a record of the number of shares of stock held by each individual shareholder in our major corporations. This could not be done economically without a numbering system being applied to a constantly changing list of shareholders.

Fundamental Requirements

Ample experience in account coding, now extending over a period of several years, indicates that the fundamental requirements of an adequate account-coding system are as follows:

1. The basic system should be simple.

2. The system should provide for adequate future growth of today's account list.

3. The number of digits in the number should be held to a minimum.

4. The number content and arrangement should facilitate manual or machine sorting of all documents.

5. The basic system, for commercial applications, should integrate account numbers with the alphabet so as to obtain a definite *relationship* between names and numbers.

6. The account number should include a mathematically-computed check digit.

7. The act of assigning an account number, including a check digit, to a new account should be a simple, positive operation.

Review of Requirements

1. *Basic Plan Should Be Simple:* The reason for this statement is fairly obvious. If the basic plan is complex, then personnel who work with the plan will not comprehend its proper application; administering such a plan becomes a continuing problem. A complex plan leads to many other problems, including errors in assigned numbers, duplicate numbers assigned to some accounts, increased sorting time, etc. Also, attempting to merge another name list into an existing list may create confusion and more errors.

2. *Adequate Growth Provision:* The plan selected should always provide for orderly growth of the original account list. This is especially true of customer lists, shareholder and employee lists. It is recognized that some vendor lists will remain relatively static, however.

3. *Minimum Number of Digits:* A number system with a minimum number of digits may save a considerable amount of clerical time and labor, when compared to an elaborate number system with more digits. In many applications, such as coding incoming vendor invoices, it is necessary to perform a "look-up" operation and manually write vendor code numbers on the face of each invoice for later keypunching and processing of payables by means of punched-card accounting. A number with a minimum number of digits will require *less time* to write—and *fewer errors* will creep in.

Also, it is obvious that each additional digit in the basic account number proportionately increases sorting time. If one account-number system utilizes five digits, and another requires the use of seven digits, sorting time for the latter *is increased 40%*. This increase in sorting time is very noticeable when mechanical card sorters are in use. Even when sorting is done on a full-scale electronic computer, with the records being read in from magnetic tape, and recorded in sorted "strings" on other magnetic tape reels, an increased number of digits or characters in the sort fields increases the overall sorting time.

4. *Number Arrangement Should Facilitate Sorting:* This is a very significant consideration. One reason for numbering accounts is to obtain easier and more rapid manual sorting numerically—or to speed machine sorting. One way to accomplish this is to include a digit in the base number which is indicative of account classifications. A case history will best serve to explain the function of such digits.

A large marketing organization was divided into nine regions which blanketed the entire United States. It was established that management wanted auxiliary sales reports *by marketing regions,* in addition to master sales reports by branches, products, etc. The customer-name list in each region ranged in size from 3,000 to 5,000 names. Here is the way the number plan for customers was worked out. We assigned blocks of numbers to customers in each region. In this way, the left-hand high-order digit will always indicate the *region code,* as in the illustration below.

Region #1	#100-000 through 199-999
Region #2	200-000 through 299-999
Region #3	300-000 through 399-999
Region #4	400-000 through 499-999
Region #5	500-000 through 599-999
Region #6	600-000 through 699-999
Region #7	700-000 through 799-999
Region #8	800-000 through 899-999
Region #9	900-000 through 999-999

Note that the left-hand digit, ranging from 1 through 9, is always the same as the region code number. This was accomplished by not using numbers beginning with zero. So, the first 99,999 numbers available are not used for sales accounting.

Now, the present list of 3,000 customers in Region #1 are assigned individual numbers beginning with #100-000 and up.

5. *Plan Should Relate Numbers to Alphabet:* The primary reason for stressing this requirement is that management invariably will prefer that all tabulated sales, purchase or statistical reports dealing with name groups *be in alphabetic sequence.*

Certain specific applications also point up the desirability of this aspect of the numbering plan selected. For example, this feature may be important if punched cards representing invoices are used for accounts receivable records. Sorting time can be saved if such cards are sorted numerically preparatory to filing them in tubs awaiting receipt of the customer's remittance. (Alphabetic sorting is very time-consuming.) If the account numbers assigned to customers have a definite relationship to a segment of the alphabet, the numerically-sorted cards can be quickly interfiled alphabetically with other cards for the same customer. Now the clerk who applies cash can locate the invoice cards by name and match a specific card with the remittance—without the necessity of first referring to a cross-index file to find the customer's account number.

6. *Account Number Should Include a Mathematically Computed Check Digit:* Reasons for this require a great deal of explanation and are covered at considerable length further on in this chapter.

7. *Number Assignment Should Be Simple:* Experience has amply proven that a vital consideration in choosing any plan is the simplicity of the daily operation and administration of

that plan. The simultaneous alphanumeric plan, detailed on subsequent pages, has failed in many installations for several reasons; one major contributing cause has been the simple fact that people who assign numbers to new accounts make too many errors, which in turn breed more errors.

Another important thing for the practitioner to remember is that it is vital that the same account number not be assigned to two different accounts. As an illustration, it is easy to imagine the confusion and complaints this will cause in either receivables or payables.

Final Consideration

When the practitioner or systems analyst is studying and considering an account-coding plan for a specific application, the final and determining factor should be the *format and arrangement of data* on the various *statistical and management reports* desired as the end result of all data-processing work.

For the purpose of amplifying the statement made above, the phrase "account coding" must include as part of its meaning more than merely the number assigned to identify each individual customer or vendor. It includes *additional* number codes necessary to designate geographical areas, territory numbers, plant locations, the relationship of subsidiary corporations to a parent corporation, and other factors. This aspect of account coding will be amplified on following pages.

CHECK DIGITS

Commercial firms now have an opportunity to profit from the mistakes made by banks since the rush began several years ago to number checking accounts in preparation for the use of electronic posting machines, high-speed sorters, computers and other devices designed to speed the flow of checks and deposits through the various bank bookkeeping operations. Many banks acted hastily and were ill-advised as to which numbering plan to select. In addition, the value of "check digits" was not well understood at first, with the result that scores of banks laboriously installed complete customer numbering systems which did not include a mathematically-computed check digit. This omission has already caused many banks to re-number all accounts, and to re-issue thousands of check books to customers.

Definition of Check Digit

A check digit refers to the inclusion of a digit to the right of a basic account number for purposes of checking the *validity* of the number. For example, manufacturers of high-speed sorting and automatic-reading equipment realized from the beginning that it would be necessary to verify, in some way, the accuracy of the machine when it is scanning and "reading" account numbers from inscribed documents. For purposes of further explanation, let us delve into the automation program embarked upon in recent years by the banks. One justification for doing this now is that the equipment and principles involved in this program are already beginning to appear in some commercial applications.

Bank Automation Program

In 1957, the American Banking Association named a committee of prominent bankers to investigate all proposed automation equipment and decide upon a means for encoding all checks and deposits which would be most suitable for rapid sorting and processing of original documents. This was called a search for a "common language," since the intent was to devise an encoding method which could be read by all types and makes of equipment and, therefore, common to all banks in the nation. Also, one objective of the program was to select a coding system utilizing numeric characters recognizable by all.

The committee's final decision, after years of study and consultations with equipment manufacturers, was in favor of special configurations of numeric characters imprinted on the face of checks or deposits in *magnetic ink* (ink with iron-oxide content). A sample check bearing the peculiar-appearing numbers referred to as "13B" type font are shown in Figure 29-1.

It is recognized that any piece of equipment can experience a malfunction occasionally. Also, it was anticipated in advance that the magnetic ink characters may be improperly applied to some checks, or other factors may cause errors when the machine scans or reads account numbers. Since a check or deposit may be posted by a computer to a customer's checking account based on the *reading* of the account number, it is vitally important to detect any of the following representative situations during the document-reading process:

1. Machine reading head interprets a 7 as a 1 due to poor placement or density of the iron-oxide particles in the magnetic ink.

2. Machine reading head interprets a 5 as a 3 due to malfunction within the machine.

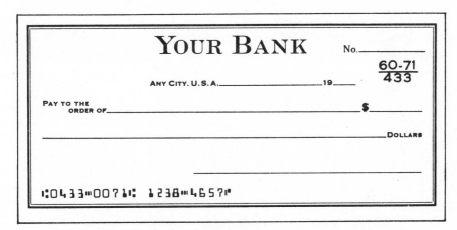

Figure 29-1
TYPE 13B MAGNETIC INK COMMON LANGUAGE NUMERALS
ADOPTED BY BANKS FOR AUTOMATION

3. Invalid numbers resulting from *manual copying* of numbers by clerks assigned to the task of coding unnumbered items.

Mathematical Formula

A mathematically computed check digit was ascertained to be the answer to the critical problem of guaranteeing the accuracy of all reading and interpreting of account numbers on documents passing through electronic sorters or input devices for computers. This concept of accuracy has now been broadened considerably to include even small units, such as document-inscribing equipment used at the very beginning of an integrated system of automatic document-handling processes. Such units now include a small electric computing device wired to calculate a check digit for each account number entered on the keyboard or read by the equipment; this enables the device to compare the internally calculated check digit with the check digit entered on the keyboard as part of the account number indexed.

Double-Add-Double Method

One long-standing method of computing a check digit is known as the "double-add-double" method. For purpose of explanation, let us select account number 12-436. Starting with the right-hand digit, we double 6 and write the result on paper. Then we add 3, double 4, add 2 and double 1. We will now examine the total obtained by adding all results together.

#12–436

Step 1..Double 6	12
Step 2..Add 3	3
Step 3..Double 4	8
Step 4..Add 2	2
Step 5..Double 1	2

$1 + 17 = 18.$

Note that the "1" in the tens column is added to the sum of the digits in the units column.

The next step is to subtract the total of the digits (18) from the nearest power of 10—in this instance, number 20; 20 minus 18 equals 2. Our mathematically computed check digit, then is 2.

Now we write the check digit to the right of the basic account number, which now appears like this: 12-436-2.

From this point on the validity of the base number, 12-436, is instantly verified as the number is scanned for sorting or posting purposes by automatic document-handling equipment. This is done by means of an electric, or electronic, computing device built inside the equipment which cross-computes as explained above. When the check digit of 2 is obtained as a result of the computation, the machine *compares* this figure with the check digit listed as part of the account number. If the two digits agree, the validity of the entire number is established.

However, suppose the reading device misreads one or more of the digits in the basic number; when this happens, the computer calculates and compares a check digit which differs from the correct check digit of 2. Since the two numbers do not agree, the item is rejected!

As an illustration of this, we will assume that the reading device scans #12-436-2, but reads the left-hand 2 as a 3. Let us now study the internal workings of the computing device.

Number Read As:	*Computer Calculations*	*Results*
13-436-2	(1) Double 6	12
	(2) Add 3	3
	(3) Double 4	8
	(4) Add 3	3
	(5) Double 1	2
	(6) Add digits in both columns	1 + 18 equals 19
	(7) 20 minus 19 equals *1, which is check digit.*	

The computed check digit of *1* calculated from the number *as read by the reading device* is now compared with the check digit of 2 appearing to the right of the base number; this instantly warns the machine of an invalid number. In this illustration, the number itself was correct, but the *reading* of the number was wrong. As explained on a previous page, the basic number itself is sometimes wrong because of manual copying.

Unusable Numbers

The double-add-double method is not 100% effective in detecting all types of transposition errors if all possible numbers in a block of numbers are used. The transposing of 09 for 90 will not be detected by the formula. However, if all numbers which include a cipher following a nine (90) are completely eliminated, then the D-A-D method is very effective against the transposition of numbers adjacent to each other. To effect this means the loss of 4% of all numbers in a five-digit account number, and a loss of 5% for all numbers in a six-digit account number.

To prevent the possibility of errors resulting from transposing figures 09 and 90, the following account numbers should be eliminated from the system:

Five-Digit Number Patterns: XX-X90
                                         XX-90X
                                         X9-0XX
                                         90-XXX

The first pattern XX-X90 indicates that all numbers in each series of 100 which end in 90 are to be deleted.

The second pattern means that numbers 900, 901, 902, etc., through 909, repeating each 1,000 numbers, must not be used.

The third pattern shows that numbers ranging from 9,000 through 9,099, in each block of 10,000 numbers are to be deleted.

The fourth pattern signals the deletion of all numbers from 90-000 through 90-999.

Summary of Unusable Numbers: The total numbers lost out of each block of 99,999 are listed below:

From 00-000 through 89-999	2,700
From 90-000 through 90-999	1,000
From 91-000 through 99-999	279
	3,979

Other Benefits of Check Digits

Use of a check digit as part of an account number can cut costs substantially on some punched-card applications. For several years now, there has been available for use a special keypunch machine with a built-in electric calculator. It can be programmed to detect any invalid number being keypunched. Here is how it works.

Let us assume that invoice cards representing vendors' invoices are being keypunched as routine procedure. Before the keypunching can begin, someone must scan the vendor's name on each invoice, refer to an alphabetic reference file and manually write the vendor account number on the invoice. It is possible, of course, to make transportation errors or other errors when reading and transcribing numbers. However, a check digit included as part of the code number will enable the keypunch machine to detect such errors. For example, suppose the correct number for a particular invoice was 23-412-0, but the number was written on the invoice incorrectly as 23-421-0. When this invalid number is punched, the internal electric calculator goes to work and calculates its own check digit on the base number of 23-421. The result, using double-add-double method, is 1. Then the calculator compares this result with the check digit of "0," which was keypunched as part of the total number. Since these two digits do not agree, the keypunch locks.

It is interesting to realize that the error in the vendor number described will not be detected at all if ordinary keypunch and key-verifier machines are in use. Reason: A verifier operator merely verifies the work done by the keypunch operator, working from the same source documents. Now, if a wrong number appears on an invoice, the keypunch operator naturally punches it *as written*. The verifier operator will necessarily do the same thing. Since they are in accord, the incorrect number will go undetected. In accounts payable procedures, this means that the wrong vendor will eventually receive payment for the invoice! Here is the explanation of this fact.

1. Invoice cards, after being keypunched and verified, are filed by due date for later payment.

2. On the due date, all invoice cards are mechanically merged with vendor Name and Address cards. Now, since account numbers are the language of such machines, the matching and merging is done on the *vendor number* in each punched card. Therefore, the invoice card bearing the incorrect number 23-421 will appear behind a Name and Address card for the vendor who has been assigned that number.

3. Next, the merged cards are placed in a tabulator which proceeds to list the data from each invoice card on the apron of a voucher check. After the last card for a vendor is processed, the machine spaces the form to the body of the check and proceeds to print vendor name, address, check number, date and check amount.

The only opportunity for management to catch such wrong payments is to match the original vendor invoices with the voucher checks and examine the invoices before signing checks.

The procedures described above are those for a tabulating machine installation. However, even if accounts payable processing is handled by a computer, the same end-result of sending the check to the wrong vendor will occur since the vendor number is the key to identifying each vendor.

Definite Savings May Be Possible

In the accounts payable department of a very large department store in the city of New York, installation of a new account-coding system for vendors, including a check digit in the numbers assigned, in conjunction with installation of self-verifying keypunch machines resulted in saving the salaries of ten verified operators. This was possible because an analysis of the job showed that other data being key-verified by these operators could be proven by other means such as pre-list or post-list totals on monetary amounts involved. Since the new system enabled the keypunch operators to prove the accuracy of all vendor numbers, the services of the verifier operators were no longer needed.

Shortcomings of Check Digits

A check digit will not detect every conceivable type of error which can occur. For example, the double-add-double formula will not warn of the following types of errors:

1. Transpositions in *adjacent columns* between *09* and *90*.
2. Alternate column transpositions. Example:

26-375-6 read as 26-573-6

3. Certain substitutions of figures between alternative columns such as *1210* for *2120,* etc.

Despite these weaknesses, the double-add-double method is known to be workable and effective. It has been in use for many years.

Other Formulas Evolved

As a result of the known weak spots in the D-A-D formula outlined above, mathematicians and people employed by the various manufacturers of electronic office equipment went to work to develop other formulas which would provide better protection against internal errors. This search for better results, plus the prestige value of developing a check-digit method which could be readily identifiable with a specific line of office equipment, brought about the development of two other major formulas, now well known and in wide use. These two methods are called the "Constant Remainder" and "Modulus 11" methods.

Constant Remainder Method

The constant remainder formula provides for calculating the complete number, including the check digit, rather than formulating the check digit as a distinct operation separate and apart from the account number.

The principle involved is that an arbitrary number from 1 to 9 is selected as the "constant remainder." 11 is then added to this constant remainder number to establish the first number. 11 is added successively to each preceding number to formulate the number list and check digits. This must be illustrated to be understood. We will arbitrarily select a constant remainder of *6* for our chart example. When we add 11 to this number, we obtain the sum of 17 for our very first number. Let us examine Figure 29-2 to see how all other numbers are successively established.

A study of the numbers appearing in the units column of the account number shows that each 11th digit is missing. This is due to the fact that the addition of 11 to any number ending in 9 causes a skip of the next successive digit. For example, when 11 is added to 39, above, the result is 50. This causes the unit "4" to be skipped.

Now we will test one of the numbers appearing on the chart. Any number, when divided by 11, must provide a remainder identical with the pre-selected Constant Remainder, or the number is not a valid one. Since we selected number 6 as the Constant Remainder when establishing the list of account numbers on the chart, all usable account numbers when divided by 11 must provide a *remainder of 6.*

Example: Account #00-027-0. This number, when divided by 11 provides a result of 24 with a remainder of *6.* Therefore, it is a valid number.

Check Digits for Simultaneous Alphanumeric System

The details and fundamentals of simultaneous alphanumerical account-coding systems are explained on subsequent pages. Briefly, a selected number interval, or gap, is used when num-

Account Number Digits						
Tens of 1,000	Thousands	Hundreds	Tens	Units	Check Digit	
					6	← Constant Remainder.
				1	7	← First number.
				2	8	
				3	9	
				5	0	
				6	1	
				7	2	
				8	3	
				9	4	
			1	0	5	
			1	1	6	
			1	2	7	
			1	3	8	
			1	4	9	
			1	6	0	
			1	7	1	
			1	8	2	
			1	9	3	
			2	0	4	
			2	1	5	
			2	2	6	
			2	3	7	
			2	4	8	
			2	5	9	
			2	7	0	, etc.

Figure 29-2
CHART DEPICTING CONSTANT REMAINDER METHOD

bering all accounts on an initial name list. This is done for the purpose of leaving groups of numbers to be assigned to new accounts in the future. The intent is to place all new names into correct alphabetic position in relation to existing names, and assign a number which will be between existing numbers. Number gaps used to accomplish this are usually divisible by 2 successively. Typical number gaps are 32-64-128-256-512, etc.

The Constant Remainder check-digit can be applied to determine all usable numbers for the gap system. For example, we will select a gap of 64. This gap is multiplied by 11 and the constant remainder is added to determine the first number.

We will use the same previously selected constant remainder of 6 to establish the numbers appearing below.

$$64 \times 11 \text{ equals } 704$$
$$\text{Add } 6 \qquad +6$$
$$\overline{}$$
$$710$$

The first usable number is 00-*071-0*.

The next number is found by adding the "gap multiple" of 704 to the first number.

$$710$$
$$+704$$
$$\overline{}$$
$$1414 = \text{second number.}$$

The number pattern will develop like this:

$$71\text{-}0$$
$$141\text{-}4$$
$$211\text{-}8$$
$$282\text{-}2$$
$$352\text{-}6$$
$$423\text{-}0, \text{ etc.}$$

Shortcomings of Constant Remainder Method

1. The formula will not expose alternate-column transposition errors.
2. About 10% of all numbers within a stated block or range of numbers cannot be used.
3. The validity of a number is determined by dividing the complete number, including the check digit, by 11. The result must leave a remainder equal to the constant remainder selected and used for establishing the entire list of account numbers.

The long division involved by this check-digit method may require measurable computer time and result in a slightly slower operation than use of the D-A-D method.

Modulus 11 Check Digit Formula

The basic purpose of this formula is to provide a positive check on transpositions of all types.

Each digit of the account number is multiplied by 2, 3, 4, 5, 6 and 7, reading the digits from right to left. The results of the individual multiplications are added and a total obtained. This total is then divided by 11. The remainder resulting from the division is *subtracted from 11;* the result is the check digit.

Example:

$$
\begin{array}{ccccccc}
 & 1 & 2 & 4 & 3 & 6 & 2 \leftarrow \text{Account number.} \\
\times & 7 & 6 & 5 & 4 & 3 & 2 \leftarrow \text{Multiplier.} \\
\hline
\end{array}
$$

$$7 + 12 + 20 + 12 + 18 + 4 = 73.$$

73 divided by 11 = 6, plus *7 remainder.*

11—remainder of 7 = 4; this is the check digit for account number 124-362-*4*.

Unusable Number

$$
\begin{array}{ccccccc}
 & 2 & 4 & 2 & 6 & 1 & 7 \leftarrow \text{Account number.} \\
\times & 7 & 6 & 5 & 4 & 3 & 2 \leftarrow \text{Multiplier.}
\end{array}
$$

$$14 + 24 + 10 + 24 + 3 + 14 = 89.$$

89 divided by 11 = 8, plus 1 remainder.

Remainder of 1 subtracted from 11 = 10. A check digit must be a single digit; therefore, the account number 242-617 is invalid.

Approximately *10% of all possible account numbers* are not usable for the above reason.

Summary

This formula will provide excellent protection against transpositions because the multiplier assigned to each successive digit of the number is different. Of course, if the account number exceeds six digits, then the multiplier pattern is repeated. Theoretically, it would now be possible to have a transposition which would not be revealed by the check-digit calculations.

THREE BASIC NUMBERING PLANS

Three different numbering systems have been developed and applied to a wide variety of name lists since the upsurge of account coding began. Each system brings with it certain benefits and disadvantages. These will be analyzed for the possible assistance of the practitioner or other people interested in account-coding principles.

Straight Numeric Plan

This plan incorporates triple benefits of simplicity, ease of understanding and ease of administration in actual daily operations. Also, precalculated check digits can be a part of account-number lists or register sheets which make it easy to assign complete account numbers (including mathematically computed check digits) to each new account.

The major disadvantage of this plan is that the assignment of consecutive numbers to new customers or vendors at random means that there is absolutely *no relationship between names and numbers*. While this is definitely not important for sorting, merging, or other paper-handling functions, it becomes highly significant when we examine a typical end-result of data processing, such as a tabulated report for management. For example, a sales report for a sales manager or marketing executive would perferably show all customers listed in alphabetic sequence from A to Z. Now, if account numbers have been assigned in numeric sequence, *regardless of new customers' last names or account titles,* then new customers belonging in the "A" group may appear after the listing of all the "Z's." Let us ascertain why this is true.

Initial Numbering: Suppose that firm "X" has 1,000 customers on the day we decide to number them. We will assign numbers in sequence as follows:

Herbert A. Aarons	0001
Robert B. Aarons	0002
Albert Baker Corp.	0003
R. L. Casey	0004
Henry Decker	0005, etc.

The last name on the list, John E. Zumwalt, is assigned #1,000. At this point we have an alphabetic list of customers properly numbered in alphabetic order. Any tabulated report prepared now would present sales figures in exact alphabetic name sequence, since account numbers were assigned consecutively to the alphabetized list. However, the problem begins with the addition of the first new name. Suppose Hubert C. Adams opens an account. He is assigned #1,001. The next new customer may be Thomas F. Walker. He is assigned #1,002. We can see now that on any sales report prepared after the addition of these two names, the sales to Adams will appear at the bottom of the list, immediately followed by Walker.

For this reason, very few commercial firms have adopted the straight numeric plan.

The General Electric Company, after a long and detailed study of the various coding systems or plans, finally adopted the straight numeric plan for its many computer installations and applications because of the plan's basic simplicity and positive control over assignment of numbers. To solve the problem of reports of various types not being in alphabetic sequence if printed in numeric sequence, the systems analysts provided a five-character sort field in each name-header record on the computer file. For example, if a customer's name is Charles L. Greenspan, the sort field contains the letters GREEN.

Since a sort on the account number will not produce reports in alphabetic sequence, the computer is instructed to sort all records on this alphabetic field which moves ABRAMS ahead of ADAMS or ADAMSON, places BROWN in front of *BURWOOD*, etc.

For a more precise alphabetic listing, this concept can be expanded to include more characters of the last name or account title, plus several letters of the first name. The systems analyst should realize, however, that the penalty paid for adoption of the straight numeric plan is computer sorting time which precedes each print run, if all names or account titles are to be in alphabetic sequence on the report.

A MODIFIED ALPHANUMERIC PLAN

One very successful alphanumeric plan makes no attempt to keep all names in exact simultaneous alphabetic and numeric sequence. The LeFebure Corporation has a long list of outstandingly successful installations in banks and commercial firms of all types. Its modified alphanumeric plan is known as "ARANS." (*A*lphabetic *R*andom *A*ccess *N*umeric *S*equence.) This account-coding plan recognizes the inherent conflict between names and numbers, yet it provides the benefits of a definite, identifiable, unchanging relationship between names and numbers.

This time-tested plan meets all objectives of a good numbering plan and actually contrives to provide most of the benefits of a straight numeric plan with the benefits of an alphanumeric system. It is simple and easily administered in actual use. It provides a completely automatic way of obtaining a mathematically computed check digit for any assigned number.

How It Works

The basic principle involved in ARANS is the assigning of a block of consecutive numbers to *small groups* of existing accounts, which are in alphabetic sequence. Let us assume that ARANS will be applied to a customer name list of 6,000 names. (It will work equally well on *any* size name list.)

The first thing that is done is to screen the name list and break it up into small groups of accounts by selecting the first two, three or, possibly, four letters *common to all surnames* in the group. And, the number of accounts established for each group of surnames depends on expected account growth, past-growth history, possibility of future mergers, and other factors. More often than not, a growth factor of TEN TIMES the present account list is provided. This means, then, that a block of 200 numbers is assigned to each grouping of twenty customer names. (100 numbers assigned to smaller groups of ten names each would provide the same basic result.)

"Screening" consists of counting about twenty names down the list and determining a convenient "break" point so that two or three letters will readily identify the next group of surnames. The first few letter-groups found in a standard 300-division alphabetic subdivision is listed below to show how this is done.

Aa	Am	Ba	Bea
Ad	Anda	Bak	Bec
Al	Andr	Bar	Bel, etc.
All	Ar	Barrett	
	At	Bas	

Note the name "Barrett" on the list. This means that the list contained approximately twenty Barretts; therefore, the entire surname is used to identify this subdivision of accounts.

In actual practice it is not possible to force an exact number of names into each subdivision. A projected grouping of twenty names each will actually result in subdivisions ranging from sixteen to twenty-two names each.

Number of Subdivisions Used

The number of alphabetic breakdowns to be evolved from the screening process is obtained simply by dividing the total number of names on the list by the number of names in each projected group; 6,000 divided by 20 equals 300 breakdowns.

Number Blocks Assigned

The next step is to assign blocks of 200 numbers each to each small group of names. (See list below.)

Alpha Breakdown	Numbers Assigned
Aa	00-001 through 00-199
Ad	00-200 through 00-399
Al	00-400 through 00-599
All	00-600 through 00-799
Am	00-800 through 00-999
Anda	01-000 through 01-199
Andr	01-200 through 01-399
Ar	01-400 through 01-599
At	01-600 through 01-799
Ba	01-800 through 01-999
Bak, etc.	02-000 through 02-199, etc.

Numbering Original Accounts

The first twenty numbers in a block are assigned to the twenty names in the alphabetic subdivision. The remaining 180 numbers are reserved for future names introduced into the list. Obviously, this makes provision for an expansion of ten times the present number of names.

Alphanumeric Relationship

If the names on the original account list are in exact alphabetic order when numbered, then the system provides an exact alphanumeric relationship between names and numbers at this point. However, let us understand that the first new name added to any subdivision list may not be in exact alphabetic position.

Examples of Number Assignments

Ada, Alexander F.	00-200
Adach, Robert L.	00-201
Adair, J. C.	00-202
Adam, John N.	00-203
Adamo, Jos. F.	00-204
Adams, C. F.	00-205
Adams, Charles	00-206
Adams, Floyd L.	00-207
Adams, Henry T.	00-208
Adams, Lilian E.	00-209
Adams, Walter I.	00-210
Adco Hydraulic, Inc.	00-211
Adele's Gift Shop	00-212
Adler, Albert	00-213
Adler, Louis	00-214
Adler, Richard B.	00-215
Adlin, Harry P.	00-216

☐ (Original Name List.)
_____
Adams, Stuart H.   00-217   ☐ (New name added.)

If we attempted to keep all names in exact alphabetic and numeric order, Stuart H. Adams would be assigned number 00-210. This plan, however, assigns numbers in straight numeric sequence to all new accounts which fall into each subdivision. The new customer, Stuart H. Adams, is placed in the "Ad" group because of the first two letters of his last name; then the next open number of 00-217 is assigned. So, we see that this plan has the simplicity of straight numerics, with the benefits of an alphabetic relationship between names and numbers.

Since we have assigned #00-217 to Mr. Adams, his name will always appear with the "Ad" group on any sorting and listing operation.

ARANS Number Register

Figure 29-3 illustrates the number register set up for the "Ad" subdivision. The sixteen numbers assigned to the original name list were posted by typing the date adjacent to the letter "O." ("O" for "opened.") The vertical red line on the left edge was drawn to indicate list of numbers assigned.

When assigning a number to a new customer, the assignment clerk merely refers to an index for the number registers, selects the "Ad" register, finds the next open number of *17* and includes this with the basic block number of 00-200 taken from the top of the sheet. Also, the

INSTRUCTIONS: ACCOUNT NUMBERS FOLLOWED BY "X" ARE NOT USEABLE NUMBERS.

Ad — ALPHA SUB-DIVISION

00-200 — STARTING NO.

ACCT. NO.	CK DIGIT	ASSIGNMENT	ACCT. NO.	CK DIGIT	ASSIGNMENT	ACCT. NO.	CK DIGIT	ASSIGNMENT	ACCT. NO.	CK DIGIT	ASSIGNMENT
00	6	9/16/6	25	3		50	1		75	8	
01	4		26	1		51	9		76	6	
02	2		27	9		52	7		77	4	
03	0		28	7		53	5		78	2	
04	8		29	5		54	3		79	0	
05	5		30	3		55	0		80	8	
06	3		31	1		56	8		81	6	
07	1		32	9		57	6		82	4	
08	9		33	7		58	4		83	2	
09	7		34	5		59	2		84	0	
10	5		35	2		60	0		85	7	
11	3		36	0		61	8		86	5	
12	1		37	8		62	6		87	3	
13	9		38	6		63	4		88	1	
14	7		39	4		64	2		89	9	
15	4		40	2		65	9		90	X	
16	2		41	0		66	7		91	5	
17	0	10/2/6	42	8		67	5		92	3	
18	8		43	6		68	3		93	1	
19	6		44	4		69	1		94	9	
20	4		45	1		70	9		95	6	
21	2		46	9		71	7		96	4	
22	0		47	7		72	5		97	2	
23	8		48	5		73	3		98	0	
24	6		49	3		74	1		99	8	

LE FEBURE CORPORATION. CEDAR RAPIDS, IOWA   FORM 9904-18

Compu-Card

ARANS ® ACCOUNT NUMBER REGISTER
DOUBLE - ADD - DOUBLE METHOD

Figure 29-3
ACCOUNT NUMBER ASSIGNMENT REGISTER WITH PRE-CALCULATED CHECK DIGITS
(Courtesy of LeFebure Corporation)

check digit, pre-figured by the D-A-D method is available at a glance. Therefore, the complete number assigned to Mr. Adams is 00-217-0.

These pre-printed register sheets are available with check digits figured by the Constant Remainder and Modulus 11 methods. The LeFebure Customer Service Division will do the screening of the names list, establish alphabetic breaks, type letters and block numbers at the top of account-register sheets, and also set up cross-reference files if desired.

Cross-Reference Records

Confusion sometimes exists as to whether an alphabetic cross-reference file is or is not needed for an account numbering installation. After analyzing the function and purpose of such files, we will see that certain conditions may warrant setting up such files.

1. If accounts are numbered for the purpose of applying a computer or punched cards to a name list, an alphabetic file of cards representing all accounts may be a necessity for number look-ups—if the account name is not recorded on the account number assignment registers.

2. Even if account names are written on assignment registers, internal operating conditions may dictate the maintenance of alphabetic reference files in adddition to assignment registers. This is something the practitioner will have to check out very carefully before making a decision.

The ARANS register sheet can be designed to accommodate the name assigned to each number; however, most installations include a separate alphabetic reference file.

3. If conventional ledger cards are in use, but accounts are numbered to obtain other benefits, it may not be necessary to set up cross-reference files. Since a number look-up can be made by direct reference to the numbered ledger cards, an additional card file would be superfluous.

Two types of look-up records are illustrated by Figures 29-4 and 29-5. The first one shows a small unit card kept in a file. Contrary to the usual cross-index card file, these cards are maintained in numeric sequence within each small alphabetic group. There is a very good reason for doing this. Assigning the same number to two accounts is one of the worst mistakes possible. Therefore, each new account card is typed or imprinted with account name and number, then filed behind the last card in the group. The number on the new card should be one digit greater than the previous number in that group. For an alphabetic reference, it is necessary to find the account card by name only, since the number is not known. The round tab on top provides a unique method of doing this. There are ten breakdowns of the alphabet represented by these tabs. Letters in each of the ten blocks represent the *first letter of first (given) names*. The letter *typed on the tab* is the middle initial. If there is no middle initial, "X" is typed on the tab.

When setting up a card for Stuart *H*. Adams, type an "H" over the letter "S" and place the card in position by number. Here is how this card can be quickly located by name for a number look-up:

1. Refer to index tab for the "Ad" group of surnames.
2. Place finger on the block of letters which include "S."
3. Now look down the "lane" of letters (from front to back) in this tab position for the middle initial "H." The card you are searching for usually will be selected instantly on the first or second try.

Figure 29-4 illustrates a more condensed type of look-up register. This register sheet is indexed down the left edge and is kept in a ring binder. The reference clerk who assigns numbers to unnumbered documents uses the left hand for locating the correct register sheet. The right hand is always free to write the number on the document. This type of sheet provides a compact register for quick reference.

Computer-Printed Lists

If a computer is available, name lists for coding purposes are usually printed by the computer from a master file kept on magnetic tape, or from direct access disks or drums.

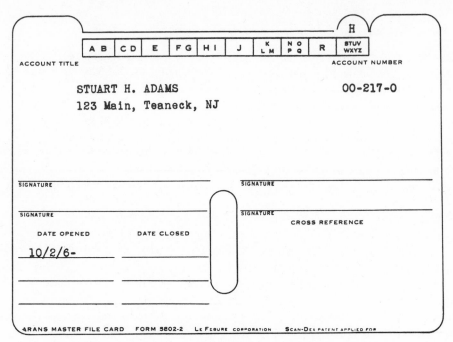

Figure 29-4
UNIT CARD ACCOUNT NUMBER "LOOK-UP" RECORD
(Courtesy of LeFebure Corporation)

The systems analyst should provide adequate and practical procedures for the temporary addition of new names and addresses to the printed coding list, since this print run is frequently quite extensive and time-consuming. If this is the situation the computer-printed list will not be repeated very often. If the coders have no reference to new names added to the list recently, coding will be slowed and coding costs will increase.

Simultaneous Alphanumeric Plan

Since the advent of account coding on a broad scale, many attempts have been made to devise systems which would make it possible to keep a constantly changing name list in exact alphabetic sequence and also maintain numeric sequence at all times. Considerable experience has now proved this to be a very difficult feat.

One of the first of such plans widely discussed was the Crockermerical plan, devised by and named for a large bank on the West Coast. This plan represented a scientific approach to the problem of assigning a number to a name based on the analysis of the letters contained in the name. The Crocker method involved a six-digit number with an alphabetic prefix. For the initial number assignment, a standard "gap" of numbers was used. This gap was determined by dividing the total number of accounts for each character of the alphabet into the six-digit number. Assigning numbers to new accounts was quite difficult. A method of interpolation was used. Numeric values were assigned to letters of the alphabet and by means of a compu-

Ad SUBDIVISION Numbers from 00-200 thru 00-399

LeFebure Corporation, Cedar Rapids, Iowa   FORM S-29947-A

A/B	C/D	E	F	G	H/I	J	K/L	M/N/O	P/Q/R	S/T/U/V	W/X/Y/Z	NAME	ADDRESS	ACCOUNT NUMBER
F												ADA, ALEXANDER F.	302 Elm, Denver, Col.	00-200-6
									L			ADACH, ROBERT L.	122 Franklin, Elmore NY	00-201-4
						C						ADAIR, J. C.	143 Lane St, Roslyn, NY	00-202-2
						N						ADAM, JOHN N.	2388 Peachtree St., Maspeth, N. Y.	00-203-0
						F						ADAMO, JOSEPH F.	1610 Bar Blvd, Belmore NY	00-204-8
	F											ADAMS, C. F.	88 Grand, Lindell, NY	00-205-5
	X											ADAMS, CHARLES	44 2nd St., Queens NY	00-206-3
		L										ADAMS, FLOYD L.	1416 H St, Wash, DC	00-207-1
					T							ADAMS, HENRY T.	3399 12th St., St Louis	00-208-9
					E							ADAMS, LILLIAN E.	45 St Joseph, Austin Tex	00-209-7
							I					ADAMS, WALTER I.	1003 E 53, Austin, Tex.	00-210-5
					I							ADCO, HYDRAULIC INC.	11 Arrow St., Mineola NY	00-211-3
				S								ADELE'S GIFT SHOP	99 5th St., Bayville NY	00-212-1
X												ADLER, ALBERT	1208 Ard St., Freeport NY	00-213-9
						X						ADLER, LOUIS	810 Woods St., Syosset NY	00-214-7
							B					ADLER, RICHARD B.	3344 F St., Dallas, Tex.	00-215-4
					P							ADLIN, HARRY P.	12,445 H Ave, Bronx, NY	00-216-2
							H					ADAMS, STUART H.	123 Main, Teaneck, NJ	00-217-0

TO FIND NAME WANTED:

Select First Letter of First Name printed at top of column. Glance down that column to locate First Letter of Second Name or Second Initial. If no Second Initial, look for "X."

Figure 29-5

ALPHABETIC NAME REGISTER FOR ACCOUNT NUMBER REFERENCES

(Courtesy of LeFebure Corporation)

tation, the new account was assigned an account number relative to its alphabetic position *between two existing accounts*. This plan was not widely copied due to the complexities and the administration problems involved.

Another plan which has never been copied to any extent involved the use of a telephone book for assigning numbers to original accounts, and also for subsequent new accounts. The theory here was that an area telephone book constituted a *master name list*. The pages were numbered and the columns were numbered. An account name appearing in the phone book was assigned a number relative to its position on the page.

Gap Plan

The "gap" plan of numbering an alphabetic list of accounts then came into being, and is in wide use today. The objective is to leave enough numbers between names so that new names can be added constantly, yet maintain the accounts *in exact alphabetic and numeric order*. To accomplish this, a selected gap is used which leaves a considerable block of unused numbers between each name when assigning numbers to an original name list. A gap may consist of any power of 2, but the most popular gaps are 32, 64, 128, 256, 512 or 1,024. In theory this plan should work perfectly. It obviously has great appeal to firms installing data processing equipment. Let us examine the mechanics of applying this numbering system to an account list.

1. Account register cards are prepared for each name on the list. These may be simple, $3'' \times 5''$ index cards, or they may consist of a deck of punched cards.

2. The cards are carefully arranged in strict alphabetic order.

3. Numbers are assigned to each card, leaving a predetermined gap or reserve supply of numbers for assignment to new accounts in the future.

Gap Example

We will select a gap of *256* for illustrative purposes. (A gap number based on a power of 2 is usually selected for reasons which will become clear as the mechanics of figuring the account number are explained.)

Here are the first few names and assigned numbers.

Abram P. Aarons	000–256
Benjamin R. Aarons	000–512
Harold L. Aaronson	000–768
Robert F. Adikes	001–024
Louis E. Allen, etc.	001–280, etc.

If there are 5,000 names on the original account list, then 1,280,000 numbers will be required to cover the list. (256 × 5,000.)

Number Assignment to a New Account

A new account is opened in the name of Adam G. Aarons. The account assignment clerk types a cross-index card with this name on it. The clerk then determines that *Adam G.* Aarons belongs alphabetically *between* Abram P. and Benjamin R. Aarons. She then calculates the account number. This is done by adding the number appearing on the cards on either side of the new account card, then dividing by 2.

Abram P. Aarons	#000–256
Adam G. Aarons	?
Benjamin Aarons	000–512
	———
	768

Dividing 768 by 2, we obtain *384*. Therefore, number 000–384 is assigned to the new account. Our list of accounts now appears as follows:

Abram P. Aarons	000–256
Adam G. Aarons	000–384
Benjamin Aarons	000–512

Now, suppose that Abram S. Aarons opens an account. His card will be placed alphabetically *after* Abram P. and *before* Adam G. Aarons.

Abram P. Aarons	000–256
Adam G. Aarons	000–384
	—————
	640

Dividing by 2, the result is *320*. Therefore, this new customer is assigned number 000–320. Numbers assigned to customers now appear as follows:

Abram P. Aarons	000–256
Abram S. Aarons	000–320
Adam G. Aarons	000–384
Benjamin Aarons	000–512

It is now apparent why the gap selected should be divisible by 2 successively. As new accounts are placed between existing accounts, the new number can be calculated without getting into fractional numbers which would be the case if a gap consisting of an odd number were selected. A recent article in a magazine dealing with office automation related procedural details pertaining to the installation of a large scale computer on shareholders' accounts in a very large New York corporation. The article casually related that a simultaneous alphanumeric plan with a gap of *500* had been selected for numbering more than one million shareholders! This undoubtedly led quickly to very difficult problems as new shareholders were placed into position alphabetically, then assigned numbers halfway between existing numbers. A gap of 500 would produce the following numbers: 500, 250, 125, 62½, 31¼, etc.

Disadvantages of Gap Plan

1. Varying with the size of the gap selected, the basic account number will contain more digits than either of the other basic plans. 10,000 accounts numbered with a gap of 256 will cover a range of 2,560,000 numbers, or seven digits.

2. *Difficult to Administer:* Assignment of numbers to new accounts is more complex with an exact simultaneous plan. Since the account number must be computed, there are opportunities for error. As a matter of fact, two things cause many errors to be reflected in the file cards and account numbers.

First, the new account card must be placed carefully in its correct position alphabetically between two existing accounts. This involves judgment and care for this step. Second, any error made in adding the two adjacent numbers, or an error in division produces a wrong account number. This alone is not so bad, until you realize that this one error breeds a continuous succession of other errors, as more new accounts are placed in position in front of and behind the card on which the first incorrect number was figured and written!

In theory it does not appear to be very difficult to position names in exact alphabetic order. However, anyone who has had experience in checking alphabetic card-and-ledger files knows that it is very unusual to find any such file actually in alphabetic order. Misfiles will range from 2% to 12%, depending on the skill, training and supervision of the people doing the filing.

Even if a new account card is correctly positioned and the number correctly figured and assigned, the nature of the system will provide many opportunities for error. For example, a common failing is to misfile the new account card one, two or three cards out of position. Suppose that the account number for Charles Adams was figured as shown below.

A. B. Adams	005–120
Charles Adams (New account)	005–248
Henry Adams	005–376

The correct number of 005–248 was entered on the file card, but filed *behind* the A. B. Adams card. Let us see what happens when Fred Adams opens an account a few weeks later. The account assignment clerk prepares the new card and correctly positions it between A. B. Adams and Henry Adams. These two numbers are added, and the result is divided by 2. The resulting number is *005–248*. This number is, therefore, routinely assigned to the Fred Adams account and the card is dropped into alphabetic position. We now have *two accounts with the same number.*

The two types of errors explained above make it easy to understand a recent analysis performed on the cross-index cards on a name list of 3,000 accounts which had been numbered with a gap plan for less than one year. Sixty-seven errors were found in numbers assigned, filing locations of cards, and in corresponding number assignments. There were *eleven instances* of the same account number being assigned to two accounts! There were *twenty-five wrong numbers assigned.* Forty-four account cards were found filed in wrong alphabetic locations. (Some of these errors were overlapping and the sum of the errors listed here will not total sixty-seven.)

3. *Sorting time* will exceed that required for plans with number systems involving fewer digits.

4. Possibly the most serious single disadvantage of a simultaneous-gap plan is the difficulty of including a check digit with the base number. It is not practical to ask an assignment clerk to perform the involved steps necessary to compute a check digit. And, due to the nature of the gap numbering plan, it is not very practical to set up a complete, pre-printed tabulated list of all possible numbers, or unit cards for each number, when the total number list may run into millions. This difficulty has been overcome in a few firms by programming an accounting machine to calculate the check digit mechanically. This means that numbers for new accounts opened during the day are held in abeyance until the machine has time to perform the calculations necessary to produce the check digits.

We should all bear in mind that there is a serious fallacy inherent in any plan which precludes the use of pre-printed lists of account numbers which include *pre-figured check digits.* Reason: If the plan requires figuring the base number itself, there is no way to detect unusable numbers in advance. And depending on the basic numbering plan selected, from 4% to 10% of all available numbers should not be used.

5. Contrary to all expectations and despite ponderous calculations of mathematical probabilities by experts, the gaps are frequently filled in surprisingly quickly after a gap system

has been installed. Customers do not follow any mathematical pattern when they decide to open accounts; and, the number gap can be misleading as to the number of new accounts which can be opened before difficulty is encountered in correctly positioning the next new name. For example, a gap of 64 may provide for *only six new names* if these names happen to fall into a descending alphabetic pattern which causes the gap number to diminish by the power of 2 each time a new name is added. Successively dividing 64 by 2, we obtain 32-16-8-4-2-1. The gap is now closed, yet the next new name may belong alphabetically between accounts numbered 2 and 1. This does happen.

An actual case history will serve to show why a gap may fill in rapidly. A Midwest bank numbered their accounts with a gap of 1,024 numbers between all accounts on the original name list. Within one year the "Sa" gap had filled in. A check-back on the account list showed the curious fact that, at the time of numbering, not one customer name existed between "Sa" and "Se," yet the local telephone book listed 624 names in this part of the book! Enough new accounts were opened subsequently in this section of the name list to close the gap.

The *AUDITGRAM* banking magazine printed a letter from a banker who had installed a gap plan and who was experiencing difficulties. The magazine published this letter and asked readers to help answer the banker's problems. Here is the substance of the banker's letter:

> We recently installed an alphanumerical numbering code on our regular checking accounts. We used a 64 gap and now find that in some instances we are running out of numbers to assign new accounts. We would like to know how to handle this problem.

The magazine received and published the following reply from the comptroller of a subscriber bank:

> We too have an alphanumerical system with a 64 gap. Running out of numbers between "Jom—" and "Joo—," we found that the only solution was to have our customer apply through the courts for a legal change of name. He is now neatly tucked away between "Jan—" and "Jaw—" but he complains that it was much easier to sign his checks with "Jones" than "Jasienesky."
>
> If you have come up with any simpler solution, we too would be glad to hear of it!

6. Name cards representing closed accounts must remain in the reference-card file indefinitely. The reason for this, again, is the method of figuring the account number. If the card for a closed account is removed, a new name may fall in exactly the same slot as the closed account name. The same number will, therefore, be assigned to the new account. This may lead to real trouble if the old account is suddenly reactivated with the old number.

Summary

Weighty evidence amassed over a period of many years leads to the conclusion that a simultaneous gap alphanumeric coding plan will eventually bog down if applied to a volatile, rapidly changing name list. This will result from an influx of new names unevenly distributed throughout the account list, and from administrative difficulties and resulting errors of many types.

On the other hand, a simultaneous-gap plan should work very well when applied to a static, long-established name list, such as some accounts payable lists.

ANOTHER SIMULTANEOUS ALPHANUMERIC PLAN

The DANS system will be of interest to students of account-coding methods. DANS means "*Diebold Alpha Numeric System*." Quoting from literature released on the system:

> DANS—A numbering system that maintains true alphabetic access to operational files. . . . Adaptable to any numbering requirement with speed and accuracy. . . . Eliminating need for gap calculations or cross-reference files.

This plan is basically a simultaneous alphanumeric gap plan, utilizing primarily a 32 gap. The plan provides visual number assignment without the necessity of computing the number after placement of the name alphabetically between two existing account names. Pre-printed register sheets are furnished which list all possible numbers on groups of pages.

	523 Thousands Block No.			*8* Approach Check Digit				
Dalton, Burt E. 866 Elm St., Denver	103	O	Dalton, John E. 716 Oak, Centerville	135	2	Dalton, T. F. 3368 Caillet, Ft. Worth	167	5
	104			136			168	
	105			137			169	
	106			138			170	
	107			139			171	
	108			140			172	
	109			141			173	
	110			142			174	
	111		Dalton, John G. 123 Main, Oakville	143	6		175	
	112			144			176	
	113			145			177	
	114			146			178	
	115		Dalton, John L. 666 Jost St., Canton	147	7		179	
	116			148			180	
	117			149			181	
	118			150			182	
Dalton, Edwin C. 1042 F St., Center City	119	6	Dalton, John W. 2024 Pine, Dallas	151	9		183	
	120			152			184	
	121			153			185	

Figure 29-6
REASONABLE FACSIMILE OF PRE-PRINTED *DANS* ACCOUNT NUMBER REGISTER SHEET

An interesting feature of the plan is the provision for "overflow" accounts. When an influx of new names has closed a gap or filled in the section of the register sheet where the next new name should be placed to keep it in alphabetic order, the new name is recorded on a special register sheet found at the back of each group of ten register sheets. Out of each 1,000 numbers, the 900's are reserved for assigning numbers to overflow accounts. So, here is a simultaneous alphanumeric system which recognizes, in advance, all the difficulties of maintaining indefinitely a volatile name list in exact alphabetic and numeric sequence. In effect, an escape-mechanism is built into the system as an integral part of it.

Analysis of DANS

The following points will assist the practitioner in analyzing and evaluating the possible application of DANS to a numbering problem.

1. There are 96 numbers pre-printed on each register sheet. With a gap of 32 numbers, one register sheet is required for *each three names* on the original account list. Numbers in the 900 group are reserved for overflow accounts. For these reasons, 9,000 names would require about 3,300 register sheets.

2. The number assignment register is used also for look-up of account numbers—if hardcopy ledger cards are not maintained for the accounts—which will be the case in almost any punched-card, punched-tape or computer installation. This has been known to cause internal conflicts. The person, or persons, who assigns numbers to new accounts may be in an entirely different department of the same building, or in a different building from personnel who are required to write numbers on source documents.

3. Check digit must be figured by assignment clerk. This is done by adding two component check digits together. Here is how it is done:

    a. A base number is assigned to each register sheet, such as *523*. This represents the "thousands block number" *(523-000)*.

    b. An "approach check digit" for this block number of 523 is typed on top of the register sheet. If the double-add-double formula is used, this digit is *8*.

    c. When a name is recorded on the register sheet on a numbered line, the check digit for the three right-hand digits is selected from a chart with numbers ranging from 000 to 999. For example, if the number assigned is 523-119, the check digit for 523, which is *8*, is read from the chart.

    d. Now the assignment clerk adds the "approach" check digit of 8 to the check digit for the serial number (523), which is 8. (8 plus 8 equals 16.) The left-hand digit is ignored, so the correct check digit for the entire number is *6*.

4. The provision for overflow accounts is an interesting feature of this numbering system. This helps keep all names in alphabetic and numeric sequence regardless of the number of new names brought into the list.

5. Sorting time is increased over that required for systems using fewer digits. Any gap plan has the effect of requiring more digits in the number than are required by straight numerics or a modified alphanumeric system. With a gap of 32, any name list exceeding approximately 3,300 accounts will require six digits in the base number.

Summary

The DANS numbering system has worked well for small to medium-sized name lists. Where it has been installed in retail receivables involving hundreds of thousands of names and numbers, mixed results have been obtained. A few users have reported difficulties in maintaining control over the large number of account-number register sheets required for the system.

ADDITIONAL CODES

Commercial-account-coding requirements frequently go considerably further than the number assigned to an individual customer or vendor. As stated before, the format and requirements of final management reports will dictate, to a very large extent, the complete numbering arrangement. A case history involving the system set up for a large chemical corporation will serve to illustrate some of the side issues to be solved.

This firm has installed punched-card accounting on receivables and sales statistics. Two primary reports are wanted at the end of each calendar month. The first report lists all sales to all customers and blankets the entire country as far as geographic locations are concerned. In addition, however, a secondary report is wanted which would list sales to a parent corporation, followed by a list of sales to *all subsidiaries* of the parent organization. Here is the way this was solved.

First, we set up a numbering system for customers which maintains a definite relationship between the alphabet and numbers assigned. This means that the primary sales report will list customers in alphabetic sequence from A through Z merely by sorting all invoice-sales cards and sales-summary cards in numeric sequence. To solve the requirements of the secondary report, we added three more digits to each customer account number. If a customer is an individual entity with no subsidiary companies involved, we add "000" to the basic account number. If a customer is a parent corporation, we select two digits from an assignment chart and include these two digits, preceded by a zero, as part of the total account number.

For example, suppose we want to assign a number to a parent corporation known as the "Acme Chemical Corporation." The block number for this alphabetic group (ARANS plan) is *00-800* and the next open serial number is 15. The basic number, then, will be 00-815-1. Next, we consult our chart for numbers to designate a parent organization. We select the next open number of *012*. The complete number assigned to Acme is now *00-815-1 012*.

Now, for each subsidiary of the Acme Chemical Corporation, we will assign a base number which designates the alphabetic position of the firm name, as usual. Then we will always add the figures *012* to each of the base numbers assigned to each subsidiary. The purpose of these three auxiliary codes is to *numerically identify* each subsidiary of the parent company for purposes of sorting sales-summary cards preparatory to running the secondary-sales report.

Summary

Coding is a fundamental requirement for a data-processing installation. It deserves as much careful planning and research as any other phase of the overall system to be designed, programmed and installed. There are two distinct aspects of the coding problem:

1. Selecting the basic numbering system and assigning numbers initially to all accounts.
2. Daily coding of various documents before they are ready for keypunching.

This latter aspect of coding may represent a substantial and continuing amount of clerical expense. Any method or procedure which can be devised to speed up this relatively slow process will be a welcome accomplishment.